AMERICANIZING THE WEST

AMERICANIZING THE WEST

Race, Immigrants, and Citizenship, 1890–1930

Frank Van Nuys

UNIVERSITY PRESS OF KANSAS

© 2002 by the University Press of Kansas
All rights reserved

Published by the University Press of Kansas (Lawrence, Kansas 66049), which was
organized by the Kansas Board of Regents and is operated and funded by Emporia State
University, Fort Hays State University, Kansas State University, Pittsburg State University,
the University of Kansas, and Wichita State University

Library of Congress Cataloging-in-Publication Data

Van Nuys, Frank, 1961–
Americanizing the West : race, immigrants, and citizenship, 1890–1930
/ Frank Van Nuys.
   p. cm.
Includes bibliographical references and index.
   ISBN 0-7006-1206-8 (alk. paper)
   1. West (U.S.)—Ethnic relations—Political aspects. 2. West
(U.S.)—Politics and government. 3. West (U.S.)—History—1890–1945.
4. Immigrants—West (U.S.)—Social conditions—19th century. 5.
Immigrants—West (U.S.)—Social conditions—20th century. 6.
Americanization—History—19th century. 7. Americanization—
History—20th century. 8. Frontier and pioneer life—West (U.S.).
9. Citizenship—West (U.S.)—History—19th century.
10. Citizenship—West (U.S.)—History—20th century. I. Title.
   F596.2.V36 2002
   978'.02—dc21
                        2002007538

British Library Cataloguing in Publication Data is available.

Printed in the United States of America
10 9 8 7 6 5 4 3 2

The paper used in this publication meets the minimum requirements of the American
National Standard for Permanence of Paper for Printed Library Materials Z39.48-1984.

For Janet and Maya

CONTENTS

ILLUSTRATIONS

PREFACE

On a sunny summer morning in 1999, 615 people from seventy-five different countries were naturalized in an impressive outdoor "Citizenship Day" ceremony in downtown Denver. I was struck by the coincidence of the pomp and solemnity of the occasion and my interest in the history of immigration and the American West. The following day, a Denver newspaper featured two of the hundreds who crossed the threshold from "alien" to citizen that September Friday: a Japanese woman and a Mexican man who had met in an English class at the Emily Griffith Opportunity School. Before becoming citizens they had become husband and wife.[1]

Although attaining citizenship inspired powerful emotions and profound reflections in the couple, their ethnic backgrounds reminded me of the tortuous paths Asians and Mexicans had trod in the annals of Western history. Immigrants from Asia and Mexico in particular have been at the center of Western conflicts regarding their identity as pioneers, Westerners, and Americans. If their lives were not nearly so freighted with distinctly "racial" tensions, immigrants from the southern and eastern reaches of Europe likewise found themselves confronting native-born hostility in the modernizing West of the early twentieth century. Asians, Mexicans, and southern and eastern Europeans—components during that era of a "new" immigration suspected by many Americans of being unassimilable—met others in the West who believed some of them could, with assistance, be transformed into desirable citizens.

Americanizing the West relates the complex of ideas and programs concerning assimilation of immigrants during an important period of twentieth-century Western history. As Western states positioned themselves as part of a maturing, postfrontier regional society within a modern nation-state, they joined in a crusade to "Americanize" the foreign-born living and working in their midst. The story of the West I tell here is not one of fistfights, gun battles, or rattling stagecoaches. Nor does it involve any heart-pounding exploits of heroic pioneers facing insurmountable odds as they forge civilization out of a "wilderness." Nor does it involve courageous Native Americans struggling to stave off conquest. This is a story of reformers and bureaucrats, employers and workers, students and teachers, agencies and commissions, bulletins and memoranda—not the material to satisfy those accustomed to romantic and picturesque depictions of the West. Yet these

xi

mundane aspects of Western history contribute quite as much as romance and legend to a fuller understanding of the region's development.

The story of Americanization in the West, I have found, is not a story of simple dichotomies. It is kaleidoscopic, with constantly shifting agendas and variations depending on time and location. It is a story encompassing social workers, state governors, wartime councils of defense, migrant laborers, unionized mine workers, corporate managers, teachers, university professors and administrators, federal officials, women's clubs, and countless other individuals and groups. The story is further complicated when the dilemma of community cohesiveness among immigrant and ethnic groups confronted the imperatives of "American" and "Western" norms and behaviors. In historian Sarah Deutsch's understatement, "The West was a messy place."[2] Boundaries between and among majority and minority groups shifted and bent, undergoing continual redefinition and renegotiation according to changes in economic conditions, population, politics, and social and cultural pressures. Ideas about race, furthermore, aided those Westerners most advantageously positioned to define who among the diverse immigrant populations could or could not become genuine American citizens. In the end, restriction and exclusion of immigrants categorized as undesirable or "nonwhite" became more compelling responses to the challenges of diversity than the uncertain results of Americanization.

Western contributions to Americanization included a number of practical applications, most notably a "home teaching" approach to assimilating immigrant women developed in California. In addition, Americanizers in Colorado fashioned an innovative, though short-lived, effort to organize "America First Societies" that would ostensibly allow immigrants themselves more initiative in guiding their own Americanization. Corporations such as the Colorado Fuel and Iron Company established some of the earliest industrial Americanization programs, and Americanizers throughout the West contributed to the adaptations of their work toward the development of general adult education.

The West also contributed the powerful racial beliefs that undergirded movements against immigration from Southern and Eastern Europe, China, and Japan. Many whites, or "Anglos" as people of northern European background were often called in the Southwestern states, influenced the national dialogue on immigration through disdainful and exploitative treatment of Mexicans and Mexican Americans. Through their perceptions of the connections between race and citizenship, Westerners played an important part in driving American policies regarding immigration and assimilation. By the end of the 1920s, with the Americanization movement largely dismissed as a failure, the West had helped consolidate the widely held assumption of American identity as fundamentally white and Anglo Saxon.

ACKNOWLEDGMENTS

Over the past decade, as I have tried to divine the historical significance of citizenship, immigration, identity, nativism, and race in the West, I have accrued many scholarly debts. Colleagues and mentors have either contributed directly to the book in terms of criticism and direction or indirectly through sage advice, encouragement, and employment. Joseph R. Conlin, in addition to editing and commenting on numerous drafts of thesis and dissertation chapters, taught me how to be a historian. Phil Roberts, my dissertation adviser at the University of Wyoming, pointed out awkward phrasing and with his consistent good cheer and unfailing optimism kept my spirits up.

For scholarly assistance, professional advice, and collegial support I would also like to acknowledge and thank Tyler Anbinder, Adrian Bantjes, Bruce Dain, Chet DeFonso, Judy DeMark, Herb Dieterich, John Egan, Richard George, Robbie Goodrich, Brian Hosmer, Barry Knight, Mike Mackey, Russ Magnaghi, William H. Moore, Howard Nicholson, Judith R. Raftery, Stan Ridgeway, Jon Saari, Virginia Scharf, Ronald Schultz, Karin Steffens, Eugene Whitehouse, and Alan Willis. A number of scholars have influenced this work through their comments at academic conferences and symposia. They include Ellen Schoening Aiken, Karen Blair, Sharon Carver, Chuck Chalberg, Roger Daniels, Neil Foley, Matthew J. Mancini, Donald J. Mrozek, and Ann Marie Woo-Sam. In addition to members of thesis and dissertation committees who read and critiqued various components of much that ultimately found its way into this work, I must thank Sarah Deutsch, Leonard Dinnerstein, and Jon Gjerde for their readings and recommendations.

Archivists and staff at several repositories around the country provided invaluable service in steering me toward pertinent collections, retrieving materials, and processing orders for photographs. Many of these helpful souls I know by name; most I do not. Those whom I did get to know, even if merely through e-mailed correspondence, are Linda M. Jordan at the Bancroft Library at the University of California, Berkeley; Terry Ketelson and Erin McDanal at the Colorado State Archives in Denver; Debra Neiswonger at the John M. Hart Library at the Colorado Historical Society in Denver; Marty Covey, David M. Hays, and Cynthia Ploucher at the Archives, University of Colorado Libraries in Boulder; Marian Smith at the Immigration and Naturalization Service in Washington, D.C.; Marie Masumoto at the Japanese

American National Museum in Los Angeles; Robert Knecht and Nancy Sherbert at the Kansas State Historical Society in Topeka; Robin Kennedy and Marcus Robyns at the Northern Michigan University and Central Upper Peninsula Archives in Marquette; Richard Ellis at the National Archives in Washington, D.C.; Kermit Hall and José L. Villegas Sr. at the New Mexico State Records Center and Archives in Santa Fe; Carol Bowers, Rick Ewig, John Hanks, Jennifer King, Lisa Olson, and Leslie Shores at the American Heritage Center at the University of Wyoming in Laramie; and Carl Hallberg at the Wyoming State Archives in Cheyenne. In addition, I wish to express my appreciation to staff at National Archives II in College Park, Maryland, the Arizona State Archives and State Library in Phoenix, Arizona State University Special Collections in Tempe, the California State Library in Sacramento, the Denver Public Library, Western History Department, the Montana State Historical Society Archives in Helena, and, in Salt Lake City, the Utah History Information Center at the Utah State Historical Society, Utah State Archives, and University of Utah's Marriott Library Special Collections.

I must thank as well the interlibrary loan staffs in Coe Library at the University of Wyoming and Olson Library at Northern Michigan University. Without their stupendous efforts to track down seemingly numberless and often obscure sources, I would have been sunk. A special note of gratitude is due to Frances Lilly, formerly of the American Historical Association, who conducted follow-up research on my behalf in Bureau of Naturalization records at the old National Archives building in Washington, D.C. Similarly, I want to thank Christi L. Hutchison for her excellent work locating and identifying relevant materials at the Wyoming State Archives. Finally, my uncle, Maxwell Van Nuys, generously provided room, board, and invaluable research assistance during several trips to Denver.

Timely sources of funding for research travel were vital ingredients in completing this book. I want to thank the University of Wyoming College of Arts and Sciences for an Independent Study Award that allowed me to visit the National Archives in Washington, D.C., and College Park, Maryland, as well as the Bancroft Library at the University of California, Berkeley, and the California State Library in Sacramento. The Charles Redd Center for Western Studies at Brigham Young University provided a key resource with the John Topham and Susan Redd Butler Faculty Research Award for 1999–2000. With the Redd Center's support, I was able to conduct meaningful research on World War I state councils of defense in Arizona, Kansas, New Mexico, and Utah.

Without the energy, expertise, and professionalism of Nancy Jackson at the University Press of Kansas, *Americanizing the West* would never have seen the light of day. It was fortuitous, indeed, for a freshly minted Ph.D. from

Wyoming to somehow come to the attention of the best acquisitions editor in the country, bar none! Nancy's enthusiasm, optimism, patience, perseverance, and suggestions have contributed immeasurably to completion of this work. I fear I cannot thank her sufficiently. Dorothea Anderson, Jessica Pigza, Susan Schott, and Sara Henderson White offered additional professional expertise in guiding this book into print. To Fred Woodward and the editorial board at the University Press of Kansas, I also desire to express my heartfelt gratitude for taking a chance on an unproven and (at the time) barely employed academic.

To family members, particularly my parents, I owe unbounded gratitude for years of moral and financial support. Finally, Janet and Maya, to whom I have dedicated this work, have endured, for sixteen and five years respectively, an absentminded, distracted, preoccupied, workaholic husband and father. To both of them I offer my apologies, but also my undying admiration, gratitude, and love. The two of you have made my sometimes rocky journey bearable by keeping me attached to a joyful world of play and talk and wonder.

None of the archivists, colleagues, editors, family members, librarians, mentors, researchers, or institutions shoulder any responsibility for errors of fact and interpretation that may appear in the pages that follow. That responsibility rests entirely with me.

INTRODUCTION

In a characteristically unequivocal statement, Theodore Roosevelt voiced a fundamental rationale behind the Americanization movement of the 1910s and 1920s. "The foreign-born population of this country," the former president declared in 1915, "must be an Americanized population. . . . It must talk the language of its native-born fellow citizens, it must possess American citizenship and American ideals."[1] University of Colorado president George Norlin echoed Roosevelt when he called on all Americans, native- and foreign-born alike, "to be in all respects and first of all Americans." Born to Swedish immigrant parents in Concordia, Kansas, in 1871, Norlin recalled that as a boy, taunted on occasion by other youngsters as a "Swede," he had "felt on the defensive because my family were immigrants and I myself had narrowly escaped being one."[2] In 1918, Governor Julius Gunter named Norlin to chair the Americanization Committee of the Colorado State Council of Defense. By speaking English, learning American history and geography, and dreaming the "dream of America—the dream of a free, unfettered life," Norlin saw the nation transcending its divisions and uniting as a single people.[3] George Norlin was one of many in the American West who put these beliefs into action and helped develop adult immigrant education programs in public schools, workplaces, churches, settlement houses, and universities. Participating in the nationwide drive to train immigrants for American citizenship, Norlin and other Westerners took part in a great reform effort, one made increasingly urgent by heavy rates of immigration and the onset of world war.

Driven by this sense of urgency, progressive reformers, industrialists, educators, and government officials strove to organize and manage the American people during World War I. To unite a nation for total war required more than patriotic rhetoric. In addition, centralizing control over complex programs in industry and government struck many as vitally necessary. The federal government set the tone with creation of such agencies as the War Industries Board to coordinate a war economy, the Food Administration to organize the efficient production and distribution of foodstuffs, and the Committee on Public Information to massage public opinion toward unquestioning support for the war effort.[4] The wrenching adjustments spawned by the war, exemplified by massive strike waves and fears concerning aliens and radicals, confirmed for reformers their belief that centralizing

1

authority in larger, presumably more efficient entities would result in a smoothly functioning social, economic, and political order. "Every progressive tendency in social organization, not to mention any of the definite economic and political forces, recognized as wholesome potencies for individual and collective advancement, point[s] to larger and larger units of integration," a University of California education instructor noted in a 1923 address. "Centralization becomes increasingly inevitable." Making citizens of millions of unnaturalized adult foreigners fit the centralizing agendas of reformers, industrialists, educators in public schools and colleges, and government officials at all levels.[5]

Beyond the naturalization of foreign-born residents, Americanization represented a far more comprehensive process of social engineering and regimentation. Solving problems that they associated with immigrants suggested to progressives a certain amount of social control and the concomitant of preserving American civilization. To address disarray in society thus required understanding by progressive reformers of both heredity and environment. Professionalization and expertise, then, as opposed to amateur do-goodism and charity, undergirded the various reform projects of the early twentieth century.[6] With American involvement in World War I, the possibilities for American experts to manage social change, and in the process advance individual careers, expanded greatly. One area in which expertise was brought to bear concerned the education of adult immigrants, the essential mission of the Americanization movement.

Although experts exerted increasing influence during the Progressive era, differences in approach to thinking about immigrants prevented the development of a coherent national immigration policy until World War I. Many hewed to racial theories to explain the apparent differences in immigrant groups. Defining even southern and eastern Europeans as racially inferior to "whites" led these thinkers to discount the efficacy of teaching immigrants English and civics in night classes and to call for restriction or exclusion. Economic concerns colored the interpretations of other experts, for instance those associated with the U.S. Immigration Commission's study, published in 1911. Although showing that unrestricted immigration was undesirable because of its economic implications, chiefly lowered wage rates leading to lower standards of living, such experts still maintained a common nativist thread by also decrying the "new" immigrants' ethnic differences. Even the most optimistic among the reformers, like the social and settlement house workers who provided much of the hands-on expertise for the Americanization movement, rarely resisted the urge to shape immigrant lives to accord with "American" standards. Inured to white, middle-class, Protestant norms, these reformers easily assumed that the immigrants wanted the advantages that they possessed.[7]

How did these progressive imperatives of centralization and social engineering pertain to Western conditions? The Americanization crusades of the 1910s and 1920s coincided with and expedited important changes in the region. As a number of historians have argued, the American West in the early twentieth century had clearly moved beyond the frontier stage and was entering a new period of frequently rapid modernization. Still, in defining a coherent regional identity, continuity vied with transformation. Even as urbanization overtook larger portions of the West after the turn of the century, homesteading entered its last and greatest period, reaching its culmination in 1913. Walter Nugent captures this ambivalent phenomenon well, stating that "the West became briefly a rare and clear case of simultaneous urban and rural growth, the dual expansion of both the very customary and the very new." A region in transition, the early-twentieth-century West resisted generalization.[8]

The West was growing up, reconciling with progress what a journalist referred to as its "pioneer conscience." Between 1914 and 1929, when the Americanization movement rose and fell, a new, increasingly urban and industrial West separated further from the remembered frontier West of lonesome homesteaders in sod houses. "In many ways," Nugent tells us, "the West became not just an exotic curiosity but an integral part of the United States" during this important period. The West, it appeared, was realizing the transition from frontier to region described by Woodrow Wilson in an 1897 magazine article. Distinctive and colorful though it was, the West in the twentieth century needed to attach itself firmly to a homogeneous national polity and a national culture.[9]

Concerns with the reliability and maturity of the Western population remained, heightened by the outbreak of World War I in 1914 and American entry into that conflict in 1917. With a war-driven economic boom on one hand, and antiwar labor and agrarian radicals apparently poised to foment revolutionary change on the other, the West could appear to be a singularly disorganized and turbulent place. Immigrants and unassimilated ethnic groups seemed peculiarly susceptible to "pro-German" propagandizing or the "un-American" ideologies and agendas of the Industrial Workers of the World (IWW) and the Non-Partisan League. Failure to assimilate the impressionable foreigners who wandered from job to job or fell for the nostrums of prairie radicalism meant that the West would remain an unruly and often uncontrollable region, a peril to national unity in a time of crisis. Immigrants, if they remained unnaturalized and unassimilated, a California state superintendent of education warned in 1916, "may become dangerous and threatening in the extreme to the very life of the republic."[10]

A profound dilemma emerged during the war as official state councils of defense assumed responsibility for Americanization in the Western states.

For progressives the war years highlighted the incompatible—and often com-
bustible—combination of tolerant Americanization, home-front mobilization,
and patriotic fervor. Key to the success of Americanization, from the Americanizers' point of view and particularly within the context of the Great War,
was speed. "Let us now 'speed up' the Americanization of our immigrants in
order to promote better national unity," a member of California's Commission
of Immigration and Housing told a convention of clubwomen in 1918. "This
is a great and necessary part of the defense program, just as necessary as is the
speeding up of industry and agriculture."[11] Most self-professed Americanizers
sincerely sought to assimilate immigrants to the national norms in which they
fervently believed. They were well-intentioned. At the same time, they meant
for the immigrants to assimilate as quickly as possible and felt a sense of
urgency that lent itself to numerous distortions and abuses.

The Americanization movement in the West represented a key element of
the progressives' "search for order" in a modernizing America. Americanization served as a mechanism to further integrate the West into an emerging
national system, one premised on increasing bureaucratization, centralization, and standardization. Westerners involved in Americanization played
significant roles in seeking an orderly society through the professional assimilation of immigrants. George Bell, at one time the executive secretary for
the California Commission of Immigration and Housing, speaking before a
national Americanization conference in 1919, cited centralization, coordination, efficiency, organization, and "uniform standards" as vital components for achieving "a unified State and Nation with a single and common
interpretation of the deeper meaning of Americanization." Definite policies,
effective organization, and direct contact with immigrants, Bell stressed,
were absolutely essential in Western states because of the "greater percent-
age" of "migratory workers" among the foreign-born.[12]

Professional Americanizers in the West worked closely with employers in
attempting to mold immigrant workers into efficient and loyal employees
and citizens. In an ongoing struggle over control, scientific managers and efficiency experts were "re-tooling" the workplace to become a symbol of the
specialized engineer's authority. Americanization fit easily into this management ethos and contest over "knowledge" between paternalistic employers
and their workers. "Radical" and "alien" interpretations of "industrial
democracy," particularly the ideas and tactics associated with the IWW and
union organizers, could be countered by corporate welfare initiatives and
conscientious Americanization efforts. On the other hand, native-born and
naturalized workers saw unionization as a far more appropriate mechanism
for Americanization, while many Americanizers sought a "middle ground"
between management's objectives and the realities behind workers' struggles.

Perceiving Americanization as a disguise for increasing control over the workplace, organized labor questioned Americanizers' motives and called for improved working conditions and wages. Once the United States entered the war, however, the IWW was crushed and criticism from labor dissipated. An intensive postwar strike wave ultimately gave way to a greater degree of begrudging acquiescence to the prerogatives of Americanization on management's terms.[13]

As another important dimension of a broader search for order, the nationalizing program of citizenship education in the West impacted the relationship between immigrants enrolled in Americanization programs and educators in public schools and universities. Among the various aspects of late-nineteenth- and early-twentieth-century cultural debates, the Americanization movement represented a seemingly objective and benign educational approach to the problems posed by immigration.[14] The formal training of adult immigrants in preparation for naturalization often reflected the more hopeful reform impulses embodied in the Progressive movement. The school teachers, administrators, and academics who made up the bulk of Americanizers in the West believed that the challenges posed by increasing immigration from southern and eastern Europe, as well as from Mexico, could best be met by education rather than restriction or repression.[15]

Americanizers often thought that the immigrants' "ultimate assimilative capabilities"[16] meant that Anglo-American culture could absorb them in time, thereby assuring economic and political stability while providing a reliable labor supply. Furthermore, the Americanization bureaucracy's growing appreciation of the need to professionalize its domain, itself a reflection of ongoing professionalization and specialization within public education, permeated the federal and state government agencies, local public schools, and universities. All those involved in "education for citizenship," bureaucrats and teachers alike, placed supreme importance on serving the broader society through their particular efforts at educating immigrants and training Americanizers.

The federal government, through the Americanization activities of the Bureau of Naturalization and other agencies, expedited and to a large extent controlled this national integrating process as it related to assimilating the foreign-born. Americanizers in the West, whether state officials, industrialists, or educators, generally welcomed national direction and willingly collaborated with federal officials in realizing a homogeneous society and culture through efficient and professional methods of assimilation, to "accomplish the solution of this problem," as a Utah Americanizer phrased it, "in the most effective way."[17] Their job, as they saw it, was to make citizens and in so doing cement their region firmly to the nation. They also bent the

Americanization movement to fit their own designs and conform to their biases and experiences as Westerners.

Americanization programs in Western states, while enjoying a considerable amount of support and direction from national leaders in the East, still maintained many distinctive attributes, some of which aided and some of which frustrated the larger processes served by Americanization. Americanizers in the West brought attitudes about race and citizenship that, while similar in many respects to views held by the typical native-born white citizen anywhere in the country, reflected unique aspects of Westerners' histories and worldviews. Above all, immigration from Asia and Mexico struck Westerners as problems unique to their region that necessitated solutions particularly well suited to Western conditions and values. Advancing the notion of a "racial frontier" between white, Anglo-American civilization and the presumed effects of contact with unassimilable Asians or racially inferior Mexicans was one such way of addressing Americanization.

Chester H. Rowell, a leading figure in the California progressive movement, consistently emphasized the maintenance of a "border between the white man's and the brown man's world" on the Pacific Coast.[18] The Chinese Exclusion Act of 1882, the Japanese-American Gentlemen's Agreement of 1907–1908, and continual attempts to bar Asian and Mexican immigration reflected this distinctly Western idea of racial frontiers. Americanization, too, was a means by which the dominant groups in the West could institutionalize the boundaries between citizens and those who either were ineligible or indifferent to citizenship. Moreover, the arguments revolving around themes of labor and capital, whether expressed by employers, workers, or Americanizers, served to accentuate the complex relationships between economic concerns and race-based understandings of nationality and citizenship.

Although not all white Westerners hewed to exclusionary ideologies like the racial frontier, many were still ambivalent about the immigrant groups in their midst. Optimistic about the nation's assimilative powers and possessed of an enduring faith in education, those involved in Americanization nonetheless feared the effects of large numbers of foreign-born residents on the republic's racial character and identity. Throughout the West, many Americanizers supported immigration restriction because of a firm belief in Anglo-American homogeneity as the basis for the nation's greatness and future prospects. "Homogeneity can only be maintained by admitting in greatest numbers those who are acceptable for assimilation with our American people," an Americanizer from Wyoming claimed in 1921. Diversity, on the other hand, represented a dangerous and exotic experiment, "a tangle of squabbling nationalities" in Roosevelt's words.[19]

Yet, there was no more diverse section of the country overall than the

West,[20] and the mix of immigrant groups residing there—Asians, Mexicans, and Europeans—meant that Eastern models for Americanization programs did not necessarily apply to situations found in the Los Angeles barrio or a Utah mining camp. Americanization programs within Western regions differed from each other according to the primary groups undergoing Americanization as well as the agenda of the Americanizers. Programs in Los Angeles or Santa Fe had clienteles different from those in Topeka or Fargo. Europeans, who constituted the bulk of the foreign-born targeted for Americanizing, could not be assimilated according to a single formula. "The foreign miner of Butte will take one line of argument," a Montana mining engineer explained, while "the semi-loyal German-American of . . . Nebraska will take another."[21]

Race complicated the matter of assimilation approaches and, in the Western context, transcended the customary assumptions of the period relating to differences among European "racial groups." Immigrants from Asia—detested by white Westerners, barred from land ownership and specific trades, presumed to be unassimilable, and ultimately defined as "ineligible to citizenship"—had little to gain from Americanization. Nonetheless, some Chinese, Japanese, and other Asian immigrants did participate, usually as adult students in English classes. Most Mexican immigrants, seeking better wages and a refuge from the strife of revolution and civil war, remained aloof from Americanization drives. In relation to Mexicans, many Americanizers in the Southwest focused on women, which often meant that entirely distinctive and complicated dilemmas of assimilation, cultural barriers, and gender had to be addressed. Regardless of the ethnic composition of the workforce, Americanization conducted by corporations associated with the West's extractive economy was as much, if not more, concerned with labor relations as with race and citizenship.

George Norlin and many of the other individuals involved in the movement to Americanize the foreign-born participated in a phenomenon that constituted a key element in modernizing and nationalizing the West. Making American citizens was tantamount to making the West thoroughly American as well. Integration into a progressive national state brought the West into a closer, more vital, less colonial relationship with the nation. Western distinctiveness still played a part in relation to the homogenizing forces; continuity and change characterized the dynamics of Americanization. In defining citizenship and addressing immigrant groups, however, the importance of race in the West impinged on the idealized conceptions Americanizers expressed about citizenship. Most Americanizers spoke in generic terms, as if anyone could be made into a citizen. "Americanization is the business of making good American citizens, the problem of acquainting all who inhabit this country with the merits of America, to the end that this knowledge may result in proper conduct and loyalty to American ideals and institutions," wrote Arch Thurman, the director of a short-lived state Americanization system in Utah. "We must all come to a new realization of what American ideals are and what institutions we wish to perpetuate. These ideals and institutions must be analyzed and interpreted in terms that touch the life of the average man."[22] When the "average man" was a native of Italy or Japan or Mexico, other, powerful political and cultural forces frequently dictated contradictory conclusions about assimilation and incorporation within the American identity. Americanization in the West, as in the nation at large, would fail to reconcile race with citizenship.

1

"THE STUFF FROM WHICH CITIZENS ARE MADE"

The Importance of Being White Pioneers

For Westerners confronting the challenges of modernity in the early 1900s, the memories of pioneer days, authentic and fabulous, betokened a golden era when rugged individuals subdued a wild country and forged a solid and orderly civilization. A rutted trail or weathered farm wagon hearkened back to intrepid men and women who had trudged across a continent in search of a new beginning in the green valley of Oregon or the alkaline Utah basin. Battlefields of the Indian Wars had become ghostly monuments with granite obelisks testifying to the courage and noble sacrifices of blue-clad soldiers. Ancient mining camps either hung on awaiting the next mineral rush or deteriorated inexorably before unremitting wind and weather. A few old pioneers remained too, embellishing their yarns, basking in adulation, and ignoring quiet mockery when they were trotted out on the Fourth of July and other patriotic occasions. The dwindling old-timers scrawled their memoirs and banded together in exclusive pioneer societies, sanctifying their singular relationship to the historical frontier and the uniquely heroic accomplishment of taming a wilderness. Sons and daughters and grandchildren, whether veterans of the Western crossing or not, likewise formed societies and laid claim to the frontier process, furthering the development of regional pride and shared memory in Western communities.[1]

As the pioneers of '49 or '59 or '76 died off, their descendants and admirers strove to sanctify the old-timers' achievements through various media of documentation. Local histories, products of a burgeoning "mugbook" industry,[2] recounted the travails and triumphs of the first settlers in heroic prose. "It has been theirs to subdue the wilderness," exulted an 1882 history of Fresno County, California, "and change it into smiling fields of bright growing grain." The hard work and sacrifice that the pioneers crowded into every day of their existence elicited awe in those who years afterward "complacently . . . talk and write and read of their deeds and exploits." The Rev. Jonathan Edwards, author of a turn-of-the-century history of Spokane County, Washington, prefaced his work with an admonishment concerning the "debt of gratitude" owed the pioneers. Not only had they come "with hearts prepared for perils and privations" and seen "the country in its virgin state," but the first settlers had selflessly wrested a civilization out of a barbarous land. "To conquer the wilderness and the Indian, whom they found in almost all his native wildness," Edwards wrote, "and make for themselves homes, and prepare the way for others, was the great task they undertook to do." Pioneers, according to Ira L. Bare, a North Platte newspaper editor who helped compile a 1920 history of Lincoln County, Nebraska, "helped blaze the path for modern civilization; the transformation of a wild and wooly West into a land of culture and refinement." Both chroniclers, the Spokane minister and the North Platte editor, summed up the pioneer legacy in classically succinct terms: "They came, they saw, they conquered."[3]

One of the Westerners most clearly associated with the Americanization movement, Dr. Grace Raymond Hebard of the University of Wyoming, reveled in the pioneer legacy. Hebard, whose family had settled in Iowa in the mid-1800s, romanticized the frontier and channeled much of her tremendous energy into commemorating pioneer accomplishments because, in part, she felt a strong personal attachment to that past. "Perhaps my greatest heritage is that I am a pioneer daughter of pioneer parents," she remarked in 1932. "Poverty and hard work can give to one what luxury and leisure never can." With obvious emotion and gratitude, she noted in a letter to a colleague that it was "a glorious and wonderful thing to be pioneers in a pioneer country in a frontier university."[4] Her publications likewise took advantage of the opportunity to proselytize on behalf of courageous trailblazers, hunters, traders, settlers, and other pioneer types.

To Hebard, the men and women she classed as "frontiersmen" were "nation builders," responsible as a class for seeking and creating a "refuge from social stagnation" in the Western reaches of the continent. "It is a wonderful history of pioneer struggles," she ruminated in *The Bozeman Trail* (1922), "of privation, of hardships, conflicts with Indians, of long and dangerous journeys to unknown parts of our country, the subduing of mountains and streams, the making of trails over trackless prairies and through treacherous passes." Despite the passing of those halcyon days and pioneer heroes, Hebard dwelt on the historical legacy bequeathed to a new West. "While we are enjoying the luxuries of this new era of the Great West," she counseled in the conclusion of her textbook on Western history, "let us not forget to honor those who endured hardships and privations, encountered dangers and peril; yes, even gave up their lives to make these things possible."[5]

Novelist Emerson Hough, also a native of Iowa, needed no convincing about America's debt to westering pioneers for conquest and the advance of civilization. Furthermore, he suggested the importance of racial identity in defining those who truly deserved the pioneer label. Hough encapsulated the allure of pioneer days with *The Covered Wagon,* first serialized in the *Satur-*

day Evening Post in 1922. For years, though, Hough had stretched and strained to adequately describe for readers the grandeur and profound significance of the West. "No fiction can ever surpass in vividness the vast, heroic drama of the West," he offered in a 1901 article, and in a history of the Old West published in 1918, Hough opened with a flourish: "The frontier! There is no word in the English language more stirring, more intimate, or more beloved. . . . It means all that America ever meant. It means the old hope of a real personal liberty, and yet a real human advance in character and achievement. To a genuine American it is the dearest word in all the world." In a passage of particular salience to Western conceptions of citizenship at that moment, Hough clarified the racial meaning of the pioneer past, a past that could only be appreciated by "genuine" Americans. The frontier, he explained, was a repository for "our comfort and our pride," a place where "we never have failed," a space in which Americans always realized their ambitions and where "we were efficient, before that hateful phrase was known." Furthermore, Hough concluded, "There we were a melting pot for character, before we came to know that odious appellation which classifies us as the melting pot of nations." Undiluted by alien culture and blood, true Americanism had made its way west and there made its last stand.[6]

Other prominent champions of the West moved well beyond Hough's suggestive language in positioning the West as a last bastion of a virile Anglo civilization. In a letter to a friend in 1893, Frederic Remington relished the prospect of a race war in which he could take his Winchesters and "get my share" of "Jews, Injuns, Chinamen, Italians, Huns—the rubbish of the world I hate." Few expressed their prejudices so bluntly, even privately, as the Eastern artist, but many agreed that frontier types and their descendants, as sociologist Edward Alsworth Ross explained, were made of sterner stuff than *"those who always stayed behind."* The lazy, slovenly, and dull—whether native stock or foreign-born—populated old, decaying New England communities, while still virile Westerners sowed prosperity and enterprise. "To-day in the recesses of the Rocky Mountains you come upon steady-eyed, eagle-faced men with tawny mustaches," Ross averred, "whose masterful, unswerving will and fierce impatience of restraint remind you of their spiritual kinsmen, the heroes of the Icelandic sagas." The governor of Minnesota, in a 1909 magazine article, interpreted the history of civilization as the "Westward march of the Aryan race, the story of the pioneers and the toilers who from time immemorial have hearkened to the call of the West." Selected by "the God of American destiny," hardy men of Northern European stock from New England, the Middle States, and the South responded to the race's innate longing to extend civilization beyond previously established frontiers.[7]

In defining an ideal individual most capable of heeding that call, race mattered. It most definitely mattered when assessing the significance of white pioneers in relation to Native Americans, African Americans, and ethnic Mexicans, nonwhite peoples who had either resided in Western places long before white penetration or had accompanied expansion-minded Europeans and Americans as slaves or laborers. Inferior peoples, most whites believed, could not benefit from Anglo-American forms of government and civilization. Thus, elimination (of Indians) or subordination (of blacks and Mexicans) emerged as the desirable alternatives. Race and the idea of "whiteness" mattered as well, especially after the mid–nineteenth century, in the face of foreign-born individuals from Asia, Latin America, and certain sections of Europe. It was these nonassimilable elements from overseas, in addition to blacks, Indians, and Mexican Americans, that threatened to undermine the achievements of a homogeneous society and culture.[8]

The importance of being white pioneers, or at least possessing a direct link to white pioneer antecedents, needs to be understood as a vital frame of reference for immigration and Americanization in Western states. If immigrants from the most backward regions of Europe, Asia, and the Western Hemisphere were deficient in pioneer qualities, then how should assimilation proceed? Furthermore, the assimilative powers of the frontier experience, presumed by some to have had a dramatic impact on early migrants from Northern and Western Europe, could have little salutary effect with the frontier fading or already vanished. Even the most optimistic among Americanization figures frequently confessed their doubts about certain groups' capacity to assimilate at all. Citizenship in a republic struck many in the increasingly urbanized, industrialized West of the early twentieth century as subject to extraordinary pressures, of which unrestricted immigration was merely one of a multitude of shocks. The social order created by the pioneers and their descendants confronted a potentially destabilizing amalgam of social, cultural, and racial diversity. Race factored mightily in constructing an American identity in the West, as it did in constructing the "other" and in determining those suitably conditioned for American citizenship.

Immigrant Wests and Racial Constructs

Within the modern, postfrontier West, thousands of immigrants and ethnic minorities resided, some scattered in small rural settlements, others concentrated in urban industrial centers, and many migrating from one labor camp to another.[9] Some had migrated directly from the point of disembarkation to the spot on the map where work or settlement awaited; others had arrived subsequent to one or more stops elsewhere. Chain migration, in which family members and relatives followed earlier migrants, was typical for many immigrant groups such as Norwegians who homesteaded in the Upper Middle West or Italians who concentrated in Little Italy in San Francisco's North Beach district. Other groups, for instance the *Volga Deutsch* in central Kansas, arrived intact as full family units and settled through formal colonization. Return migration occurred with considerable frequency among certain groups, and many immigrants made the journey between home village and the United States several times. Others returned to the "old country" and never came back. More intended to go back someday but decided their future lay in America. Continual mobility typified immigrant and ethnic life within the United States as well. European, Asian, and Mexican workers and families joined the thousands of native-born white and black Westerners who moved from job to job, becoming part-time residents of city neighborhoods or migrant labor camps in a continuous progression.[10]

The immigrant experience in the West, whether rural, urban, or a combination thereof, was a story of both change and continuity. Life in the United States often militated against wholesale transplantation of traditional forms of family or community structure. On the other hand, immigrants strove to uphold traditions while constantly adapting to the exigencies and uncertainties of life in a rapidly developing region.[11] The varieties of ethnic experience reflected in the diverse communities and attitudes toward change influenced the immigrants' own claims to pioneer status, their identities as ethnics and Westerners, and their responses to discriminatory treatment by members of the host society. Ethnic "mugbooks," such as a turn-of-the-century publication devoted to the role of Italians in the development of Colorado, documented the contributions made to early frontier societies by foreign-born pioneers.

Members of immigrant communities went to considerable lengths to organize ethnic organizations at the local, state, and national levels. For example, the Japanese Association of America (JAA) was organized in the wake of an upsurge in anti-Asian activity in California after 1900. Officially formed with Japanese government support in 1908, the JAA spread throughout the country and into Canada and served as a buffer of sorts between Japanese immigrants and the host society. Open only to males and typically led by the most successful immigrants in the community, the Japanese associations provided similar services, such as fund-raising, documents, interpreters, legal aid, insurance, and welfare, as many ethnic charities, fraternal associations, women's clubs, mutual aid societies, and political clubs did for other immigrant communities. Immigrants throughout the West also established societies based on home regions, churches and synagogues, and language schools.

A host of similar processes and institutions impacted each group, community, neighborhood, family, and individual in every conceivable manner while varying over space and time. Ethnic associations, clubs, saloons, religious institutions, and schools offered both confirmation of group identity and a transition zone between immigrants and the host society.[12]

For the foreign-born and many of their children, the ethnic group formed the core of their identity. Indeed, powerful forces from within the group often worked against assimilation. The immigrants' family and community traditions bumped against the designs of the activist state. Corporate ideals transplanted from the old country clashed with liberal ideals in the United States, while the community arrayed itself against the individual. Allegiance to nation of origin, religious creed, tradition, family, and language provided safety and reassurance in a frequently hostile and menacing new environment. Nonetheless, one could adhere to traditional loyalties while simultaneously drawing toward American citizenship and devotion to the United States. Through this process of ethnic group formation, or "ethnicization," the foreign-born in Western places often developed a complementary identity, one that conflated multiple loyalties and addressed Americanization on pluralist terms. In the face of official agendas typically at variance with pluralism, however, forging a complementary identity within the pressure-cooker contexts of war and resurgent nativism would prove difficult at best. Increasingly, immigrants and ethnics confronted hardening attitudes concerning Americanism. Regardless of birthplace or background, they were told that one was either unequivocally American or not American at all and thus deserving of the severe condemnation reserved for the disloyal. For many, the reassurance once promised through ethnic identity would be shattered by the unrelenting pressure to conform to a single cultural model.[13]

The heightened urgency relating to immigration and assimilation that characterized the 1910s and 1920s intensified cultural tensions that had long impacted Western communities. To better grasp how nonimmigrant Westerners in the early twentieth century perceived the diversity around them, it is necessary to consider more widespread attitudes about race and immigration after 1880, which, in the manner of previous nativist movements, weighed "new" immigrants from southern and eastern Europe, Asia, and Mexico against an idealized American identity. The fact that a nation could possess a fairly uniform racial character constituted a truism for many Americans thinking and writing about immigration in the late nineteenth and early twentieth centuries. For instance, one writer maintained in 1890 that "every nation manifestly has a character of its own as distinct as those of the individuals who compose it." Basic to many Americans' conception of an ideal national character was the assumption that at some point in the hazy past America enjoyed the benefits of a homogeneous population.[14]

Furthermore, immigration and nativist responses to changes in its composition influenced the developing mythology of the West. The creation of Western societies, whether detailed in mugbook histories, dime novels, or motion pictures, was portrayed as fundamentally the product of white pioneering. Given that premise, alien and unassimilable foreigners, devoid of pioneer qualities, portended doom for the survival of this most American of American regions. Extending the argument to its logical end, American racial identity, construed as "white" and Anglo-Saxon, had to be salvaged for future generations. The "old stock" in the East were already coping with an inundation of "new" Europeans supposedly determined to underlive and outbreed the declining Yankees. Meanwhile, the "Far West," as Nebraska-born Edward A. Ross claimed, stood alone as "that last asylum of the native-born." It could not, then, be the asylum for the "tempest-tost" from the backwaters of Europe. Most definitely, the West, so soon after the conquest and relocation of the Indians, could not freely offer its wide-open spaces to blacks, Asians, or Mexicans.[15]

American identity thus depended on the maintenance of cultural and racial homogeneity and the defense of an "American race." Confronting diversity in the West prompted members of the dominant society to formulate constructions of other peoples' racial identities and capacities for assimilation in relation to widely accepted assumptions about race and citizenship. Racial constructs aided in the categorization of immigrants and minorities as either unassailably white and thus possessed of proper citizenship qualities or decidedly nonwhite and therefore undesirable as possible citizens. Not a few observed the growing diversity and feared for the future. "When we consider the influence of immigration, it is by no means reassuring to reflect that so large a share of it is pouring into the formative West," wrote Josiah Strong, the Congregationalist home missionary and Social Gospel advocate whose best-selling 1885 book, *Our Country*, cataloged the anxieties of white, Anglo-Saxon Protestants in a rapidly changing industrial society.

Strong, who had presided over a frontier congregation in Cheyenne, Wyoming, in the early 1870s, argued that the West lay unusually prone to the evils of greed and the concentration of wealth, socialism, the saloon, Mormonism, and Roman Catholicism, as well as immigration. "These forces of evil, which are severely trying the established institutions of the East, are brought to bear with increased power upon the plastic and formative society of the West. It is like subjecting a child to evil influences, for resistance to which the full strength of mature years is none too great." Although no best-seller, a little volume published by a San Francisco lawyer in 1896 echoed the

concerns of Strong and placed the West at the center of the nation's immigration dilemma. In *Immigration Fallacies,* John Chetwood Jr. alluded to the
perception that, with the closing of the frontier and impending loss of the
public lands, the country was rapidly being deprived of its "great national
safety valve." As tempting as it might appear to divert the vast numbers of
immigrants then arriving in crowded Eastern ports to the Western prairies,
Chetwood cautioned that the dubious character of that immigrant tide demanded a numerical restriction.[16]

Beyond a generic rendering of the evils to which immigration and its associated effects subjected the West, anxious observers participated in the
great national debates on immigration from Europe, seeking to define the
racial qualities of different groups and how those attributes would impact
Western societies. Although recent historians of immigration have argued
compellingly for the need to dispense with the "old" and "new" immigration
as categories, in the context of the late nineteenth and early twentieth centuries, "old" versus "new" was an important rhetorical distinction.[17] An 1891
editorial in the *Nation* noted how the 1890 immigration was shifting toward
more Italians, Poles, Hungarians, Russians, Austrians, and Bohemians and
fewer Germans, Scandinavians, English, Scotch, Irish, Dutch, and Swiss.
Several months later a Treasury Department report prompted further comment in a second editorial in the *Nation,* which observed that "the flood
which is already so enormous is steadily and rapidly increasing in quantity."
As for quality, the figures showed "a distinct deterioration" regarding social
condition because "it [the "new" immigration] is not related to us in race or
language, but has habits of thought and behavior radically foreign to those
which have so far prevailed in the United States."[18]

What this amorphous mass of "radically foreign" immigrants would do to
the United States if allowed to "flood" the republic filled many a page in the
nation's newspapers and periodical press, as well as hundreds of books, congressional debates, and convention proceedings. Nativist organizations, such
as the anti-Catholic American Protective Association, founded in Iowa in
1887, and the Immigration Restriction League, formed by New England
elites in 1894, agitated against "un-American" influences and lobbied for
changes in immigration law. It was widely assumed, moreover, that the vast
majority of the "new" immigrants had no intention of becoming assimilated.
One writer summarized the indictments in a 1904 article for *Overland
Monthly.* Congregated in urban colonies, "neither the adults nor their children have any opportunity to learn what constitutes true Americanism," he
began. "They live as they lived at home or even worse; they talk as they talked
at home; they think as they thought at home; and to them the President is
only a king by another name." Lacking education, the new immigrants nat-

urally drifted into crime. Being paupers, they also lacked the foundation to become good citizens. Others perceived the colonies of uneducated and impoverished immigrants from southern and eastern Europe in clear terms of race and citizenship. "We who are here owe our democracy to selected races," Congressman William Kent of California announced in the House of Representatives in 1915. "We owe our democracy to races that have long struggled for constitutional liberty and who know what it means. . . . It is necessary that we carefully select our citizenship."[19]

In a 1919 study of public education, Ellwood P. Cubberley, dean of the School of Education at Stanford University, expounded on the distinctions he and many "old stock" Americans had made between European immigrants. On the "old" immigration from England, Ireland, Germany, and Scandinavia, Cubberley noted little difficulty in assimilation to American ways. "All were from race stock not very different from our own, and all possessed courage, initiative, intelligence, adaptability, and self-reliance to a great degree." Each group added to "our national life" through its unique qualities. For Cubberley, the "new" immigrants from southern and eastern Europe, "largely illiterate, docile, lacking in initiative, and almost wholly without the Anglo-Saxon conceptions of righteousness, liberty, law, order, public decency, and government," had diluted the nation's racial stock, corrupted politics, undermined social conditions, and disrupted public education. Foreign folkways and languages had supplanted American ones, while the nation struggled "to absorb and assimilate" the numberless hordes of "new peoples." As with so many commentators on the new immigration, Cubberley could not resist making a digestive metaphor, describing the problem as "a serious case of racial indigestion."[20]

Individuals closely involved with immigrant education, like Cubberley, but inclined toward a relatively more liberal approach to Americanization, struggled as well with preconceptions and prejudices toward southern and eastern Europeans. Ethel Richardson, the director of the California Commission of Immigration and Housing's Bureau of Education, expressed harsh judgments regarding Armenians and Germans from Russia living in Fresno during World War I. Armenians "exhibit certain antisocial traits which stand in the way of their being easily assimilated," she reported, while "isolation and the consequent inbreeding" had rendered the "Russian-German" population "static." Grace Raymond Hebard's remarks to a meeting of the Wyoming Federation of Women's Clubs in 1916 offer another example of much conventional wisdom regarding European immigrants among progressive Westerners. A University of Wyoming professor and Americanization teacher, Hebard first enlightened the clubwomen about the fundamental differences between the class of immigrants—"advanced in in-

Colorado Fuel and Iron Company miners outside boardinghouse, ca. 1900. *Colorado Fuel and Iron Company Sociological Department Report for 1901–1902,* 14. Colorado Historical Society.

dustry, skilled in agriculture, and above the average in intelligence"—which had once predominated with those now coming from "southeast continental Europe," who were "less educated . . . not skilled in industry," impoverished, and lacking in ambition. "Americanization and citizenship are two identical words to the majority of the American born citizens," she then pointed out, yet "under conditions as they now exist, the two words are as far apart as the North and South pole." Immigrants, Hebard continued, "should be made to feel that citizenship is a favor and not a right."[21]

For many white Westerners, particularly those living in the Pacific Coast states, concerns regarding racial homogeneity did not focus entirely on southern and eastern Europeans. To Chester H. Rowell, a newspaper editor and leading progressive from Fresno, and many of his contemporaries on the West Coast, the admission of unassimilable Asian immigrants menaced the very survival of western civilization. Poised to defend that civilization at its last outpost on the Pacific, Californians and other Westerners added a compelling ingredient to the era's cultural debates—the racial frontier. This was the idea of the frontier as not just a historical model explaining American development, but as a palpable physical and ideological barrier between "American" civilization and foreign influence, especially that emanating from the Far East and represented by immigrants from China and Japan. "Californians are vividly conscious of their position as the warders of the Western mark," Rowell explained. "They hold not merely a political and geographic, but a racial, frontier—the border between the white man's and the brown man's world."[22]

Racial frontier rhetoric defined Asian immigrants as permanently outside of the American experience. In practical terms, the erection of barriers to unwanted immigration from Asia between 1882 and 1924, couched in the language of the racial frontier, was a predominantly Western variation on the national obsession with cultural and ethnic homogeneity. The Chinese Exclusion Act of 1882 prohibited the importation of Chinese laborers for ten years while providing exemptions, in line with an 1880 Sino-American commercial treaty, for government officials, teachers, students, merchants, and travelers. In 1884, Congress amended the exclusion measure to broaden the definition of "laborer" to include Chinese from such places as Hong Kong that were not part of China and in 1888 barred Chinese laborers from reentering the United States unless they had family or property in the country. The Scott Act, also passed in 1888, barred reentry for laborers even if temporarily out of the United States and intent on returning. The 1892 Geary Act extended exclusion for ten more years and established a requirement for certificates of residence for Chinese immigrants. Another ten-year extension of the Chinese Exclusion Act passed in 1902 and, finally, Chinese laborers were excluded indefinitely in 1904. The 1902 and 1904 legislation also succeeded in extending coverage of the exclusion laws to all U.S. possessions, including the Philippines and Hawaii.[23]

Excitement concerning Japanese immigration, which had dissipated after renewal of the Chinese Exclusion Act in 1902, reappeared and became a permanent fixture on the West Coast by 1905. The Gentlemen's Agreement of 1907–1908, actually a series of notes between the U.S. ambassador to Japan and the Japanese foreign minister, conceded that only merchants, farmers, students, diplomats, tourists, and Japanese residents of the United States returning from visits to Japan qualified for passports. The Japanese government agreed to prevent the issuance of passports to all laborers or to those holding passports to other countries.[24] Not surprisingly, the Gentlemen's Agreement did little to quiet the anti-Japanese movement, which thrived on allegations of the smuggling of Japanese laborers over the Canadian and Mexican borders, the supposed flooding of the Pacific Coast states with "picture brides," and the presumedly increasing control of California's rich agricultural lands by Japanese farmers.

In 1907, California's legislators first began to seriously consider blocking ownership by and restricting the option of leasing agricultural land to "aliens ineligible to citizenship." Between 1907 and 1911, Republican presidents Theodore Roosevelt and William Howard Taft managed to convince the legislature to back down in the interests of international comity. In 1913, however, Democratic president Woodrow Wilson and Secretary of State William Jennings Bryan failed to prevent passage of an alien land law that implicitly targeted Japanese immigrants. The Alien Land Act of 1913 prohibited ownership of land by "aliens ineligible to citizenship" and limited leases to three years. Hiram W. Johnson, California's progressive Republican governor, pointed out that U.S. naturalization law did the actual discriminating against the Japanese and thereby absolved the state of any responsibility should Japan protest against the Alien Land Act.[25]

California voters, through the initiative process, revised the Alien Land Act in 1920 to remove even the limited leasing privileges provided in the 1913 law and make it more difficult for Japanese immigrants to possess land as guardians of their American-born citizen children or as stockholders in American-controlled land companies. The legislature added an amendment in 1923 that outlawed cropping contracts, in which white landowners had allowed Japanese farmers to work a section of land for wages. Legal challenges to the California alien land law ultimately came to naught, while Arizona, Washington, Louisiana, New Mexico, Idaho, Montana, Oregon, and Kansas enacted similar legislation between 1917 and 1925.[26]

Efforts to achieve the exclusion of Japanese immigration altogether continued apace. An "Asian barred zone," created as part of the federal Immigration Act of 1917, effectively excluded all "Asiatic immigration" with the exception of the Chinese, who were already excluded, and the Japanese, regulated by the Gentlemen's Agreement. Exempting government officials, missionaries, teachers, doctors, lawyers, students, artists, authors, merchants, and travelers, the Asian barred zone was designed to prevent the influx of Hindu and East Indian immigrant labor to the West Coast.[27] Hiram Johnson, now a senator, led efforts, beginning in 1921, to organize a unified West Coast campaign to achieve total exclusion of Japanese immigrants. The landmark Immigration Act of 1924 (also known as the National Origins Act) represented the climax of nearly a quarter century of effort by California's anti-Japanese movement by excluding entirely aliens who were not eligible for naturalization.

As with southern and eastern Europeans, Chinese and Japanese immigrants represented an unassimilable mass, guaranteed to flood the Pacific Coast states and territories specifically, if not the entire West and, ultimately, the nation. Asian immigrant communities, like other minorities, were typically relegated to relatively well-defined ethnic enclaves. Moreover, unlike immigrants from Europe, Africa, or Latin America, newcomers from China and Japan could not become citizens, a proscription based on ambiguous legal definitions of Asian racial identity. Asians' inability to become naturalized American citizens helped reinforce the boundaries between them and a dominant society that needed little convincing of Asian unassimilability.

To clearly establish the boundaries of the racial frontier, figures in the anti-Asian movements of the late nineteenth and early twentieth centuries repeatedly discussed the unalterable differences between Asian and American civilizations. A congressional committee that traveled to San Francisco in 1879 tersely summed up the indictment against the Chinese immigrant and civilization: "He is not *for* us. He is not *of* us." That same year, during debate on a bill to restrict commercial activities for Chinese in the United States and prohibit the employment of Chinese labor, Senator James H. Slater of Oregon declared, "It is a conflict between different races, between different and antagonistic civilizations, and is as irrepressible as that other conflict [between whites and blacks] which has caused so much trouble and disaster in this country." Noting that Americans had completed their crossing of the North American continent and now faced the oldest nation and civilization in the world, Slater warned that the "antagonism of race and civilization" forbade mixing the two peoples, which would only result in "irritation and discontent."

In 1882, Senator John F. Miller of California, whose bill ultimately became the original Chinese Exclusion Act, reiterated the crucial point that civilization's westward march had been consummated on the Pacific Coast. Discoursing on Chinese history, the senator insisted that the Chinese had "remained the same through all the changes of the world," impervious to western "literature, art, science, or religion." Any effort to merge two such "radically antagonistic" civilizations as the Chinese and the American would thus prove as impossible as mixing oil and water. The proof, Miller observed, lay in the Chinese "colonies" on the Pacific Coast. They were "changeless, fixed, and unalterable," he announced—even the children born on American soil. Former San Francisco mayor and future U.S. senator James D. Phelan sounded a similar tocsin in 1902, observing that the Chinese still in California after nearly twenty years of exclusion remained "a permanently foreign element. . . . it has been clearly demonstrated that they can not, for the deep and ineradicable reasons of race and mental organizations, assimilate with our own people, and be molded as are other races into strong and composite American stock."[28]

Combating Chinese immigration, which supposedly emanated from a stolid and static civilization and a weak nation in terms of international con-

James D. Phelan, U.S. senator from California, 1915–1921, and inveterate foe of Asian immigration. Bancroft Library, University of California.

cerns, required less mental torture for those constructing the racial frontier than addressing immigration from Japan, a rapidly modernizing society and an increasingly powerful presence on the world stage. Nonetheless, anti-Japanese leaders and followers did their best to portray their concerns as an irrepressible conflict between civilizations as well. Chester Rowell and numerous other Western exclusionists held that Japanese "race pride" resulted in irresolvable complications when arrayed "against the white man's race exclusiveness." Such a demanding state of affairs could only be alleviated through the erection of a barrier between two proud civilizations. A favorite anti-Japanese theme meant to buttress the dichotomous relationship between the two nations involved Japanese loyalty to the homeland. Senator Phelan, in testimony before a House committee in 1919, insisted that "their allegiance is to the Mikado, and that vast number of Japanese on the western coast now would rise as a man in case of conflict between the United States and Japan."[29]

Establishing the boundaries of western civilization required defining Asian immigrants as belonging to irremediably different civilizations. To further underscore the importance of keeping the Chinese and Japanese apart from it, Anglo-Saxon civilization required definition as well. "They [in California and on the Pacific Coast]," Senator Miller proclaimed in 1882, "are forming and building up American institutions based upon Anglo-Saxon civilization. They have seen and understand that there can be no stability to their institutions and government unless based on one civilization." "The Anglo-Saxon is not the only civilization, but it is confessedly the highest one," a writer in the *Overland Monthly* announced in 1886. Therefore, Americans possessed a national duty to protect their civilization by, if necessary, restricting or excluding immigration of those from lesser civilizations. Once defined, anti-Asian theorists and practitioners proclaimed the absolute necessity to defend American or Anglo-Saxon civilization in the interests of self-preservation and clearly delineated the barriers beyond which Asians should not cross.

For instance, the report of the 1879 House committee called for stopping the onslaught of Chinese immigrant labor at the Sierra Nevadas, deeming the task "a case of self-preservation—a question of who shall abandon the fertile fields of the Pacific coast; the proud white Caucasian, or his inferior in mind and and [*sic*] body and soul?" Some years later, a senator from Montana also implied a connection between the notion of national self-preservation and the maintenance of a racial frontier when he acknowledged a theoretical foundation, based on "the universal brotherhood of the human race," for denying a nation the "right to use its frontier as an element of protection." On the practical level, however, situated "in the hard experience of human life," the senator expressed support for the 1892 bill extending exclusion for another ten years on the basis of protection for labor and industry via "a national frontier." Confessing that prejudice played a central role in Westerners' demands for exclusion, a Colorado newspaper nonetheless maintained that "it rests upon a well-defined instinct of self-preservation."[30]

Finally, self-styled racial theorists in the West denied to Asians, coming as they did from antagonistic civilizations and unassimilable by definition, the status of immigrant. The influx of Chinese and Japanese, avatars of the racial frontier said over and over, was not immigration, but an "invasion." In 1902, for instance, James D. Phelan provided a Senate committee with a history lesson, replete with military metaphors, regarding the displacement of "the sons and daughters of the pioneers" in California by "these invaders . . . from a foreign land." Fourteen years hence, Phelan, now a senator, complained, "We on the Pacific coast have been holding back, in the matter of the Chinese and the Japanese, a real, silent, but overwhelming invasion. They are accomplishing by silence and diplomatic means what they dare not attempt by open and forceful means." Though misunderstood and unappreciated, Phelan and his fellow defenders of western civilization on the Pacific coast were "saving this country from Asiatic contamination." To Phelan every indication, from the Japanese immigrants' "mastery of the land" to "their great fecundity," revealed "their plan to establish a little Japan permanently in California, which would ultimately colonize the entire Pacific coast." Stop the influx and the threat of Japanese expansion, symbolized by invaders in the guise of immigrants, would be stopped.[31]

By articulating the insoluble differences between East and West, anti-Asian individuals and organizations constructed the foundation of the racial frontier, bolstering an ethnocentric national identity that clearly situated Asian immigrants beyond that frontier's physical and ideological boundaries. The architects of the racial frontier symbolized these differences by painting Chinese civilization as hopelessly retrograde and antagonistic in relation to the ever-advancing West and Japan as a proud and dangerous competitor whose emigrants formed, as did the Chinese before them, a silent, invading army of occupation. Embracing the putative value of a monocultural civilization, opponents of Asian immigration proclaimed their patriotic desires to man the ramparts and preserve the sanctity of their Anglo-Saxon or American world.

After the turn of the century, as Westerners gradually secured a curtailment of most Asian immigration, the numbers of immigrants from Mexico steadily increased. A U.S. senator from Texas, many years before migrant labor from south of the border became a pressing issue, formulated a critique of the Mexican that was strikingly similar to the racial frontier rhetoric of

Japanese agricultural workers in California, early twentieth century. Japanese American National Museum (gift of Henry Chihiro Mikami)

anti-Asian nativists. "We know that the people over there are aliens to us in blood, aliens to us in their social habits and political education, aliens to us in every sense of the word," Samuel B. Maxie announced during a debate on the floor of the House of Representatives in 1877. For decades thereafter, many Westerners would maintain that unchecked Mexican immigration presented a distinct threat to the maintenance of a homogeneous society because of the virtual impossibility of assimilation ever taking place.

University of California economist Paul S. Taylor, in his study of Mexican labor in the late 1920s, noted that the most persistent objections to Mexicans on the part of Anglos still pertained to the perception of the laborers as "an alien people." "Of all the foreign stocks represented in any considerable numbers in our population," University of California zoologist Samuel J. Holmes claimed, "the Mexicans appear to be the least assimilable." For evidence, Holmes pointed to New Mexico Hispanics, including state legislators, unable to speak English despite living in the United States for generations. A military officer with extensive experience on the Southwestern frontier reported to the federal Bureau of Education that Mexican immigrants and American citizens of Mexican descent represented an "exception" to the "great melting pot of American Amalgamation."[32]

Several factors, outlined in studies from the period, explained why ethnic Mexicans stood outside the nation's supposedly irresistible symbol of assimilation. Obvious to many, the itinerant nature of the immigrants' jobs in Western agriculture and industry operated against effective assimilation. Mexican migrant farm laborers "are not permanent, do not acquire land or establish themselves in little cabin homesteads, but remain nomadic and outside of American civilization," concluded Bureau of Commerce and Labor investigator Victor S. Clark in 1908. Three years later, the federal immigration commission acknowledged the difficulty of assimilation, but discounted any importance so long as the laborers quickly returned to Mexico. Unlike Asian immigrants, sojourners from Mexico could become naturalized American citizens. On the other hand, white Americans generally agreed that the Mexican laborer, whether an immigrant or an American citizen by treaty or birth, represented an inferior type of human being.[33]

Anglo interpretations of Mexican political life enhanced the notion that migratory laborers destabilized social arrangements and prevented the qualities of citizenship from taking root. Having never known what democracy was, the Mexican immigrant came to the United States unschooled in proper civic ideals and subject to the attractions of radical panaceas or charismatic autocrats. "He has been raised on the triangular [M]exican mixture of feudal obedience, communal lawlessness and a skeletal framework of government which appears to be somewhat democratic," reasoned a night school teacher from California. "His apperceptive mass is a sum of these things, while the spirit of democracy is entirely absent." On the other hand, Mexican immigrants possessed powerful patriotic sentiments toward their troubled homeland, which created additional difficulties in making citizens of them in the United States. "To change the Mexican immigrant's loyalty from his native to his adopted country requires a realignment of organized sentiment," University of Southern California sociologist Emory Bogardus explained, and the typical experiences that most confronted in the United States did little to "arouse his desires to become a citizen."[34]

A number of particularly adept students of Mexican immigration discussed the significance of the Mexican immigrant's folk culture in relation to adjusting to the demands of life in urban-industrial America. Although cultural customs and folkways were frequently interpreted by Anglos as racial traits, discerning observers, such as the Mexican-born sociologist Manuel Gamio and economist Paul S. Taylor, presented more subtle analyses. Gamio, in an investigation conducted in the late 1920s, discussed contact in terms of largely aboriginal and mestizo cultures making an abrupt change once they met the "modern, integrated, and homogeneous civilization" of the United States. This disorienting collision of preindustrial peoples with industrial society was complicated by the presence of Mexican-American culture, which, though "American nominally," was nonetheless traditionally

Mexican in intellectual and emotional respects. In addition, cultural differences and difficulties of assimilation were accentuated by isolation in urban barrios or company colonies situated away from American towns, a condition explored by Taylor in his study of sugar beet *colonias* along the front range of Colorado. "The disparity between the company colonies and the American towns," Taylor noted, "is further accentuated to the eye by the fact that the colony houses are of adobe construction, rectangular, and usually flat-roofed—picturesque villages of an alien culture set down in the midst of the fields."[35]

Discrimination accompanied and intensified the residential segregation of Mexicans in the West. According to Carey McWilliams, writing in the late 1940s, Mexican immigrants faced a more restrictive environment in terms of where in Western communities they could live, at what jobs they could work, and with whom they could associate "than in the northern industrial communities where a different pattern of acculturation prevails." The intensity and persistence of discrimination in the Southwest, McWilliams believed, worked against the adoption or incorporation of "Anglo-American" values and cultural norms. Indeed, as a Mexican high school student explained to Paul S. Taylor, white attitudes caused Mexican nationals to resist becoming American citizens. "I don't know whether I will become a citizen," the student informed Taylor. "Because of the race prejudice against my people I doubt if citizenship would be any advantage."[36]

Taylor's young informant understood that Anglo observers, whether opposed to immigration from Mexico or not, saw race as the central determinant in defining the ethnic Mexican's place in Western society. "We regard them as Mexicans," an Imperial Valley employment agent explained. "I have never attempted to draw a line between white and black Mexicans. We have different ideas as to white and black in the West." A former congressman from San Antonio elaborated on the meaning of ethnic Mexicans' place in the cotton belt: "There are probably 250,000 Mexicans in Texas who were born in the state but they are 'Mexicans' just as blacks are Negroes though they may have five generations of American ancestors."[37] The labeling of all Mexican immigrants and Americans of Mexican descent as simply another undifferentiated mass of nonwhite labor typified attitudes among Western employers, labor leaders, opinion makers, politicians, and the general public. A concise but telling statement by a Texas cotton grower summed up the prevailing sentiment on Mexicans and race: "We feel toward the Mexicans just like toward the nigger, but not so much." Those inclined to examine the racial composition of the Mexican immigrant population more closely also expressed concern at the preponderance of Indians and mestizos. "They are Indians in physique, temperament, character, and mentality," noted the author of a federal government report in

1908. Emory Bogardus echoed a typical Anglo assumption about Mexicans possessing a mixed Indian-Spanish ancestry, arguing that the "Indian elements are dominant" in mestizos.[38]

Assumptions regarding the social and cultural attributes of Mexican immigrants accompanied the economic and racial critiques. Senator William E. Borah of Idaho put the case succinctly: "Their ideals and ideas are quite different from ours." Even sympathetic and progressive observers, such as Bogardus, subscribed to certain stereotypes concerning Mexican character. For instance, having cautioned against stereotyping in his 1934 study of Mexican immigrants, he referred to Mexicans as "a siesta-loving people." Bogardus addressed other aspects of the Mexican laborer's social and cultural characteristics, summing up community organization as "an organized, loose arrangement, resting on daily needs, and taking little thought of the morrow." The "mañana spirit," as Bogardus termed it, while perhaps identifiable as a roughly eloquent "plea against a hectic machine age," prevented the "hacienda-minded" peon from learning responsibility and thrift. Regarding health and hygiene, Bogardus faulted irresponsible American employers and an indifferent American public for the deplorable conditions of Mexican immigrant camps and communities but characterized the "average Mexican immigrant" as "uninstructed." In terms of morals, the sociologist explained the Mexicans' shortcomings as a result of a simple, preindustrial "life organization" confronting the "complex social conditions" of urban, industrial America.[39]

The solution to the problem of assimilating Mexican immigrants, according to some, lay in education and social amelioration: "With adequate childhood backgrounds and later training in hygiene and sanitation the Mexican peon as a class responds as well to satisfactory standards as do any people of similar culture levels," noted Bogardus. In California and other sections of the American Southwest, many Americanizers zeroed in on Mexican immigrant women as the key to assimilating the largest growing segment of the immigrant population in that region. As they did with southern and eastern Europeans, Americanizers occupied an ambivalent position in relation to Mexican immigrants. Situated between restrictionists—principally labor unions and organized nativists—and agricultural and industrial employers hoping to keep the tide of cheap labor flowing, Americanizers in California and the Southwest tried to salve their own doubts about Hispanics with assurances that they had the power to work a profound transformation through the seemingly isolated Mexican women in the barrios. An indication that Americanizers believed they could effect a tremendous impact on assimilation in general by turning Mexican mothers into near copies of proper "American" housewives is seen in a comment by Amanda Matthews Chase, a "home teacher" in Los Angeles. "One class of Mexican women,"

Mexican mine workers in Arizona. Arizona Historical Society, Tucson.

Chase explained in 1917, "a timid, sloppy, baby-submerged lot to begin with, now take an honorable place on general school programs with songs and recitations in English." Once the Mexican women had been taught English, hygiene, proper diet, table-setting, and similar "skills," Americanizers hoped, the Mexican family as a whole would cease endangering cultural homogeneity. In particular, the Mexican mother, as the presumed transmitter of values within the family, would serve as a conduit of American ways to the second generation even if she and her husband failed to become completely Americanized themselves.[40]

Conclusion

A number of historians have concluded that immigrants in the West acculturated more rapidly and were accepted more readily by Anglo-Americans than was typically the case east of the Mississippi.[41] This may be true of some immigrant groups, for instance those from northern and western Europe who had arrived prior to 1880 or certain elements among the "new" immigrants who may have abandoned old ways of thought and behavior more readily in a bid for acceptance. On the other hand, Mennonites from central and eastern Europe who settled on the Great Plains clung tenaciously to traditional cultural forms such as language, while Asian and Mexican immigrants faced unrelenting nativist pressures. The idea that the more open society of the West resulted in easier acculturation and greater acceptance seems to explain little in relation to either the exceptionally strong ethnic identities of certain groups or the itinerant immigrant labor force toiling away in Western mines and mills after 1900. Nor does it apply very realistically to non-Europeans. Rather than any clear tendencies toward unencumbered acculturation, much of the evidence concerning immigrants and ethnics in Western communities shows ambivalence in attitudes toward Americanization, a dialectical relationship between continuity and change, and infinite variations on the theme of the transition from immigrant to ethnic groups.[42]

As for native-born Americans and many "old" immigrants who had staked their claims to the pioneer tradition, attitudes toward newly arriving immigrants from Europe, Asia, and Mexico ran the gamut from terror to toleration. To say that the foreign-born found a greater measure of acceptance in the postfrontier West is debatable. More apparent is a sense among concerned Westerners that they better understood the singular conditions that their maturing societies faced. "The misfortune is that the people in the east do not know what we know here," Loring Pickering, a San Francisco newspaper publisher, informed a congressional committee in 1879. Pickering's testimony concerned the dangerous effects of Chinese immigration, but suggests as well a prevailing sense among Westerners that they inhabited a unique region and confronted particular challenges that "people in the east" could not possibly comprehend and appreciate.[43] Decades later, many Westerners in the Americanization movement also brought attitudes regarding racial and ethnic differences based on histories that they perceived as distinct from Eastern experiences. What white Westerners had heard and read and been told about the meaning of their past had enormous repercussions for the ethnic and racial groups that they sought to control. Immigrants and minority groups, defined by white Westerners as the "other," performed a vital function for those individuals most concerned with shaping themselves as white pioneers and crafting their vision of the West as their land of opportunity and a "white man's country." Their self-definitions shaped by pioneer experiences in what they remembered as an unruly frontier, Western Americanizers felt a responsibility to incorporate the foreign-born on terms conducive to sustaining a "civilized" West.

Citizenship and American identity were frequently defined by Westerners in racialized terms, and assimilation was deemed either possible or impossible according to the racial characteristics of various immigrant groups. Southern and eastern Europeans, as Grace Raymond Hebard of Wyoming put it, were seen as "a large foreign element whose habits of thought and behavior are radically different from those which the founders of the nation hoped to establish."[44] Chinese, Japanese, and other Asians, according to "racial frontier" rhetoric, could never assimilate into American civilization and must remain permanently outside of the American experience. Asians, as U.S. Senator James D. Phelan of California testified in relation to Japanese immigrants, were "not made of the stuff from which American citizens are made."[45] Providing the labor that, along with government subsidies, developed the Southwest after 1900, Mexican immigrants were stereotyped by nativists as indolent, undependable, and docile. Not all Americanizers subscribed so openly to the stereotypes. Yet, finding Mexican civilization wanting, they tried to reshape Mexican immigrants to fit the reformers' preconceived ideas of proper American lifestyles and behaviors.

If indeed the presence of certain racial types would undermine the nation's racial and cultural homogeneity, it could only follow that the same groups presented a clear and present danger to the nation's civic health. As committed as they were to citizenship training, some Americanizers had to confront their doubts about the capacity of many immigrants in the West to assimilate. Meanwhile, the status of Asian immigrants in terms of naturalization remained unsettled until a 1922 Supreme Court decision confirmed earlier rulings defining them as neither white nor black and thus ineligible to citizenship. Until that time, however, Asian nationals were reported as registering for and attending Americanization classes in some Western locales. Impoverished, mistreated, and segregated, Mexicans residing in the United States remained attached to their homeland, to which they often returned.

Consequently, Mexican immigrants had very low rates of naturalization and were therefore deemed by some observers as impervious to the melting pot's otherwise powerful appeal. Nonetheless, in southern California and the remainder of the American Southwest, the Americanization movement, especially after World War I, focused on Mexican immigrants.

For decades, American-born migrants of predominantly Anglo-Saxon and Protestant backgrounds had interacted and competed with immigrant and ethnic communities, which they frequently perceived as peculiar if not dangerous enclaves antithetical to American cultural norms. Drawn to the West by an open environment and presumably limitless resources, both American-born and foreign-born settlers carried cultural systems seen as indispensable to the successful transplantation of civilization. The "West," however defined, represented grand avenues of opportunity but also a potential battleground over contested meanings of Americanism. Those groups who, from the point of view of many native-born Americans, avoided the Americanizing influences of Western environments and institutions threatened the nation's homogeneity and identity. They did so by retreating to remote corners of the region, cordoning themselves off in enclaves to perpetuate alien ways. Stubbornly persisting in loyalties to the ethnic group, to countries left behind, to languages, and to churches, immigrants clustered in colonies defied the American creed of undivided devotion to a republic of individuals. If deemed racially fit and properly guided away from the disunifying and disorganizing ways of tradition and ethnic allegiance, immigrants would soon appreciate the supreme importance of the individual's personal relationship with the nation's history and institutions, best achieved through appropriating the language and ideals of America.

2

PROGRESSIVES, AMERICANIZATION, AND WAR

Progressive Americanization and the California
Commission of Immigration and Housing

Training immigrants in English and civics as a means to facilitate assimilation and expedite naturalization had been taking place for decades before 1910, but usually in an unofficial capacity by private charitable organizations or ethnic associations. Government-supported adult immigrant education, which has been studied most often within the context of large Eastern and Midwestern cities with substantial immigrant populations, actually originated in San Francisco. In 1856 the city began devoting some local resources to citizenship classes and special programs for religious, linguistic, and racial minorities. A short-lived adult school—a joint venture of the city school board and the Roman Catholic Church—operated in 1856 and 1857. In 1860, decades before most Eastern cities did the same, the school board established evening schools for adult immigrants, even providing a separate school for the Chinese from 1861 to 1870, when political pressure forced its closure. California lawmakers, with the 1879 constitution, became the first in the Union to formally recognize evening schools as part of the state's public school system. A 1908 amendment to the state constitution allowed the use of state monies to fund evening classes. Two years later, with the election of Hiram Johnson as governor, progressive Republicans came to power in California. Ultimately, Johnson's administration would consolidate the tradition of adult immigrant education in a new state agency, the California Commission of Immigration and Housing.[1]

The advent of Americanization activity in California and parts of the West corresponded to the broader currents of reform percolating to the surface of American public life in the early 1900s. In the West, progressivism typically emerged as a response to corporate domination of state politics and corruption in city governments. Progressives in California sought to curtail the power of the Southern Pacific Railroad's political machine; elsewhere reformers battled other railroad companies, mining corporations, and stockgrowers' associations. In addition, a rapidly growing urban population strained some local governments' capacities to provide basic services, leading to innovative changes in the management of a number of Western cities. At

the state level, reform administrations succeeded in enacting initiative, refer-
endum, and recall measures, direct primaries, woman suffrage, corporate
regulation, labor laws, conservation, and temperance and prohibition.[2]

By eliminating corruption from politics and imposing discipline and restraint on both business and labor, progressive reformers sought to tame
Western society of its frontier characteristics. Informed by expertise and devoted to efficiency, progressives hoped to forge a unified and mature New
West, an equal partner in an emerging national culture rather than an ex-
ploitable colony. Assimilation of the "new" immigrant, if composed of the
proper raw material for citizenship, held considerable promise in bringing
order out of the chaotic conditions that seemed to plague Western labor
camps and cities. To pessimists, a journalist from Topeka wrote in 1904, the
immigrant "is as great a bugaboo as the ghosts and hobgoblins of their extreme youth." Aware of "nothing but the immigrant himself," he continued
"they lose sight of the size and assimilative powers of this land of ours. . . .
While the immigrant may not be the menace to our Nation that the pes-
simist makes out, he yet presents a problem—the problem of his assimilation and transformation into a good American citizen."[3] Guardedly
optimistic, reformers perceived in Americanization a road toward social cohesion and stability.

Progressives' reactions to the "immigration problem" were as diverse as the
impulses that fostered reformers' overall approaches to the ills of a modernizing nation.[4] Treating social problems, for many reformers, did not necessi-
tate reassessing assumptions on race and immigration. The progressive
sociologist Edward Alsworth Ross, in a xenophobic outburst for which he
later expressed some regret, asserted that "the cheap stucco manikins from
Southeastern Europe do not really take the place of the unbegotten sons of
the granite men who fell at Gettysburg and Cold Harbor." He derided the
"flood of immigration" as "the beaten members of beaten breeds." Ross also
advocated eugenics and coined the phrase "race suicide" to describe the impact of the declining birth rate of America's "native-stock" white population.
In 1906, Chester Rowell, soon to become a leading figure in California's progressive Republican insurgency, issued a stern warning about racial mixing
and race suicide for readers of his Fresno newspaper. Rowell, an intellectual
well versed in mainstream racial theorizing, explained how the crossing of
Spanish conquistadors with California's "Digger Indian," Greeks with Turks
and Tartars, and the "original Aryan race" with "the aboriginal black blood
of India" had resulted in "your servile peon," "your track-walking Greek,"
and "your low-caste Hindu," respectively. "And just these three wrecks of
once proud races," by which he meant the Castilian Spaniard, the Greeks of
Athens and Sparta, and the Aryans, "are being imported, to repeat the same

process here. It is the most dangerous possible form of race suicide, and must be stopped."[5]

While displaying considerable optimism about the power of education to effect assimilation, Western reformers involved with the Americanization movement often betrayed their fear that many immigrants were unassimilable. The progressives' dilemma was made more compelling by wide disagreement over the precise meaning of Americanization. Some adhered to an Anglo-conformist approach, often simply termed Americanization or Anglo-Americanization. "Americanization" theory, according to sociologist William Carlson Smith, writing in the 1930s, meant that "all immigrants should divest themselves of their heritages immediately and take over a standardized American pattern for their lives." Ellwood P. Cubberley of Stanford University believed that the task of educators centered on eroding the group cohesiveness of the "new" immigrants, "to assimilate and amalgamate these people as a part of our American race." Future Bureau of Indian Affairs director John Collier, an employee of the California Commission of Immigration and Housing in 1919–1920, sarcastically defined Anglo-Americanization as "the taking over of the richly variegated cultural life of the many peoples coming to our shores and reducing them all to a deadly, dull Puritan drab." Despite such criticism, many reformers involved in the organized aspects of Americanization, believing that material progress and social order depended on homogeneity, adhered to Anglo-conformist conceptions of assimilation.[6]

If a significant proportion of progressive Americanizers hoped to reshape aliens into citizens through conformity to a presumptive Anglo-American cultural model, most had a broader understanding of assimilation. The high-minded ideal of an American "melting pot," derived from the play of that name written in 1908 by the English Jewish immigrant Israel Zangwill, has persisted as the most durable mainstream sentiment regarding Americanization in the United States. The melting pot theory, explained the liberal Americanizer and pluralist Isaac Berkson in 1920, "is apprehensive of lack of culture much more than it is of a diversified culture, and is, therefore, not so quick to condemn the old heritage which the immigrant brings with him. It tries rather to preserve the old while the new is being formed."[7] Arch M. Thurman, state director of Americanization in Utah after World War I, typified many Western progressives' embrace of the melting pot ideology. "Americanization is the union of native and foreign-born in all the most fundamental relationships and activities of our national life," Thurman argued. By uniting new citizens with the native-born, Americanization promised to broaden the national experience through "a mutual giving and taking of contributions from both new and older Americans." George Lewis Bell, an attorney from Berkeley and the California Commission of Immigration and

Housing's executive officer, exhorted a statewide meeting of clubwomen to "utilize these old-world forces so as to make iron sides for this melting pot." Thurman and Bell represented what appears to be the predominant attitude on the part of Americanization workers in the West: that assimilation required some inclusion of immigrants' perspectives and traditions.[8]

Tolerant of and receptive to the infusion of certain immigrant cultural contributions, then, the "melting pot" nonetheless assumed a homogeneous end: a composite, unified, American populace, melted as in a crucible to form a single element. Many champions of the melting pot idea, like Theodore Roosevelt, still trumpeted the principle that one was either unequivocally American or "not an American at all." Meanwhile, a few liberal progressives opposed the beliefs in either Anglo-conformity or a melting pot. Thinkers such as Horace Kallen and Randolph Bourne posited alternative ideals of cultural pluralism and cosmopolitan nationalism. They saw America, in Kallen's words, as "a multiplicity in a unity, an orchestration of mankind," and decried what Bourne called "the imposition of its own [Anglo-American] culture upon the minority peoples."[9] Kallen's "Democracy Versus the Melting Pot," which first appeared in the *Nation* in 1915, confirmed pluralism and heterogeneity as part of the era's cultural debates. Regardless of how hard nativists or Americanizers tried, Kallen contended, an individual's ethnic ties could not be sundered. In a famous statement, Kallen said, "Men may change their clothes, their politics, their wives, their religions, their philosophies, to a greater or lesser extent: they cannot change their grandfathers."

Bourne's "trans-nationalism" differed somewhat from Kallen's cultural pluralism, which, as several scholars have shown, was premised on descent rather than consent—not unlike Anglo-conformity. Instead of merely preserving cultural or ethnic differences, Bourne cultivated the idea of multiple citizenship, a cosmopolitan alternative to Anglo-Saxon hegemony. Influenced by American pragmatists William James, Josiah Royce, and John Dewey, Bourne wanted a decentralized, dynamic, and pluralistic American democracy, a polity always in the process of creation. Provocative as pluralist theories of assimilation undoubtedly were at the time, few individuals engaged in actual citizenship education, in the West or elsewhere, applied pluralist theories to their work.[10]

Much of the impetus for progressive Americanization originated with the settlement house movement, a fact that underscores most Americanizers' preference for melting pot approaches to assimilation. Urban settlement house reformers and social workers in the East and Midwest established night school classes for immigrants during the 1890s and the first decade of the twentieth century. In many urban centers of the West, settlements with similar "Americanization schools" appeared as well. North Side Neighborhood House in Denver, for instance, which opened in 1904, held English classes at night for Italian men.[11] A number of leading Americanizers in California also had extensive backgrounds in settlement work. The Reverend Dana Bartlett established citizenship classes at his Bethlehem Mission in Los Angeles, where, as a 1912 magazine article stated, "to-day the American is being created." College Settlement in Los Angeles, at which future "home teacher" Amanda Matthews Chase did work, opened a night school in 1903 that was soon incorporated into the city school system. Emory S. Bogardus began his Americanizing activities as a settlement worker at Northwestern University before moving on to Los Angeles, where he taught courses on immigration and Americanization at the University of Southern California. Simon Lubin, destined to become the head of the California Commission of Immigration and Housing, had studied immigrant communities as a settlement worker in New York City and Boston. In a similar vein, other Western reformers entered Americanization work through the YMCA, which started night school classes in Tacoma, Washington, in 1910 and sponsored immigration conferences on the West Coast in 1912 and 1913.[12]

With the exception of California, public schools entered the adult immigrant education field relatively late. New York City began its night school program in 1901, Chicago followed suit in 1903, Detroit initiated a program in 1906, and other Eastern and Midwestern cities soon followed. The early professional efforts of settlement workers and urban public schools were soon augmented by patriotic organizations, such as the National Society of the Sons of the American Revolution, which formed a Committee on Information for Aliens at its national conference, held at Denver, in 1907. State government support of Americanization in the East also began in 1907, when New Jersey authorized school boards to direct evening classes for immigrants. Several state agencies designed to address problems related to immigration were created as a result of the 1911 publication of the U.S. Immigration Commission's reports. New York State's Bureau of Industries and Immigration, the California State Commission of Immigration and Housing, and similar bodies in New Jersey, Massachusetts, Pennsylvania, and Rhode Island investigated conditions and suggested legislation as well as proposed and in some cases implemented Americanization programs. Usually led and staffed by individuals associated with settlement houses, these state agencies sought to address growing demands for immigration restriction by carrying out a "domestic immigration policy" focused on geographical dispersion, protection, education, and relief.[13]

The North American Civic League for Immigrants (NACL), formed in New York City in 1907, soon became tantamount to a national clearinghouse for Americanization. It coordinated the efforts of the patriotic organizations and concerned itself with cultivating efficiency and good behavior among immigrant laborers. In addition, the league organized immigrant aid centers in Boston, New York, Philadelphia, Chicago, Los Angeles, and other cities, lobbied for Americanization programs in public schools, offered lectures, and distributed pamphlets. An energetic young lawyer and social worker named Frances Kellor emerged through her affiliation with the NACL to become the leading national figure in the Americanization movement. As secretary of the New York–New Jersey Committee of the NACL and chief investigator of the New York State Bureau of Industries and Immigration, Kellor developed a powerful stake in Americanization between 1907 and 1914. In these years, she exhibited her close association with both industry leaders and progressive reformers by deftly mixing scientific management techniques with calls for achieving cultural unity through education. Kellor toiled ceaselessly to coordinate schools, industry, private organizations, public agencies, and any institution interested in the work, hoping to forge an unassailable and professional Americanization movement. Her mobilization of American institutions to acculturate immigrants along professional, scientific lines played convincingly to a public anxious about immigration's effects on the nation's cultural health yet optimistic about experts' abilities to efficiently mold them into citizens.[14]

At the time Americanization began attracting greater national attention, chiefly through the exertions of Frances Kellor and other Easterners, California had the longest-running adult immigrant education system in the country. In 1913 progressive reformers established an agency that, as part of its immigrant protection responsibilities, would coordinate Americanization in the Golden State. An assumption that the recent opening of the Panama Canal presaged a likely boom in European immigration to the West Coast influenced, in some measure, the formation of the California Commission of Immigration and Housing (CCIH). This prospect of a dramatic jump in immigrant numbers guided the thinking of West Coast reformers attending immigration conferences sponsored by the YMCA at Tacoma in 1912 and San Francisco in 1913. Speakers at the meetings sounded a humanitarian concern for immigrants' well-being and expressed a desire to avoid having East Coast slums replicated in the Far West. Creation of the new commission was inspired as well by a 1912 national Progressive Party platform plank on immigration drafted by Frances Kellor and Jane Addams. To ensure greater opportunity for immigrant workers and protect them from the greedy and unscrupulous, the plank endorsed "Governmental action to encourage the distribution of immigrants away from the congested cities, to rigidly supervise all private agencies dealing with them and to promote their assimilation, education, and advancement."[15]

Although the commission came into existence as a committed expositor of "mutual accommodation" between natives and immigrants, its creation also reflected the ambivalence many reformers displayed about immigrants and race. California's progressive Republicans, led by Governor Hiram Johnson, intended to achieve political objectives by making inroads among urban, working-class, foreign-born voters by creating an agency devoted to those constituents. In much the same way, passage of the Alien Land Act of 1913 sought to salvage a rural voting bloc disaffected by the presumed domination by Japanese immigrants of choice agricultural lands. Hardly immune to the traditional anti-Asian sentiments in the state, progressives from California led in the drives for alien land legislation and the exclusion of Japanese immigrants. In 1911 Governor Johnson had quashed anti-Japanese land legislation on behalf of the Taft administration, which feared a diplomatic breach with Japan. Two years later, with Democrat Woodrow Wilson assuming the presidency, Johnson reversed course and signed a discriminatory alien land act. Interestingly, the main section of the act referred to the right of "aliens eligible to citizenship" to own agricultural land; this statement, of course, was an implicit denial of such rights to Japanese and other Asian immigrants. In a small concession, "aliens ineligible to citizenship" were allowed to lease land for up to three years. The point here is that in a single legislative session, California's progressive administration bolstered its political bona fides by, on one hand, creating an agency committed to immigrant aid and education and, on the other, reassuring white Californians that unassimilable Japanese immigrants would not take over the state's farmlands.[16]

The California Commission of Immigration and Housing, created within the ambivalent political setting of both accommodation and rejection of immigrants in 1913, approached its mission with a cosmopolitan "melting pot" approach. Heading the CCIH and establishing its liberal tone was Simon Lubin, a Sacramento merchant and Harvard-trained economist who had drafted the legislation creating the agency. Lubin advanced a "domestic immigration policy" at odds with the emphases on restriction and deportation favored by nativists. Lubin argued instead for protecting immigrants from abuse and exploitation, distributing the immigrant population more widely, maintaining appropriate standards for health, sanitation, housing, education and justice, and offering programs to educate immigrants for citizenship. Section 6 of the act creating the commission, signed into law by Johnson on 13 June 1913, dealt specifically with immigrant education, announcing at the outset the new body's mandate to cooperate with all "proper authorities and organizations . . . with the object in view of bringing to the immigrant the best opportunities for acquiring education and citizenship." In addition to procuring lists of school-age immigrant children in order to facilitate enforcement of a compulsory education law, the CCIH was charged "to devise methods for the proper instruction of adult and minor aliens in the English language and other subjects," in particular those stressing citizenship rights and duties. Acknowledging the peculiar nature of California's agricultural labor system and the existence of pockets of rural poverty, the act also demanded the extension of educational opportunities to immigrant children and adults in labor camps and other remote sections of the state.[17]

To these ends, a Bureau of Immigrant Education was formed and another of the original commission members, Mary S. Gibson, assumed responsibility for the commission's Americanization programs. As the commission's staff was small, Gibson, a former schoolteacher and prominent clubwoman from Los Angeles, worked closely with the State Department of Public Instruction, the State Board of Education, the University of California Extension Division, numerous local school authorities, and her extensive network of women's club contacts. Volunteers, rather than bureaucrats, would conceive and direct much of the commission's Americanization work in California during Gibson's tenure. "It is to her clear vision, to her energy and enthusiasm and her readiness to sacrifice her personal interests in her service to this undertaking," the commission proclaimed upon her retirement in 1922, "that the State owes, in a very great measure, its present far-reaching policy in the education of the foreign-born." The head of Americanization work for the National American Woman Suffrage Association dubbed Gibson "the fairy godmother of the Pacific Coast, so far as the immigrant is concerned."

At the outset of her tenure in 1913, however, immigrant education in California faced a potentially demoralizing situation, with an estimated 10 percent of foreign-born whites illiterate in any language. Soon after its creation, the commission surveyed adult immigrant education programs in San Francisco, Sacramento, and Los Angeles. In San Francisco, which had supported adult education since 1860, Gibson nonetheless found private agencies operating classes rather than the city. In Los Angeles, on the other hand, the public schools provided night classes, and those students who passed competency tests in English and civics were granted diplomas that were regularly accepted by judges in lieu of courtroom tests for naturalization. Inspired by the successes in Los Angeles, Gibson lobbied for the standardization of adult classes along similar lines as well as state Americanization textbooks and teacher training programs.[18]

Americanization in California was also brought directly into the homes of immigrants. Aided by the Home Teacher Act of 1915, Gibson and her subordinates in the Bureau of Immigrant Education initiated an innovative "home education" plan for immigrants and their children. Specifically, the legislation permitted school districts to employ a licensed home teacher for every five hundred students attending classes daily. According to the commission, conditions within immigrant communities had created the need for home teaching. Family problems, such as the second generation's growing loss of respect for their parents and the ignorance and timidity of foreign-born women, required enlightened intervention by dedicated Americanizers. When visiting immigrant children's homes, therefore, home teachers were authorized to discuss such topics as school attendance, sanitation, and citizenship rights and duties.

Tacitly, the home teacher law was aimed at immigrant women, an aspect of Americanization given added urgency by the enfranchisement of California women in 1911. As freshly minted voters and citizens seeking to redefine the very nature of citizenship, politically active women in California, many of them progressives, quite naturally felt attracted to Americanization as a vehicle to further transform women's public lives. By joining the Americanization movement, native-born women citizens could play a vital role in constructing citizenship for immigrant women, leading them to greater independence and moral authority both within the home and within the community at large. In addition, home teachers tried to bring immigrant mothers together for classes in English and domestic responsibilities, thereby defining women's citizenship for immigrants according to white, progressive, middle-class norms.[19]

Whether in the school, at the workplace, or inside the home, progressives perceived Americanization as a tool for realizing greater control over a dynamic and frequently chaotic society. Progressives often spoke about assimilation in fairly open and tolerant tones, but their optimism was qualified by conventional racial assumptions and the fears of a fragmented citizenry. Liberal approaches to Americanization in the West, exemplified by the California Commission of Immigration and Housing, would be challenged by the pressures of forging wartime unity.

Western Progressives, Councils of Defense, and Wartime Americanization

With the outbreak of World War I in the summer of 1914, interest in Americanization, fueled by suspicions of immigrant disloyalty, was transformed into a national public crusade. The humanitarian reform impulses embodied in the Americanization work of the California Commission of Immigration and Housing waned as the movement edged toward more centralized and nationalistic manifestations. In a symbolic realization of Americanization's increasing centralization, Frances Kellor's New York–New Jersey Committee of the NACL left the parent organization and changed its name to the Committee for Immigrants in America. The committee soon became "the general consulting headquarters for immigrant and Americanization work throughout the country" and provided the impetus, initial funding, and staffing for the newly created Division of Immigrant Education in the Department of Interior's Bureau of Education. That Bureau, in September 1915, inaugurated its so-called "America First" campaign to forge cooperation among chambers of commerce, corporations, patriotic societies, fraternal orders, and educators.[20]

Competition, as opposed to cooperation, characterized the relationship between the Bureau of Education and the Department of Labor's Bureau of Naturalization, which began sponsoring citizenship education through the public schools and holding discussions concerning the coordinated nationalization of Americanization in 1914. "The proposition of a coöperative movement on the part of the public schools with the Bureau of Naturalization," Commissioner of Naturalization Richard K. Campbell reported, "was not only heartily indorsed, but the bureau was urged by . . . educators to take the lead in this educational work so vital to citizenship and to formulate a course of instruction adaptable to the candidates for citizenship." In addition, Campbell noted the "unanimous indorsement" of the cooperation between schools and bureaucrats on the part of federal judges. By spring 1916, the bureau claimed cooperation with public schools in six hundred cities and towns in forty-four states, had sent the names of 130,000 citizenship candidates and their wives to the schools, plus personal letters to each of the declarants, petitioners, and wives thereof, and distributed an Outline Course in Citizenship and a Syllabus of the Naturalization Law nationwide.[21]

Generally speaking, federal bureaucrats' endorsement of education for Americanization reflected the progressives' faith in the power of education as well as education reformers' recognition of environmental forces in shaping individuals. In this regard, then, much World War I–era Americanization did not ignore the students' culture and environment. Many Americanizers talked of meeting students halfway and avoiding impositions of their own norms and cultural biases. Federal Commissioner of Education Philander P. Claxton offers a clear rhetorical example of this attitude:

> Americanization is a process of education, of winning the mind and heart through instruction and enlightenment. From the very nature of the thing it can make little or no use of force. It must depend rather on the attractive power and the sweet reasonableness of the thing itself. Were it to resort to force by that very act it would destroy its spirit and cease to be American. It would cease to be American if it should be-

come narrow and fixed and exclusive, losing its faith in humanity and rejecting vital and enriching elements from any source whatever.

Immigrant education, compassionately applied and sensitive to the students' environment, would certainly result in the unity for which the American people longed. Americanizers believed this assertion. "The school," stated Frank V. Thompson, superintendent of public schools in Boston and author of one of the Carnegie Corporation studies of Americanization, "both public and private, may and we hope will become a powerful influence for a progressive unification in our continually renewed diversity of citizenship." Officials in the bureaus of education and naturalization saw themselves as key facilitators for public schools and other Americanizers. Through efficient, democratic, and humane methods, progressives convinced themselves that they could indeed forge national unity.[22]

Under optimum conditions, crafting a more orderly, unified society by tenderly stirring away at the melting pot was a Herculean challenge for progressive Americanizers. To meet immigrant pupils halfway and eschew coercion while a nation girded for the increasing likelihood of war complicated matters, to say the least. A certain uneasiness and sense of foreboding appeared within reformist circles, a fear, as a February 1916 editorial in the *Independent* stated, "that we shall deal emotionally, thoughtlessly and more or less ridiculously with the practical problem of converting our millions of unnaturalized aliens into Americanized American citizens." Because the country had not created anything resembling a systematic program of assimilation up to that moment, immigrants would be exposed to "all the excesses of virtue unrestrained by common sense." The desire to speed things up would, with certainty, lead to "foolish" and "unjust" methods. Most reformers, however, entertained misgivings about un-Americanized immigrants and not the potential for excessive enthusiasm and abuses on the part of well-intentioned and patriotic Americanizers. "It [Americanization] is also a duty we owe to ourselves," an editorial writer in the *Outlook* declared. "Unless we perform it the United States will cease to be a Nation and will become a mere congeries of detached racial groups."[23]

Appreciating the grave dangers that separation into "racial groups" portended for the Republic, Americanizers embarked on their crusade. At a Bureau of Naturalization–sponsored ceremony in Philadelphia in May 1915, President Woodrow Wilson admonished several thousand freshly naturalized citizens to "become in every respect and with every purpose of your will thorough Americans." Wilson's remarks reflected, on one hand, an increasing amount of rhetoric critical of alleged tendencies on the part of the foreign-born to maintain attachments to their homelands.[24] In addition, the

Unidentified group with American flags, Butte, Montana, ca. 1915. Montana Historical Society, Helena.

president's comments comprised a significant element of the administration's pragmatic campaigning on behalf of preparedness for possible entry into the war, wherein the education of the immigrant became an even larger concern.

Augmenting the federal government's agenda to further centralize immigrant citizenship education, the Committee for Immigrants in America organized an Americanization Day celebration to take place across the nation on 4 July 1915. A National Americanization Day Committee designed the event to both officially welcome immigrants and stress national unity. To stimulate enthusiasm, the committee sponsored a prize contest for the best statement on "What America Means and How to Americanize the Immigrant" along with the best plan for a citizenship celebration on the Fourth. In addition, letters from the federal commissioners of immigration and education were sent to mayors and school officials, posters placed in railroad stations and factories, and press releases provided to news bureaus nationwide. At elaborate receptions on the day itself, speakers—having been provided with data and suggestions by the committee—explained the need for Americanization Day and the meaning of Americanization. Schoolchildren sang patriotic songs, newly naturalized citizens made speeches of gratitude, and, in some instances, officials conducted naturalization ceremonies.[25]

In an attempt to feed off the enthusiasm generated by Americanization Day, the indefatigable Kellor and her organization, now called the National Americanization Committee (NAC), organized the first National Conference on Immigration and Americanization, which met in Philadelphia in

January 1916. "The great immediate task before us," Kellor wrote on the eve of the conference, "is Americanization, the welding of the many races and classes in this country into one enduring, steadfast nation." Once convened, the conference resolved to eliminate duplication of effort and concentrate on forming a definite national program while instituting a special committee to plan means by which to achieve those objectives.[26] Kellor's National Americanization Committee continued until 1919 as a national clearinghouse, orchestrating Americanization Day and other patriotic celebrations, sponsoring more immigration and Americanization conferences, soliciting help from women's clubs and patriotic societies, and forming and financing the Immigration Committee of the U.S. Chamber of Commerce.

After the United States entered the war, the NAC enjoyed what one historian terms "a quasi-governmental status." The NAC staff was "hired" as one-dollar-a-year "special collaborators" by the Bureau of Education, while Kellor became a "special advisor" to the bureau commissioner and supervisor of a new Division of Immigrant Education section, called the War Work Extension (later absorbed by a reorganized Immigrant Education Division, which was renamed the Americanization Division). The extension, as described by Commissioner of Education Philander P. Claxton, was established to supplement the division's purely educational exertions by "undertaking the larger phases of the work which depend less on class instruction in English and other subjects, but which can be done through the foreign language press, racial societies and clubs, popular lectures, lantern and moving picture illustrations, games, festivals, special celebrations, exhibitions and personal contact." The NAC also backed the National Committee of One Hundred, appointed in September 1916 by Commissioner Claxton, "to act as an Advisory body and as a representative Council of the organizations and agencies cooperating with the Bureau."[27]

As part of the preparedness campaigns, Congress in August 1916 authorized formation of the Council of National Defense (CND) to organize production of food and munitions and assess the prospects for effective mobilization of the nation's resources. With American entry into the war, state councils of defense were formed, either through executive appointment or legislative action, and the Council of National Defense organized a State Councils Section to assist in coordinating wartime activities in the states. The state councils, frequently assisted by county and community councils, would manage the home fronts, overseeing production and conservation of fuel and food, mobilizing labor, coordinating the sale of war bonds, and investigating alleged disloyalty. Ultimately, the CND would designate its affiliated state councils as the official bodies responsible for wartime Americanization of the foreign-born. The Council of National Defense system showed exceptional promise in linking even the most obscure crossroads village to the national war effort and fostering a unified national outlook.[28]

A week after Congress declared war, an executive order created the Committee on Public Information (CPI), composed of the secretaries of state, war, and the navy and directed by George Creel, a former journalist and progressive activist from Denver. Creel saw the CPI as a publicity bureau geared to articulate America's democratic purpose in going to war as well as explain the government's war policies to the American people. As with the CND, the CPI would seek to enhance Americans' feelings of unity and nationhood through involvement in an intensified campaign for Americanism. Concerning immigrants, Creel had published an article in early 1916 entitled "The Hopes of the Hyphenated," in which he laid the blame for the masses of unassimilated foreigners on the federal government and the native-born American population at large. "In the activities of hyphenated societies and a foreign-language press, expressed by seditious attacks upon the Government and bold disruptions of industry, there is plain evidence that the melting-pot has not been melting," Creel wrote.

The lack of allegiance to the United States characteristic of "great masses of aliens" constituted "a domestic peril that threatens the permanence of American institutions as gravely as any menace of foreign foe." For further proof of this parlous state of affairs Creel noted both the millions who had returned to Europe and the millions who had remained in America but shown no "formal evidence of any desire for citizenship." "No record of failure," Creel concluded, "was ever written so plainly." To redress the "record of failure," Creel's agency included a Foreign Language Newspaper Division, which monitored the content of such publications throughout the nation. Another Denver reformer, Josephine A. Roche, directed the CPI's Division of Work with the Foreign Born, which was created in May 1918. Roche's division, which absorbed the functions of the Foreign Language Newspaper Division, concerned itself more broadly with cultivating immigrant loyalty through organizing foreign groups into patriotic societies, distributing war news and propaganda, and providing speakers and translations of CPI pamphlets.[29]

As the national government mobilized to fight in Europe and foster unity and cohesion on the home front, leaders in a number of Western states responded quickly to the war crisis. In some cases, state governments acted with extraordinary verve. Colorado, for instance, bolted from the starting gate on mobilization when Governor Julius Gunter appointed what Coloradans claimed as the nation's first State War Council and called out thousands of National Guard members a week before the United States formally declared war on Germany and Austria-Hungary. Officials in Kansas, on the basis of an emergency food conference in Governor Arthur Capper's office in March, also laid claim to having the first state council of defense. "Kansas buckled her armor at the next formal meeting on April 17," Capper recalled, "and outlined a program so comprehensive and practicable that it afterwards was adopted, with few modifications, in the organization of the National Council of Defense and served as a model for the organization of other state councils." Other Western states, if less bold in asserting a role as pioneers in organizing councils of defense, nonetheless followed suit during the first several weeks of the war.[30]

The alacrity with which state governments mobilized for World War I has struck some historians as indicative of Westerners' desire to prove themselves unequivocally loyal. In an interesting passage, the authors of a Colorado history survey argue that, because most Americans knew more about the state's inglorious record of industrial warfare than its "thriving cities or its imposing resources," the "eagerness for war" signified "a special desire for acceptance by the nation." To take, or at least claim, the vanguard in the nation's new crusade would demonstrate Westerners' maturity and earn the respect of sadly misinformed citizens in the East. "How better to assure future stability," these authors write, "than to expose European minorities to massive Americanization programs and to centralize control of economic activity in the hands of business leaders?" The fact that a significant portion of the votes in Congress against President Wilson's request for a declaration of war also emanated from the West added some grist for anyone inclined to question the regional commitment to the cause.[31]

Although accusations of disloyalty attached to Western states or particular groups within the region were infrequent and rendered insignificant by their outrageous and intemperate claims, Westerners took them seriously and responded with official denunciations. Lingering questions regarding the loyalty of the Latter-day Saints in Utah prompted the Mormon Church, which has been described as "intertwined with" the Utah State Council of Defense, to publish a tract defending the state and church. Compiled by Benjamin Goddard of the Latter-day Saints' Bureau of Information, the pamphlet documented evidence of Utah's loyalty during the Civil War, the Spanish-American War, the Philippines campaigns, and World War I. "Although constant reference is made in this treatise to the loyalty of the Mormon people, mainly because of the persistent falsehoods circulated by hireling agitators in the East," Goddard wrote, "it should be stated that the citizens of Utah, irrespective of creed, party or color, are working unitedly in all war activities and are responding nobly to every call of the government."[32]

In New Mexico, race and culture had greater potential than religion to unsettle "hireling agitators" or self-appointed loyalty watchdogs. In August 1918, a letter to the editor of the *North American Review*, signed by "Henry

Wray" of Kansas City, Missouri, sought to cast doubt on the loyalty of ethnic Mexicans in New Mexico. Concerned with the 1916 cross-border raids of Pancho Villa and continuing revolutionary unrest in Mexico, Wray asserted that the Southwest lay exposed to invasion by an army of "degenerate" Mexicans convinced that the "cowardly gringo" would not fight. Rehashing claims of German intrigues given a semblance of credence by the Zimmerman telegram affair of 1917, the writer warned that "a few German officers and some German gold effectively placed could assemble this army and start it northward." With a citizenship preponderantly Mexican in origin and sentiment and where schools, churches, the legislature, and the courts conducted business in Spanish, New Mexico had "remained Mexican in every sense of the word." The small, devout, and secretive sect of Penitentes, Wray went on, were in actuality "a powerful political organization" committed to restoring New Mexico to Mexican statehood. "A state of treason exists in this part of our country," the writer concluded ominously.[33]

New Mexicans reacted with righteous indignation to Wray's letter. In a telegram to the *North American Review,* Senator Albert B. Fall demanded an apology to readers and the people of his state for publication of the "heterogeneous, fantastic mixture of ignorant, malicious and false statements and slanders." New Mexico's representative in Congress, W. B. Walton, made a comprehensive reply on the floor of the House of Representatives. "Were it not that some of the people of the United States have seemed to be in absolute ignorance of conditions in the West, and especially the Southwest," Walton began, "I would not expend the breath necessary to make an answer to this classic in libel and epic in vicious slander." Walton then reminded his colleagues of New Mexico's loyalty during the Civil War and, more pointedly, in the Spanish-American War and the recent disturbances with the Villistas. "Thousands of Spanish-American youths are now proudly wearing the khaki of the American Army," and Spanish-American citizens had invested millions of dollars in Liberty Bonds and War Savings Stamps. The congressman also refuted Wray's claims about Spanish language use and the Penitentes. In defending New Mexico, however, Walton indulged in a fair degree of cultural mythmaking concerning the Southwest, ignoring the thousands of non-Spanish ethnic Mexicans (about whom "Henry Wray" was actually most concerned) then residing and working in the state. Walton described the "Spanish-Americans of New Mexico" as "descendants of the Conquistadores, who wrested the Southwest from the savage tribes of Indians. The blood of nobility flows in their veins." The journal, which received dozens of other letters protesting the Wray letter and defending New Mexicans' loyalty and patriotism, did indeed apologize and agreed with Fall that the letter should never have been published.[34]

From 1917 through the early months of 1919, those responsible for managing home front affairs in the West usually faced more momentous challenges than responding to malicious falsehoods about regional loyalty. Formation of state councils of defense in the West possessed potentially disorienting implications for Western progressivism, particularly in terms of fostering unity at the likely expense of civil liberties. Many of the Western governors in office at the time either identified as progressives or, if not reformers themselves, had accommodated to political change. Progressive Republican Washington E. Lindsey was governor of New Mexico, where a special legislative session in early May 1917 created the State Council of Defense (of which four of eight members were Hispanic). Elected governor in 1918, Octaviano A. Larrazolo, once a Democrat, entered office in 1919 as a progressive Republican inclined to emphasize ethnic issues and the interests of New Mexico's Spanish-speaking constituents. New Mexico succeeded better than most states in the West at keeping a lid on unrest and overzealous displays of patriotic scapegoating. Progressives in Kansas, on the other hand, led by Governor Arthur Capper, strained during the war years to reconcile their principled support for individual rights with the need to bolster patriotism and loyalty through increased government regulation of thought and speech. Not surprisingly, despite the likelihood of disenchanting individualistic Kansans, both ethnic and native-born, the State Council of Defense had little inclination to resist pressures to equate loyalty with conformity. Similarly, other progressives in the West, particularly when associated with the state councils, privileged patriotic duty over an individual's constitutional right to express dissent.[35]

A proclamation issued on 20 April 1917 by Governor Thomas E. Campbell and the Arizona State Council of Defense called for a united front on the part of aliens and citizens. "Let us be considerate of those who have been subjects of nations with which we are now at war," Campbell and the council admonished. Requests for unity and consideration could not, however, assuage the distrust and hostility many Westerners felt toward the foreign-born. The historical tensions between immigrant and ethnic communities and the larger society and state in the West reached a crescendo during the Great War. The United States's entry into the war had a tremendous impact on ethnic minorities throughout the region, and hostility toward German, Austrian, and non–northern European immigrants and ethnics predominated. "There are two possible sorts of human beings in America to-day— foreigners and citizens," intoned an article in the official publication of the Kansas State Council of Defense. "Of these it is the duty of citizens to be loyal; foreigners will be taken care of as they deserve, according to their actions." Grace Raymond Hebard, who served the Wyoming State Council of

Grace Raymond Hebard and unidentified student demonstrate their patriotism, ca. 1917. American Heritage Center, University of Wyoming.

Defense as a traveling speaker, paid tribute in a March 1918 address to "faithful Germans" but also sounded a Rooseveltian note: "There is no such thing as an American-German. Either they are for us or against, and they can not be both American and German."[36]

Hysteria and mob violence, based on authentic and rumored acts of disloyalty and suspicion, reigned in many areas of the West in the first weeks after the United States declared war. A man who shouted a toast to the kaiser in a Thermopolis, Wyoming, bar in April 1917 was hung from a beam, then cut down, revived, and forced to kneel and kiss an American flag before being run out of town. In Colorado, municipal authorities placed armed guards around water systems, National Guard patrols were stationed near reservoirs and power plants, warnings appeared concerning ground glass in German sausages, and a wireless station was supposedly operating on behalf of the Kaiser atop one of the state's highest peaks. When authorities were alerted to a gathering of bearded, suspicious-looking men, armed guards broke into what turned out to be a Grand Army of the Republic (Union Civil War veterans) meeting.[37]

Throughout the war years the Council of National Defense exhorted its state affiliates to strengthen the loyalty of German-speaking residents with, as a January 1918 bulletin phrased it, "the utmost tact and understanding." Nevertheless, the historical record for the period is replete with numerous examples of frequently tactless and thoughtless treatment of German and other ethnic minorities. Western states, among them Colorado, Montana, Nebraska, North Dakota, and South Dakota, restricted or banned the teaching of German in public schools and pressured parochial schools to cease instruction in German. A superintendent of schools near Grand Junction, Colorado, was reportedly tarred and feathered for using a book that contained favorable references to Germany, while a Colorado University prep school sponsored a "book burning" rally. German-language newspapers endured accusations of disloyalty and pressure to translate articles into English or cease publication. Zealous patriots forced the reluctant to purchase war bonds, while court dockets brimmed with prosecutions under state and federal sedition and espionage laws.

In pronouncing sentence upon a German Lutheran pastor convicted under the Espionage Act, a North Dakota federal district judge lashed out at the foreign-born. The "basic wrong of these thousands of little islands of foreigners," the judge lectured, was "that instead of trying to remove the foreign life out of their souls, and to build up an American life in them, they have striven studiously from year to year, to stifle American life, and to make foreignness perpetual. That is disloyalty." Harassment and arrests of putatively pro-German individuals occurred throughout the war years, often under the guise of quasi-official actions undertaken by 100 Percent American Clubs, vigilance committees, Minute Men, and Loyalty Leagues. With its notorious sedition law of 1918 (upon which the federal Sedition Act of 1918 was based), out-of-control State Council of Defense, and paranoid harassment of the Industrial Workers of the World, Montana, according to that state's leading historian, outdid every state in the nation in patriotic excess.[38]

The reactions toward unassimilated foreigners occurred within a wartime context that also witnessed increased local, state, and federal government powers. Authorities monitored the foreign-language press, registered noncitizens and enemy aliens, expedited extralegal harassment and persecution of allegedly disloyal citizens and aliens, and pressed for the passage of English-only laws. Alongside the intensified emotions and fears shaped by wartime, Americanization entered the public mind to an extent not apparent before 1917. Nonetheless, with the confusion sown by rival federal agencies and numerous private or semiprivate organizations vying for recognition and influence, the Council of National Defense and its affiliated state councils responded cautiously in officially entering the Americanization field. In late 1917, the National Committee of One Hundred, which advised the Bureau of Education on behalf of private organizations, requested an endorsement of its policies by the Council of National Defense along with a cooperative arrangement with the state councils. Once the Council of National Defense approved the request and the State Councils Section worked out the details with the Bureau of Education, the state councils became the official state agencies conducting the bureau's national Americanization program.

Thus, in February 1918, the State Councils Section belatedly encouraged states to take on Americanization work and form Americanization committees composed of representatives of the state council of defense, the woman's committee of the state council, employers of alien labor, the state board of education, and voluntary agencies involved in Americanization. In subsequent correspondence the State Councils Section urged states to include representatives of organized labor and the foreign-born on Americanization committees and appoint a state Americanization director. Finally, states were advised to inspire patriotism through the foreign-language press and speaking campaigns, promote the organization of English classes in night schools and factories, encourage aliens to become citizens, and centralize Americanization efforts through the state councils. In a letter addressed to President Wilson and signed by Secretary of War and CND chairman Newton D. Baker, the State Councils Section boosted the state councils as the vanguard of national Americanization work. "The existence of this great national system," the Baker letter claimed, "valuable for each and every government department, makes, of course, for economy of effort and renders unnecessary the creation of much local federal machinery which would otherwise have to be set up for the performance of specific tasks."[39]

State councils in the West responded to the State Councils Section's urgings in different ways. In response to a letter from James C. Stephens of the University of Colorado Extension Division in January 1918, Governor Julius Gunter had called in members of the Coal Survey Committee, composed of "the heads of the principal coal companies of Colorado," and asked them to help. The governor also wrote to the Boards of County Commissioners in counties with large numbers of foreigners, asking them to assist and set aside at least $150 for Americanization work. Finally, in March 1918, Governor Gunter named Professor George Norlin, acting president of the University of Colorado, to chair the Americanization Committee of the Colorado State Council of Defense. In its official newsletter, the council announced that the new committee would assist the Council of National Defense and federal Bureau of Education "in the task of welding the many residents in this country of foreign nativity or origin into a unified American people back of the fighting-line." Once constituted, the committee appointed Stephens to direct Americanization efforts in Colorado. Stephens, along with two assistants, concentrated on organizing so-called America First Societies in immigrant communities, principally in Denver, Pueblo, and a number of mining camps. The America First Societies functioned as organizations through which loyalty to American government and ideals could be strengthened and maintained as well as vehicles for classes in English and citizenship.[40]

Through the spring and summer of 1918, other state councils in the West incorporated Americanization into their official agendas. Inspired by the Department of Interior's Washington conference on Americanization in early May 1918, the Utah State Council of Defense appointed a permanent Committee on Americanization, chaired by the state superintendent of public instruction.[41] The Arizona legislature, in a special session, enacted a bill organizing a new Arizona State Council of Defense in June 1918 that included a section appropriating $3,000 for a survey and report of Americanization needs in the state. The Arizonans also passed a bill, with a $25,000 appropriation for the first year, providing night schools in districts where fifteen or more persons who were at least sixteen years old and did not read and write or speak English desired instruction.[42] In July, the director of the Kansas State Council of Defense proposed forming a committee composed primarily of naturalized citizens to conduct an Americanization campaign. Through a subcommittee on Americanization, the Kansas council's Committee on Public Relations took charge of the work. In New Mexico, Americanization programs were organized under the direction of the state superintendent of public instruction, who also served as the state council's

Professor George Norlin, president of the University of Colorado and chair of the Committee on Americanization of the Colorado State Council of Defense. Archives, University of Colorado at Boulder Libraries, Norlin Collection.

educational director.[43] In a number of states, including Montana and Nebraska, a large measure of Americanization work fell to the women's committees of the state councils.[44]

State councils of defense entered an Americanization arena in which settlement houses, public schools, university extension divisions, and federal bureaus already cooperated and often collided. Colorado's Committee on Americanization had to assert its prerogatives as the official wartime body in charge of immigrant education. Problems of centralization and control were most apparent in Denver, where the Denver Opportunity School had been cooperating with the Bureau of Naturalization on adult immigrant education since 1916. Yet the school and the Americanization committee worked out a mutually satisfactory cooperative arrangement. A more pressing dilemma emerged with Denver University, which desired to establish a Peoples' Institute and conduct Americanization programs independently of the Americanization committee. "It is clear to me," George Norlin informed Governor Gunter, "that if the work of Americanization is to be properly done it must be directed generally, if not specifically, by a single authorized agency and that this authorized agency cannot delegate the work to any other or lose control of it to any extent." To drive home that point, the State Council of Defense asked all county councils of defense, chambers of commerce, and boards of education to consult with the Committee on Americanization before proceeding with any form of Americanization. While not wanting to displace agencies engaged in "effective Americanization work," the state council hoped to achieve "greater harmony and concentration of effort" through prior consultation.[45]

Many Americanizers operating through the state councils of defense found themselves assessing the loyalties of various foreign-born groups and pondering means by which to break through walls of ignorance and distrust. A preoccupation with the menace posed by alleged pro-German spies and agitators, in some cases, colored the thoughts of state authorities. The Nebraska State Council of Defense, for instance, published and distributed a slightly revised version of a patriotic address first given at a "Naturalization Night" gathering at the Commercial Club in Omaha in February 1917. The Prussian-born speaker, C. J. Ernst, an official with the Chicago, Burlington, and Quincy Railroad, focused on naturalized German Americans in his remarks. "When our country is at war, no matter with whom," Ernst declared, "every one of us belongs and can only belong to one of two classes. We are today either loyal citizens of this our native or adopted land, or else we are traitors. The neutral or 'half-baked' citizen, in time of war, is an impossible conception."

Impressed by a meeting in Washington with the National Council of Defense, L. H. Farnsworth, the chairman of the Utah State Council of Defense, reported to his colleagues the grave danger presented by German-language newspapers and parochial schools: "To counteract this influence and this German propaganda there must be a vigorous and far-reaching activity among all loyal citizens, and it would seem to me that loyal Americans of German birth must see to it by their own work, among their own people, that such conditions cannot and must not prevail. The American people will not stand for it." In a September 1918 report, Colorado's James Stephens reported that the response to the America First Societies had been very positive, with just one or two instances of opposition. Stephens suspected that the resistance to Americanization indicated "the presence of enemy sentiment," but noted efforts being undertaken "to combat these conditions, and it is hoped that all suspicion and reluctance will soon be overcome."[46]

Ernst's anxiety about "half-baked" citizens, Farnsworth's concerns with "German propaganda," and Stephens's comments regarding "enemy sentiment" raise questions about the connection between Americanization and the assaults on ethnic groups, German Americans in particular, that characterized much home front sentiment during the war years. The problem of loyalty frequently centered on language, an issue the Colorado Committee on Americanization confronted during the busy summer of 1918. Victor Neuhaus, editor of the German-language *Colorado Herold* laid the problem before the State Council of Defense in June. Reassuring members of the council that the newspaper would preach the virtues of Americanism, Neuhaus asked for an official endorsement to print the newspaper in both German and English. "With the proper cooperation this paper might be made into a powerful instrumentality in the Americanization process," the editor hinted. The Council of Defense referred the matter to the Committee on Americanization, which recommended refusing such an endorsement.

Still awaiting a reply, an uneasy Neuhaus reiterated his desire for assistance in influencing his readers who could best be reached through their native language. Neuhaus's second letter was likewise referred to the Committee on Americanization. In a communication to the Executive Committee, Dr. Norlin expressed appreciation for Neuhaus's offer to aid Americanization but pointed out that "since it is a function and duty of the Committee to promote the study and use of the language of this Country, the Committee doubts whether . . . the Colorado Herold should be encouraged to publish in the German language." Moreover, to endorse a newspaper, regardless of the language in which it published, would put the committee and the Council of Defense on record as approving "the general policy of such paper." Apprised of the committee's decision, Neuhaus, to the great satisfaction of Norlin and members of the Council of Defense, soon began publishing in English only.[47]

Responding in a more general way to the use of foreign languages, the Colorado State Council of Defense referred proposed poster copy to the Committee on Americanization in late July 1918. Prompted in part by reports of difficulties concerning German language use, the council proposed the following text:

> Every Loyal and Patriotic
> AMERICAN
> Is Requested To Use The
> AMERICAN LANGUAGE
> At All Times
> IF YOU DON'T KNOW IT
> LEARN IT!

Concerned with the demanding tone of the initial draft, Dr. Norlin and the Committee on Americanization revised the copy to read:

> EVERY LOYAL AMERICAN
> SHOULD USE THE
> AMERICAN LANGUAGE
> IT IS THE LANGUAGE OF
> YOUR COUNTRY
> IF YOU DON'T KNOW IT—
> LET US HELP YOU LEARN IT

Once printed, the posters were distributed through county councils of defense for display in workplaces, post offices, courthouses, and other "prominent places." In addition, county councils and religious denominations that used German in their schools and church services received copies of a general letter that emphasized the avoidance of provocation "by greater wisdom and thoughtfulness on both sides." The committee admonished patriotic and "level-headed citizens" to do all in their power to prevent the excesses of equally patriotic but "hot-headed" colleagues. Seeking to make a distinction between actual disloyalty in word or deed and "mere suspicions," the committee pointed out that attacks and threats "directed against those suspected of pro-Germanism add to the difficulties of those who are seeking to preserve the community peace and keep the machinery of industry moving smoothly and efficiently." On the other hand, the letter reiterated the necessity for people of German birth and descent to avoid arousing suspicion, even if unfounded. The best way to accomplish that objective, according to the committee, lay in discontinuing the teaching of German in parochial schools and limiting the use of the language in religious services.[48]

In Kansas, pacifist traditions and antiwar sentiments underwent a quick transformation, and the State Council of Defense puzzled over problems of "slackers," German Americans, and disloyalty. The Committee on Public Relations, chaired by Chancellor Frank Strong of Kansas University, formed a subcommittee on Americanization and selected Dr. Martin Graebner of St. John's College in Winfield as state Americanization chairman. The emphasis in Kansas, as in other states, lay on the use of English and the voluntary relinquishing of German. "Of organized resistance there was scarcely a trace, and our foreign-born population was never, apparently, a real menace to our success," Graebner reported in January 1919. Nonetheless, a united effort on behalf of winning the war depended on "unity of language."

The inability to speak English on the part of foreign-born residents and citizens, Graebner explained, "rendered the utterance of disloyal remarks comparatively safe, and . . . had a tendency to provoke mob violence on the part of the more hot-headed members of society." Naturally, then, the Committee on Americanization desired to restrict the use of German but strove to do so "in harmony with the American spirit," eschewing the "harsh and autocratic methods" employed in other states. Graebner's committee held conferences with leaders of foreign-language organizations, primarily ministers and officials with the German Lutheran, Baptist, Methodist, and Mennonite churches. "We left the details in their hands, trusting them that the seed we had sown would yield fruit in abundance." Graebner congratulated the Committee on Americanization for effecting expanded use of English among German Americans in Kansas "without forsaking true American principles of liberty and justice, and without losing the good will of the Kansas people."[49]

The State Councils Section singled out the Washington State Council of Defense for its constructive, noncoercive approach to potential disloyalty and sedition. Led by Democratic governor Ernest Lister and Dr. Henry Suzzallo, president of the state university, who served as chairman, the state council in Washington, from the CND's perspective, placed strong emphasis on stimulating patriotism rather than repression. Be that as it may, Lister, Suzzallo, and other officials in Washington State spared no effort in aiding lumber companies determined to stamp out radical labor agitation, particularly the troublesome Industrial Workers of the World. Whatever restraint may have obtained in Washington was not apparent in Montana, where reformers had failed to curb the unbridled economic and political power of the Anaconda Copper Mining Company. Patriotic fervor took a violent turn in August 1917, when IWW organizer Frank Little was lynched during a miners' strike in Butte. During a special session early in 1918, the Montana legislature, encouraged by Governor Samuel V. Stewart and the State Council of Defense, passed a criminal syndicalism statute and sedition law aimed at suppressing allegedly treasonous speech by Wobblies and other dissenters. An amendment to the federal Espionage Act of 1917, first introduced by one of Montana's U.S. senators shortly after the lynching episode in Butte, was enacted in May 1918. For its part, the Montana State Council of Defense acted in many respects as a political arm of the Anaconda Company and condoned extralegal investigations, harassment, and punishment of "slackers," pro-Germans, and presumed Wobblies by overzealous patriots throughout the state.[50]

Progressive Americanization, largely predicated on moderate "melting pot" notions about assimilation, struggled to sustain the more tolerant strains of American principles while simultaneously seeking to forge a loyal new citizenry, speaking and thinking in one language. The dilemma was particularly acute in California, which, with the State Council of Defense most notable for its incompetence, continued to rely on the progressive Commission of Immigration and Housing to manage Americanization programs. Within just a few years of its organization, preparedness campaigns and wartime exigencies had compelled the CCIH to advertise its Americanization program as a crucial ingredient in the state's contribution to Allied victory and national unity, while at the same time holding fast to its philosophy of mutual accommodation between Americanizers and immigrants. Americanization involved far more than teaching English, the commissioners announced in a pamphlet outlining its program, and to be democratic, Americanization had to be inclusive, allowing representatives of the foreign-born and labor to contribute ideas. "No program, however excellent," the pamphlet warned, "can have its best success when handed down ready-made from above. . . . the program . . . must be an elastic thing, subject to modification by advancing experience."[51]

The commission's plans for wartime Americanization reflected its goal of inclusion and depended on the cooperation of several bodies. Americanization chairmen in each county sought out foreign group leaders and expedited the formation of committees and subcommittees, which were to be composed of representatives from immigrant groups, labor, employers, Americanization organizations, and education authorities. In addition to evening schools, home teaching, and mothers' classes, the CCIH and those cooperating with it published propaganda in English and foreign languages, sponsored films and patriotic programs, conducted poster, song, essay, and drama competitions, provided special library services, and lobbied for improved housing and sanitation measures. When it came to public exhortation, the commission advised English speakers to stress the democratic obligations of the native-born, the impact of race prejudice on national unity, and foreign-born contributions to the armed forces and American history. Foreign-language speakers, they suggested, should emphasize America's war and peace aims, the "advantages of democracy," the obligations of citizenship, and the necessity to learn English. Schools throughout the state were pressed to offer effective instruction for teachers and to inculcate proper citizenship values and decent treatment of the foreign-born. Industry and churches, according to the CCIH plan, had specific roles to play as well. For example, it fell upon both employers and employees to "co-operate in improving industrial conditions and in raising them to American standards, so that no opportunity will be afforded seditious or malicious agitators to use unsatisfactory conditions as pretexts in stirring up labor troubles."[52]

The adaptation of the California Commission of Immigration and Housing's mission to the exigencies of the home front demonstrated the dilemma of progressive Americanization in relation to wartime pressures and continuing agitation for immigration restriction and exclusion. Likewise, the advent of state councils of defense as official agents of Americanization raised troubling questions about the future of progressive Americanization. Generally speaking, the war brought a basic paradox to reformers. Although the conflict expedited the progressive search for order, it also generated dangerous emotions attached to nationalism and patriotism. "War necessitates organization, system, routine, and discipline. The choice is between efficiency and defeat," journalist and Council of National Defense staff member Frederick Lewis Allen wrote in April 1917. "The only way to fight Prussianism is with Prussian tools. The danger is lest we forget the lesson of Prussia: that the bad brother of discipline is tyranny—which our fathers fought to put down and our immigrants came to our shores to escape." In the end, the United States did not slide into an absolute tyranny, but civil liberties guaranteed by the Constitution frequently gave way to demands for loyalty and conformity.[53]

For many immigrants who had sought an escape from Prussian-style tyranny, the war years proved especially difficult. The pressure to become Americanized intensified well beyond anything previously experienced. The manner in which many among the growing ranks of Americanizers conducted their crusade alienated and frightened the foreign-born. A naturalized citizen herself, Professor Sarka B. Hrbkova of Nebraska had considerable insight regarding the "yawning, unbridged chasm that separates the alien from the native born American." In a pamphlet on Americanization published by the Nebraska State Council of Defense in 1919, Hrbkova acknowledged the complexity in assimilating peoples from diverse European backgrounds but also underscored what she considered the common and fundamental meaning of America to them. "It is indeed a problem," she wrote, "to make Americans of these surging, ebbing, responsive, sullen, singing, cursing, sorrowing, carousing, harmonious, disputatious elements, some coming from lands of liberal thought, others from age-old autocra-

Three Italian workers "preparing for citizenship" in southeastern Kansas, ca. 1917. From Loren Stiles Minckley, *Americanization Through Education*, 255. Kansas State Historical Society.

cies—all of them with dreams of a more or less realisable Utopia, which the magic word 'America' spells to them."

For optimists like Hrbkova, Americanization presented the opportunity for allowing the foreign-born to contribute the "highest expression" of their unique cultures to an ever-developing American civilization. "These inestimable contributions should not be crushed out in our effort to remake the immigrant, to shape him, overnight, so to speak, in the form of the kind of American who gets spoiled in the making." Hrbkova, like other progressives, used terms such as "cement" and "weld" in describing the unifying effects of successful Americanizing. Unfortunately, Hrbkova's vision of bridging the chasm between the alien and native-born had less impact on public sentiment than insistence on more forcibly cementing and welding the nation together through demonstrable 100 percent Americanism. It was within this context that progressive Americanizers in the West attempted to keep their programs afloat after the war.[54]

Postwar Americanization in the West

In the weeks following the conclusion of hostilities in Europe, federal agencies admonished states to carry on in forging a united America. Shortly after Armistice Day, the commissioner of naturalization lectured chairmen of state councils of defense to broaden their organizations' cooperation with public schools and take "affirmative action" to break down the barriers "between the foreigners, the citizenry, and citizenship" that wartime conditions had revealed. Meanwhile, the Council of National Defense resolved in December 1918 to recommend that state legislatures authorize continuation of state councils of defense to aid in postwar readjustment. Secretary of the Interior Franklin K. Lane, who also served as chairman of a new Field Division of the CND, warned Governor Arthur Capper of Kansas that "a failure to secure statutory authorization will appear to be a definite refusal by the highest authority of the State to recognize the State Council as an official body." The director of the Field Division instructed members of state councils that, whether or not legislatures extended the lives of their organizations, "the Americanization work . . . be placed upon a permanent footing." In addition, the federal Bureau of Education convened another national Americanization conference in May 1919.[55]

As it turned out, state legislatures throughout the country refused to appropriate funds to continue state councils of defense, thereby endangering many official Americanization programs. "The end of the war brought an end to our Americanization work, followed soon after by the dissolution of the State Council," the state Americanization chairman in Kansas ruefully reported. "Our joy at the victorious termination of the great war was mingled with a little regret that, more than likely, all organized Americanization work would thereby also find its termination. We were convinced that it ought not to stop, but should be carried on with increased vigor, as a regular function of government." Kansas State Council of Defense secretary J. C. Mohler, in a report to new governor Henry J. Allen in January 1919, urged an effort "to facilitate the establishment of night classes and all other mediums for teaching Aliens the English language and for other men assisting them in becoming American citizens." Mohler recommended establishing an Americanization committee to further the work. A bill to continue Americanization work failed to pass both houses of the Kansas legislature in 1919, although bills compelling the use of English in instruction in all schools did become law.[56]

An act establishing state-funded Americanization schools did pass in Montana, becoming law in February 1919. In New Mexico, the legislature enacted a law providing night schools with paid instructors for "illiterate or semiliterate adult persons."[57] The Utah legislature passed an American Legion–backed compulsory education measure in 1919, which required aliens between sixteen and forty-five years of age and unable to speak, read, or write English at a fifth grade level to attend public night school classes. A 1921 amendment tacked on a ten-dollar registration fee and lowered the age requirement to thirty-five.[58] "The war has brought clearly and forcibly before us the fact that we were either asleep or gone on a journey on this question of Americanization," the Wyoming State Board of Education acknowledged in its 1918 report. Failure to enact "proper legislation" putting in place "an effective system of Americanizing these foreigners" would call the people's patriotism into question. "Wyoming should enroll herself among the most progressive and patriotic States and enact such legislation as will safeguard the character of her citizenship." The 1919 Wyoming legislature passed a compulsory evening school bill drafted by James R. Coxen, chairman of the Americanization Committee of the State Council of Defense. Governor Robert M. Carey, however, vetoed the measure because compelling those over eighteen to attend school conflicted with the state constitution. Nonetheless, two years later, the Wyoming State Board of Education received the legislature's authorization to organize Americanization classes through county school boards and establish teaching standards.[59]

In Arizona, state-backed Americanization efforts initiated during the war continued for several years. An informal survey conducted in 1918 by Mulford Winsor, chairman of the Americanization Committee of the Arizona State Council of Defense, suggested to him a strong desire on the part of the foreign-born to cooperate in becoming Americanized. In an issue of its official bulletin that was devoted to Americanization, the council reported hopefully on the opening of night schools throughout Arizona. The State Committee on Americanization Work in Arizona was formed in January 1919 by joining the Americanization committees of the State Council of Defense and the Woman's Committee. Besides members representing the State Board of Education, the University of Arizona, patriotic societies, employers, labor unions, and several additional organizations, the committee boasted six representatives of foreign-born groups, specifically Latin Americans, Italians, Greeks, Slavs, Chinese, and Japanese.[60]

In a pamphlet and bulletin produced in 1920, the committee listed its accomplishments and documented its goals, reporting that more than three thousand pupils representing twenty nationalities enrolled in the state-funded English classes in 1918–1919. In addition, the committee furnished publicity and lessons, organized local Americanization committees, maintained a Speakers' Bureau, and arranged for the statewide observance of "Americanization Sunday" on 5 October 1919. Arizonans of Mexican descent had "actively assisted" Americanization work as night school teachers, interpreters, and local committee members. As for future plans, largely dependent on further appropriations from the legislature, the committee hoped, among other things, to supply more printed matter in Spanish, arrange a statewide Americanization conference, and increase the number of trained Americanization teachers. Above all, the committee desired to "safeguard the work of Americanization from all suspicion of political, religious or other propaganda, and prevent unwise, extreme and hysterical methods of work in this field—a danger which is indicated by the experience of other states—from gaining a foothold." The committee also expressed a desire to reach immigrant women through visiting public health nurses and home demonstration agents.[61]

The legislature's inconsistency in providing funds hampered Arizona's ambitious plans for a comprehensive Americanization program. Arizona lawmakers did not provide an appropriation for Americanization when wartime funding expired at the end of June 1919, which meant there was no funding for the 1920–1922 biennium. In 1921, lawmakers did include $20,000 to defray expenses for conducting classes in the 1922–1924 biennium. The next legislature, meeting in 1923, again neglected to continue funding, prompting State Superintendent of Public Instruction C. O. Case to respond forcefully in his 1926 report: "This is entirely an educational problem and calls for a united effort of all the educational forces in our State backed by the financial aid that can come only through an appropriation by our State Legislature. I feel that there should be created in the State Department of Education a department for the furtherance of Americanization, which program would include the eradication of illiteracy, with a State Supervisor in the office of the State Superintendent of Public Instruction and a competent field worker to organize in each county branch educational forces for this work." Case's plea failed to achieve the desired results and subsequent reports made no mention of Americanization.[62]

The truncated attempt in Arizona to forge a permanent Americanization system had a parallel in California. The California State Americanization Committee was formed in 1919, with the Commission of Immigration and Housing's Simon Lubin as chair, to coordinate all state programs along the lines of "Community Americanization." The CCIH, State Board of Education, and the Extension Division of the State University united to organize communities, develop adult education in English and civics, and train Americanizers and community workers. Ethel Richardson, hired by Mary S. Gibson as director of immigrant education in 1917, supervised the training of Americanizers and home teachers, while the Extension Division was authorized to offer Americanization education courses and certify teachers. "Americanization Institutes" began in Los Angeles in November 1919, leading to greater interest, according to the commission, in community/neighborhood organization as the most effective means to accomplish Americanization goals.

On the recommendation of Carol Aronovici, the commission's new director of housing, a young social worker from New York City named John Collier was contracted to conduct the lectures to prospective Americanization teachers. Upon completion of the institutes in December 1919, the CCIH, in conjunction with the University of California Extension Division, hired Collier as its director of community organization. Collier's responsibilities included the further development of an Americanization education system, training teachers and community workers, and organizing school-based community centers statewide. The University of California began offering courses in Americanization and community work at Berkeley, Los Angeles, and through extension at San Francisco and Oakland in 1920.[63]

By 1920, the CCIH had developed what the State Councils Section of the Council of National Defense had earlier described as "decidedly the best" state immigrant education system in the country, with evening classes for adults, home education for immigrant women, and a promising program for training and credentialing professional Americanizers. Problems of coordination, financing, and preparation remained, however, as Mary Gibson pointed out in her capacity as chair of the General Federation of Women's Clubs Americanization Committee. "Although many federal and national bodies have undertaken to lead in Americanization, no one attacks the subject in the large," she lamented. Focusing narrowly on language instruction, literacy, and naturalization, too many Americanizers neglected such vital national interests as the "Americanization" of industry and the immigrants' environment. Noting the disparate aims and methods as well as underfinancing of the Bureau of Education and Bureau of Naturalization, Gibson called for leadership and funding for a successful Americanization campaign. The commitment made to conserving food and fuel during the war was sorely lacking in relation to Americanization, Gibson complained. Instead, "it was merely tossed to the general public with instructions to Americanize the foreign population, to do this for the salvation of our country." Leave the teaching to professional teachers, many more of whom needed to be trained, she advised, and rely upon social workers, immigrants' experiences, history, and other disciplines.[64]

Gibson's frustrated pleas for leadership, money, and teachers came too late and reflected the waning of progressive optimism regarding immigrants in California and the West. Coercive strains mixed uncomfortably with the commission's social worker approach in the immediate postwar years. The legislature passed laws making citizenship and English instruction for immigrants mandatory—though without enforcement provisions—between 1919 and 1923. In 1920, after conservative business elements backed by *Los Angeles Times* publisher Harry Chandler accused Lubin of protecting Wobblies and communists, the legislature cut the commission's appropriation. In October 1920, the CCIH board voted to cut staff and end its publicity and community development programs. John Collier resigned and began turning his attention to the preservation of Native American cultures. The State Americanization Committee quickly faded away as responsibility for immigrant education in California was passed on to the new Division of Adult Education, headed by Ethel Richardson, within the State Department of Education. With the election of conservative Republican Friend W. Richardson in 1922, the CCIH's days as the nerve center of Americanization came to an end. Governor Richardson removed labor leader Paul Scharrenberg from the commission, which led to Lubin's resignation as well. By the late 1920s, after numerous reorganizations, a fragmented Americanization system was what remained of the CCIH's efforts.[65]

In its 1923 report, the commissioners, under fire from the forces of conservative reaction in the state and within the context of the rising tide of restriction sentiment nationwide, offered an epitaph for progressive Americanization:

> The Commission found that Americanization was not flag raising and "patriotic" howling; that it was not suppression of speech and honest opinion; that it was more than teaching English to foreigners. Americanization, it found, is the encouragement to decent living, and making possible the attainment of decent standards. It involves the development of national ideals and standards and the schooling of all residents, foreign-born as well as native-born, in those ideals and standards.

Lubin's sympathetic attitude toward immigrants was well articulated in the same document. "From the first," the report proclaimed, establishing a clear demarcation between its "melting pot" methods and the war-spawned coercion of superpatriots, "the Commission took its stand against that form of assimilation which hands to the immigrant some things which he is supposed to swallow." Instead, commission-backed Americanization "placed equal emphasis upon the things he can give us." Moreover, the commissioners claimed, they "sought to encourage the preservation and development of the best national cultural elements" of each group. "Only by preserving and developing these heritages and combining them with the cultural elements which are distinctly American can the foreign-born be given their rightful place in the tasks of our nation."[66]

The commission's tolerance had virtually no effect on Californians' on-going campaign against Asian immigrants, primarily the Japanese. Senator James D. Phelan, the McClatchy and Hearst newspaper enterprises, the American Legion, and pioneer societies led the agitation for a 1920 ballot initiative to close loopholes in the 1913 Alien Land Act. Besides barring leases, the initiative measure forebade any transfer of land to Japanese; prohibited landholding, through lease or purchase, by corporations controlled by Japanese; and outlawed guardianships by issei on behalf of their citizen offspring. Simultaneously, Phelan ran for reelection to the U.S. Senate on the slogan "Keep California White." Although Phelan lost, the initiative triumphed by a three to one margin. Voters' approval of the Alien Land Act of 1920 further symbolized the ambivalence of progressives in terms of race and citizenship. Via a mechanism of direct democracy produced by progressive reform, the California electorate took the next significant step toward exclusion of Japanese immigrants. The all-embracing rhetoric of Americanizers in the CCIH was belied by the continued rejection of nonwhite Asians as "ineligible to citizenship."[67]

Conclusion

When the California Commission of Immigration and Housing was created in 1913, Americanization was emerging as an important component of the progressive crusade to reshape the nation's social relations. Adhering to the "melting pot" dream of welding multiple nationalities into a united people, reformers exhibited a qualified optimism that generously funded educational programs could make aliens into citizens. With American entry into the war in April 1917, the education of aliens in the ways of America and preparation for the august responsibilities of citizenship had taken on additional importance. As the movement blended into the war effort, a crowded field of Americanization organizations drafted plans, organized conferences, conducted surveys, trained teachers, and exhorted immigrants. Americanization during wartime highlighted the ambivalent positions taken by progressives toward assimilation. Education for citizenship appealed to reformers' optimistic hopes that the foreign-born would, in the main, embrace Americanism and contribute wholeheartedly to the war effort. At the same time, the intense pressures of patriotic fervor heightened the fears of the irremediable damage that could be done to national unity by the unassimilated and unnaturalized.

"Americanization is the process of making a united America," a commentary appearing in the official bulletin of the Arizona State Council of Defense announced several weeks after the armistice. "Americanization is more than teaching an immigrant the English language. It is the reconstitution of his civic consciousness. It is an adjustment of all his attitudes of mind, of his ideas, habits of thinking, traditions, customs and ideals to American standards. It is the elimination of all in him that is anti-American and the preservation and stimulation of all that is capable of becoming American. It is the appropriation of every element which can contribute to the upbuilding of a greater American civilization." The native-born, it was acknowledged, needed to lead and live according to American ideals, too. Nonetheless, rhetoric that focused upon reconstitution, adjustment, elimination, stimulation, and appropriation on the part of the immigrant signified the paradoxes facing progressive Americanizers at that moment. For all the references to mutual accommodation and "immigrant gifts," the pressures of war emphasized the responsibility of the foreign-born to do all of the melting in the melting pot.[68]

Unfortunately for liberal Americanizers who remained committed to their cosmopolitan ideals, the fervid nationalism and 100 percent Americanism stoked by the war continued to find outlets after the armistice. An explosion of labor unrest, featuring a general strike in Seattle, and the antiradical and anticommunist raids of the so-called Red Scare occupied much of the nation's attention during the tumultuous year of 1919. In addition, race riots in Chicago and other cities and an upsurge of lynch law demonstrated the tensions engendered by increasing black migration out of the South and the determination to sustain white supremacy by any means at hand. The newly formed American Legion, a resurgent Ku Klux Klan, and other superpatriot groups kept up the pressure on nonconformists, aliens, labor agitators, bootleggers, and a host of other perceived threats to Americanism and community morality. Emotions provoked by wartime exhortations to patriotic exertion were not easily dissipated, and the unassimilated foreign-born offered ready-made objects of scorn and resentment.

Manifestations of these heightened social and cultural tensions abounded in the West. A postwar American Legion antialien campaign in Utah, for instance, focused on the Greeks, who many native-born resented for maintaining their own schools, language, and newspapers, plus leaving industrial labor to start their own businesses. Attacks stepped up with Greek, Irish, Italian, and Slavic miners' participation in a 1922 coal strike and peaked with major outbreaks of Klan intimidation in 1924.[69] The Klan found especially fertile ground in Texas, Oklahoma, and other areas of the old Southwest, where even border cities with long traditions of relatively benign race relations, such as El Paso, were not immune to recruitment by the Invisible Empire. Tensions concerning enforcement of prohibition and vice laws, a crime wave, and increasing numbers of both Anglo migrants from the deep South and Mexican immigrants combined with fallout from the Mexican

Revolution and World War I vigilantism to spawn formation of a Ku Klux Klan chapter in El Paso.

Beginning in 1921, the Klan also achieved significant success in recruiting on the Pacific Coast, with particularly active and seemingly powerful chapters in Los Angeles, Portland, and Seattle. Attracting thousands of native-born, white Protestants, the fraternal order soon impacted municipal and state politics with emotional appeals to "One Hundred Percent Americanism" as a bulwark against the Roman Catholic Church, Jews, blacks, immigrants, immorality, corruption, and crime. The Klan became a real political force in Oregon, helping elect a governor and U.S. senator and influencing the passage of nativist measures such as an alien land act directed at Japanese immigrants and an anti-Catholic compulsory public school attendance law (struck down by the U.S. Supreme Court in the *Pierce v. Society of Sisters* decision of 1925). The Denver-based Klan in Colorado achieved extraordinary power as well, with more than thirty-five thousand members at its peak in 1924, when voters elected a Klan-influenced governor and state assembly.[70]

As war and revolution slid further from Americans' immediate concerns, 100 percent Americanism diminished in intensity. The Ku Klux Klan, riven by internal dissension and exposed in numerous places as corrupt and incompetent, collapsed with crushing suddenness after 1924. Nonetheless, manifestations of nativism, while rarely violent, complicated efforts by Western progressives to maintain unappreciated and underfunded educational programs. Progressive reformers, in a sense, wanted to achieve something similar to what the Klan and superpatriots desired: a law-abiding, moral, and orderly society. Americanization conceived as a vital element in a rational and progressive reordering of American society had been decimated, however, by the passions of wartime patriotism and fear. Events and emotions colored many Americans' perceptions about immigrants during these years, and even some of the most committed and hopeful Americanizers would succumb to the fear that so uneasily accompanied their belief in education's salutary effects. By 1924, Americanization as a meliorative program of assimilation lay in tatters, a symbol of the overall fading of reform.

3

"SANE INFORMATION ON CAPITAL AND LABOR"

Employers, Unions, and "New" Immigrants

Transforming alien workers into loyal citizens during the war and the tense years that followed highlighted the entanglement of race and citizenship with problems of economics, class, and ideology that had long plagued the West. With an island pattern of settlement and the cyclical and seasonal nature of work in corporate, natural resource–based industries, the Western economy, although dynamic, was less mature than longer settled regions to the east. Even on the eve of World War I, itinerant, unskilled labor remained a prominent part of the Western workforce. Moreover, the federal census for 1910 showed that the majority of unskilled laborers in Western mines, mills, and smelters were new immigrants from southern and eastern Europe. Many more worked on the railroads that served industrial centers throughout the region and the nation. Railroads and large-scale farms, according to the Immigration Commission's 1911 report, also employed seasonal workers culled "from the general migratory labor supply of the Western States." Increasingly drawn from Asian and ethnic Mexican populations, such laborers typically spent a few months in the orchards and fields, then cast about for seasonal jobs with the railroads and construction camps, often congregating in predominantly male ethnic enclaves in the cities. Thus, while the foreign-born made up smaller percentages of Western states' overall populations than they did in the East, they were alternately concentrated in industrial centers or migrating from job to job.[1]

Whether transient or relatively sedentary, immigrant labor presented unique problems but also appeared to offer tangible benefits to employers. The mobility of new immigrant workers along with their general inability to speak English made organization into effective unions extremely difficult. Organization among mine workers and other labor in the West had flourished when skilled workers of American birth or from Northern Europe had predominated. The greater diversity that resulted from the "new" immigration from Europe, Asia, and Mexico after the turn of the century provided a potential obstacle to effective union organizing. The Union Pacific Coal Mines centered around Rock Springs, Wyoming, as one example, consciously hired from a variety of ethnic groups to keep labor unions from forming. Companies often relied on private employment agencies and independent labor contractors to procure the cheap, unorganized migrant labor that fed the industrial machine of the West. Nor were agents averse to exploiting inter- and intraethnic antagonisms on behalf of management, for instance when a labor contractor imported mainland Greeks to break a Carbon County, Utah, copper strike led by islanders from Crete in 1912. The influx of different groups, in Utah for example, frequently began with strikebreaking: Finns, Italians, and Slavs for English, Welsh, Irish, and Americans in the 1890s, Greeks for Italians and Yugoslavians in 1903, and Mexicans for Greeks in 1922.[2]

While immigrant laborers could not always be counted on for strikebreaking and often played leading roles in fomenting conflict with capitalists, employers throughout the West displayed a preference for seemingly unorganizable and tractable foreign-born workers. In *The Old World in the New*, one of the most widely read and authoritative nativist works of the period, University of Wisconsin sociologist Edward Alsworth Ross described Italians as "migratory job-hunters rather than homeseekers." Because Italian laborers were mostly illiterate peasants lacking in trade union experience, Ross argued, "they are very hard to reach and to bring into line. So far as they are transients, who are not staking their future on the industry, they are loath to pay union dues and to run the risk of having to strike." Chinese labor, reduced to increasing insignificance by exclusion, took on an almost mythological status among large-scale farm operators in California. At a 1907 agricultural convention, one California farm owner fondly recalled the "patient, plodding, and uncomplaining" Chinese. He characterized Japanese farm laborers, on the other hand, as "a tricky and cunning lot, who break contracts and become quite independent." The allegedly docile Chinese of yore, whom Chester Rowell termed a "labor machine," stuck to contracts even under poor conditions and lacked the ambition to demand higher wages or farm on their own. "The Chinese virtues are business virtues," Rowell liked to point out, "and the Japanese faults are business faults." The federal Immigration Commission noted that the Chinese, widely praised as "careful workmen, faithful to the employer, uncomplaining, easily satisfied with regard to living quarters, and not ambitious to learn new processes and to establish themselves as independent farmers," were "used in the older agricultural district as the standard by which others are measured."[3]

For those supportive of employers' desire for tractable labor, Mexicans and Mexican Americans could appear especially virtuous from a business standpoint. Labor demands in the Southwest had coincided with the mass emigration of peasants from Porfirian Mexico and the restrictions on Asian labor migration resulting from the Chinese exclusion laws of 1882 through 1904 and the Gentlemen's Agreement of 1907–1908 that aimed at stopping the flow of Japanese laborers. Characterizing ethnic Mexicans as particularly suited to backbreaking manual labor and agreeable to low wages, employers justified their widespread use in agriculture and industry. "They work well and are contented in the desert, where Europeans and Orientals either become dissatisfied or prove unable to withstand the climate," claimed a federal Bureau of Labor report in 1908. According to the 1911 report of the commissioner-general of immigration, Mexican labor in the Southwest "met an economic condition demanding laborers who could stand the heat and other discomforts of that particular section. The peon makes a satisfactory track hand, for the reasons that he is docile, ignorant, and nonclannish to an extent which makes it possible that one or more men shall quit or be discharged and others remain at work; moreover, he is willing to work for a low wage."[4]

About 10 percent of the Mexican population—probably more than one million people—fled to the United States between 1910 and 1920 during the Mexican Revolution. The continuing development of Southwestern mining and irrigated agriculture, mobilization for World War I, and labor shortages eased the impact of such a large influx on the United States. Employer demands for Mexican workers were further expedited by a special waiver to the restrictive Immigration Act of 1917, which enacted a literacy test requirement for all aliens over sixteen years of age and an eight-dollar head tax upon entry into the United States. Pressure exerted by Southwestern agriculture, railroad, and mining interests prompted the Department of Labor to waive the literacy test, head tax, and contract labor provisions for Mexican immigrants as part of a temporary admission program that lasted from May 1917 to March 1921. In the 1920s, religious, political, and economic violence, food shortages, and inadequate wages in Mexico corresponded with an economic boom and the restriction of European immigration in the United States to produce a continued high demand for Mexican labor. Employers' satisfaction rested, then, on a widely held perception that Mexican laborers, despite requiring considerable supervision, provided a cheap and plentiful force of workers who knew their place. "Mexican laborers do not possess initiative," an Imperial Valley grower asserted in 1927, "but that's no criticism of them from our point of view."[5]

From the point of view of organized labor, immigrants from southern and eastern Europe, Asia, and Mexico had a debilitating impact on white workers. The importation of low-wage, foreign-born laborers, officials with the American Federation of Labor and other mainstream unions maintained, sapped the morale of American workers and depressed wages throughout the West. Opponents of Chinese immigration, for instance, frequently alluded to the demoralizing effect of Chinese "cheap" labor on white labor in both

Japanese miners employed by the Colorado Fuel and Iron Company in New Mexico. *Colorado Fuel and Iron Company Sociological Department Report for 1901–1902,* 12. Colorado Historical Society.

economic and cultural terms. A memorial to the president and Congress drafted at an anti-Chinese convention in 1901, and read by James D. Phelan to a Senate committee several months later, reiterated that "American labor should not be exposed to the destructive competition of aliens who do not, will not, and can not take up the burdens of American citizenship, whose presence is an economic blight and a patriotic danger." While denunciations of Chinese labor never entirely disappeared once exclusion became indefinite after 1904, most anti-Asian rhetoric shifted to the Japanese. The *San Francisco Chronicle* informed its readers in 1905 that the "bumptious, disagreeable and unreliable" Japanese laborer posed the most serious threat ever to face the white worker. Left unchecked, Japanese immigration would force "the American laborer . . . into hoboism and criminality."[6]

The power to exclude workers deemed dangerous because of racial or ethnic difference became an urgent imperative, one reflected in tensions between persistent, often unionized, laborers and transient, often immigrant, workers. Examples of these tensions between "home guards" and "bindlestiffs" in the West are abundant. Powerful unions in San Francisco played leading roles in campaigns against Chinese and Japanese workers while excluding Italian laborers who employers used to break strikes. English-speaking miners in the Cripple Creek district of Colorado kept new immigrants out of the mines and out of the unions. With the violent and devastating strike of 1903–1904, many of these older, skilled, unionized miners left and were replaced by southern and eastern Europeans. The Butte Miners' Union ultimately unraveled, partly as a result of hostility between Irish workers who dominated the union and eastern Europeans seen as strikebreaking tools of the Anaconda Copper Company. In the copper mines of Arizona, unionized "Anglo" miners differentiated the value of their work from "Mexican labor," as such menial tasks as construction, wood chopping, and water hauling were termed. From the late 1890s, local Western Federation of Miners unions in Arizona displayed a consistent anti-Mexican bias as part of their organizing efforts.[7]

Localized efforts to integrate unions or develop cross-cultural coalitions were squelched by union leaders and crushed by employers. In California, for instance, when Oxnard beet workers struck in 1902 and 1903, Japanese and Mexican unions, combined into the Japanese-Mexican Labor Association, won the approbation of white unionists in the Los Angeles area. Unfortunately, when the same ethnic unions applied to the American Federation of Labor as the Sugar Beet and Farm Laborers' Union of Oxnard, they were refused a charter. Therefore, it came as little surprise when, at the AFL's national convention in San Francisco in November 1904, Samuel Gompers declared, "It is your mission here in San Francisco to guard the Western Gate of the continent from being thrown open to those who would undermine our very civilization." Such rhetoric was music to the ears of most California labor organizations, and they were gratified when the convention endorsed exclusion resolutions against the Japanese. Responding to Arizona copper companies' implementation of a newly enacted territorial eight-hour-day law on behalf of Anglo employees only, Mexican, Italian, and Slavic workers, organizing through their respective fraternal societies, coordinated a strike in the Clifton-Morenci district in 1903. The cross-cultural action lasted for several weeks, despite the lack of official backing by Anglo unions, members of which stayed on the job. A dam break during a strikers' march brought a tragic end to the strike, killing fifty. In the aftermath, strike leaders were convicted for impeding the copper companies' operations and sentenced to lengthy prison terms.[8]

The contempt with which many Anglo workers in Arizona held ethnic Mexicans took political forms as well. A 1909 literacy law requiring voters to demonstrate their ability to read and write English effectively disfranchised many Mexican Americans. Chiefly backed by a Democratic-labor coalition forged by future governor George W. P. Hunt, the Arizona statute had a marked similarity to progressive approaches in the South, where disfranchisement of blacks had been a prelude to reform. Progressivism in Arizona was both anticorporate and anti-Mexican, thus making an alliance between the Democratic Party and Anglo labor unions rather logical. In response to mining companies hiring Mexicans and other foreign workers, voters in 1914 approved an initiative, backed by labor organizations, that required 80 percent of workers hired by employers with at least five employees to be citizens. Although the Supreme Court upheld a San Francisco District Court ruling that the "80 percent citizenship law" violated the Fourteenth Amendment, passage of the measure indicated the popularity in Arizona of excluding immigrant labor, Mexicans in particular, from the mines. Likewise, Arizona's 1916 enactment of an alien land act, modeled on California's 1913 law aimed at Japanese immigrants, demonstrated the depth of support for discriminatory legislation.[9]

The Clifton-Morenci copper strike of 1915–1916 (and earlier strikes at Globe-Miami and Ray) confirmed Mexican and Mexican American copper workers' determination to confront employers. By the same token, the Mexican workers' activism further complicated relations between Anglo and Hispanic workers and exposed the limitations of the progressive-labor coalition's anticorporate agenda. Companies treated Mexican strikers harshly because Anglo unionists in both the Western Federation of Miners and the Arizona State Federation of Labor provided tepid support at best and even aided in the repression. The strike of 1915–1916 was similar to the walkout in 1903, with interethnic coordination of local clubs and fraternal societies bringing support for the Mexicans from Finns, Spaniards, Italians, Austrians, and Poles. George W. P. Hunt, now governor, intervened on behalf of the strikers, an unusual action in its own right but especially so because of his history of supporting anti-Mexican legislation such as the 80 percent law. Mexicans, Mexican Americans, and southern and eastern Europeans constituted the vast majority of strikers when ten thousand copper workers went out at Clifton-Morenci again in summer 1917. Organized, as usual, outside of established Anglo unions, Hispanic workers endured low wages (Clifton-Morenci employees were the worst paid in Arizona copper and the dual wage system was particularly noticeable) combined with high wartime inflation and company price gouging at stores and with rents. Racial oppression exacerbated already intolerable treatment by the mining companies. Members of a presidential Mediation Commission and Anglo labor leaders described Mexican and Mexican American strikers as out of control and in need of organized labor's discipline (even though excluded by Anglo unions).[10]

Working-class constructions of what constituted the "American race," typically filtered through the AFL and its affiliates, had a significant impact on defining the place of certain immigrant and ethnic groups in the West. Nonwhite and non-Anglo workers found acceptance within established unions difficult; even union support for their own actions against employers was unlikely. Indeed, much of the push for control of immigration came from the top in the organized labor hierarchy. American Federation of Labor leaders Samuel Gompers and William Green even used that organization's relationship with its Mexican counterpart, the *Confederación Regional Obrera Mexicana* (CROM), to try influencing the Mexican government to restrict emigration of Mexican workers. Throughout the 1920s, the AFL also stood out as one of the most persistent advocates of applying national origin quotas to Mexico as well as Central and South America.[11] Although it may be true, as some historians suggest, that employers manipulated working-class racism to facilitate social control, the AFL and other racially exclusive labor unions had their own reasons to protect their "white" working-class privileges. "New" immigrants from across the Atlantic and Pacific, Mexicans, and African Americans were seen as distinct threats to "real" American labor's precarious stands on wages and working conditions (a view bolstered by management's propensity to use these groups as strikebreakers).[12]

The "Wobbly Menace": Labor Radicalism in the West

Although most skilled, white workers joined racially exclusive craft unions, the uncertainties of Western economics also drove a large number of workers into a potentially more radical and inclusive type of organization. The popularity of militant industrial unions among the Western workforce has been ascribed to the West's widely dispersed natural resource–based industries. Exploitation of abundant natural resources in Western fields, forests, and mines had expedited the rise of industrial capitalism during the last third of the nineteenth century, and economic expansion came with stunning rapidity to specific, frequently isolated locales with a heterogeneous and mobile workforce. If they entered the public consciousness at all, these islands of urbanization and industrialization situated within the sparsely settled hinterlands often did so as disturbing examples of working-class unrest and violent conflict between employers and wage laborers. For example, the Coeur d'Alene mining district in the panhandle of Idaho had become synonymous with labor-management conflict and violence since a battle between a miners' union and a mine owners' association over wage reductions in 1892. It was in response to the convictions of union members for criminal conspiracy during this strike that the Western Federation of Miners (WFM) was formed in Butte, Montana, in May 1893. Forged in the mold of a traditional trade union emphasizing recognition and the right to bargain over wages and hours, the WFM confronted powerful mine owners, judges, and state and federal authorities in a series of violent episodes that transformed many union members into radical opponents of capitalism.[13]

Enduring assaults by employers and government for two decades after its founding, the WFM turned increasingly to socialism. Unlike its counterpart in the coalfields, the United Mine Workers of America, the WFM disdained cooperation with or organization among "new" immigrants. Nonetheless, leaders in the WFM ultimately advocated an inclusive mode of unionism, an alliance of all industrial workers regardless of skill, nationality, religion, or race. The union's influence predominated in Chicago between 27 June and 8 July 1905 when William D. Haywood and other WFM officials helped organize the Industrial Workers of the World (IWW). Committed to class struggle and the realization of a cooperative commonwealth in which toilers would own the means of production, the IWW, or Wobblies, offered all workers a radical alternative to the exclusive craft-dominated unionism and accommodation with capitalism of the American Federation of Labor.[14]

Whether native- or foreign-born, uprooted and transient workers subjected to the indignities and vagaries of the West's economic conditions appeared to be the most likely beneficiaries of the Wobblies' efforts. An IWW official writing in one of the union's periodicals in 1914 celebrated the revolutionary spirit that Wobblies assumed to be a natural condition among the mobile, exploited, and despised "timber beasts," harvest hands, and construction laborers in the West:

> The nomadic worker of the West embodies the very spirit of the I.W.W. His cheerful cynicism, his frank and outspoken contempt for most of the conventions of bourgeois society . . . make him an admirable exemplar of the iconoclastic doctrines of revolutionary unionism. His anomalous position, half industrial slave, half vagabond adventurer, leaves him infinitely less servile than his fellow worker of the East.

Some historians have claimed that the IWW set itself even further apart from the mainstream of union organizing by welcoming immigrants from Southern and Eastern Europe, Asia, and Mexico, Mexican Americans, and blacks, as well as native-born whites and immigrants from Northern and Western Europe. The truth is more complicated, as individual Wobblies expressed racial prejudice and specific locals collapsed due to interethnic tensions. An

IWW local in Tonopah, Nevada, supported Japanese exclusion, and some members even favored cutting off immigration from Europe. Upon the IWW's return to active organizing in Western mining regions in 1917, the union still focused on Anglo and Irish workers rather than Mexicans and southern and eastern Europeans.[15]

Desultory Wobbly attempts leading strikes in mining regions of Nevada and among Pacific Northwest lumber workers garnered few tangible results. Public notoriety increased dramatically when, in 1909, the IWW initiated a series of legendary free-speech fights designed to aid organizing efforts among migratory workers and challenge established authority's attempts to suppress such organizing. At Spokane, the employment center for the Coeur d'Alene mines as well as lumber and farm labor camps, Wobbly soapbox speakers exhorted workers to join the union and refuse to deal with exploitative employment bureaus. The die was cast for subsequent free-speech conflicts when the Spokane city council passed an ordinance prohibiting street-corner orations by Wobblies. Speakers (including nineteen-year-old Elizabeth Gurley Flynn) took to the soapboxes in defiance of the ordinance and were promptly arrested and jailed, with hundreds enduring brutal treatment at the hands of police and jailers. The pattern was repeated in other Western cities, most notably San Diego in 1912, where citizen vigilantes reveled in unprovoked beatings of nonviolent Wobblies. The free-speech campaigns gained the IWW considerable amounts of publicity and hundreds of recruits but little in the way of concrete gains in camps and mills.[16]

The Wobblies' colorful activities coincided with several violent incidents prior to the outbreak of World War I. A bomb blast that leveled the offices of the virulently antiunion *Los Angeles Times* in 1910, killing twenty employees, appeared to raise the stakes in the war between labor and capital to a deadly level. To the dismay of many in the labor movement, the two union activists brought to trial for the bombing, John J. and James B. McNamara of the AFL, admitted their guilt. Additional notoriety came to the West's labor struggles in August 1913, with an incident in the northern Sacramento Valley known as the "Wheatland riot."

The "riot" took place on the Durst Hop Ranch, where Wobblies had been organizing among migrant farm workers. Inhumane treatment in the fields plus poor housing and sanitation in the workers' overcrowded camps compelled nearly three thousand hop pickers and their families to gather for a Sunday night mass meeting. Near the end of the peaceful gathering, at which Wobbly organizer Richard "Blackie" Ford spoke and the crowd sang IWW songs, Yuba County law officers arrived and immediately provoked a violent confrontation by attempting to arrest Ford and firing a warning blast with a shotgun. In the ensuing melee five people were killed—two workers, two sheriff's deputies, and the Yuba County district attorney—and dozens were injured. Ascribing responsibility to the IWW, deputies and detectives arbitrarily arrested and jailed migrants and Wobblies throughout the state. Ford and Herman D. Suhr were convicted of murder and sentenced to life in prison. An investigation by the California Commission of Immigration and Housing led to more effective state regulation of labor camp conditions but did not make the Wobblies go away.[17]

Although the IWW made some inroads with Mexican laborers, a number of whom were involved with the Wheatland incident, observers at the time attributed little if any radical political threat to Mexican immigrant workers. Still, some nativists used fear of the Wobblies and the turmoil of the Mexican Revolution as another particular in the bill of indictment against them. "Villa, Huerta, Orozco, Carranza, and their bands and the conditions of Mexico now are exhibits of Mexican character," declared John Box, a Texas congressman and inveterate foe of immigration from south of the border. In Texas and other parts of the Southwest, immigrant workers and Mexican Americans with ties to revolutionary activity in Mexico did join tenant and worker organizations such as the Land League of America and the Socialist Party.

Racial violence between Tejano and Mexican raiders and Anglos in South Texas revolved around the *Plan de San Diego,* a document that called for the violent liberation of the Southwest by an army of Indians, Mexicans, Japanese, and African Americans. Inspiration for the uprising, which began in 1915, was traced to Ricardo Flores Magón, an exiled Mexican anarchist based in Los Angeles and publisher of the revolutionary Mexican Liberal Party's (PLM) newspaper, *Regeneración.* A failed insurrection across the border in Baja California in 1911 had led to the arrest and conviction of Magón and other PLM leaders on charges of violating U.S. neutrality laws. Cross-border raids into New Mexico by followers of Pancho Villa in 1916 added fuel to fears of radical revolution and race war in the Southwest. The prevailing climate of superpatriotism and suspicion generated by America's entry into World War I intensified nativist and antiradical pressure on ethnic Mexican communities. The Wilson administration used Military Intelligence Division agents to keep watch on both the IWW and PLM in the Southwest. An intelligence report from May 1917 asserted that anarchistic *Magonistas* were organizing Mexicans for the IWW "under the guise of dances."[18]

The episode that, above all others, riveted the public's gaze on labor relations in the West occurred in the southern Colorado coalfields in April 1914. The United Mine Workers of America (UMWA) had, in the fall of 1913, called a strike on behalf of ethnically diverse and previously unorganized coal miners against the Rockefeller-controlled Colorado Fuel and Iron

Company (CF&I) and other mine operators. Issues for which strikers sought redress included union recognition, the removal of armed guards from company property, enforcement of state-mandated safety regulations, an eight-hour workday, and a 10 percent wage increase. According to CF&I officials, rank-and-file miners were contented and the strike was an unnecessary and illegal attempt to impose the "closed shop" by radicals from outside the state. Nonetheless, a walkout by thousands of miners took place on 23 September 1913, and the UMWA set up tent camps to house striking workers and families evicted from company housing.

Striking miners and operators were both armed, and in October Colorado's governor ordered state militia into the southern coalfields to quell violence that had resulted in the murder of several nonunion employees. The strike dragged on through the winter and early spring until, on 20 April 1914, a gun battle escalated into a rout of strikers and their families from a tent colony at Ludlow. Militia troops torched the camp, inadvertently killing two women and eleven children who suffocated in a hole beneath one of the burned-over tents. More violence followed the Ludlow "massacre" until federal troops were sent in and calm restored. According to mine operators, the tragedy at Ludlow was provoked by armed and violent strikers, and they refused to accede to any settlement that included recognition of the UMWA, which terminated the strike in December 1914. Public outrage and a U.S. Commission on Industrial Relations investigation was directed at John D. Rockefeller Jr. and the coal operators. The most immediate result for coal miners, steel plant operatives, and other wage workers was a CF&I Industrial Representation Plan meant to circumvent union recognition while providing expanded social services and benefits.[19]

War in Europe revived agriculture and industry, most noticeably in the previously depressed farming and natural resource belts of the West. War-driven prosperity, however, did not bring peace to the workplace or an end to violence waged in the name of the toiling masses. A Preparedness Day parade in San Francisco on 22 July 1916 was marred by a bomb explosion, which killed ten and wounded forty bystanders. Radical labor activists Tom Mooney and Warren K. Billings, despite insufficient evidence, were convicted of murder, with Mooney being sentenced to death. A few months after the San Francisco bombing violence rocked the Pacific Northwest. Lumber companies, although enjoying the profits generated by war orders, remained, as labor historian Melvyn Dubofsky put it, "fiercely competitive, practicing nineteenth-century capitalism in a twentieth-century world and continuing to misuse their employees and combat labor unions." Employers' determination to forge an uncompromising "open-shop" regime and the IWW's resolve to organize lumber workers reached a violent crescendo at

Everett, Washington. The Wobblies' free-speech tactics met with weeks of violent retribution by middle-class vigilantes, capped by the 5 November 1916 assault by gun-toting citizens on 250 Wobblies arriving at the city's Puget Sound dock. Five Wobblies and two deputies died in the crossfire, with an unknown number of IWW passengers drowned after falling overboard during the melee. Although seventy-four Wobblies were arrested and indicted for murder upon their return to Seattle, federal authorities refused to intervene on behalf of the IWW in bringing any of the Everett employers and vigilantes to justice.[20]

Within six months of American intervention, nearly three thousand strikes occurred. The labor unrest in 1917 was motivated by a number of developments, starting with the tightening of labor markets created by mobilization, conscription, and the near suspension of immigration from Europe. Inflation accompanied the growing demand for labor, and unions were determined to achieve substantive gains, even in the face of employers' equal determination to defend the "open shop." Finally, the reshaping of the workplace prompted by wartime, particularly in terms of greater diversity along the lines of ethnicity, race, and gender, accentuated the chaos of rapid industrial mobilization.[21] The IWW, representative of the radicalization of Western migrant workers, stood poised to exploit the economic boom and tightening labor markets on behalf of the laboring masses. With an estimated 100,000 members, the organization appeared to be peaking at just the right time.

To better organize agricultural labor on the Great Plains, the IWW had founded the Agricultural Workers' Organization (AWO) in Kansas City in April 1915. The AWO enjoyed almost immediate success in securing members among migratory harvest workers in Oklahoma, Kansas, North and South Dakota, and California, as well as lumberjacks in Minnesota and Washington (an Oil Workers' Industrial Union attempted to organize pipeliners in northern Texas, Oklahoma, and southern Kansas). Organizing harvest workers in 1917, the Wobblies enjoyed successes in the Dakotas. In the Pacific Northwest, the Wobblies organized the Lumber Workers' Industrial Union No. 500 in Spokane in March 1917 and, with a strike, quickly secured the eight-hour day and increased wages for lumber workers in northern Idaho and eastern Washington. The first months of the war appeared to hold some promise for realizing the IWW's vision of industrial democracy.[22]

Yet the Wobblies' dedication to class war, along with zealous opposition to militarism and patriotism, left them exposed to employers determined to destroy them and to waves of public hysteria regarding subversion. "Hanging is too good for the I.W.W., the pro-German, the pacifist and the anarchist who is [sic] attempting to thwart the government in its prosecution of our righteous war against the brutal foe that is at war with nearly all mankind," a Utah mining industry publication declared. An industry-wide walkout called by the Wobblies for 17 July 1917 in the Pacific Northwest spawned a rare display of unity on the part of employers, who formed a Lumbermen's Protective Association to combat the eight-hour-day drive. Most lumbermen and state authorities believed, as the Washington State Council of Defense phrased it, that "the greater part of the agitation was un-questionably fomented by pro-German agents and irresponsible foreigners who were at heart enemies of democratic government." The Wobblies called off the general strike in August, but workers continued to "strike on the job," hobbling the lumber industry's ability to satisfy intense wartime demand. In November 1917, an Omaha newspaper added to the perception of the IWW as unpatriotic by seeking to associate the organization with the Bolshevik revolution in Russia, excoriating Wobblies as "brazen advocates of disorder" and "malcontents and apostles of disloyalty."[23]

Assaults on the IWW took on increasingly brutal and even bizarre mani-festations. In Butte, the old WFM Local 1 (or Butte Miners' Union) had ef-fectively become a company union, helping the Anaconda Copper Company blacklist undesirable workers and suppress the Wobblies and other radicals. On the occasion of the annual Miners' Union Day celebration in June 1914, thousands of disaffected miners rioted, destroying Local 1's head-quarters. Amid the turmoil emerged the unaffiliated Butte Mine Workers' Union. Company officials, WFM officials, and Samuel Gompers convinced themselves that the IWW was responsible for the ongoing unrest. In late summer 1914, Montana governor Samuel V. Stewart placed the city of Butte and Silver Bow County under martial law, which facilitated the crushing of both the independent Miners' Union and WFM Local 1.

With union control in Butte terminated, opportunities for the IWW to organize disgruntled copper miners there improved. That situation ripened with American entry into the war and blossomed with the Speculator mine tragedy of 8 June 1917. Fire and poisonous gases snuffed out the lives of 164 miners that day, but also revived Butte's dormant labor activism. Wobbly or-ganizers led in the formation of a new independent organization, the Metal Mine Workers' Union, and thousands of miners struck three days after the fire. Faced with the intransigence of the Anaconda, they stayed off the job through the summer, then returned to the mines only to malinger. In the midst of the strike, IWW organizer Frank Little was lynched by masked vig-ilantes. By the end of the year, federal troops patrolled the streets of Butte, and the Metal Mine Workers' Union had called off the strike.[24]

In Arizona, where copper miners had never enjoyed the fleeting period of labor strength seen in Butte, the IWW found fertile fields for organizing and succeeded in forming independent unions as well as infiltrating locals of the AFL-affiliated successor to the WFM, the International Union of Mine, Mill, and Smelter Workers (IUMMSW). Wobblies succeeded extraordinarily well in Bisbee and other mining districts, with over six thousand members and 125 paid organizers in Metal Mine Workers' Industrial Union No. 800 by the time the United States joined the war. Inspired by the Butte miners' walkouts after the Speculator disaster, both the IWW and IUMMSW called strikes in late June 1917. Intransigent employers refused to make any concessions, characterizing the conflict as subversion by the IWW and German agents. "There will be no compromise because you cannot compromise with a rattlesnake," declared Phelps Dodge Corporation president Walter Douglas. "That goes for both the International Union and the I.W.W.'s." Organized into vigilante organizations, mine owners, businessmen, conservative union members, and law officers in Jerome and Bisbee arrested and deported hundreds of suspected IWW agitators in July 1917. The twelve hundred Bisbee deportees, loaded onto boxcars and later stranded in the New Mexico desert, spent weeks as refugees in a Columbus, New Mexico, army camp. Contrary to vigilante claims that their victims were mostly alien enemies, Mexicans, and IWW subversives, almost half were American citizens, most were neither German nor Mexican, and a number were businessmen and AFL members. Nonetheless, with the deportation and exaggerated claims of IWW influence, the Phelps Dodge Corporation achieved its broader goal of crushing union labor in the mining towns of Arizona, which included increased hiring of cheaper, nonunion Mexican labor.[25]

As local vigilantes took the law into their own hands in Montana and Arizona (with copycat deportations recorded from Missouri to California), officials expressed their frustration with the IWW and an urgent desire for the federal government to take a strong position in dealing with Wobbly treason. Following the Bisbee deportation, James S. Douglas of the Phelps Dodge Corporation insisted that "just now there could be nothing done by our Council of Defense that is of more importance than to call to the attention of our government a condition which now exists in this State, and throughout the west, brought about by the activities of this treasonable organization." Determined to destroy the IWW's ability to further hamper war production, a group of Western governors dispatched California Commission of Immigration and Housing secretary George Bell to Washington, D.C., to impress upon the Wilson administration the necessity for federal action to suppress the Wobbly menace. In a meeting with the Council of National Defense, Bell argued that the federal government, to both head off further vigilante law and crush the IWW, should intern Wobbly "subversives" for the duration, censor all mention of the IWW from newspapers and magazines, and then compel employers to improve conditions in their workplaces.

Although deigning to resort to measures of doubtful constitutionality, federal authorities did fashion a comprehensive assault on the IWW through the Departments of War, Justice, and Labor. To prevent possible IWW-inspired disruption of war production, federal troops were dispatched in summer 1917 to patrol mining districts in Arizona and Montana, timber regions in western Washington and Oregon, as well as farms in eastern Washington. The War Department also organized the Loyal Legion of Loggers and Lumbermen, composed of thousands of soldier-workers, as a labor relations alternative to the IWW and AFL. On 5 September 1917 Justice Department agents raided IWW offices and the homes of union officials in Chicago and around the country. Within weeks of the raids, federal grand juries in Chicago, Fresno, Sacramento, Wichita, and Omaha indicted 166 IWW members for criminal conspiracies to undermine the war effort. Meanwhile, the Labor Department, assisted by the American Federation of Labor and a federal mediation commission, worked to bring recalcitrant Western lumbermen and mine owners to their senses and grant the eight-hour day and bargain with a loyal, legitimate labor union. Employers, distrustful of federal officials and reformers and contemptuous of even the AFL, either acquiesced in the organization of compliant "company" unions, such as the Loyal Legion of Loggers and Lumbermen, or circumvented agreements forged by federal mediators and carried on business as usual.[26]

The fear with which employers in Western mines and forests regarded the IWW during the war was manifested in alternate guises on the plains and in agricultural sectors. In an episode known as the Green Corn Rebellion, several hundred Oklahoma tenant farmers belonging to a group called the Working Class Union defied the draft in an armed revolt in August 1917, earning for their troubles state and federal prison terms of up to ten years. Antiradical reaction to the Green Corn Rebellion in Oklahoma focused on Socialists and the IWW, which was accused, erroneously, of directing the uprising. Agrarian political revolt arose in North Dakota and Minnesota during the war years as well, manifested through the Non-Partisan League (NPL). Tracing its ancestry to the Populists and similar agrarian movements that had sought to organize on the basis of farmers' resentments of middlemen and bankers, the NPL, founded by the charismatic Arthur C. Townley in North Dakota in 1915, proposed state-owned and -operated processing, marketing, and credit institutions that would compete with private elevators, mills, packing plants, insurance companies, and banks. After its stunning electoral successes in North Dakota in 1916, which included a league-backed candidate becoming governor, the NPL spread into Montana, Colorado, Idaho,

Minnesota, and Wisconsin. Although the league officially backed the government once the country entered the war, it remained critical of "profiteers" and "Big Business." Press misrepresentations of a Robert M. La Follette speech at a September 1917 conference sponsored by the Non-Partisan League in St. Paul led to widespread questioning of the organization's loyalty, and the NPL joined the IWW in the public mind as a haven for radicals, "slackers," pro-Germans, and Bolsheviks.[27]

The issue of loyalty may have redounded to the NPL's benefit in North Dakota, where intemperate attacks on "pro-Germans" and "foreigners," often coupled with calls for "accelerated Americanization," did not prevent NPL triumphs in the 1918 elections. Elsewhere, even in states where the nonpartisan movement made little headway, rumor held sway. A labor camp investigator for the California Commission of Immigration and Housing depicted the NPL as "honeycombed with I.W.W.s, Socialists, and pro-Germans" who were "continually violating laws of patriotic citizenship, forming alliances that are seditious, and when checked by indignant patriots or state authorities, they pour the vials of their treasonable displeasure upon the United States as a whole." In February 1918, the executive manager of the Federal Reserve Bank in Kansas City sent Kansas governor Arthur Capper a "Personal and Confidential" letter, noting that information had come to that office about an NPL organizer named Hayward ("prominent in I.W.W. circles, and who, it is stated is now lodged in jail in Chicago") trying to organize farmers. "We have reports that workers for this league are now traveling throughout the states of Kansas and Oklahoma in automobiles, spreading the wildest sort of anti-government propaganda—with what success we do not know." Capper responded that he had not heard anything and doubted that the Non-Partisan League would be tolerated in Kansas. "Sentiment in Kansas has crystallized very rapidly in favor of a vigorous and aggressive prosecution of the war," Capper wrote. The governor reassured his correspondent that his administration and the people of the state would "not tolerate any society or organization in Kansas that is not absolutely right on the war question," and that the U.S. District Attorney in Kansas City, Kansas, had special agents throughout the state keeping an eye out for antigovernment types.[28]

Capper then alerted the chairmen of the county councils in a form letter, stating that "proselyting of any sort against the government is rankest treason in this war for self preservation. . . . It is our first duty to keep a vigilant lookout in our home communities for evidences of these crafty activities of a cunning and conscienceless foe while the National Government is so desperately engaged with this powerful and satanic enemy 3,000 miles [from] home." The letters were published in newspapers, prompting some replies by

NPL supporters as well as backers of government policy. One informant reported that a man had tried to solicit farmers around Hope, Kansas, the previous fall. With the exception of a German Baptist community with an antigovernment pastor, he had had little success. The pastor was gone but the organizer had returned to the area. "So far as seditious remarks from these farmers themselves, I have only heard of a few; but we know that some of them are trying to except their sons without cause and they are not buying liberty bonds as they should." A "thorough investigation of the Non Partisan League in this community should be had. . . . We have too large a German settlement to take any chances and if taken in hand now can be easily controlled."

A hog farmer and NPL member from Sterling told Capper that the disloyalty accusations were nonsense. "The league is a patriotic organization from cellar to garret . . . and I defy any man to find a more loyal or patriotic group of men anywhere, and they are not patriotic for profits either." Farmers, through political action, were seeking the same objectives as the president and governor: to win the war against Prussianism and oppose special interests at home. A farmer from Ellsworth who claimed he had been the first NPL organizer in Kansas welcomed the investigation because "it would prove to the state that it is an honest, loyal, and needed organization. . . . To think of me as a pro-german, is ridiculous and you know that farmers are not I.W.W.'s." Capper responded to NPL defenders that the federal government had requested the investigation and no evidence of disloyalty had thus far been unearthed. "If the league is a thoroughly loyal organization its members need have no fear of the inquiry which the government officials have asked the Council of Defense to make." Over several months Capper kept having to answer inquiries about the NPL in roughly the same manner: that an investigation was under way, but no evidence had yet turned up.[29]

Lack of evidence may have protected alleged Non-Partisan League activists in Kansas, but the same could not be said for the Wobblies rounded up by federal authorities in the 1917 raids. In Chicago on 31 August 1918, IWW leader William D. Haywood and eighty-two codefendants were convicted of disloyalty, sabotage, and sedition and sentenced by Judge Kennesaw Mountain Landis to between five and twenty years in federal prison. Subsequent trials in Sacramento and Kansas City, Kansas, sent more Wobblies to prison (although charges against sixty-four Wobblies were eventually dropped in Omaha). The assault on the IWW in federal courthouses brought wartime harassment of radicals to a climax, but only presaged further dire consequences for Wobblies and others in the immediate postwar period. Although not directed by the IWW, the Seattle general strike of February 1919 provoked more fear of the "Wobbly menace" as an ingredient of

Bolshevik revolution in America. In November 1919, an Armistice Day gun battle between Wobblies and American Legionnaires in Centralia, Washington, followed by the lynching of Wesley Everest, a Wobbly and World War I veteran, underscored the raw tensions made possible by years of labor unrest and patriotic fervor.[30]

Fear of anarchy and revolution also fed the nationwide spasm of anti-radical reaction known as the Red Scare, which featured the federal Justice Department's "Palmer raids" in November 1919 and January 1920. Designed to nab alien members of "Bolshevik" groups, namely members of the Union of Russian Workers, the Communist Labor Party, and the Communist Party, the raids were inspired by an earlier series of roundups and prosecutions of Wobblies in the Pacific Northwest. In an effort to rid the country of dangerous foreign-born radicals, federal authorities used an antiradical provision of the Immigration Act of 1917 and a 1918 law ascribing mere membership in subversive organizations as a deportable offense. The combination of federal convictions and deportations of foreign-born members, along with prosecutions by states under criminal syndicalism statutes, practically destroyed the IWW as a labor organization. Nonetheless, in the immediate postwar years, remnants of the IWW continued to play a role in ongoing strife between capital and labor, leading strikes among maritime workers in Portland in 1922 and San Pedro in 1923 and coal miners in Colorado in 1927–1928.[31]

Industrial Americanization

From the point of view of employers and most government officials, the fields, lumber camps, mines, mills, and factories endured an unrelenting assault by radical agitators, particularly IWW organizers. The persistent threat of un-American ideals and subversive doctrines contained even greater dangers when spread among impressionable immigrants. Several months after the Bisbee deportation, Hywel Davies, a federal labor administrator in Arizona, explained the continuing appeal of the Wobblies among foreign-born miners. Davies blamed "Americans of anarchistic disposition" for "this pernicious and disloyal campaign, which is undermining and poisoning the poor ignorant alien industrial worker, thus creating false hopes and expectations of a sort of Bolsheviki success, when they make their next attempt at an industrial strike." When unable to alleviate poor conditions, legitimate trade unionism, such as that practiced by the IUMMSW, was jettisoned by alien workers deluded by the radical nostrums of the Wobblies. "There are in Bisbee," Davies noted, "four organizers of that body [the IWW], inoculating the

Miners with English teacher, Jerome, Arizona, ca. 1919. Arizona Collection, Arizona State
University Libraries.

idle and discontented with the virus of radicalism and 'direct action', by en-
couraging the despondent that 'The Day' is not far distant when they will
overturn the whole industrial machinery of this and other Western states."
Davies suggested that if the IUMMSW could not successfully educate workers to the wartime necessity of loyalty and solidarity, then perhaps the Department of Labor's Publicity Bureau should step in. He also recommended
a campaign to strengthen cooperation between employers and trade unionists "that will safeguard the industry from the inebriate pipe dreams of the
disloyal I.W.W. crew." The Immigration Bureau and Department of Justice
could assist by going after "active disloyal aliens" and "deluded American citizens" respectively.[32]

     In addition, the possibility of foreign-born Western workers turning to
radicalism reinforced the imperatives of assimilation. Although far from accurate, a National Committee of One Hundred claim that "I.W.W. members are largely alien" reflected the growing sense that wartime production
and interclass unity stood dangerously exposed to the "national menace" of
Wobbly agitation. Upon being placed in charge of wartime Americanization
in the state, University of Colorado president George Norlin reiterated to
Governor Julius Gunter the vital necessity of building loyalty among for-

eign-born workers. "Being ignorant of our language, of our government, of our ideals and the principles for which we fight, he is devoted to one cause alone, that of Labor against Capital, and is easily led into mutterings, slackness, strikes, etc.; and we may be sure that our enemies are taking every advantage of this attitude of mind and spending money freely to encourage it." Norlin received confirmation of his concerns from Director of Americanization James C. Stephens, who reported on a conversation held with a Bulgarian "anarchist" in Colorado's northern coalfields. Alarmed by the Bulgarian's characterization of the war as a sacrifice of "the common people . . . for the benefit of capitalists," Stephens warned Norlin that "a situation like this holds possibilities of great harm. There are undoubtedly many such situations in our State." To combat those seeking to enlist the immigrant worker "in the war of class against class" in Colorado, Norlin recommended applying as much in the way of state and federal resources as possible to "organize and conduct classes in the centers where foreign labor is employed, send them speakers, circulate literature in their individual languages, and bring to bear every sound influence which we can command."[33]

In the postwar years, labor strife and a steadily intensifying atmosphere of intolerance inspired further attempts to foster enthusiasm for educational work among the foreign-born. A week after the armistice, James C. Stephens had noted growing discontent among workers around the world, a phenomenon made more pressing by the Bolshevik revolution in Russia and anarchy throughout central Europe. "Traces of this same discontent may be seen in the restlessness of the working classes of this country," he warned members of the Colorado State Council of Defense, "the cause of which can be reached only through a widespread educational movement for the masses such as the Americanization movement." In a January 1919 letter to the secretary of the council, Stephens elaborated on why Americanization was an essential component in the struggle against radicalism. "The foreign-born and those of foreign parentage are peculiarly susceptible to this agitation," he asserted, because they received much of their information about the United States from "the leaders of their respective nationalities who have a fairly good command of English and who oftentimes get their ideas in turn from the most radical among native-born Americans." Precluding further radicalization of the immigrant working class and preventing "a serious upheaval" required education for citizenship "in order that they may take an intelligent part in the government of their adopted country." In a Labor Day speech in 1919, the Wyoming state labor commissioner warned that, by leaving unassimilated foreigners "to their own conceptions of America, gained through the inspiration of the enemies of order, these thousands can be made a public menace." Educators and right-thinking citizens had the responsibility to steer immigrants toward the "patriotic spirit necessary in good citizens."[34]

It has been noted that, in addition to prompting increased repression of radicals by the federal government, "the Wobblies greatly stimulated the drive to Americanize the immigrant." Even before the war, membership in the IWW provided a benchmark for naturalization of alleged radicals. Loyalty to the Wobblies could not be reconciled with loyalty to the United States. As the organization was defined by authorities as representative of bad citizenship, aliens who belonged to it had no reason to expect favorable rulings on naturalization. Understood as a direct assault on the IWW, a provision of the 1917 Immigration Act providing for deportation of those "advocating or teaching the unlawful destruction of property" was built on established procedures in naturalization courts. Denial of naturalization petitions and deportation could only impact the small but dangerous minority of incorrigibles. To inoculate the uninstructed and vulnerable worker against the virus of radicalism required a comprehensive and focused effort of industrial Americanization.[35]

Corporate involvement in "industrial Americanization" had developed steadily after 1910, overseen to some extent by the Committee on Immigration of the U.S. Chamber of Commerce. For the Sociological Department of the Ford Motor Company, Americanization meant, in addition to enrollment in the Ford English School, inuring new workers to the discipline and efficiency of the factory system. Moreover, cleanliness of body, home, and mind would exhibit the successful appropriation of "American" habits and values, a prerequisite for participation in Ford's Five Dollar Day and profit-sharing arrangements. Like the various patriotic organizations and government commissions, industrialists also hoped to influence immigrant workers away from radicalism and, in so doing, used Americanization as part of an evolving welfare capitalism. In Gary, Indiana, for instance, Americanization, assimilation, and unionization were key questions as adherence to the status quo by steel corporations fed growing labor unrest. A "propaganda of domesticity" sponsored by the steel companies to improve living conditions and to Americanize immigrants' values was undertaken by Neighborhood House, a Presbyterian settlement house. In addition to the Neighborhood House activities, the corporations directly sponsored Americanization via English classes, health services, and visiting nurses (who also inquired into the immigrants' morals). Company paternalism in the form of putatively dissent-proof propaganda proved no substitute for decent hours and wages, however, and Gary descended into the violence and chaos of the Great Steel Strike of 1919.

For another example, large corporations with plants in Milwaukee, such as International Harvester, developed welfare programs that included classes in English, citizenship, and safety. Wary of criticism and concerned about costs, major firms generally entered such employee welfare schemes voluntarily, though progressive legislation regarding workplace safety, sanitation, and compensation in states like Wisconsin certainly motivated industrialists to look after all employees, immigrant and native-born alike. Factory-based English classes at Ford, International Harvester, the Colorado Fuel and Iron Company, and many others were often taught by YMCA instructors utilizing a curriculum designed by the Y's industrial education expert, Dr. Peter Roberts. Most immigrants trained under this system completed only the introductory course of practical job-oriented English lessons related to home, consumption, and industry. Some went on to the intermediate level, which had students reading basic history, geography, and civics texts, while a choice few made it to the advanced stage of preparation for naturalization and citizenship. International Harvester began English classes at its plants using Roberts's methods in 1910, concentrating on simple lessons revolving around themes of discipline, welfare, and safety. Teaching immigrants posed unique problems, of course, given barriers of language and culture, yet the most socially conscious businesses went to great lengths to educate foreign-born workers, from employing interpreters to showing motion pictures.[36]

Once the United States entered the war, the comparatively light touch of Peter Roberts's settlement worker approach was supplanted at International Harvester and other large factories by the militance now espoused by the Council of National Defense. Patriotic bureaucrats and businessmen tried to impose their broader agenda of national unity and 100 percent loyalty on industrial welfare programs that theretofore had been chiefly concerned with company loyalty and constructive labor relations. A Bureau of Education memorandum distributed nationwide to state councils of defense and industries called for a "Pro-American Drive" in plants that employed immigrants. "Anti-American propaganda," the bureau announced, "is spreading among persons of foreign origin in industrial centers according to reports from authentic sources. The purpose of this propaganda is to make the un-Americanized population anti-American in spirit and thereby to affect the winning of the war." To address the menace presented by alien workers who, poisoned by "insidious influences," could delay or sabotage production, the bureau advised industry to cooperate with the public education system in establishing night schools and factory classes. Given the emergency situation, however, such a program needed to proceed well beyond lessons in English and civics. With the bureau's assistance, plants could establish "a campaign of patriotic education," organized by "a real American who is a natural leader." Industries were advised to concentrate on organizing "'America First' Committees of Minute Men" among native- and foreign-born employees, foremen, and superintendents who could report on and counter disloyalty in the workplace.[37]

Typically, many industries simply arranged for the Americanization of foreign workers in conjunction with public schools. The Colorado Fuel and Iron Company began experiments with night classes taught by public school teachers in 1901 and, in the Iron Range region of Minnesota, mining companies helped initiate night schools as early as 1908. According to the school superintendent of Virginia, Minnesota, by 1914 classes met from three to five nights per week, two hours a night, with afternoon classes provided for night shift workers. Teachers were culled from the regular day school faculty and "visual and dramatic methods of instruction" were preferred. Some educators involved with industry saw daytime factory classes as advantageous because workmen could derive the many benefits of lessons in English and citizenship and forgo the fatigue and time away from family necessitated by enrollment in night schools. "The noon factory class takes the instruction to him in the plant and becomes a part of his daily life, to which he expects to give a measure of his time and energy," explained a junior high school principal from Grand Rapids, Michigan. "Employers, where the [factory school] plan has been tried, become enthusiastic over the English classes," a national magazine reported. "They find loyalty to the company goes hand in hand with loyalty to the country."[38]

English and citizenship classes, in school or factory, also appeared to be a more effective means to inspire other foreign workers, family, and friends to seek instruction and not be left out of something their more earnest compatriots had already begun. The superintendent of public schools in Frontenac, a coal mining community in southeastern Kansas, published a book treating various aspects of Americanization. For adult immigrants who had children, Loren Stiles Minckley suggested visiting days at which parents gathered at the school to become acquainted with teachers, listen to their progeny recite their lessons, and receive invitations to attend night school and learn English. Public entertainments, such as Christmas pageants, socials, and picnics, likewise built up a relationship between adult immigrants and the public schools. "They know very well that there is not much chance for them to adopt American ways, but they all want their children to go to the front in American ideas," Minckley explained. "This desire for the children to be good pupils in the public schools brings them in touch with American ways. . . . The foreigner's whole ambition is for his children's success, although he be a miner down upon his hands and knees digging coal out of the earth to feed and clothe his boy and girl." For those immigrants without children, mostly young, single males, Minckley advocated night school but acknowledged the difficulties in interesting those most in need of basic instruction.[39]

The federal bureaucracy and national leaders of the Americanization drive did all they could to advance cooperation between industrialists, businessmen, labor unions, public schools, and experts like themselves. Frances Kellor, as the power behind the National Americanization Committee, preached for Americanization as part and parcel of industrial preparedness in the months leading to American entry into the war. "Until our language and American citizenship accompany the pay envelope," she declared in a typical pronouncement, "our cities will not be American cities—nor the United States a united nation."[40] In addition, National Conferences on Americanization through Education, also referred to as America First Conferences, were initiated by the Bureau of Education, in cooperation with its National Committee of One Hundred, in February 1917. Skeptical progressives commented on the predominance of the "subalterns of industry and the noncoms of the chambers of commerce" and conspicuous absence of labor representatives at the conferences held in Washington, D.C., in 1918 and 1919. The bureau also involved the U.S. Chamber of Commerce's Committee on Immigration, hoping above all to "bring into relation employers and educators."[41]

Throughout the war and the critical years that followed, federal agencies bombarded industries, chambers of commerce, public schools, state councils of defense, and anyone else remotely associated with industrial Americanization with memoranda, letters, bulletins, and circulars. To further the causes of citizenship, patriotism, and industrial cooperation, factories and other employers of foreign-born labor received continual reminders to advance English language and citizenship instruction through patriotic speeches, Flag Day celebrations, distribution of Americanization literature, noon-hour and night school classes, and the establishment of Plant Americanization Committees. The latter, according to a Council of National Defense circular letter, were "to include members designated by the foreign-born employees themselves, subject to the approval of the employer as to their loyalty." Once constituted, such Plant Americanization Committees could distribute Americanization information in different languages and keep authorities apprised of the educational measures required for effective work among foreign-born workers. The Bureau of Education, in advocating its "America First" campaign, advised industries to reward employees who regularly attended night schools with bonuses, wage increases, and preference in receiving promotions.[42]

The "America First" drive also sought to interest labor unions in promoting night schools, appealing to the idea of "a more homogeneous body of organized labor" and the reduction of accidents. Despite the government's efforts, union leaders frequently expressed their dissatisfaction with the close collaboration between Americanizers and industrialists. Organized labor enjoyed an improved bargaining position in the war years, thanks to sharply increased production, labor shortages, and inflation. Union membership doubled between 1917 and 1920, offering an alternative Americanizing force to factory and classroom for untold numbers of immigrant workers. From the point of view of union leaders, foreign-born workers assimilated through unionization, and in organizing workers during the war, union leaders appealed—as did government agencies and industries—in terms of democracy and patriotism. Unions also conducted English and civics classes, for example at the Labor Temple Evening High School in Los Angeles. In broader terms, unionization allowed for the socialization of new immigrants to the labor movement and some acculturation in relation to the wider working-class culture. Immigrant workers framed their struggle for industrial democracy with an amalgam of ethnic identity and class consciousness, often linking Old World nationalism to American patriotism as they understood it. In that sense, whether marching in a May Day parade, organizing a union, participating in a strike, or sitting in a classroom, immigrants could become Americanized on workers' terms.[43]

The question of Americanization also became intertwined with the emergence of a workers' control movement in the postwar period. Industrial Americanization was a vital component of industrialists' early-twentieth-century managerial reforms. Corporate welfare programs, personnel management, and the scientific management techniques invented by Frederick Winslow Taylor were designed to transform workers into orderly, efficient, sober, thrifty, and contented industrial laborers. Much to management's consternation, immigrants' preindustrial work habits, typified by irregular exertion, quitting, "blue Mondays," and drinking binges, along with unionization and strikes, shaped workers' responses to the efficiency experts' attempts to implement scientific management.

Industries nationwide rolled out their American Plan, which encompassed scientific management and corporate welfare, including grievance procedures and employee representation plans meant to increase productivity, reduce turnover, decrease strife, and undercut support for unionization. However, because the rationalization of industry assaulted skilled workers' traditional control of the workplace, created more chaos, such as chronic unemployment, in workers' lives, and corresponded with a rising cost of living, immigrant participation in strikes and radicalism actually increased. Many workers, immigrant and native-born, participated in the massive strike wave of the 1910s and early 1920s with the understanding that they were upholding basic American working-class traditions rather than engaging in revolution. They thought they had embarked on a crusade to bring democracy to industry and appropriate a long-denied share of economic power. Employers and the public at large, unfortunately, saw the unrest in the light of the fears engendered by war and revolution abroad. Unions and their immigrant members endured crushing defeats in mass production industries between 1919 and 1922.[44]

Sympathetic Americanizers had an understanding of unions' significance as Americanizing forces that often bore more similarity to the viewpoint of labor leaders than industrial managers. Frank B. Lenz, the immigration secretary of the YMCA in San Francisco, praised labor organizations because the "union teaches the immigrant self government. . . . It throws different nationalities into united groups, so that the foreign nationality of any one of them becomes lost. They then adopt the common way of thinking and acting, which is American." Assimilated union members with whom foreigners came into contact became models of correct "American" behavior, and union policies that members be U.S. citizens or "have declared their intention of becoming one" induced the "foreigner to become naturalized." Through accepted union activities on behalf of the "immigrant's wages . . . hours and . . . physical working conditions," the unions paved the way for the foreign-born "to adopt the American social and moral standard of living."

As labor arbitrator and University of Toledo professor William M. Leiserson explained in one of the Carnegie Foundation studies of Americanization, union membership "furnished [the immigrant] a practical school in citizenship, giving him practice in voting, elections, and law-making, teaching parliamentary practices, methods of law-making, obedience to the agreements of the union and the employers . . . and introducing him to judicial processes and methods" of arbitration set up by such agreements. The "efficient and successful" trade union was, according to Leiserson, "a miniature republic" in which the immigrant worker received practical training in democratic citizenship. "A trade union needs to engage in no Americanizing or proselytizing campaigns to make Americans of immigrant workmen," Leiserson concluded. By uniting all workers in a given industry, the well-run union "imperceptibly fuses native and foreign born into a common folk."[45]

Working-class Americanization was extraordinarily dynamic. Employers, Americanizers, middle-class ethnic community leaders, labor unions, and radicals all shaped the process. At the same time, the immigrant worker presumably possessed a considerable amount of leeway to "invent" his or her own American identity. Nonetheless, race could and did inject itself into the mix, signifying the constraints impeding immigrants who lacked the requisite attribute of "whiteness." In the wake of the Clifton-Morenci strike of 1917, for example, an official with the Arizona State Federation of Labor commented that participation in a recognized labor organization would assist in the Americanization of Mexican and Mexican-American workers. The irony, of course, lay in the long-established policies of excluding Hispanics from membership in such unions. In time, southern and eastern Europeans could and would gain acceptance and acknowledgment as "white" workers, but Western opposition and hostility toward Asian and Hispanic labor still militated against genuine acceptance of all workers as workers.[46]

The camps and towns owned by mining corporations and agribusiness concerns illustrate industrial Americanization in a Western context. One of the most prominent mine, smelter, and mill operators, the Colorado Fuel and Iron Company (CF&I), originated with the construction of a small steelworks at Pueblo by the Colorado Coal and Iron Company, an affiliate of the Denver and Rio Grande Railway Company, in 1881. The Colorado Fuel Company, a rival coal mining concern owned by John C. Osgood and a group of investors from Iowa and Denver, absorbed the struggling firm in 1892, thereby creating the Colorado Fuel and Iron Company. John D. Rockefeller and eastern investors gained control in 1903, while George Jay Gould, principal stockholder in the Denver and Rio Grande Railroad, assumed a similar status with the CF&I. John D. Rockefeller Jr. assumed control in 1907, with Lamont Montgomery Bowers as chief executive officer from 1908 to 1915.[47]

After the Ludlow massacre, new CEO Jesse Floyd Welborn implemented the Industrial Representation Plan, developed by former Canadian minister of labor (and future prime minister) William L. MacKenzie King. John D. Rockefeller Jr. had hired Mackenzie King in summer 1914 to plan an alternative to the striking United Mine Workers of America (UMWA). The plan, which offered employee boards for each mine and a company-wide employee/employer board, was approved by coal mine workers in October 1915 and put into effect 1 January 1916. Steelworkers in Pueblo approved the plan in May 1916, as did iron mine workers at Sunrise, Wyoming, in October. All CF&I plans were consolidated in 1921. Clearly, the CF&I management hoped the Industrial Representation Plan would lessen class consciousness and strengthen the relationship and identification of employees and their families with the company. For its part, the CF&I would not relinquish any real power or control. Furthermore, initiating a strike and membership and/or participation in the IWW were causes for immediate dismissal.[48]

Though not specifically geared toward citizenship training, the CF&I, through its Sociological Department, had for years been providing night school classes for its employees. The department, in its first report (1901–1902), noted the challenges in administering services to workers spread out

YMCA instructor and Americanization class for steelworkers in Pueblo, Colorado, ca. 1920. *Colorado Fuel and Iron Company Industrial Bulletin,* 27 April 1920. Colorado Historical Society.

along the front range of the Rockies from Wyoming to New Mexico. Representing thirty-two nationalities and speaking twenty-seven different languages, employees and their families "clung . . . most tenaciously" to traditional ways. "Neither is it strange," the report continued, "that their ideals differ from the common American standard, that they possess many and strong prejudices, and that their suspicions are easily and quickly aroused." The Sociological Department opened the first night schools, taught by regular public school teachers, in fall 1901, which proved most popular among Italian workers, who, along with a few Mexicans, Austrians, and Slavs, studied English, mathematics, and an occasional lesson in geography or history. The following year, the department reported on a camp night school in New Mexico "composed almost wholly of Japanese who proved themselves very industrious pupils." Until the 1903–1904 miners' strike shut down operations, steel workers in Pueblo had the opportunity to attend a six-month evening course at the company's normal and industrial school. In the 1906–1907 report, the department commented on the "varying success" of night school classes in the camps, as the "average foreign miner doesn't feel like applying himself to study after a hard day's work underground. However, the more ambitious derive great benefit from the schools."[49]

In one of the early Sociological Department reports, the Colorado Fuel and Iron Company clarified why it went to the trouble of providing social and educational services to its widely scattered workforce. Churches and public schools had to be supplemented by concerned corporations, who alone possessed the means to address the comprehensive needs of the entire community of workers and their families. The company, moreover, defined those needs in a manner most befitting its desire for a stable, orderly, and permanent class of employees. "The need in our coal fields," the Sociological Department pointed out, "is for better mothers and wives; better cooks and home-makers; so that husbands will not be driven to the saloon for comfortable quarters or an appetizing meal." As the company expected their workers' male children to work in the mines and mills, technical training in the schools had to assume as much, if not more, importance in the public schools. "This work and the providing of a healthy social and intellectual life for the adults cannot all be done by the public school nor yet by the church, nor by the men themselves," the report concluded. "Much of it must be done by the great corporations controlling the coal fields, for they have the means and control the situation." Through paternalism, the CF&I intended to mold its workers into capable, competent, and, above all, contented citizens and employees. In time, Americanization would take its place among the tools available to the company for maintaining its precarious hold on the loyalty of its polyglot communities.[50]

Under the Industrial Representation Plan, the company offered the YMCA the opportunity to administer the social centers and educational and social welfare programs in the camps. Thus, in October 1916, the Y's Dr. Peter Roberts toured the company's camps and Pueblo steelworks to organize classes in English and citizenship for employees and their wives. Loyalty to the company became intertwined with loyalty to the country when the United States entered the World War. "Any man who tries to persuade us to quit work or limit production," an editorial in the company's industrial relations magazine suggested, "is not our friend or the friend of our country. He is helping the enemy." The CF&I's Americanization efforts soon merged with the America First Society program of the Colorado State Council of Defense. After quarantines prompted by the influenza epidemic that struck Colorado in October 1918 were lifted, the America First societies were reorganized and English and citizenship classes resumed.[51]

With dissolution of the State Council of Defense after the war, the CF&I maintained its night school classes, as before, in conjunction with public schools and the YMCA. The company even managed to briefly continue the

Steelworkers and teacher in Colorado Fuel and Iron Company citizenship class, Pueblo, Colorado, 1924. *Colorado Fuel and Iron Company Industrial Bulletin,* 15 February 1924. Colorado Historical Society.

America First Society programs. A February 1924 issue of the company's *Industrial Bulletin* included a glowing report on a citizenship class at one of the Pueblo steel plants. "Only praise is due those who have the patience and the courage and are willing to make the necessary effort" to complete the rigorous requirements for American citizenship, the *Bulletin* declared. A veteran Pueblo public school teacher guided students through the basics of English, American history, and government. Fourteen steel workers, hailing from Austria, Hungary, Italy, Russia, and Slovenia, completed the course, and, because of the thoroughness with which they had passed the instructor's examinations and received diplomas, they were "excused in court from the examination on government."[52]

Accompanied by other aspects of corporate welfare, such as improvements to company housing and profit sharing, the CF&I's Americanization programs aimed to undercut the appeals of labor organizers and firmly attach workers and families to the company. The extent to which the company succeeded is difficult to ascertain. John D. Rockefeller Jr. and the CF&I management hailed the Industrial Representation Plan as a success, but workers, as shown during disputes in 1917, 1919, and 1921–1922, continued to look to the United Mine Workers of America. With demand for coal plummeting in the 1920s, employees endured mine closures and wage cuts. Increasingly dissatisfied with both the Industrial Representation Plan and the UMWA, some turned to the IWW, which attempted to manage a walkout in the southern fields in 1927–1928. The plan was abandoned in the coal mines in 1933 because of section 7a of the National Industrial Recovery Act, which required company recognition of an independent union, in this case the UMWA.[53]

The St. Louis, Rocky Mountain and Pacific Company also implemented a broadly conceived Americanization strategy in its coal mining towns in Colfax County, New Mexico. In a fascinating report written by company "welfare manager" Horace W. Kruse in 1920, the philosophy and practice of industrial Americanization in a Western mining center is revealed. Diagnosing the fundamental problems as ethnic group allegiance, self-segregation, and adherence to "the habits and customs peculiar to their own lands," Kruse prescribed education, "the ultimate end being Americanization," as the key to the "accomplishment of the whole general plan of welfare work." Before any mention of night schools or citizenship papers, however, the company's welfare staff commenced a campaign "to show these people what it meant to live in America," beginning with "the first requisite in American living—to keep clean." To correct the crowded and dirty conditions in which many of the employees lived, the company cleaned and painted houses, provided garbage cans, and fenced in each family's yard. Unfortunately, the tenants hung their laundry, carpets, and clothing on the new fences, "a picturesque thing, but one of appalling disorder." Thus, the company installed clotheslines and poles, "but the problem of disorder was by no means solved."[54]

It is interesting to note Kruse's focus on transforming immigrant workers' lifestyles from disorder to order. As with progressive reformers and the rising cadre of industrial efficiency experts and engineers, social workers like Kruse defined their mission in terms of essentially rescuing disorderly, unassimilated souls from chaotic modes of thought and behavior. Americanism meant order, which had to be revealed through concrete examples of right living: clean homes, paint, ash cans, fences, and clotheslines. Even then, the task required "endless patience," and the subsidized provision of cellars and coal bins, electric lights, running water, and the planting of trees and lawns augmented the previous beautification measures. "Each family," Kruse noted, "had to be visited and impressed with the fact that order was a requirement." Being careful "not to antagonize," but instead "to rouse in them a worthy pride," the company's Americanizers showed their tenants and employees "what it meant to live in America."[55]

Once the outward signs of cleanliness and order had been established, traveling nurses assumed the responsibility of dealing with the "more delicate problem of reconstructing the inner conditions of the homes." Like home teachers in California, the company's traveling nurses, with "utmost tact and skill," instructed immigrant mothers and their families in the importance of American standards in health and hygiene. Children, too, received the gospel of cleanliness at school, receiving prizes and a school picnic for diligently cleaning their faces and hands and brushing their hair. "Surely the work of Americanization finds its greatest success in educating the children," Kruse commented. "They carry the influence into the homes and into the future."[56]

For those adult employees who so desired, the company subsidized their attendance at night school for instruction in English and in preparation for naturalization. As with virtually everyone involved with Americanization, Kruse noted how "the drifting tendencies of the men" made regular attendance a rarity. Moreover, the difficulties in securing "suitable teachers" impeded the work. Practicality and simplicity had to prevail in order to convince the foreign worker that English would provide a "great advantage . . . over his own language." Contrary to what a number of industries had done during and after the war, Kruse advised against paying workers for the time spent in class or offering bonuses to attend. Instead, "he should be shown the advantages of being able to speak our language and have it made clear that he cannot share in the privileges of citizenship until he has proved himself worthy of them." Defining foreigners as "emotional" and "impressionable," Kruse cautioned against instilling the impression that one should attend night school merely to please an employer. Complete Americanization was a "complex matter" with multiple approaches, "a slow and thorough process" by necessity. "There can be no doubt about the first steps—the influence of American living conditions, instruction in the English language, and most effective of all, the education of the rising generation."[57]

Finally, to address the tendencies of the foreign groups to segregate, the St. Louis, Rocky Mountain and Pacific Company endeavored to provide "a common ground where the different nationalities could meet for recreation and enjoyment." With national prohibition in effect, the company converted former saloons into "community houses," with soda fountains, dance halls, libraries and reading rooms, kitchen, game rooms, and barber shops. Dances, motion pictures, concerts, socials, and club meetings, according to Kruse, "enliven the town spirit and promote a desired mingling of nationalities under wholesome, happy conditions."[58]

All the company's welfare work, from sprucing up workers' houses and yards to teaching English in night schools and building community centers, was conducted in a spirit of paternalistic benevolence. "The Company recognized," Kruse concluded, "that it could aid materially in moulding the character and aiding the development of its alien units by shaping their lives along the lines of civic and social usefulness." Americanization, for the St. Louis, Rocky Mountain and Pacific Company and others like it, was synonymous with establishing order in the lives of workers. Orderly workers appeared to industrial Americanizers, quite logically, as contented and loyal. Although expensive, improving conditions at work and home for foreign laborers promised long-term payoffs of industrial peace. The commitment, however, had to be permanent and the devotion to work with the foreign-born genuine. "The work of Americanization must not be spasmodic; it must be sustained. Above all, there must be vision. No one has a right to undertake it who does not believe in foreigners."[59]

Americanization work among Mexican laborers and their families in citrus worker villages in Orange County, California, revealed rationales similar in many respects to those advanced by mining companies in the interior. George B. Hodgkin, an employee with the Industrial Relations Department of the California Fruit Growers' Exchange, described an experiment in community Americanization financed by a growers' association and nearby public schools in La Habra and Fullerton. Druzilla Mackey, an experienced home teacher hired in 1919 by the La Habra Citrus Growers Association for their Campo Colorado *colonia,* combined several roles. "If she fails to gain entrée into a home in one of her capacities," Hodgkin noted, "she has a number of other official capacities to turn to—teacher of women's and men's classes, truant officer, house inspector, employment manager, nurse, etc." With the exception of religion, Hodgkin depicted the camp's Americanization teacher as the "supreme directress of all the activities of the community," marveling at the transformation presumably effected by her expertise and example. "Within a few weeks after this work was started this Camp of sixty odd families, nearly all of whom were strangers to one another, had become a harmonious community all working together," he wrote in a November 1921 article. As in the Colfax County mining camps, the Americanization program in Campo Colorado began with a cleanup campaign, complete with the construction of fences around yards. With the camp taking on "a more orderly, attractive appearance," Americanization progressed rapidly. According to an enthusiastic Hodgkin, residents pledged to assist in the construction of a bathhouse and laundry, established a mutual heath insurance society, organized orchestras, and screened educational films.[60]

In educational terms, the residents of Campo Colorado benefited from English lessons that enhanced the Mexican men's efficiency in the fields and allowed "the women . . . to wisely order their groceries in English and to care for the baby and call the doctor, etc." The supervisor of immigrant education for Los Angeles, Ruby Baughman, prepared a curriculum explicitly designed for citrus workers, with lessons revolving around the progression of the planting, harvesting, packing, and marketing of the fruits "and back again finally to the wages paid to the Mexicans." Teaching English to the Mexican laborer in Orange County was less an academic exercise than a practical tool "that will help him in his work and make a better worker of him." Above all, improved conditions and well-organized and effective

Americanization meant that the growers had been "well supplied with a permanent and reliable labor force."[61]

In other parts of the West, employers of immigrant labor also attempted to make better workers and citizens through various means of Americanization. The Immigration Committee of the U.S. Chamber of Commerce reported on many of these programs in the pages of its bulletin. In Phoenix, the Chamber of Commerce helped inaugurate "War Americanization activities among foreign-born residents in mining camps of Arizona." Meanwhile, industrial plants cooperated with the Omaha Commercial Club's Americanization Committee, which organized "Naturalization Nights" at the club's headquarters. Held every three months in conjunction with the federal district court's naturalization hearings, from fifty to seventy-five applicants presented final papers to the judge and clerk of the court and listened to talks by prominent citizens who offered advice for the new citizens. "These foreigners thus call up our business men to get information of all kinds and a splendid relationship is engendered," the Commercial Club reported. "The foreigners are at first timid. Now they see we are trying to help them and do not wish to use them for any other purpose than to make citizens of them. We have kept politics outside all our activity and will continue to do so." In the 1920s, the Union Pacific Coal Company hired Jessie Mc-Diarmid, a former Hull House resident, to coordinate Americanization for workers and their families in polyglot Rock Springs, Wyoming. McDiarmid edited the company's Americanization magazine and organized recreational activities for the wives of mine workers. A firm believer in the "immigrant gifts" philosophy, McDiarmid learned a great deal more than she perhaps had anticipated about the immigrants' lives, for instance through participation in a traditional tea ceremony with a Japanese immigrant woman.[62]

Whether or not the Union Pacific or other Western employers shared Mc-Diarmid's outlook on the contributions of the foreign-born, the bottom line remained cooperative relations in the workplace, improved efficiency, loyalty, and order, all of which flowed toward more earnings for the company. Industrial Americanization, from the perspective of the Colorado Fuel and Iron Company, benefited the enterprise in a number of ways. "Workmen drawn from every quarter of the globe begin to develop common interests and common sympathies when a medium of communication is established," the CF&I's *Industrial Bulletin* remarked at the outset of the firm's Americanization drive in 1916. "Mutual dislike and suspicion melt away with the coming of better understanding. The heterogeneous population of the mining camp is welded into a public spirited community. With knowledge of American history and institutions comes a desire for American citizenship. In the mine and shop, safety rules and working regulations can be made intelligible to all, thus reducing accidents and increasing efficiency and earning capacity." In the broader scheme of things, industrial Americanization in the West satisfied the desire of reformers, educators, and businessmen to push the region further along the road to greater maturity and acceptance. Welding an Americanized workforce into place hopefully would assist the nation as a whole by removing the Western propensity for radicalism and violence.[63]

For workers, the presumed benefits of Americanization as a complement to corporate welfare programs were not as clear. Having the house painted by the company, getting a pay raise, enjoying subsidized medical treatment, learning English, dancing at the community house, or getting one's citizenship papers must have had very real and often poignant meaning for foreign workers and families. Communities may indeed have become more tightly knit, and safety on the shop floor or in the mine may have improved markedly. Yet, industrial Americanization emerged in the West as an employer prerogative manifestly designed to steer immigrant laborers away from organizing outside the purview of the company. For Mexicans and other "non-whites" in particular, company exertions on their behalf did not alter in any appreciable way the relationship between the dominant society and the "aliens" undergoing Americanization. Residents of the *colonias* in Southern California understood that the growers desired a fixed and reliable labor supply. The pressure to transform oneself culturally, however, could appear too great a sacrifice when the transformation still left one on the wrong side of the racial divide. Americanization in rural labor camps such as Campo Colorado, while satisfying in the main for both Anglo townspeople and Mexican villagers, had little impact on the social gulf separating Anglos from Mexicans.[64]

Professional Americanizers, whether employed by government or corporations, occupied a middle ground in conducting programs aimed primarily at workers. Collaborating with councils of defense, industries, chambers of commerce, and public schools, Americanization workers in the West implemented the means whereby immigrant workers became responsible citizens possessed of realistic conceptions concerning labor relations. The California Commission of Immigration and Housing, for example, envisioned a large part of its role as guiding labor and employer toward common ground on Americanism. In its stated goals for Americanization during the war emergency, the CCIH included the following objective: "That employers and employees should co-operate in improving industrial conditions and in raising them to American standards, so that no opportunity will be afforded seditious or malicious agitators to use unsatisfactory conditions as pretexts in stirring up labor troubles." Augmenting the intensified campaign to improve working conditions, the commission also utilized a foreign language agent

program that, during the war especially, became an industrial spying operation. What one student of the CCIH termed "labor espionage" by commission labor camp investigators and foreign language agents began after the
1913 Wheatland riot. Investigators reported to executive secretary George
Bell and after he left the agency in 1917, directly to commission chairman
Simon Lubin. To spy on Wobblies, the CCIH also employed a onetime
Alaska Fishers' Union officer, J. Vance Thompson, whose often fanciful reports on the IWW and Non-Partisan League played a role in the development of state and federal suppression efforts.[65]

Although not charged with spying on labor activists, Utah Americanization director Arch Thurman perceived the challenges of industrial Americanization as momentous in their implications. "Most of the aliens in Utah
are settled in the industrial centers and mining camps," Thurman pointed
out in a 1920 report. "This complicates the problem somewhat, because under such conditions they can maintain their Old World traditions and customs, many of which are inimical to our own." To alleviate the problem
required sustained work on the part of the state's fledgling Americanization
system. "If we do not undertake the duty of giving to these people an opportunity to know American ideals, American institutions, and what is in
store for them as citizens of this great republic," Thurman argued, "those
who are preaching discontent as the only means of escape from the economic
burdens of present civilization, will take advantage of the ignorance of these
people, and will instill into them un-American ideas, with the result that our
free institutions will be in danger."[66]

Americanization workers in Colorado also approached the problem from
the standpoint of countering the radical menace lurking within the immigrant working class. In summer 1918, under the auspices of the state council's Committee on Americanization and Colorado University's Extension
Division, James C. Stephens and two assistants organized chapters of the
America First Society of Colorado for the foreign-born in Pueblo, Denver,
Leadville, and a number of mining camps on the Western Slope. Through a
cooperative agreement, a Colorado Fuel and Iron Company YMCA worker
organized several chapters in Las Animas and Huerfano counties. "Before organizing one of the chapters," Stephens explained, "the leaders of the nationality or nationalities concerned are consulted." Once five or six leaders
were chosen to serve as an Executive Committee, with a president, vice president, and secretary, a new chapter could be formed. "The Societies work in
co-operation with the Americanization Committee," Stephens reported in
September 1918, "but are self-governing, the main impetus for their growth
coming from themselves." At the outset of the organizing drive, Stephens
held out great promise for its success. "The Italians, Greeks, and Slavs of

AMERICA FIRST SOCIETY

AUTHORIZED BY
THE STATE COUNCIL OF DEFENSE

The object of this Society is to oppose to the enemies of liberty and justice everywhere a solid front of one hundred million Americans, united in loyalty to one Language, one Country, one Flag.

ITS MOTTO: *He that is not for America is against America.*

PLEDGE OF MEMBERSHIP: I pledge myself to be first of all an American; to promote with all my power a knowledge of the language, the government and the ideals of this country; and to support her by my every word and act in her struggle for the freedom of mankind.

33   Signed: ....

"America First Cards" used by Committee on Americanization in Colorado during World War I. Julius C. Gunter Papers, Colorado State Archives.

Pueblo," he recorded in spring 1918, "as they grasp the idea of the America First Society are taking to it with great enthusiasm." Each chapter, Stephens informed Governor Gunter, would "serve as propaganda centers" through which to instruct foreigners about the war, American government and ideals, and "what foreign labor can do to help bring about victory." Members of the America First Society also signed pledge cards proclaiming their absolute loyalty and support of the nation and intention to promote knowledge of its language, government, and ideals. To further inspire Americanization within immigrant working families, Junior America First Societies were organized among schoolchildren in Colorado Fuel and Iron Company camps.[67]

The Committee on Americanization also intended to conduct classes in English, American history, and citizenship through the America First Societies. Stephens and his fellow organizers encouraged the Executive Committees of each chapter or local industries to conduct rough surveys of those in need of citizenship or English instruction or both. Once prepared to begin classes, notices were sent out to individuals identified as prospective students, with "additional urging" for those failing to respond or attend classes. Stephens later reported that the classes were conducted on two or three evenings a week, typically financed by the local school board and taught by local teachers. "No expense is incurred by the foreigner who attends the class," he noted, and the Naturalization Bureau supplied free textbooks. The director, while cognizant of the potential difficulty of providing teachers in the most inaccessible mining camps, held out great promise for the educational programs.[68]

In late September 1918, Stephens reported considerable progress to the Council of Defense. Thirty-two chapters of the America First Society had been organized, including five in Pueblo, one in Leadville, four in Denver, eight in Las Animas County, five in Huerfano County, seven in the Telluride area, one at Silverton, and one at Eureka. The immigrants in larger urban areas were organized along separate national lines, with Yugoslav, Slovak, Greek, and two Italian chapters in Pueblo and Slav, Italian, Greek, and "German-Russian" chapters in Denver. In communities where smaller numbers of different nationalities lived, such as the coal mining camps in Las Animas and Huerfano counties, Stephens had organized multinational chapters. "The proposition of Americanization in Colorado is a very difficult one," he acknowledged, "owing to the great distances to be covered and the great difficulty of reaching many of the metal mining camps," two of which had America First Societies but could only be accessed by long aerial trams during the winter. Nonetheless, about five thousand individuals had enrolled in the societies, and Stephens projected that sixty or seventy thousand people would eventually belong to seventy or seventy-five chapters. As it turned out, however, no additional America First Society chapters would be successfully organized. The influenza epidemic hit Colorado in the fall of 1918, leading to a ban on public meetings that seriously disrupted the committee's attempts to organize new America First Societies and classes and maintain existing ones. With the end of the war in November 1918 also came the likelihood that the State Council of Defense would be dismantled.[69]

On 1 January 1920, within a year of the disbanding of the State Council of Defense, the *Denver Post* featured a series of essays on Americanization by prominent Coloradans, including Dr. Norlin and Emily Griffith, the principal of the Denver Opportunity School. For the most part moderate admonitions for the foreign-born to learn English and become citizens, the essays were framed by more militant expressions of antiradicalism: "Instead of Letting the 'I.W.W.' Run the Country, Let's Run the 'I.W.W.'—Out! Remember That I.W.W. Also Means 'I WILL WRECK.'" The juxtaposition of relatively measured efforts at persuasion with bombastic reminders of dangerous Wobblies symbolized the contradictions of the Americanization drive among immigrant workers. Industrial Americanization in the West, while often conducted with good intentions and apparently sound methods, was primarily geared toward management's control of the workplace and workers. The imperatives of wartime unity, which fostered the militant 100 percent Americanism of the Red Scare, came to define much that passed for

America First Society meeting at Segundo, Colorado, ca. 1919. *Colorado Fuel and Iron Company Industrial Bulletin,* 30 April 1919. Colorado Historical Society.

Americanization in industrial settings. For a growing number of liberals in the early 1920s, Americanization had been effectively co-opted and distorted by patriotic societies, chambers of commerce, and outside agencies, such as the YMCA, which cooperated closely with industry. They argued, with some justification, that professional Americanizers served as corporations' allies in imposing social control on immigrant workers. On the other hand, the professional Americanizers either employed by or in agreement with corporations possessed genuine faith that their work would hasten the day when class divisions, along with the racial and ethnic animosities that disrupted working-class lives, would be eradicated.[70]

Conclusion

The itinerant workers who were buffeted by cyclical and seasonal unemployment and, if settled in one place, frequently segregated by custom and law symbolized the regional distinctiveness of Western labor. Because of the predominance of natural resource–based industries, moreover, organization into industrial unions like the militant Industrial Workers of the World typified much of the region's labor activity. In addition, the First World War's impact on Western economies, signified by booms in agriculture and manufacturing, was coupled with harassment and prosecution of labor militants. The end of the war brought canceled government contracts, rapid economic contraction, numerous strikes, and repression of radicals and labor activists. Americanization in the West, then, paralleled a period rife with violent class conflict—the Ludlow Massacre in 1914, the "deportation" of hundreds of Wobblies from Bisbee, Arizona, into the New Mexico desert in 1917, a wave of strikes between 1919 and 1922. The height of Americanization activity coincided with the Red Scare and a precipitous decline of union labor's influence in industrial affairs.

Both industrialists and Western labor unions embraced Americanization but did so with very different ideas about the term's meaning. For the former, Americanization meant more than English and citizenship classes and naturalization; it meant acceptance of management's program of employee relations. Corporations like the Colorado Fuel and Iron Company provided citizenship classes as part of corporate welfare programs meant to undercut the appeal of radical unions like the Industrial Workers of the World. Labor unions offered alternative definitions of Americanism to Western miners, railroad workers, and other industrial laborers through organizing drives, strikes, and educational programs. Union membership became the vital first step in a process of transforming newly arrived, non-English-speaking laborers from potential strikebreakers into self-respecting "American" workers. Union leadership argued that Americanization only arrived with unionization, but largely unwilling to admit "new" immigrants into membership and identified with restriction and exclusion, organized labor, as a columnist in the *New Republic* put it, "played straight into the employers' hands."[71] Race and ethnicity, though masked behind the generic commentaries and humane actions of Americanizers, still had profound impacts on labor relations in the West. For the most part, then, industry controlled the debate on Americanizing immigrants, especially after the routing of radicals and fizzling of union activism by the early 1920s. Immigrants themselves set individual or group agendas frequently contrary to what either industry, organized labor, or Americanization experts thought was best for them.

For progressives, American involvement in the Great War provided further opportunity to fashion a nation notable for its discipline, generosity, can-do spirit, and high moral tone. With big business as a partner, the government strove to forge an efficient wartime state, modern and businesslike in its orientation. Alien disloyalty and working-class unrest knew no geographical limitations, but the Western reaches of the nation at war appeared to offer continual and disturbing examples of overt anti-Americanism,

menacing radicalism, and reactionary vigilantism. Industrial Americanization made sense for companies coping either with multinational workforces
or racial groups that the dominant community found offensive. Whether
situated within or outside the industrial arena, Americanizers saw Americanization in the idealistic terms of a means to transcend class divisions and
bridge gaps between racial and ethnic groups. It was "a movement," as
George Bell of California stated, "to make everyone in industry, whether native born or foreign born, whether a member of the management or of the
manual working force, a *real American*." A visitor to the Denver Opportunity School, in a letter to a Colorado business paper, noted that "as I looked
at these foreign people it seemed to me there could be no better Americanization work than what was going on." The foreign men who took instructor Arthur G. Hoel's classes, the observer continued, besides learning
American history, laws, and citizenship responsibilities, "received sane information on capital and labor."[72]

4

"EDUCATION FOR CITIZENSHIP"

English, Citizenship, and Night Schools

In November 1917, 165 flag-carrying members of Alfred G. Hoel's Opportunity School classes marched behind a Grand Army of the Republic drum corps and took their seats on the stage at a Colorado Education Association meeting in Denver. After patriotic songs and speeches, federal Chief Naturalization Examiner Paul Lee Ellerbe took the podium and extolled the effects of "Education for Citizenship" upon the nation's preparedness and Denver's immigrant population. "We lead our aliens to citizenship," Ellerbe declared, "but it is only men like Mr. Hoel who can make them drink of the spirit of it." Upon addressing the audience of twenty-five hundred, Ellerbe conducted an examination of three male students—natives of England, Italy, and Sweden respectively. Afterward, Ellerbe informed his superior in Washington that 90 to 95 percent of Denver's naturalization applicants, estimated at six hundred pupils, had attended Hoel's classes by fall 1917. Mr. Hoel, the examiner boasted, "has instructed bankers, jewelers, merchants of all kinds, university graduates, professional men, engineers, artists, cooks, waiters, street sweepers, and laborers."[1]

For Western educators like Alfred Hoel, Americanization represented a great crusade to weld the nation together through the teaching of a common language, citizenship classes, and naturalization proceedings. It mattered little whether the work was conducted among hundreds or thousands of foreign-born in populated urban centers or among a scattered few in remote corners of the West. Grace Raymond Hebard, who became Albany County, Wyoming's official Americanizer during the war, saw her task of making citizens of a relatively small number of immigrants as the realization of a patriotic mission. "I wish to make it a religion," she informed one correspondent, "for a time at least. My idea is that one cannot be a real christian until he is a patriot." Nina Mitchell Crow, a teacher at a one-room country school near Coalwood, Powder River County, Montana, interpreted the importance of her rigorous Americanization work with a half-dozen Bulgarian men. Crow held evening Americanization meetings, either at the schoolhouse or in the men's homes. "I took them and their peculiar ways seriously," she reported, "I never patronized them. I tried to make them see that I was a dependable

Citizenship instructor Arthur G. Hoel with Americanization class at Denver Opportunity School. *Rocky Mountain News,* 27 February 1916. Colorado Historical Society.

friend to them. They thought I knew everything. I filled out their business papers; was private secretary to all; prescribed for their sick babies; called on them, ate their dreadful meals; slept in their hard beds." The Montana teacher's hard work and sacrifices, from her point of view, were necessary guides in transporting a handful of immigrant men to the promised land of American citizenship. "To live among these people, to be helpful and never superior, is the right way."[2]

In certain urbanized sectors of the West, where social and cultural diversity assumed more significance in terms of nonwhite immigrants than on the high plains, educators also perceived Americanization as the path toward order. Ruby Baughman, an immigrant education specialist with public schools in Los Angeles, emphasized the complex interweaving of race and economics in southern California. "In addition to the immigrant groups found in other sections of the country," Baughman observed in a 1921 article, "the Mexican and the Oriental tangle the threads of race prejudice and commercial competition through the warp of integration." The unwelcomed but necessary Mexican migrant worker, in particular, could benefit from basic educational services, Baughman argued, "but he does not know his need of it and his industrial foster nation has not perceived clearly that he must have it." Assimilation to American ways and adjustment to the complicated realities of southern California's economic system, with its spasmodic patterns of seasonal work and unemployment, were "peculiarly matters of education."[3]

Whether in Wyoming, Montana, or southern California, in day schools, night schools, or through home teaching, with European, Mexican, or Asian pupils, English language instruction stood apart as the number one priority in Americanization programs during the war and afterward. Americanizers constantly recited a collection of facts gleaned from the 1910 census to support their case for systematic instruction in English as the basis for a sound assimilation policy: according to the data collected, there were 13 million immigrants ten years of age and older living in the United States, of whom 3 million did not speak English. Underscoring the urgency for adult immigrant education programs, over 2.5 million of the non-English-speaking immigrants were twenty-one or older. Yet, as Frank V. Thompson, superintendent of public schools in Boston and author of a Carnegie Corporation study of Americanization, pointed out, that meant the remaining 7 million immigrants from non-English-speaking nations who did speak English must have learned somewhere, mostly outside of the schools. Thompson, while acknowledging that immigrants possessed an understandably "strong inherent hostility to all attempts to suppress their language," maintained that newcomers to America had "a moral and easily recognized obligation" to "make reasonable effort to conform to the customs and become acquainted with the language of the nation receiving them." An Armenian-born Americanizer in St. Louis, while arguing that learning English had no direct relationship to loyalty to America, agreed that "the teaching of English to immigrants is indispensable to their welfare and necessary for the safety of our democracy."[4]

Similarly, Americanizers in the West expressed their beliefs in the immigrants' obligation to learn English. According to the director of the Americanization Committee of the Arizona Council of Defense,

The first requirement, in the effort to weld these many races and nationalities into a unified American people, adapted to our standards, appreciative of our national customs, in consonance with our national ideals, is education, and that education must be begun by the teaching of the English language. The knowledge of the English language is the open sesame by which those speaking a foreign tongue may gain a clear insight into and comprehension of the principles upon which true American citizenship is based, and therefore it becomes the chief foundation stone of the Americanization movement. It must be accomplished, however, by a sympathetic understanding of the characteristics, the peculiarities and the needs of the various immigrant races, and a real desire to assist them.

Arch M. Thurman, the director of Americanization in Utah, noted that twenty-eight thousand adults in that state could not "speak or read the English language with sufficient ability to carry on the ordinary relations of American life." Utah's ethnic minorities, most of whom lived in industrial and mining centers, remained "generally in national groups where their business relations, their amusements, and their ordinary life processes are carried on in accordance with old world customs and through the medium of their native language." Assimilation, Thurman argued, had to begin with English. "Without this 'tool,' our ideals and institutions will remain unknown to these newcomers." In a statement of principles, conferees at a wartime education conference in New Mexico enunciated their stand on English and Americanization: "We believe that the English language should be the first means of Americanization and should be the medium of communication between all citizens." The New Mexicans announced their support for suspending German language instruction during the crisis and teaching "all immigrants" to read and speak English "as a means of impressing them with the importance of citizenship." Hoping to phrase the idea in a way she assumed her audience could comprehend, a home teacher in Los Angeles stressed—through an interpreter—the extreme significance of learning English to a group of Italian women: "Now it is you who have come to live in our country. So it is for you to learn English, in order that we may know you and appreciate you and like you. You have come to our house to be part of our family—so you should learn the language of our house, which is English."[5]

Though many commentators drove home the point that learning English constituted the first and most important step for immigrants to undertake, they expressed concern as well for a number of problems inherent in teaching the foreign-born. "Instructors have generally been left to their own devices," noted Frank V. Thompson, "with the injunction to teach English and maintain classes of a satisfactory size." Most school systems, according to critics, delegated adult immigrant English classes to unsupervised, untrained, poorly paid teachers. In addition, English teachers often neglected to alter lesson plans designed for children so as to appeal to adults, frequently resulting in alarming rates of absenteeism.[6] To obviate such flaws, the Bureau of Education's Division of Immigrant Education, in its suggestions for implementing programs, stressed the importance of classifying students. Ability to speak English constituted the "first test," which was supposed to help the teacher separate the learners into beginner, intermediate, and advanced classes. From there, the students—particularly beginners—could be further subdivided by nationality to prevent ethnic tensions and the persistence of "foreign mental attitudes." If the number of students allowed, the division advised applying a "third test" that involved separating illiterates and poorly educated immigrants. Other options involved separating the "mentally dull and stupid pupils . . . from the alert, bright ones," women from men, and older from younger students. "Where numbers are inadequate to justify separation in classes," the division's standards recommended, "group pupils according to suggestions above mentioned and teach each group separately as much as possible."[7]

Students from English-speaking countries and others who had mastered the language to some degree advanced to basic instruction in American civics and history in preparation for naturalization. "Every foreigner who comes among us must be led to discover America," professed Grace Raymond Hebard. "When the foreigner has learned to read, he has only come within sight of land. Discovery of America will not be complete until he has learned to enter fully the life and ideals of our country." A thirty-three-year-old Croatian in Kansas City, Kansas, described his "discovery of America" through citizenship training in the early 1920s:

> In my six Months atending the nigth scool I can say I learned great many things witch will be of great help to me every day in the life. As the clas began We start under stand the Goverment of the United States and a constitution by witch the great republic is Governd. and all other section and articles releted to it, we allso read about the Father of the Contry George Washington Abraham Lincoln and many other famous men and women of the land. we also read teh history form the fonder Christopher Columbus Pilgrims and to present.

The superintendent of public schools in Frontenac, Kansas, explained the rationale behind beginning citizenship courses with the intricacies of the Constitution. By copying the preamble and articles of the document, students learned "to write English as well as to read it and at the same time it began to create a spirit of patriotism." Moreover, the naturalization examinations in district courts focused heavily on understanding the American system of government, so there was an obvious practicality in spending a considerable amount of class time on constitutional provisions. "It seems quite difficult to get the adults out and hold them in the night school," the superintendent admitted. "In order to do this the subject has to be made practical and interesting." Lessons based on the Constitution had clear political benefits as well. Explanations of the legislative, executive, and judicial branches of the national government offered prospective citizens appropriate guidance in becoming functioning participants in a democratic system.[8]

"However, teaching the adult foreigners to read the Constitution of the United States in order that they may be able to vote is not Americanizing them," argued Arizona's superintendent of public instruction in a 1926 report. "To make desirable citizens of these people we must educate them in the aims and ideals of our government and inspire in them a desire to become patriotic, self-respecting citizens of our Country, our State and the community in which they are located." Thus, in addition to basic treatments of government and history, citizenship training could also include elementary lessons on proper citizen behavior. For example, a Division of Immigrant Education syllabus suggested opening with a lesson on "The Citizen—How He Lives," which, as a means for improving students' English skills, included discussions of food and nutrition, clothing, water, and fresh air. To accustom the class to appropriate civic responsibilities involving these necessities of life, the syllabus proposed, for instance, discussing the "responsibility of every individual in preventing pollution of air." Other lessons drove home the point that "the Citizen's Community" served its citizens, while every citizen had obligations to the community in such areas as fire protection and prevention and the support of public schools. Finally, the syllabus, after reinforcing the relation between the students' work and citizenship, suggested lessons designed "to show the greatness of America and the devotion of its citizens," the meaning of "American Citizenship," and the logistics of becoming a citizen.[9]

While some progressives dismissed education as an effective means by which to assimilate adult immigrants, almost all Americanizers were, by whatever definition used, progressives. Generally speaking, they exhibited a characteristic optimism in relation to the Americanization movement, believing that their well-intentioned and professionally grounded efforts could quiet the growing demand for restriction on the basis of national origins. Success at this challenging endeavor would prove that American society, even in the case of its most marginal elements, could be engineered and made to work. Failure would simply play into the hands of groups like the Immigration Restriction League, which, though composed of many leading progressives, represented to liberal Americanizers the forces of intolerant reaction. Restrictionists, whether middle-class progressives, labor leaders, or old stock elites, took to dismissing Americanization as ineffective and dominated by sentimentalists. As demands for closing the gates to "inferior" racial stocks from Asia, Mexico, and southern and eastern Europe typically rested on "scientific" findings, organized Americanization education's emphasis shifted as well to encompass a scientific approach. Reformers increasingly perceived the school in broader, environmental terms, concluding that the nation's schools required enlightened, businesslike methods to do their jobs efficiently. The schools needed progressive expertise, and, in the case of adult immigrants, they needed to move beyond lessons in English and civics.[10]

Settlement residents and progressives involved in education reform reinterpreted the school as a means not only to teach the "three R's" but also to socialize students to a wide range of life experiences and attitudes. When it came to the children of immigrants, progressive educators struggled valiantly to provide a better environment, through settlement house programs for instance, to counteract the lure of the street. For adult immigrants, simply relying on a few classroom lessons left too much to chance. "We are assuming too much," wrote one Americanizer, "when we conclude that the formal schooling of the immigrant will automatically solve the problem of Americanization. Not only the school, but the home, the church, the street, the playground, the moving picture, the job, are factors which determine the character and tendencies of the citizen." In progressive formulations, education for citizenship needed to be broadly construed. Thus, many Americanizers conceived of the school as a community center, an idea derived in large part from the settlement house movement. Participants in a national conference sponsored by the Bureau of Education in May 1919 attempted to sustain enthusiasm for the movement by emphasizing the big picture. "Many valuable suggestions were put forward," noted a correspondent for the *Nation,* "for increasing the efficiency of the public school as the great American solvent, all tending to the thesis that the public school should be developed into the community centre where alien adults, as well as alien children, should find the gateway to merging in the body politic."[11]

Arch M. Thurman, who directed Utah's Americanization efforts from 1919 to 1921, exemplified the broad construction of immigrant instruction, exhorting educators throughout the state to accept the responsibility of bringing the foreign-born "into full citizenship." Born in Provo in 1885, Thurman earned his bachelor's degree from Brigham Young University, where he became assistant director of the teacher training department after graduating in 1914. Thurman served the state as chairman of the Utah County Council of Defense and, beginning in August 1918, executive secretary of the Utah State Council of Defense. He was named state director of Americanization in the Utah Department of Public Instruction in 1919, but the position was terminated by the legislature two years later. Thurman advocated an "immigrant gifts" approach similar to much settlement worker rhetoric. "We who were born in this country," Thurman admonished in a 1920 pamphlet, "must come to realize that these newcomers do not come empty-handed, but that they bring to us their arts, their crafts, their appreciation of the beautiful; and above all, their life-long passion for recognition and participation in the affairs of government." A "social problem" with a "direct bearing on our national life," Americanization also constituted an educational project requiring leadership of the schools. By working closely to-

Arch M. Thurman, director of Americanization programs for the state of Utah, 1919–1921. Used by permission, Utah State Historical Society.

gether, schools, industries, community and commercial organizations, city and county officials, churches, fraternal orders, and patriotic societies could unite in effectively presenting "American opportunities and obligations" to immigrants. With the national government supporting the effort through suggestions of uniform standards and methods, Utah, having passed an Americanization law, would soon solve the problem of the unassimilated foreign-born "in the most effective way."[12]

Compulsory attendance laws for adult aliens, a key provision of Utah's 1919 Americanization statute, would not strike all observers as the "most effective way" to further assimilation. Critics have charged that even liberal Americanizers in the settlements and public schools engaged the immigrants in what one historian terms "the unfair exchange." At some point, the reformers expected the immigrants to cast off their Old World cultural attachments and embrace Americanism as defined by their middle-class WASP instructors.[13] Certainly, the imperatives of stimulating patriotism and achieving enhanced efficiency and social stability during the period of the war and its aftermath placed intense pressures on even the most cosmopolitan educators. Nonetheless, the broad conception of citizenship to which certain representative Americanizers adhered must be considered in reaching a balanced assessment of citizenship education.

Emory S. Bogardus was, like Arch Thurman, another Western-based educator whose broad conception of Americanization does not necessarily square with later criticism of Americanizers' methods and objectives. Bogardus began his Americanizing activities as a settlement worker at Northwestern University before moving on to Los Angeles, where he taught courses on immigration and Americanization at the University of Southern California. "Americanization begins with an examination of American traits and ends with the perfecting of an assimilation movement that includes young and old; white, yellow, red, and black; native-born and foreign-born," he averred. "It has four fundamental sets of characteristics: liberty and initiative, union and co-operation, democracy and justice, internationalism and brotherhood." On the face of it, these expressions do not connote an "unfair exchange" between omniscient teachers and empty-vessel immigrants. Americanization, properly understood, Bogardus continued, must begin with the native-born, who needed to cultivate far more sympathy not only for immigrants but also for Indians, blacks, Asians, Mexicans, and even "mountaineers" in Appalachia.[14]

Education for Americanization, as explained by Thurman and Bogardus, reflected the progressives' faith in the power of education as well as education reformers' recognition of environmental forces in shaping individuals. For the most part, the rhetoric of Americanization expounded by professional educators in the West tended to be sympathetic. For instance, in its 1920 bulletin, the State Committee of Americanization Work in Arizona stressed that educators could not expect immigrants to relinquish love of their native language and country of birth. Anyone who could do so "would indeed make a poor citizen of any country." Compulsion to learn English and become naturalized served no useful purpose in shaping new citizens of the foreign-born. "The foreigner who is here to stay will no doubt be better off as a citizen, and needs only to have this fact impressed upon him." Loren Stiles Minckley, a school administrator in southeastern Kansas, insisted that "the interest of the foreigner must be at heart."[15]

In a wartime speech to the California Federation of Women's Clubs, George Bell, the executive secretary of the California Commission of Immigration and Housing, praised evening schools as "the potential birthplace of a great cosmopolitan democracy." During a visit to Boston in September 1918, Wyoming's Grace Raymond Hebard asked, "Is the melting pot melting?" Answering her own question, she pointed out the self-segregation of

Boston's foreign population. "There should be no foreign quarter," she declared, and then helpfully explained her Americanization philosophy: "I instruct at night in the fundamentals and ideals of United States history, show them the difference between liberty and license and prepare them for American citizenship." Ethel Richardson, who oversaw immigrant education in California as an assistant superintendent of public instruction, informed a National Education Association meeting in 1922 that "the business of the night school" was "to create an environment in which the pupil can live an American life."[16]

In their speeches, Bell, Hebard, and Richardson acknowledged the vital role night schools played in educating the foreign-born for citizenship. Indeed, most of the adult immigrants who did see the inside of a schoolroom did so at night. The federal Americanization bureaucracy, while cognizant of how local conditions necessitated variations, stood at the ready to advise night school administrators and teachers. An experimental procedure, titled "Standards and Methods in the Education of Immigrants" and prepared by the Education Bureau's H. H. Wheaton, offered suggestions, for instance, on how to organize and administer a citizenship education program. The document included guidance on procuring and appropriating funding from local and state authorities, supervising immigrant education at both the state and municipal levels, determining policies for the appointment, qualifications, and salaries of teachers, scheduling classes, and publicizing a citizenship education program.[17]

The most fundamental problems for educators lay in convincing prospective citizens to enroll in night school and, once enrolled, keeping them interested. A member of the Woman's Committee of the county defense council in Jerome, Arizona, had the "bright idea" of using "the moving picture theatre, patronized almost exclusively by the Mexican people, for educational work." Spanish-language slides were projected onto the screen "giving information in regard to war work, advertising evening schools, etc. This suggestion can easily be copied in other places." Leaders in the Americanization drive offered numerous suggestions on these questions as well. Frances Kellor stressed the efficacy of reaching the foreign-born through the agencies with which they came into regular contact: jobs, stores, homes, even saloons. It was imperative, too, to utilize the foreign-language press, employers, chambers of commerce, churches, courts, visiting nurses, and libraries. "Neighborhood celebrations and dances can be held by social agencies in order to present the reasons for attending night schools to the guests, and *interesting them in trying it*." Maintaining regular attendance, Kellor argued, depended on opening enough night schools to service all immigrant neighborhoods. "The sessions, especially in beginning classes, must be short, and there must be some form of recreation every evening." Night school teachers, according to Kellor, needed to be "vigorous and interested" and given to "dramatic" methods of instruction.[18]

Emory S. Bogardus agreed that night schools held exceptional promise but decried the customary practice of regular day school teachers undertaking evening classes as overload assignments. Resourceful, specially trained instructors, relieved of full-time teaching during the day, could better display the necessary vigor, interest, and drama. "Evening-school teachers could be placed on a par with the day-school force, and as high a standard of teaching ability and as much vigor of effort could thereby be secured as are now found in the day schools," advised a specialist with the Bureau of Education. Comprehensive day and night teaching assignments could even be reorganized "on a shift-basis, thereby following the regular practise in an industrial plant." In 1916, however, only California specified evening schools as part of the state school system, providing regular grants, reckoning each two-hour session as a half day, and operating evening schools coextensively with day schools. Even the Americanization fervor of the war years did little to impel administrators to devote more than token resources toward night school programs.[19]

Americanizing Immigrant Women

English and civics for Americanization, though usually taught by women at night in public schools and other settings, was explicitly geared toward males. Prior to 1922, immigrant women, if married, automatically became citizens once their husbands were naturalized. Section three of the Expatriation Act of 1907 decreed that "any American woman who marries a foreigner shall take the nationality of her husband," regardless of her residence. Reflecting concerns about immigration, dual citizenship, naturalization, family unity, and the patriotism of women, the law awakened many feminists to the tenuous and arbitrary nature of women's citizenship.[20] In suffrage states before the ratification of the Nineteenth Amendment, loss of citizenship via marriage had particularly unsettling implications. Grace Raymond Hebard treated this problem in a 1918 article that appeared in a Washington State suffrage journal. "If the woman [who marries a foreigner] should chance to live in the state where woman suffrage is granted and should marry a man who had not completed his naturalization," she warned, "she not only would become a foreigner, but her right of suffrage would be taken from her." Likewise, immigrant women who were naturalized automatically when they either married an American or their husbands became citizens gained the franchise without any requirements to receive training for such a responsibility.[21]

When the Nineteenth Amendment became part of the Constitution in late summer 1920, the stakes for native-born women increased. For women involved in Americanization, the nationwide suffrage triumph also underscored the crying need to assimilate more foreign women. "With the coming of universal suffrage, comes also the vote of foreign women whose husband has been naturalized," Hebard pointed out in a talk to Wyoming clubwomen in 1920. "Separate citizen[ship] should be required of these women, subject to the same training and examination in American government, language and history as is required for the male foreigner."[22] Congress responded, albeit slowly, to newly enfranchised women's demands for independent citizenship. Pressed by the Women's Joint Congressional Committee, Congress passed the 1922 Cable Act, which allowed native-born wives of aliens to keep their premarital citizenship and alien women to pursue citizenship independently. Resident wives of males ineligible for citizenship (i.e., Asians) continued to be denationalized by marriage, while foreign women were still barred from naturalization if married to an alien ineligible for citizenship or were themselves ineligible.[23]

Even before passage of the Cable Act, many Americanizers zeroed in on immigrant women as essential components in the construction of a more unified citizenry. "The immigrant woman has hitherto been a neglected factor in our civilization," opined the *Immigrants in America Review*. "Little notice is taken of the degree to which she becomes assimilated, slight provision is made for her instruction, she is not thought of in connection with citizenship, and her needs and interests receive but scanty consideration in the development of our communities." Surveying the situation during the war, the National Americanization Committee (NAC) documented a series of obstacles that many Americanizers believed prevented immigrant women from becoming assimilated. Old-world notions held by foreign-born husbands and fathers concerning women's place, in combination with the "unneighborliness of native families," exacerbated immigrant women's isolation.

Often illiterate in their own language, the ignorance of English left such women more dependent on children and husbands. Reduced to the drudgery of cooking and washing for families and lodgers and often compelled to work outside the home as well, immigrant women were "overburdened with labor." Poorly nourished, ill-informed, and frightened, the Americanizers' stereotypical immigrant female languished in unsanitary housing and abject poverty. To solve the problem of the immigrant woman, the NAC recommended a largely top-down program, beginning with the appointment of a "Woman's Americanization Committee" representing schools, industry, social welfare agencies, and city governments. By standardizing methods and acting as an information clearinghouse, these bodies could "give direction to work of bringing about Americanization." Moreover, afternoon women's classes could be started by "educational authorities" to teach "American standards of living by means of the language lessons"; home teachers could be employed to "sympathetically and patiently try to correct un-American home standards"; and employers, legislators, and the foreign-language press could all do much toward alleviating the plight of immigrant women.[24]

Whether Americanizers in the West could ever hope to witness the desire on the part of the various groups suggested by the NAC to offer support and, more important, devote the necessary financial resources to Americanizing women was a key question. Regardless, advocates believed that the stakes were exceedingly high. In recommending the founding of night schools during a 1918 talk to a Daughters of the American Revolution chapter in Fort Collins, Colorado, Grace Raymond Hebard emphasized the need to Americanize the alien's wife. "She must be educated," Dr. Hebard declared, "and receive more recognition and [s]ome of the principles of Americanization must be ground into her." English and civics played key roles in grinding the principles of Americanization into foreign-born women, but expediting the adjustment to an appropriate "American" lifestyle often stood out as the central objective. Concerned Americanizers made constant references to the need for proper models of "American" homes to impress upon immigrant women the importance of cleanliness and order. "Domestic education," as a YMCA leader in California put it, "would put particular emphasis upon the importance of educating women along the lines of sanitation, hygiene, foods, home nursing, and sewing." In the Southwest, the home economics emphasis appealed to Anglo educators convinced of Mexicans' and Mexican Americans' shortcomings in proper homemaking and hygiene. Evening school classes for "Spanish-American" women, the New Mexico Department of Education's journal advised, had to be planned in such a way "that better standards may be developed."[25]

Making citizens of immigrant women called forth the energies of various agencies and organizations, which meant a further broadening of how "education for citizenship" could be construed. "The Extension Divisions of Agricultural Colleges are in a splendid position," a federal official pointed out to a professor in Idaho, "through the field agents of their Home Economics Departments, to further the Americanization work by teaching the value of citizenship." As a sidelight to their demonstrations, the extension division agents could proselytize on the opportunities provided by the Bureau of Naturalization and public schools. In addition, home economics instructors could do much to aid in establishing citizenship classes where none yet existed.[26]

Established women's organizations such as the General Federation of Women's Clubs (GFWC) and the Women's Christian Temperance Union

(WCTU) also weighed in on the Americanization of immigrant women. In terms of Americanization, moreover, members of women's clubs believed that American mothers possessed an innate understanding of the problems of their immigrant sisters. In a report on illiteracy at the Wyoming federation's 1925 convention, Bertha Van Devender exhorted her compatriots to reach out to immigrant mothers. "Club women everywhere will find their largest field of usefulness in working with the non-English speaking mother. There are so many things for her to learn if she would train her children to become the good American citizens we wish them to be."[27] In the era of Prohibition, the WCTU augmented the theme of motherhood as a philosophical underpinning of good citizenship and a motivation for service to define citizenship for the foreign-born in terms of faith and sobriety. In Kansas, for instance, the state WCTU saw immigrants as fit subjects of study and service, but emphasized the potential for evangelization and the need, as the revised 1924 state handbook put it, "to teach the foreign women the principles of total abstinence that their children may grow up total abstainers, and thus help safeguard the Eighteenth Amendment to bring to them American ideals in home and civic life."[28]

The maternalism inherent in the exhortations of middle-class women in women's clubs or the WCTU affected official policies relating to training immigrant women. In his speech to California clubwomen, George Bell of the California Commission of Immigration and Housing identified the immigrants' homes as "the real cradles of American patriotism and democracy." While children could be assimilated in day schools and immigrant men Americanized through the workplace and night schools, reaching those foreign-born wives and mothers who were not part of the workforce required the use of home teachers. Commission member Mary S. Gibson's hometown of Los Angeles provided the first major test for home teaching, beginning in the summer of 1915.

After conducting a census of immigrant communities and preparing detailed plans for coordinating the various Americanizing agencies in Los Angeles, only one group, the Daughters of the American Revolution, responded by sponsoring a home teacher, who then volunteered her services to the public schools. The teacher, Amanda Mathews Chase, worked at the Amelia Street School in a largely Mexican and Japanese neighborhood. In suggestions published in a commission manual, Chase urged constant visits to mothers at home and the scheduling of monthly social functions for all mothers in the neighborhood. She also recommended, in addition to and in conjunction with English lessons, instructing immigrant women in cooking, cleaning, laundering, sewing, mending, weaving, sanitation, personal hygiene, and patriotism. "Make yourself loved," she admonished, "just as if you had moved into a new

Immigrant women and teacher, southern California, 1920s. Ethel Richardson, "Doing the Thing That Couldn't Be Done," *Survey,* 1 June 1926.

town where you wished to be a social success, or as if you were a new minister, just come to the parish. Your situation is somewhat similar to both, and the affection of the neighborhood is a big asset for your success in Americanizing it." Concerned as well with immigrants' economic welfare, home teachers endeavored to instruct mothers on protecting themselves and their families through lessons on their rights as consumers, tenants, and employees.[29]

Other home teachers in the state imparted advice similar to Chase's. Rebecca Jacobs, who chaired the Committee of Americanization of the Council of Jewish Women in San Francisco, described the home teacher's duties thus: "She explains the value of fresh air and sunshine, the need of proper ventilation, sanitation, and the use of disinfectants. She teaches hygiene, she gives simple home remedies for slight illnesses, and urges calling upon the clinics in the neighborhood for more serious cases." The home teacher also stressed punctuality, compulsory education and curfew laws, and "food values," which meant convincing immigrant mothers to add more cereals and green vegetables to family meals while reducing the amount of meat. As a means to inure immigrant women to an appropriate American work ethic

and sense of sacrifice, Frances A. Patten, a home teacher working out of the
Mission Road School in Los Angeles, composed songs such as the following,
sung to the tune of "Tramp, Tramp, Tramp, the Boys are Marching":

> We are working every day,
> So our boys and girls can play.
>> We are working for our homes and country, too;
> We like to wash, to sew, to cook,
> We like to write, or read a book,
>> We are working, working, working every day.

> Work, work, work,
> We're always working,
>> Working for our boys and girls,
> Working for our boys and girls,
> For our homes and country too—
>> We are working, working, working every day.

The effort to bring the immigrant woman into a fuller—though nonetheless
domestic—Americanized life left little to chance. "Nothing is left undone,"
Jacobs stated, "which can and will implant in the mind of the mother the
idea that the state, the home and the school must be so closely linked that
nothing can destroy the chain." It took a village, in other words, to Americanize an immigrant mother.[30]

Californians' determination to forge an unbreakable chain linking foreign-
born mothers to state and school had parallels in other Western communities.
Americanization work organized by county chairmen of the Woman's Committee of the Kansas State Council of Defense, for example, consisted of assistance for home demonstration agents teaching foreign-born women. One
southeastern Kansas county, according to the official report of the Woman's
Committee, had "a large settlement of Mexicans, and these homes were all
visited" by the chairman and others. "The Mexican women responded to the
assistance offered them and eagerly accepted the Americanization of their
homes and families." Such Americanization appears to have consisted primarily of the registration of mothers and babies for the county's child welfare
programs. "In view of the need of Mexican railroad labor and the large number of these foreign families in Kansas, an urgent necessity was seen for extended child-welfare work among these strangers, who were so much in need
of sanitary enlightenment and a better understanding of our customs and
modes of life." Helen Roberts, a teacher at the Arizona State Normal School
and member of the State Americanization Committee, helped organize a

"Mother's Club" among Mexican immigrant women in the Phoenix area. The committee, in its list of objectives, hoped to "extend the organization of foreign women into groups for social life, preparation for intelligent voting, instruction in the care of children, home nursing, and household arts."[31]

The philosophy of home teaching in California and similar programs elsewhere was closely tied to the rhetoric of maternalism that the General Federation of Women's Clubs and other women's organizations avowed. In addition, maternalism was an important influence on public policy formation and progressive educational reform. Home teachers took part in a widespread reform project to craft a progressive society built on strong families, which in turn needed strong, capable, engaged mothers as their foundation. In family solidarity lay the hope for achieving the orderly society so central to the vision of progressive reformers and educators. To achieve this new, maternalist order, communities had to have certified, professional educators working through public schools to make citizens and "American" mothers of foreign women. Lessons in English and housekeeping appeared to the reformers as the most important tools to that end.[32]

Differences in class and ethnicity, however, did much to hamper female Americanizers' attempts to build cultural bridges between themselves and foreign-born women. Given public sanction to enter private homes, home teachers, seemingly unaware of immigrant women's network of extended families, groups, and clubs, saw immigrant mothers as isolated and in need of immersion in American middle-class culture. The home teachers were not inviting the immigrant mothers into the middle class, however, as they still perceived them as clients limited to the roles of wife and mother and possibly as a domestic or worker in light industry. Home teachers, especially those in southern California, tried to temper the intrusiveness of their work by establishing a "neighborhood cottage" program. Teachers would fix up schoolrooms to replicate the typical "American" home as a model, on one hand, and as a gathering place, on the other, for immigrant women from different ethnic groups. Ruby Baughman, who supervised adult immigrant education for the Los Angeles public schools, lauded the "little rooms or houses" as intimate spaces where immigrant "housemothers" could be drawn "out from the shell of shyness or fear or distrust or loneliness."[33]

While some support for a home economics emphasis—whether for daughters or mothers—certainly existed among certain traditionalist immigrants, others would contest the imposition of home economics and various forms of vocational education. Critics of California's home teaching system have argued that, while the Americanizers saw themselves as effective connections between immigrant women and the public schools, in effect they served as agents of social control. In relation to Mexican women, Americanization programs represented an effort to change the immigrants' cultural values, to soften them up, as it were, to accept a prescribed role in the "American industrial order." Success or failure depended on the mother, and getting her out of the home so as to inculcate American values became an imperative. Thus, home teachers ironically used visits to immigrant homes to create enough trust to take the mother out to attend classes. Then, once mothers were in the classroom, they were taught traditional homemaking skills that they could utilize in transforming their homes into proper working-class models.[34]

Of greater concern, through home teaching, "neighborhood cottages," or other means, programs that focused on teaching immigrant women how to keep house served a growing Hispanic population. In that respect, Americanization in southern California and other areas of the Southwest often suggested an intentional effort to relegate Mexican and Mexican-American women to low-paying jobs and economic dependence. In addition to improving the Mexican immigrants' home lives, training in domestic skills prepared Chicanas for work as domestic servants and other occupations demanded by middle-class Anglo women. Indeed, the content and lesson plans of home teachers throughout California revolved around attaching instruction in English to household tasks. In terms of citizenship, running an efficient "American" home, becoming an informed consumer, and stabilizing her working-class family struck many home teachers as the immigrant mother's essential functions.[35]

For the Americanizers, however, what they sought to achieve through home teaching was not social control, but socialization. From their point of view, they were aiding in the strengthening of community, creating bonds between the foreign-born adult and the larger American world around them. The home teacher, according to Ethel Richardson, "knows the forces which can be utilized in bringing about a closer union between the foreign-born and native-born." For their part, immigrant women were not the passive receptacles that social control theories predicate. Interaction did occur, for instance when an Americanization teacher in Los Angeles surveyed her students on what types of English words they actually needed to learn, then used her findings to construct a series of lessons. The focus on practical or vocational applications in Americanization was not always imposed from above, but on occasion reflected demand on the part of adult immigrant students.[36]

Lacking much documentation on the actual sentiments of the immigrants themselves, historians unfortunately are handicapped in making definitive judgments on whether relationships between home teachers and immigrant women were constructive or destructive. To characterize home teaching and classes for mothers as pure and simple top-down social control sidesteps the complexity of the actual interactions between many teachers and their for-

Home teacher visiting Mexican mother, 1920s. Ethel Richardson, "Doing the Thing That Couldn't Be Done," *Survey,* 1 June 1926.

eign-born pupils. Just the same, white, middle-class home teachers, in centering lessons on such areas as diet, health, and hygiene, were trying to effect a cultural transformation that they assumed Mexican women and families could achieve in no other way. An Americanizer who taught in Mexican labor camps at La Habra, California, believed that such instruction meant "indirect contact with a deep, overflowing, sympathetic source of human action where American ideals, ambitions, attitudes and aspirations for clean, pure, healthful thinking and living are born." That approach may very well have constituted social control, but it also reflected the progressive certainty shared by many Americanizers that the Americanization of the home depended on reaching the immigrant mother.[37]

Universities and the Question of Professionalization

Emory S. Bogardus, Grace Raymond Hebard, James C. Stephens, Arch Thurman, home teachers in California, and many other Americanizers conducted their programs under the auspices of the West's land-grant universities and normal schools. University programs and Americanization had a logical connection, given progressives' faith in education and belief in specialized expertise as the most effective means of democratic social control. Education possessed clear political uses for reformers, and the universities, having dispensed with the classical subjects of nineteenth-century higher learning, had shifted their concerns to practical training in political science, economics, and sociology. Public policy, in its creation and application, rested increasingly on trained experts and scientific methodology, and progressives turned to the universities as partners in governing.[38]

Extension divisions at state universities appeared to be especially well appointed for Americanization work and held particular appeal to those seeking to construct programs that could reach into even the most remote communities in the West. The war, moreover, struck many in higher education as a golden opportunity to highlight the universities' comprehensive service to the public. The role of the university in rendering war service, according to a remarkable University of Utah Extension Division document, rested on how patriotic experts would "make their knowledge and training available as a source of information, influence, and inspiration in the national service and defense." The extension division was uniquely qualified and equipped to disseminate information and mold public opinion, for instance in shaping points of view with "facts as to what Americanism is and how it has become what it is." The unnamed author then arrived at an important insight, one that underscored the larger significance of Americanization in the West: "To keep the ideals of America vital and fresh must be somebody's task as we submit to the process of being made into an efficient machine for the national service and defense." In effect, it was time for a new, modern West to submit to this process of creating a greater, more efficient and rational nation, and to submit as well to the expertise of its modern institutions, notably the universities. "An effect of the participation of all the parts of the country in the work for the national service and defense will be that the point of view and the character of the activity of each of the parts will become nationalized to an extent never before true. Such effect is to be desired."[39]

University extension work in Americanization easily fit within the model of nationalization through education advanced by the University of Utah. Occasionally, extension division projects in citizenship training displayed some potential to evolve into sophisticated long-term programs. In coordination with the State Council of Defense and the chamber of commerce in Kansas City, Kansas, the extension division of the state university in Lawrence organized adult classes in that city. According to the director of Americanization work in Kansas during the war, the university organized eleven classes in Kansas City with an average enrollment of fourteen; three of the classes had both men and women enrolled. A professor by the name of T. J. Smart was appointed to the extension division faculty as community adviser, with responsibility to develop "the indirect forces for adult education and Americanization." Smart concentrated on the southern and eastern portions of the state, visiting city and county school superintendents, YMCAs, and YWCAs. After the war, the Americanization program in Kansas City continued as a joint effort of the city's public schools, the chamber of commerce, and the university. "This year [1920–1921] it is our hope to enlist all available forces in putting on a city-wide and thorough Americanization Campaign, continuous throughout the year," noted a document describing the Kansas City program. The methods used by the university and its school and business colleagues varied. A significant portion of the program involved holding noon-hour meetings during the fall and spring at which large numbers of immigrant workers employed at Kansas City packing plants listened to patriotic speeches. In addition, Americanizers helped in the organization of "Class-Study groups," which presented community programs with singing, speeches, and "appropriate" motion pictures, plus public school programs and contests designed to allow children to further influence their immigrant parents.[40]

In Western states, as occurred throughout the country in the waning years of Americanization enthusiasm, professional training of teachers became a growing preoccupation that universities and normal schools seemed prepared to address. Teacher training provided one key to legitimizing Americanization as something more than a mere movement; it would become a profession, an educational career track with "a distinct pedagogy . . . and a very distinct methodology." Yet, a 1920 study of immigrant education ruefully noted that only five of fifty state normal schools and colleges were offering extension work in teacher training or retraining during the 1918–1919 academic year. Happily, summer school courses in Americanization teaching appeared in 1919 at several normal schools as well as at Columbia, Harvard, Johns Hopkins, and the University of Chicago. The extension divisions also endeavored to professionalize Americanization by establishing teacher training programs. Although considered superficial and incoherent by some critics, these early attempts at instituting teacher training seemed to bode well for the developing profession.[41]

"The aliens are here," Arch Thurman wrote in the 1920 report of the Utah superintendent of public instruction, "and our task is to take care of them. Our generosity should match our responsibility in this regard." The Utah Americanization law of 1919 authorized school districts "to establish and maintain Americanization classes for the education of adult aliens in matters of English language, citizenship, history, and other subjects that will help make of our alien population desirable citizens." With the law in place, Thurman reported that sixty-three Americanization classes were conducted by public schools, with a total enrollment of 2,016. Of sixty-nine teachers "regularly engaged in Americanization work," eight were employed specifically for that purpose, while the majority were regular schoolteachers. "All teachers were selected by the school authorities because of special ability and interest in Americanization work" with no special certification required. Before interest flagged, the University of Utah offered summer school training courses in 1919 and 1920. Brigham Young University and the Agricultural College at Logan (now Utah State University) also conducted such courses. "At the present time," Thurman noted, "the University Extension is endeavoring to interest teachers throughout the state in more thorough preparation for this particular type of teaching."[42]

A pamphlet for the University of Colorado Extension Division's "Americanization Course" in summer 1920 clearly reflected the concern with producing more qualified instructors: "Although not limited to them, the course will be of special value to public school teachers, who will be needed more and more in this line of work; for our public school system is, without doubt, the greatest Americanization agency that exists today." The University of Utah's Extension Division produced a pamphlet of "Suggestions for Americanization Teachers," written by Raymond D. Harriman, an instructor in ancient languages and member of the state Americanization Committee. Harriman's pamphlet included a bibliography and reading course on immigration, naturalization, and Americanization, guidelines for classifying students, and various methods for teaching English. Among several general suggestions, Harriman urged teachers to "put yourself in his [the immigrant student's] place. Can you imagine your own feeling in a strange land attempting to learn a strange language from a strange teacher who may be very dull, especially after a day's hard work?" These pamphlets clearly demonstrate the interest Western educators had in training Americanizers yet do not indicate to what extent young men and women attending the universities and normal schools shared that interest. Although Grace Raymond Hebard trained several Americanizers in Wyoming, the state's director of vocational education, in an April 1920 letter to federal Director of Citizenship Raymond Crist, admitted that "up to this time there has been little or no demand for it [a teaching methods course] on the part of our students."[43]

Mary Gibson, in her capacity as a member of the California Commission of Immigration and Housing, also worked hard to establish training of home teachers as a generally accepted professional specialty within California's educational establishment. This effort began when Ruby Baughman, a member of the faculty at the state normal school in Los Angeles, was hired to direct a new municipal department of immigrant education in 1916. Baughman, who had previously taught immigrant children in Butte and Helena, Montana, set up weekend conferences for home teacher training through the normal school and extension divisions of the University of California, Southern Branch (now the University of California, Los Angeles). Baughman also taught a two-credit course on Americanization during summer 1919. The University of California at Berkeley offered summer session courses, taught by Oakland educator Ethel Swain, from 1923 to 1930, and the State of California introduced a specialized credential in teaching of citizenship for adults in 1925. By then the emphasis tended toward quantitative methodologies rather than the broader, reform character of earlier years. Home teachers in California tried as well to build a professional culture of associations, conferences, and journals, but little came of their efforts. By the late 1920s, Americanization and home teaching had been absorbed by the movement toward general adult education.[44]

The attempt to further home teaching's status as a profession was a reflection of progressives' search for order through organization and efficiency. Male leaders in progressive era educational reform, such as Stanford University's Ellwood P. Cubberley, emphasized specialization, standardization, and scientific management as the paths to adapting the schools to better serve a complex, industrial society. Yet, home teaching's development as a profession was hampered by conservative state governments that cut budgets for Americanization and the reduction of its client base through immigration restriction. For home teachers especially, a contradiction also emerged because of the increasing bureaucratization of the social welfare field. The pressure to maintain clinical detachment in treating one's "case load" did not mesh with home teachers' backgrounds in female-dominated, benevolent social work premised on personal contact. Were home teachers generalists stuck in a field becoming increasingly specialized and inflexible, or could they defend their jack-of-all-trades approaches as specialties worthy of professional recognition and training? The ambiguous experience of home teachers paralleled that of female social workers and Americanizers generally. Striving to create a respected niche for themselves as public professionals, home teachers struggled to transcend the perception of all female benevolence as private and voluntary.[45]

The challenge that home teachers and other Americanization educators faced in being taken seriously as professionals was evident in other ways. An opinion by the Arizona attorney general on that state's 1918 Americanization law held that teaching English and citizenship to foreign adults did not require a state teachers' certificate. Americanization was not the same as "ordinary school teaching," and volunteers who showed "special aptitude for this particular form of teaching" had proven to be up to the task throughout the country. "It is a great advantage to those in charge of the night schools to be able to avail themselves of the services of suitable teachers, certified or not." The notion that uncredentialed volunteers could teach adult immigrants as well as professionally trained and certified instructors carried an assumption that women made up the vast majority of Americanization teachers. In that respect, the attorney general's opinion indicated the dilemma of the feminization of Americanization.

Administrators of public school systems and leaders in the state educational establishments, most of whom were men, held an expectation that any upstanding, patriotic woman could teach a citizenship class. This attitude underscored the problem of trying to coordinate and professionalize an emerging field dominated by women in the midst of enthusiasm for an idea that drew so many volunteers and amateurs, most of whom were women too. "There are hundreds of people in the State of California alone who are engaged in trying to Americanize something or somebody," remarked Mary Gibson in a report to her colleagues. "They are amateurs whose motives are worthy of all respect but whose methods are hardly sufficient." Gibson and the California Commission of Immigration and Housing, like Americanizers throughout the West and nation, sought in vain to enhance the professional status of immigrant education and differentiate its efforts from those of primarily female volunteers.[46]

In spite of an uncertain supply of instructors and the difficulties confronted in creating a professional niche, enthusiasm for teaching English and civics to the foreign-born did not dissipate right away in the West. Even on the eve of the Immigration Act of 1924, an Americanization teachers' conference took place in Denver. A letter from Chief Naturalization Examiner Paul Armstrong to the Commissioner of Naturalization that spring reported on organizing Americanization teachers in Denver into a conference to meet at least monthly. Armstrong also noted demand for an Americanization Institute during the upcoming summer session at the State Teachers College at Greeley. "It is felt," he wrote, "that there will be a great deal of interest in the work because of the number of Americanization classes throughout Colorado operating at the present time, both in the cities and in the rural districts." Also reflecting this sense of great things yet to come, the University of Utah's Harriman reminded budding Americanization teachers that the ultimate objective of their endeavors rested on teaching citizenship to foreigners. "No greater returns in teaching can be found," he concluded, "than in a citizenship class well taught." For many similarly motivated educators in the West, despite the myriad frustrations associated with poor funding, lukewarm support, and fluctuating attendance, "a citizenship class well taught" provided a tangible goal and, on occasion, cause for genuine satisfaction.[47]

Fear and Optimism: The Americanization Career of Grace Raymond Hebard

University-based Americanizers typically operated in conjunction with wartime councils of defense (as in Colorado), with state agencies (as in California), or with public schools. The University of Wyoming professor and Americanizer Grace Raymond Hebard stands out because, aside from assistance provided by Bureau of Naturalization examiners, she conducted what amounted to a freelance operation, with university backing, in Laramie between 1917 and 1919. Of all Grace Hebard's accomplishments, which included service on the University of Wyoming Board of Trustees, a Ph.D. (through correspondence study) from Illinois Wesleyan University, admission to the Wyoming bar, the authorship of several historical monographs and textbooks, directorship of the university's department of political economy, and the marking of historical sites throughout the state, she reportedly valued her Americanization work as "perhaps most precious." The chief naturalization examiner from Denver, under whose jurisdiction naturalization in Wyoming lay, told of Hebard's dedication in a 1918 article in the *Outlook*:

> When they [naturalization petitioners] are admitted in March and September, nobody comes from afar to welcome them; but there is a gleam of the dream in the eyes of a woman who watches them come in. She has taught nearly all of them. They hold certificates of graduation issued by her, countersigned by the chief naturalization examiner on behalf of the United States, respected by the Court; and they give an excellent account of themselves. . . . There is a steady attendance now of six or eight, and not the least of the stars in the crown of the Naturalization Service is the citizenship class of Laramie, Wyoming.

Hebard's accomplishment in almost single-handedly constructing an Americanization movement in Wyoming even impressed the Easterners who made up the National Americanization Committee, who informed Mary Antin, the immigrant Americanizer from Boston, that Hebard "carried on the most notable work of the sort in the State."[48]

Although Dr. Hebard's involvement with Americanization in Wyoming began relatively late in her career, evidence of her interest in educating immigrants dates from at least 1896, when she published an article entitled

"Immigration and Needed Ballot Reform" in the *Illinois Wesleyan Magazine.* "The danger which threatens us," she warned, "is the growth in our population of a large foreign element whose habits of thought and behavior are radically different from those which the founders of the nation hoped to establish." This contention that "Southern and Eastern Europeans" lacked the necessary requisites to simply ease into the American social and economic order without somehow disrupting it constituted conventional wisdom in the 1890s. Notably, Hebard cited the famed economist and statistician Francis Amasa Walker, whose writings during that decade gave intellectual credence to nativists for years to come. She expressed as well the very common alarm that this class of immigrants, while certainly possessed of some desirable individuals, had a tendency to produce anarchists and rebels. Yet Hebard, convinced of the transforming powers of education, suggested a means to forestall otherwise inevitable and irrevocable damage to the republic. Thus, she concluded, "the only way in which we can protect ourselves is to educate this heterogeneous mass, so blind to the duties of patriotism that they are unable to distinguish the red flag, typical of society unregulated by any principles of government, from the red, white and blue—a perfect national emblem. We must change this mass into a homogeneous population, and this can be accomplished only by grafting into the hearts of the aliens who have determined to make these lands their lands, the highest conception of citizenship, the reverence for a constitution which gives them their liberties."[49]

Her 1896 discussion of the immigrant problem provides considerable insight into a well-developed ideology of American nationalism. At the outset, Hebard made clear the crucial and obvious legacy of immigration to the United States. "To whom do we owe our Nation's unparalleled success?" she asked. "Certainly not," the future author of *Sacajawea* responded, "to the native tribes which have resisted civilization ever since Columbus claimed the land by right of discovery. No, no, it is not to them; it is to the immigrants." With the aid of a table showing the number and nationality of immigrants in 1882, 1891, and 1892, Hebard proceeded to point out the large increases in immigration from Russia, Poland, Italy, and other southern and eastern European sources. Then, in an assertion she believed "apparent" from "these figures," Dr. Hebard stated "that the *quality* of this immigration is deteriorating." As a result, she concluded in a manner typical of late-nineteenth-century American writings on immigration, "vast numbers of people unfamiliar with our habits or political thoughts and actions" would become voters and low-wage competitors with "our workingmen."[50]

After lauding the pre-1870 immigration as sufficiently composed of the "better classes," Hebard lamented: "Today we are receiving the dregs of all nations. America has been well called the dumping ground for all of the old world, and from this steaming heap of refuse population made up of the scum of communities, we see arising hideous disease, debasing crime, drod and drivel of the asylums, degrading pauperism and bloody rebellion, and in place of citizenship, anarchy and socialism." Pausing to suggest the educational remedy needed to homogenize these motley hordes, Hebard suggested that without citizenship, there could be no patriotism. On the other hand, the overwhelming numbers of virtually unassimilable immigrants posed a logistical problem in training "the incomers into ethical harmony with the fundamental principles of its [America's] own individual life." "The great ship of State—citizenship," she cautioned, "is not overcrowded, but there is a superabundance of steerage passengers." Finally, Dr. Hebard decried the nation's "loose naturalization laws," which, she claimed, put too much political power "into the hands of ignorant voters" and "their often unscrupulous leaders." "There should be a Department of Naturalization," she suggested, because the seriousness of the problem demanded cabinet-level attention. Furthermore, "In each state there should be one officer responsible to the Secretary of Naturalization." Hebard had several other suggestions, including the imposition of educational and property qualifications for voters, before closing her article.[51] What is interesting from a historical perspective is both the harshness of her descriptions of the new immigrants and the occasional glimmer of optimism that education—albeit in tandem with severe restrictions on the number of such immigrants allowed into the country—could transform most of them into desirable citizens.

There is no clear evidence that Dr. Hebard applied her intense interest in naturalization and immigration issues in a practical way before 1916. It is probable, though, that she treated her classes in sociology and political economy at the University of Wyoming to discourses resonant of her 1896 article.[52] For the period after January 1916, however, one can find numerous clippings, letters, and references to Americanization in Hebard's papers. Between January and April of that year, she requested and received a number of documents from the Committee for Immigrants in America and other entities for her sociology class. In May, she wrote Paul Lee Ellerbe, the chief naturalization examiner in the Bureau of Naturalization's Denver office, having noticed his reference to citizenship training for foreigners in a Cheyenne newspaper, and asked him for more printed material. "If I were living in Cheyenne," she closed, "I would be very glad to offer my services for Saturday evening teaching of this subject."[53]

As it turned out, not living in Cheyenne did not prevent Dr. Hebard from ultimately offering her services. Having followed with keen interest the developing national push for Americanization, Hebard, by the autumn of

1916, felt prepared to bring the issue before Wyoming's citizenry. In the weeks leading up to an early October address on the "Americanization of the Immigrant" presented to the Wyoming Federation of Women's Clubs (WFWC) in Sheridan, she also busied herself with a plan to involve the University of Wyoming in an Americanization program in Laramie. The city's public schools had evidently ignored the Bureau of Naturalization's prodding to start night classes for immigrants, so Hebard, in consultation with Chief Examiner Ellerbe, District Court Judge Volney J. Tidball, and university president Clyde A. Duniway, began laying the foundation for the classes. In addition, the president of the university's YMCA expressed to Dr. Hebard his organization's willingness "to take up this work of helping to instruct the Immigrant." Ellerbe agreed with Hebard that securing the cooperation of such groups as Wyoming's women's clubs and the university's YMCA would be helpful, but in specific reference to Laramie, he felt that "after it [the class] is started it will be a one-man job and will not take much time at that."[54]

Hebard opened her talk in Sheridan by explaining the shift in countries of origin for the majority of immigrants—from the "old" immigration from northern and western Europe to the "new" immigration from southern and eastern Europe. In doing so, she resorted to several myths and stereotypes. The British, French, German, and Scandinavian immigrants that predominated until the late nineteenth century were welcomed by the native-born with open arms, assisted in finding homes and work, "and the little red school house was built for the betterment of their children." With the additional leavening of intermarriage, the "old" immigrants became Americans and, according to Hebard, "the word hyphenated-American is an unknown term in their vocabulary." On the other hand, the generally uneducated, unskilled, and impoverished peoples arriving from southern and eastern Europe, even when naturalized, "have been content to do the most menial class of labor and live in the most dejected environment."[55]

Warning that the prospective postwar influx of European immigrants could be "unprecedented," Hebard addressed a fundamental concern regarding naturalization and citizenship. Although a majority of immigrants became naturalized, that result did not necessarily translate into the creation of good citizens. While most American-born citizens understood Americanization and citizenship as identical, for many immigrants wrestling with conflicting loyalties during wartime, "the two words are as far apart as the North and South pole." The best means by which to close the gap between the formalities of naturalization and the spirit of Americanism, Hebard stressed, was education. "Public schools throughout the U.S. are being used for night schools for the training of the alien in Americanization, which means the reading of the English language, the study of . . . U.S. History and the principles of our government," she pointed out. Thousands of applicants for citizenship anxiously sought instruction but could find nowhere to turn "for enlightenment." Hebard then appealed to her fellow clubwomen "to help Americanize the immigrant citizen, that he may be a more intelligent and better citizen and in this way we may have an unparallel[ed] preparedness in time of foreign conflict." Inspired by her address ("the treat of the evening"), the delegates proceeded to endorse a resolution in support of Americanization.[56]

"The iron is hot," Hebard wrote Ellerbe after her successful weekend in Sheridan, "and I believe can be welded into a satisfactory shape, if you will tell me what to do, and let me know what you can do." In reply, Ellerbe suggested persuading public schools in sections of the state with "an appreciable proportion of alien population to install classes in citizenship." He hoped to see classes started "at once" in Cheyenne, Laramie, Rawlins, Sundance, Casper, Sheridan, Rock Springs, Newcastle, and Kemmerer. Ellerbe later journeyed to Laramie to discuss citizenship education for immigrants with university president Duniway. Ellerbe's visit was, according to a letter he wrote to the *Laramie Daily Boomerang,* a follow-up to a conversation he held with Dr. Hebard in September, during which he "found her enthusiastically interested in the subject." Despite the small number of immigrant residents in Albany County, Ellerbe believed, as did Judge Tidball, that "the need for such a class is nevertheless very real." As the Laramie public schools had failed to act upon the bureau's request to implement an adult immigrant education program, Duniway informed Ellerbe "that the University of Wyoming would undertake the conduct of a citizenship class," to be taught by Dr. Hebard. Ellerbe informed the professor that he would furnish her with the names of those filing petitions for naturalization. He also suggested that Hebard arrange with the clerk of the district court in Laramie to refer declarants and petitioners directly to her. To Mrs. Walter McNab Miller in New York City, Hebard noted her intention to get the state's public schools to ultimately take on the work, then gushed: "I love the work because it is along the line of citizenship and this is my one hobby. I only wish I might be able to do national work on this account." The first letters to prospective students went out on 1 December 1916.[57]

A spring 1917 article from a National American Woman Suffrage Association publication, the *National Suffrage News,* and documents from Hebard's papers provide a glimpse at how her classes actually operated. Hebard's initial citizenship course covered ten weeks—two hours of class one evening each week—during that winter, "a severe test," the article presumed, "of the desire to become good American citizens." The first lesson began with the students memorizing the song "America," then writing an essay on "what the Hymn means." Hebard, in addition to explaining the process of naturalization, had the class describe "why and under what conditions" they had immigrated to the United States and also discuss the meaning of liberty. Each week focused on a particular theme—citizenship, one of the three branches of the federal government, an overview of American history, Wyoming and city government—before ending with a review and discussion of "Citizenship Privileges and Duties." In addition to "the academic treatment of her subject, Dr. Hebard never let a lesson pass without a patriotic stimulus," from "special study" of American presidents to "lessons in democratic ideals from the Revolutionary and Civil Wars." An American flag, "with a picture of Washington in its folds," hung behind the instructor throughout.[58]

At the district court in Laramie on 8 March 1917—with one of Dr. Hebard's sociology classes on hand—Judge Tidball, a former Hebard pupil, and naturalization examiner Frederick C. Emmerich quizzed the professor's three foreign students. Afterward, Tidball expressed his wish that "all native-born Americans could answer the questions as well, and with as full understanding." At the end of the examination in district court, "Dr. Hebard pinned a small silk flag upon the coat or dress of each one of the class" and reminded them that their first duty as new citizens might entail defending the emblem "even at the sacrifice of life." A lawyer in attendance, moved by the ceremony, assured Hebard, "Although you have no sons to send to war, you certainly have made three patriotic loyal citizens out of that number of aliens." Significantly, one of the professor's patriotic citizens was Ferdinand Hansen, a German from Rock River, who when asked if he would fight against his former homeland if the United States entered the war replied in the affirmative, "without any hesitation, but with a troubled brow." Accompanying the one-page article, a photograph showed Dr. Hebard standing on the courthouse steps with Judge Tidball, Emmerich, the clerk of court, and her three students, identified as "German, Irishman, Englishman."[59]

Considering her views about southern and eastern Europeans, Dr. Hebard had very little direct contact with immigrants from those parts of the globe. Yugoslavians, Czechs, Slovaks, Poles, Turks, Greeks, and Italians inhabited the coal mining camps in southwestern Wyoming, but Hebard's citizenship students generally came from the British Isles, Germany, and the Scandinavian countries. Of fifty-three students listed on enrollment cards found in her papers, one was Greek and another Syrian. Of the remaining fifty-one, eleven were English, eleven Swedish, seven Norwegian, six German, three Canadian, three Scotch, two Danish, one Belgian, one Irish, one British West Indian, one Swiss, and one Mexican. The other three were American women married to immigrants, who by law were citizens of their husbands' nations of origin until the men became American citizens. It is unlikely that these three and the five foreign-born wives included in the enrollment cards

Grace Raymond Hebard with three of her Americanization students shortly after they were granted U.S. citizenship, 8 March 1917, Laramie, Wyoming. American Heritage Center, University of Wyoming.

actually took Dr. Hebard's course, thereby leaving forty-five bona fide students. Otherwise, only three of Hebard's immigrant scholars were women, the widowed Englishwoman Louisa Banner, her single daughter Kate, and Jennie McLay, a forty-two-year-old teacher from Canada. Most of the students worked for the Union Pacific railroad as engineers, machinists, car inspectors or repairers, tie hacks, rip track workers, and hostlers. Others noted their occupations as laborers, carpenters, and ranchers, with one each being a shepherd, teamster, barber, merchant, and miner.[60]

During the summer of 1917, Hebard augmented her normal teaching load by conducting more "classes in Americanization." By November, according to the *Woman Citizen,* she had already "achieved a nation-wide fame" in "bringing America to many a foreigner." Moreover, Dr. Hebard wasted little time in taking her message about Americanization on the road. As the federally appointed head of Wyoming's War Lecture Bureau, she traversed the state giving talks not only on Americanization but also on food conservation and women's role in war work. In a presentation before the state board of education in November 1917, she "made a strong plea for some action toward the Americanization of emigrant foreigners in this country, and the removing of the hyphen from their designation in advance of their being made citizens." She pushed the board to provide free instruction for Wyoming's foreign residents in English, American and Wyoming history, and government. Alas, on this occasion, the board could only sympathize with Hebard's wishes, confessing that a lack of funds prevented the implementation of a state-run Americanization program.[61]

Hebard continued teaching citizenship classes to naturalization petitioners as well as a course on Americanization methods to about twenty normal school students at the University of Wyoming in fall 1918.[62] An attack of acute indigestion prevented her from attending the naturalization of five of her students in March 1919, and she subsequently informed correspondents that she had taught her last naturalization class.[63] Nonetheless, she put considerable effort into immigrant issues and Americanization for the remainder of her life. For example, immediately following the armistice, the University of Wyoming's Division of Correspondence Study offered "Political Economy XIII: Americanization," taught by Dr. Hebard. "As a future preparedness for national unity," her course description stated, "naturalization of the alien should mean more than a human voting machine, it must mean being an American with all hyphens eliminated." The course, designed for regular university students, not immigrants seeking naturalization papers, offered a brief history of immigration and a description of "what our government is now doing to Americanize the foreigner." Soon thereafter, Dr. Hebard began teaching a two-credit course, required of political economy majors, called "Americanization and Reconstruction." Reflective of widespread postwar concerns about labor radicalism, the catalogue course description pointed out that "the problem of making the immigrant an American before he is naturalized involves important labor conditions which are allied with the period of reconstruction always necessary after a war." An Americanization measure passed by the Wyoming legislature in 1921 provided the pretext for a summer school class in naturalization and citizenship, planned "to meet the new demand of those who are expecting to teach in night schools."[64]

Responses of immigrant students and prospective Americanizers to Hebard's classes suggest that she made a positive impression. A letter "from a member of my first Americanization class" thanked Hebard "for the work you have done and the interest you have taken in us." The correspondent continued: "I consider that we have been singularly fortunate . . . that your public spiritedness and patriotism prompted you to assume the task. . . . Personally, I came to the classes at first with a feeling that I was pretty well acquainted with the needful subjects, and that it would not be necessary for me to attend, but at the first lesson I formed a different concept of Citizenship from your enthusiasm and Patriotism." Kate Banner, the young Englishwoman whose mother and brother Hebard also "Americanized," thanked the teacher for "your kindness in making things so pleasant for us, especially Mother." In 1929, the University of Wyoming's student newspaper, *The Branding Iron,* in a story about Dr. Hebard's fortieth year at the school, reported, "Many of our citizens of foreign birth speak gratefully of this service whenever her name is mentioned in their presence."[65] Thus, in contrast to Hebard's often harsh comments about certain immigrant groups, it must be acknowledged that she made a concerted and conscientious effort to ease their assimilation into American life. Even if one questions her embrace of homogeneity—and one does so at the risk of yanking Dr. Hebard out of context—her underlying optimism contrasts favorably with much of the raw chauvinism and xenophobia passing as patriotism during and after World War I. One can only guess at whether more contact with southern and eastern Europeans in her classes would have confirmed her prejudices or softened her views.

Hebard's impact must also be considered in relation to the native-born American students who, under her tutelage, confidently strode forth from Laramie to teach the immigrant in communities all around Wyoming and elsewhere. In 1929, for instance, Hebard witnessed a naturalization examination of applicants trained by "my one-time student" J. E. Thayer. "The way they answered and the earnestness with which they went to their task," she informed Thayer, "showed very clearly that their instructor had been very painstaking and that he had obtained their respect and confidence." "As a student in your classes in Americanization and Sociology during the past summer term," A. L. Burgoon, a school district superintendent in Lincoln County, Wyoming, wrote in 1922, "I wish to express my appreciation for the vision and inspiration you have given me." And from a nun in Indiana, delighted at Dr. Hebard's prompt reply to her request for information, a sincere, even touching, note of gratitude: "I know I should be very proud and happy to have made as many good citizens for our beloved country as you have done."[66]

Conclusion

To those educators devoted to the cause of Americanization, that was exactly the point—to make good American citizens. Considered by many of her contemporaries as "a path breaker" in "making American citizens,"[67] Grace Raymond Hebard, through her career as an Americanizer, represents a paradox in America's historical treatment of immigrants. Although welcomed as a crucial supply of manual labor, the southern and eastern Europeans, Asians, and Mexicans repelled many "old stock" Americans like Hebard. They lacked the proper individualistic and democratic traditions, seemed particularly susceptible to following the red flags of radicalism, and stood apart as racially and culturally alien to the standards believed inherent to true Americans in a "white" republic. Even though many at the time and since have rightly criticized them for their zealotry and prejudice, the Americanizers generally conducted their crusade as a sincere and well-intentioned educational endeavor. In tandem with their fear of the effects of the "new" immigration, they somehow sustained an abiding optimism in the efficacy of "education for citizenship."[68]

That education customarily began with teaching non-English-speaking immigrants the "language of America." Learning "to speak American English," as recited in a citizenship textbook lesson, "means a better opportunity and a better home for me in America. It means a better job for me. It means a better chance for my children. It means a better America." Speaking English in his home, at his job, and to his wife and children, moreover, demonstrated the immigrant's sincerity in seeking citizenship.[69] With an adequate understanding of the language, the immigrant could partake of instruction in citizenship fundamentals. As naturalization required some command of the facts and conceptual framework of American government, the Constitution became a tool for inculcating the principles of a representative democracy. Citizenship education also involved training for patriotic and responsible participation in the political and civic spheres, as well as acceptable behaviors and lifestyles. As an elemental component of progressives' designs to create a humane, orderly, and unified society, Americanization also encouraged the idea of the school as a community center. Professional educators, employers, government officials, churches, private organizations, and anybody with a sincere and sympathetic interest in aiding the foreigner had an opportunity, if not an obligation, to assist.

Keeping the interest of the adult foreigner at heart, furthermore, would enhance the prospects for achieving the ultimate goal of education for citizenship—a nation united through common ideals and principles. Many Westerners involved in the movement shared this desire to unite the nation through a careful and compassionate application of Americanization methods. To fulfill those desires required resources and trained personnel, and throughout the era of heightened interest in Americanization, immigrant night schools remained a poor stepchild of public school systems. Carol Aronovici, who directed Americanization work in Minnesota before taking charge of housing programs with the California Commission of Immigration and Housing, summarized the problems. "The main difficulties," he reported, "are to be found in the lack of facilities for learning English, the low grade of teachers provided, the hours and conditions under which teaching must be done, the failure to employ teachers with experience in handling foreign adults, and above all the fact that most adult foreigners during their first years in the United States must earn their living in ill-paid and exhausting occupations which leave them physically unfit for any mental effort."[70]

Factory schools conducted in relation to the revolving shifts of the male workforce provided one possibly effective alternative, while other Americanizers directed greater attention to the immigrant woman in the home. Home teachers in California signified the growing concern with the supposedly isolated immigrant mother, a figure increasingly identified as key to the successful acculturation of immigrant families in general. Home teachers, in guiding the cultural assimilation of immigrant women, many of whom were Mexican, concentrated on teaching household skills along with English. The fact that home teaching had the appearance of preparing immigrant women for prescribed domestic roles and service occupations points to a process of social control. Practitioners of home teaching obviously saw their mission more idealistically. "In and out through this network of integration and assimilation, the home teacher weaves a thread of vital and personal contacts," wrote Ruby Baughman, who directed the work of home teachers in Los Angeles. "She perhaps more than any other agency ties the homes of the neighborhood not only to the school and to each other but also to all the general civic and social agencies which those homes need. . . . her work is humanly simple because it is simply human."[71]

Americanizers based in Western universities saw their role in similar terms. No longer a remote repository of erudite learning, the modern university had become a laboratory for the study and application of political, economic, and social change. A journalist for a national publication commented on the practical significance of universities in the West in 1917: "The Western university is not merely a place for the scholar; it is a workshop for the student. Reaching into the ultimate life of the community, it is called on to advise regarding the community's health, to develop natural resources, to be in a large sense a co-laborer in everything that affects complete advancement."[72] Because Americanization affected advancement, it made a great deal of sense for Western universities to take leading roles in the campaign. Moreover, the expertise and training provided through extension divisions and normal schools enhanced the incorporation of Western societies as part of an increasingly efficient and modern nation-state. Western universities and normal schools participated as well in the attempted professionalization of education for citizenship, a project that had mixed results. Nonetheless, in the long term, efforts to more effectively train home teachers in California and other Americanizers in Western colleges contributed to the successful development of general adult education. In the short term, a number of short-lived Americanization training programs in the West produced dedicated instructors inured to the ideal of "a citizenship class well taught."

Whether or not they taught well, Americanizers in the West affected an indeterminate number of adult immigrant pupils during the years of World War I and the readjustment that followed. Many educators' lives were improved, too, by their interactions with these students. While Grace Raymond Hebard and other Westerners were often dismissive of "new" immigrants, their sincerity in hoping to ease even the most benighted alien into the American mainstream frequently shone through as well. Reporting to the state chapter of the Daughters of the American Revolution (of which she was state regent in 1916), Hebard spoke eloquently about educating immigrants while simultaneously enriching their own lives, noting that "in helping them, we can gleam glimpses of light ourselves."[73]

Grace Raymond Hebard displayed the same devotion and zeal other native-born Western educators brought to the Americanization classroom. Unlike the others, she became mildly famous in relation to her work. For the historian, Hebard symbolizes the ambivalence so characteristic of the Americanization movement. Making citizens was, as she put it, "a work of love and patriotism,"[74] but it was a labor of love derived, to a significant degree, from fear. Not to Americanize the aliens, even the small numbers residing in southeastern Wyoming, placed the potential fate of the nation in the hands of radicals or degenerates. Hebard never reconciled her disdain for the new immigrant groups with her optimism that education could help sustain the presumed homogeneity of the American people. She defined citizenship in terms of racial assumptions altogether common to those of her generation, thereby limiting her vision to that of a "melting pot" for the many who qualified, with restriction or exclusion for some who did not. As a self-professed "daughter of pioneers," Hebard nonetheless made a small but significant contribution to modernizing and nationalizing the West as a prophet and practitioner of Americanization. Other Westerners joined her in the task of "education for citizenship," furthering the integration of their maturing region in a modern nation.

5

"OUR GOVERNMENT THINKS WE CAN"

The Bureau of Naturalization in the West

Country schoolteachers on the prairies, night school instructors in mining communities, state education officials, university professors, and many other Western Americanizers cooperated closely with the federal Americanization bureaucracy. As the presumptive last frontier, the West had effectively been "constructed" by the federal government, which had provided land grants and loans for railroads, homesteading laws for settlers, plus incentives and subsidies for urban growth and industry. Moreover, the national government managed the lives of conquered Native Americans and the development and conservation of natural resources, rangelands, national parks, and forests.[1] Regardless of the issue at hand, the West and Washington had found themselves locked in an often uneasy embrace. With Americanization, the ambivalence that federal bureaucrats, state officials, and citizenship teachers often felt for each other reflected this pervasive Western theme. Generally speaking, however, the officials and teachers welcomed the assistance of federal naturalization examiners with open arms and wished for more attention than the understaffed and distance-challenged bureaus could provide. Nonetheless, tensions emerged between teachers, state officials, and federal bureaucrats as well as between regional examiners trying to cope with the peculiar needs of Western communities and their bosses in Washington, ever desirous of following the letter of regulations.

Western conditions could strain the government's best efforts to sustain adequate contact with school administrators, teachers, and immigrants. Distance constituted the most obvious challenge to federal naturalization examiners and limited their opportunities to make frequent contact with Americanizers in the most far-flung outposts of each district. In 1920, the Bureau of Naturalization had eleven district offices, each headed by a chief naturalization examiner and staffed by a small number of naturalization examiners and clerks. Only five district offices were situated west of the Mississippi River: District No. 7 at St. Louis, which had jurisdiction over Kansas, Nebraska, and Oklahoma; District No. 8, headquartered at St. Paul, which oversaw North and South Dakota; District No. 9 at Denver, which administered Wyoming, Colorado, New Mexico, Utah, and southern Idaho;

District No. 10 at San Francisco, with jurisdiction over Arizona, California, Nevada, and one county in Oregon; and District No. 11 at Seattle, which covered Washington, Oregon, northern Idaho, and Montana.[2]

Manning the Denver office as chief examiner, Paul Lee Ellerbe oversaw the Bureau of Naturalization's activities in the Rocky Mountain region during the period of intensified interest in Americanization. Publicizing the bureau's lately inaugurated citizenship training program in a Denver newspaper in February 1916, Ellerbe underscored the importance of training applicants properly and professionally, thereby negating the baleful influences of "the anarchist, the agitator and the more ignorant and vicious of their own kind." He explained the significance of citizenship to the immigrants by recounting a visit to naturalization court at Burlington, far out on the dry prairie of eastern Colorado. Thirty applicants (he did not say of what nationality or nationalities) filled the small courtroom, of whom about twenty-five had filed for homesteads. "They filled the courtroom at Burlington that day," Ellerbe wrote, "and they sat so quietly that the sizzling of the radiators could be heard. Surely citizenship with them was no light matter. They won or lost their stake in the country, their land, as they were granted or denied naturalization." The ignorance of the simple immigrant farmers that day struck Ellerbe as "complete, unqualified, absolute." Only a systematic effort to educate for citizenship, expedited by the Bureau of Naturalization, might improve such a doleful situation. "Perhaps we can assimilate the Russian Jew, the Bulgarian and the Czech, and perhaps we cannot," Ellerbe ruefully concluded. "Just now our government thinks we can. Let us help it."[3]

As just one small example of the government's determination to assimilate immigrants and make citizens, in late winter 1919, the Bureau of Naturalization undertook a letter-writing campaign to interest universities and colleges throughout the United States in initiating or expanding citizenship classes for adult immigrants. "The Federal Government desires to bring to your attention," the letters began, "an important phase of the movement for the education in our language and citizenship responsibilities of the permanent foreign-born residents of the United States, with particular emphasis upon those who are coming into citizenship." To university extension divisions in the West and elsewhere, the bureau offered its support "in forming the nucleus for subsequent development" of their work as Americanizing agents. On copies of the letters provided to field offices, the commissioner urged chief naturalization examiners to "please call on the addressee and secure the support of the Bureau's program." In addition to the letters, the bureau sent free copies of its revised textbook and teacher's manual.[4]

In a follow-up several weeks later, the Naturalization Bureau advised the extension divisions to have their workers observe public school citizenship classes in which the agency's official textbook was in use, making recommendations for improving the book, teaching methods, attendance, and other aspects. "*Affirmative action* may be taken by the University's agents through extending the interest in the union now existing between the Federal Government and the States through the public-school systems." This form of "affirmative action," the bureau suggested, could be advanced through contacting foreigners not then attending classes and convincing them to do so by emphasizing the issuance of free textbooks and certificates of graduation. Besides evaluating classes and corralling additional students, the extensions would undoubtedly gather the right kind of information to put into place effective Americanization teacher training courses. "All this," the bureau assured its colleagues in higher education, "can only result in a national plan of unified action by all the State Universities."[5]

The Bureau of Education's Division of Immigrant Education, like its rival agency, also inundated colleges and universities with inquiries. One such barrage elicited 147 responses from 425 "institutions of higher learning." Of those replying, only 14 offered specific courses on immigration, and according to a bureau memorandum, "practically all of these discuss the question in a purely academic manner, devoting relatively little attention to the more practical and pressing problem of what to do with the immigrant now that he is here." In an effort to rectify this sorry state of affairs, the bureau had prepared a training syllabus entitled "Professional Training Course for Social Service among Immigrants." Indicative of the particular importance that the division placed upon universities and colleges as training centers for Americanizers was a statement by special collaborator Frederic Ernest Farrington, published in a bureau report in 1916. "The fields are already ripe unto the harvest," Farrington declared, "but trained and competent laborers are few. . . . Upon our colleges and universities, therefore, devolves the responsibility of preparing these workers, of giving them breadth of vision, and catholicity of purpose, in short training them for their tasks."[6]

With advice and exhortation, officials with federal bureaus labored long and hard to sustain momentum on Americanization. The form letters to universities represent a minute portion of the tremendous volume of correspondence, circulars, textbooks, instructional aids, and other materials mailed to Americanizers everywhere. Perhaps more impressive, particularly in the West, Bureau of Naturalization employees spent weeks on the road, keeping tabs on citizenship education and conducting naturalization examinations in district courts. The federal government's responsibility for citizenship training and naturalization in Montana, for example, fell under the jurisdiction of the Naturalization Bureau's Seattle office. Examiner Paul B. Phillips, therefore, had to make the most of his routine trips for naturalizing court dates by also visiting university campuses and attending education conferences. Phillips began one such itinerary in spring 1919 by taking in a meeting of county superintendents at Missoula, at which he consulted with the superintendents and gave a fifteen-minute talk. Included in his remarks was an appeal for cooperation between the Naturalization Service, county superintendents, and the courts, premised on an "Educational Court Order," which basically ordered judges to remind naturalization declarants and petitioners about night school classes. He also "emphasized the desire of the Bureau that every rural school as well as every city school should be a power house for Americanization whither the alien may unfailingly turn for assistance." In closing his brief remarks, Phillips essentially warned the superintendents that examiners would be visiting them whenever naturalization hearings occurred in their counties.[7]

While in Missoula, Phillips visited with University of Montana president Edward O. Sisson, who was "anxious that the University cooperate with the efforts of the Bureau of Naturalization along Americanization lines to the fullest extent possible." No real extension division, however, existed at the university, although establishment of a public service division was then under consideration by the state Board of Education. The two also discussed the more likely service of training teachers for citizenship instruction, as, according to Phillips, "their country school teachers are not competent to teach civics and citizenship in a great many of the districts." Dean of journalism Arthur L. Stone, head of the school's semblance of an extension division, expressed interest in putting on an institute in citizenship training during the upcoming summer session. Stone later informed director of citizenship Raymond Crist that the teacher training conference during the summer of 1919 was indeed "an unquestioned success," thanks in large part to the assistance of the Seattle office, particularly the aid rendered by Phillips.[8]

From Missoula, Phillips ventured to Bozeman to confer with extension division director Fred S. Cooley at the College of Agriculture and Fine Arts of Montana. Cooley noted that the county Farm Bureaus offered the most practical way of reaching citizenship candidates who happened to be farmers, while Phillips explained to Cooley the "'educational court order' . . . linking up the machinery of the Courts with the public schools," which hopefully would soon be in operation in all fifty Montana counties. Phillips also ascertained Cooley's willingness to send letters to all rural applicants for citizenship—farmers, ranchers, and homesteaders—directing them toward public schools, if provided with monthly lists by the bureau.[9]

The following day, 1 April 1919, found Phillips in Butte with acting president Charles H. Clapp of the Montana State School of Mines. Finding the tiny school ("The enrollment is about 80 students") lacking an extension division, Phillips conversed with Clapp about the school's success in reaching immigrant mine workers in Butte. "President Clapp said that until recently the School of Mines, though in a large city owing its existence entirely to the mining industry, has been unable to get well in touch with the workingmen who work underground." Clapp assured Phillips, however, that the school would soon succeed in reaching the underground workers with safety and training materials, within which night school literature would be inserted. The professor placed much hope for improvement on the expected creation by the state of a bureau of mines. Several weeks later, Raymond Crist, the bureau's director of citizenship, congratulated Clapp on "reaching the above-ground workers in the smelters" and lauded his "desire to keep up this and in addition to get in touch more and more with those workers who are employed below ground." Crist mentioned too the "Act of Congress" approved by President Wilson on 9 May 1918, by which the bureau's federal textbook would be distributed free to candidates for citizenship attending public school classes. Clapp assured Chief Naturalization Examiner Jonathan Speed Smith that once Montana's Board of Examiners passed on the legislature's two-year appropriation for a state Board of Mines and Metallurgy, the School of Mines was ready to cooperate "to advertise and assist in the work of Americanization." "As you are probably aware, the problem is one of considerable complexity owing to the suspicion which the miners have of the propaganda of the companies, but I am certain that this suspicion can be overcome and that greater education of miners and smelter workers can be brought about."[10]

Phillips returned in July and attended an Americanization conference at the University of Montana in Missoula. On 15 July, Phillips spoke to an audience numbering over a hundred—"mostly Montana lady school teachers," he wrote in his report to Chief Examiner Smith. He stressed the distinction between patriotism and Americanization, describing the former as "an enthusiasm" or "emotion," while defining Americanization as "an intellectual process, a process of understanding and reason, which should bear fruit in the form of patriotism." Americanization, in the best progressive tradition, involved "the whole sphere of education." Phillips discussed the movement in very broad terms: surveys of social, economic, and industrial conditions, state housing laws, community activities such as sings, Fourth of July celebrations, pageants, parades, movies, speakers, libraries, and public schools. He explained in detail the fostering of Americanization through the courts, night schools, home teaching, factory schools, and the wide variety of interested organizations. To a somewhat smaller group the following day, Phillips explored in more depth the Americanization efforts of the Bureau of Naturalization.[11]

The dedication to their mission exhibited by peripatetic examiners like Paul B. Phillips did not always translate into successful programs or grateful acquiescence to the bureau's wishes on the part of local authorities. Prior to American entry into the war, bureau employees, from examiners to the commissioner of naturalization, spent a year and a half in an attempt to open night schools in Prescott, Arizona. Extensive correspondence and two visits by naturalization examiner Frederick Jones revealed significant interest in the problem on the part of school superintendents and the judge of the Yavapai County Superior Court. Difficulties concerning funding and a local perception that the town's small foreign-born population had little interest in citizenship classes impeded the bureau in its determination to bring Prescott into "this national work." George A. Crutchfield, chief naturalization examiner in the bureau's San Francisco office, ventured to Prescott himself in February 1917 and consulted with the city and county school superintendents, the superior court judge, and leading businessmen. As the town could boast no large corporations or mining concerns, it had a relatively small number of aliens, mostly Mexican laborers and Italian dairy farmers. As Crutchfield related the situation to the commissioner of naturalization, the Italians "could not attend a night class because their milking was done then." The judgment on the part of the committee in Prescott concerning the Mexican residents is revealing. "It was conceded on all sides," Crutchfield wrote, "that nothing could be done with the adult alien Mexicans. As a rule they take no interest in civic matters, and there was said not to be the slightest chance that they could be induced to attend a night class for instruction." A meeting with two hundred members of the Merchants Luncheon Club provided similar elite perceptions about the hopelessness of starting night school classes in Prescott.[12]

An examiner in Utah reported on towns not cooperating with the bureau's efforts, whether incidentally or intentionally, to Chief Examiner Paul Armstrong in May 1919. For instance, at Brigham City approximately one hundred unnaturalized agricultural laborers—"mostly Hindoos"—were simply too scattered to organize into classes. Nor had classes been organized at Eureka for about one thousand unnaturalized foreign miners because of the influenza epidemic and labor strife. Hopefully, Armstrong relayed to naturalization commissioner Richard K. Campbell, an Americanization act passed by Utah's legislature would result in the organization of more classes the following year, and, indeed, at Murray, where the American Smelting and Refining Company employed roughly three hundred foreign-born, a class had recently been organized in the public schools. After a visit to Rock Springs, Wyoming, in December 1919, Armstrong informed James R. Coxen, state director of vocational education at the University in Laramie, that "arrangements have been finally made to establish a night school for adult foreigners." Although the Rock Springs School Board offered no help, the superintendent was "willing to go ahead with the work on the assurance of a committee which I had called together" to raise money. "I hope that the citizens of Rock Springs, in spite of the attitude of the school board, will go ahead on a large scale to make this one of the largest and flourishing classes in the State of Wyoming," Armstrong wrote.[13]

The commissioner of naturalization in Washington demonstrated some concern with the practice, common in much of the West, of naturalizing court judges accepting citizenship applicants' certificates of graduation, provided by the public schools or Americanization instructors, in lieu of rigorous courtroom examinations. Courts in Los Angeles, reportedly with the approval of federal authorities, routinely accepted diplomas provided to applicants who had completed citizenship classes as substitutes for public examination. As the *National Suffrage News* noted in a report on Dr. Hebard's activities, her students' certificates eliminated the need for a courtroom examination, "an infinite relief to the foreigners, who find a court examination under strange surroundings a trying, sometimes even a disastrous ordeal."[14]

Potential disaster, in the view of naturalization officials in Washington, lay not in the prospective citizens' court day jitters but in the law-bending by regional examiners. "To recognize a certificate as entitling the alien to admission to citizenship is illegal," Commissioner Campbell reminded Paul Lee Ellerbe in November 1917. The chief examiner reassured the central office that instructions pertaining to certificates would "be very carefully and strictly followed." Nevertheless, Ellerbe wrote, "No certificate of graduation is entitled to any consideration whatever by any court in this district until it has been countersigned by me, and that not under any circumstances have I countersigned a single certificate unless I was convinced that the holder thereof was educationally qualified for admission to citizenship in a very unusual degree." He then explained that of the forty-three citizenship classes then being conducted in his district, almost all issued graduation certificates and almost all were recognized by naturalization courts as substitutes for examinations when countersigned. "It is . . . impossible," Ellerbe argued, "for a member of this service to examine in person every petitioner whose certificate of graduation is sent to me for countersignature. . . . I am morally certain that the citizenship instructors and I together have increased the knowledge of these applicants ten fold, and that they are educationally fully qualified for admission to citizenship." In concluding his appeal, Ellerbe begged the bureau to "bear in mind the difficulties with which we have to contend in a district of this geographical size and sparse population," which demanded a certain amount of instruction by correspondence as well as "a missionary spirit."[15]

Chief naturalization examiner Paul Lee Ellerbe (in center) at work in the Bureau of Naturalization's regional office in Denver, ca. 1916. *Rocky Mountain News,* 27 February 1916. Colorado Historical Society.

Unimpressed, Campbell responded that Ellerbe had no authority "to countersign any certificate of graduation unless it is based upon a *personal* examination of the candidate by yourself or a member of your station showing him personally qualified to assume the responsibilities of citizenship." According to the commissioner, accepting the public schools' certificates of graduation for citizenship students constituted a "fiction" and placed the bureau in an awkward position regarding naturalization statutes.[16] "You have gone entirely beyond the limits of any sanction or intimation or desire upon the part of the Bureau in taking this action," Commissioner Campbell scolded. "The Bureau cannot from your statement, other than view your action as most short-sighted and ill considered and taken without the sanction and advice of the Bureau, and in its complete ignorance that you contemplated such a departure." An obviously agitated Campbell charged Ellerbe with subordinating the legal requirements of naturalization "to an overzealous desire to stimulate the growth of what is admittedly a most desirable relationship, a closer relation between the public schools and this Bureau in its Americanization work." A chastened Ellerbe promised to withhold countersignatures until certificate holders had been personally examined by a member of the Naturalization Service.[17]

Two years later, however, in a letter to a Wyoming official, Raymond

Crist, now the Department of Labor's director of citizenship, lauded new federal government–supplied certificates of proficiency and graduation. In the Bureau of Naturalization's report for the 1920 fiscal year, Crist explained the efficacy of the certificates of proficiency being used to hold the attention of candidates having their first papers but not yet eligible for citizenship. The official graduation certificate, according to Crist, "usually relieves the applicant of the educational examination in court which he so much dreads." The change in policy required the bureau to examine candidates before having the chief naturalization examiner's office deliver certificates to school authorities. Some courts then accepted the certificates in lieu of a courtroom examination. "The practice of making the presentation of these certificates an occasion of public ceremony has grown," the director of citizenship noted, "and is developing into an integral feature in this national force for raising up a loyal Americanism and displacing opposing spirits." The official graduation certificate, described by Crist as "a badge of distinction," also displayed some ability of the naturalization bureaucracy in Washington to adjust to conditions in the field.[18]

Nonetheless, misunderstandings also occurred between state and federal officials involved in the immigrant education push. Despite frequent contact with representatives of the Bureau of Naturalization, James R. Coxen, the state director of vocational education in Wyoming, complained to Crist that "suggestions for specific means of cooperation have always been lacking." Coxen suggested that many Americanizers at the state level believed federal declarations of cooperation rang hollow:

> Your Agents have been in Wyoming repeatedly, and have been in Laramie a number of times, but with the exception of one visit from Mr. Armstrong about two years ago, none of them have ever taken the trouble to look me up or to find out anything about the work which we are trying to do. The opinion has been expressed by a number of people in this section that your people do not really wish to work with the educational forces in the various states. I hardly think this can be true, but up to this time there certainly has been no cooperation between your forces and our own.

Crist hastened to ease Coxen's concerns: "It is greatly regretted that the erroneous impression that this division does not really wish to work with the educational forces in the various states had gained credence, since in every possible way we are supporting all efforts put forth by the public-school system for the education of alien candidates for citizenship." Recent creation of the Division of Citizenship Training, he reassured, would go far toward rectification. Crist pointed out as well that the bureau's furnishing of supplies to public school officials and teachers, lists of declarants, and personal letters to candidates "all seem to be specific cooperation. All that is required is a statement from them or from you that a class has been organized and needs these supplies and assistance."[19]

Finally, the federal government's relentless but fruitless attempts to incorporate all Americanization programs under its control often frustrated local Americanizers. For example, Dolly Dean Burgess, "chairman" of the American citizenship department for the Montana Federation of Women's Clubs, received a note from Commissioner of Naturalization Raymond F. Crist in November 1927. Crist informed Burgess that, regrettably, he could not dispatch copies of the federal textbook on citizenship training to her because of a law limiting distribution to declarants and petitioners enrolled in the public schools' citizenship education classes. An angry Burgess returned the letter after typing this comment at the bottom: "I will never ask the Bureau to help me again on my Naturalization work. *Your technicality kills your usefulness.*"[20]

On the whole, though, Americanizers at the state level, whether volunteers or employed by universities, state councils of defense, or education offices, worked well with the examiners from Denver, San Francisco, or Seattle. The presumed boundaries between state and federal jurisdictions in fact often blurred as, for instance, university program administrators and naturalization officials negotiated their respective roles. Just such a smudging of responsibilities occurred after the University of Colorado began offering citizenship classes statewide through its extension division. Responding both to the Bureau of Naturalization's appeal to extension divisions nationwide early in 1919 and the legislature's failure to appropriate funds for the Committee on Americanization of the State Council of Defense, Professor George Norlin (the chairman of the committee) informed Chief Examiner Armstrong that the university's extension division would continue the work under its director, James C. Stephens. When Stephens left the university shortly thereafter, Dr. Loran D. Osborn assumed responsibilities for both the division and Americanization work conducted through the university. Extension division Americanizers, moreover, continued in their capacity as de facto agents of the Naturalization Bureau, thus further obscuring the lines between federal and state backing for citizenship training. "Let the Extension Division of the University, inasmuch as it is an educational institution, take as its special part in the enterprise the systematic supervision of all the Americanization classes," Osborn suggested to the Bureau of Naturalization's Paul Armstrong. "It of course would be desirable for you to render these classes any help that you could, but the understanding would be that the responsibility for the educational aspects of the work would rest primarily with the University." University and naturalization bureaucrats agreed, then, that combining forces promised expeditious results.[21]

Given the degree to which teachers and bureaucrats cooperated in the West, it is not entirely surprising that confusion arose over such issues as funding Americanizers' travel and the mailing of information. Professor Norlin, in his capacity as chairman of the Committee on Americanization in Colorado, appealed to Secretary of the Interior Franklin K. Lane for financial support, specifically for transportation and mail franking. "One of the first things that we are planning to do," Norlin informed the secretary, "is to send to all centers of the foreign population in the State men of unquestioned loyalty who can speak to the foreigners in their own language and do so effectively." Lane replied that the Department of the Interior could not subsidize speakers' traveling expenses, but he held out the hope that Congress would pass legislation containing "a sufficient appropriation to enable us to assist the several States in carrying on the Americanization program."[22]

Frustrated Hopes for Centralization

Paul Lee Ellerbe's request that, because "our government thinks we can," citizens help assimilate possibly unassimilable immigrants will not go down as one of the most inspiring Americanization pep talks. As with many colleagues in the Americanization field, Ellerbe at times exhibited his ambivalence about the foreign-born. Nevertheless, in the context of his time and place, he was reasonably optimistic that Americanization could succeed if the federal government made an even stronger commitment to the crusade by centralizing its direction. That, as it turned out, constituted the central question for the movement as it related to the federal government's role.

This desire for greater centralization and efficiency was also expressed by George Bell at the May 1919 Americanization Conference in Washington, D.C. Bell, former executive secretary for both the California Commission of Immigration and Housing and the War Labor Policies Board based in New York City, maintained that each state must create a centralized agency or commission and coordinate its work with the federal government. The several states' task would be made easier, however, if there was but one federal agency or department in charge. "To the actual workers in the field," Bell pointed out, "it has been most confusing and discouraging to receive during the past two years diverse and often conflicting letters, bulletins, pamphlets, and programs from several different bureaus in Washington. . . . The army of Americanization workers have felt much as the scattered armies in France must have felt before they had a unified command and an organized staff under Gen.

Foch." Carol Aronovici, who, prior to accepting a position managing housing programs for the CCIH, had directed Americanization efforts in Minnesota, echoed Bell's concerns. "One hesitates to suggest which department of the federal government should be in full and exclusive charge of the work," Aronovici stated, "but a unification of functions is necessary and the department most vitally concerned with the problem and best equipped to carry out a consistent, constructive policy should be intrusted with the responsibility of promoting the education and granting the privilege of citizenship."[23]

Increasing friction between the Bureaus of Education and Naturalization, however, frustrated the hopes of Aronovici, Bell, and other leading Americanizers to completely federalize immigrant education through the hoped-for creation of a single bureau of citizenship and Americanization. The Bureau of Naturalization possessed some advantage in having its examiners in the field, establishing personal networks with educators, district court judges, and state officials. A congressional act of 9 May 1918, the chief naturalization examiner in Seattle informed the secretary of the Montana Council of Defense, "entrusted the government's Americanization program to this [Naturalization] Bureau." In point of fact, the 1918 statute, an amendment to the basic naturalization law that had created the Bureau of Immigration and Naturalization in 1906, only authorized reimbursement for the cost of publishing the bureau's citizenship textbook. Nonetheless, many Americanizers perceived the Bureau of Naturalization as the most important federal agency in relation to their efforts. James C. Stephens, director of Americanization in Colorado during the war, pointed to the bureau as "the only agency carrying on a country-wide work which has a consistent program and offers real help to state and local agencies which it asks to cooperate with it."[24]

On the other hand, the Bureau of Naturalization exhibited less concern with the overall effectiveness of its educational programs, gearing its efforts toward preparing immigrants for naturalization procedures instead. The bureau's citizenship textbook, compiled by then deputy commissioner Raymond Crist and published in 1918, exemplified its chief concern in naturalizing the foreign-born. Chock-full of moralistic and patriotic homilies, the text eschewed information of concrete relevance for abstract peans to America's greatness and the students' duties to attend night school, learn English, be quiet, polite, clean, and punctual, and respect the teacher and fellow pupils. A long lesson concerning the "Story of the United States Government" consumed well over half of the textbook. Any citizenship student (or citizen, for that matter) possessing an inordinate facility with English could read a considerable amount about the discovery of America, the Indians, and the lives of Washington, Lincoln, and Longfellow. The textbook also reprinted and discussed the Constitution, reiterated the process of becoming a naturalized American citizen, and, in a section of more than fifty pages, explained the history and structure of the national government. This section included a comprehensive survey of all the executive departments, with each of their constituent bureaus and services.[25]

Officials with the Bureau of Naturalization wanted to believe that they had the imprimatur bestowed by Congress to take complete charge of Americanization. The lack of focus on sound educational methods, unfortunately, allowed their chief bureaucratic rival to sustain its claim to a legitimate national stake in the crusade. The Bureau of Education, inspired as it was by Frances Kellor and guided by the broad concerns of its specialist in immigrant education, Harrison H. Wheaton, hoped to synthesize the best methods of immigrant education from around the nation and devise a standardized program. Textbooks produced by the Bureau of Education, in contrast to that published by the Naturalization Bureau, reflected some educators' growing realization that Americanization required a greater level of sympathy toward immigrants' desires. Largely written by Columbia University professor Henry H. Goldberger (himself an immigrant from Czechoslovakia), *Teaching English to the Foreign Born: A Teacher's Handbook* and *Training Teachers for Americanization* stressed the organization of classes in more informal settings and teaching English in such a way as to be useful to immigrants in their daily lives at work and home. Although respectful of immigrant contributions, the Bureau of Education texts nonetheless reflected the duality so characteristic of Americanization in the World War I period by exhorting teachers to be 100 percent Americans, thereby setting the right sort of example.[26]

The duplication of effort on the part of the two federal bureaus, according to Commissioner of Education P. P. Claxton, "produced more or less confusion in the minds of school boards and superintendents and was . . . resented by them." Although the Bureau of Naturalization had an obligation "to provide for the technical instruction necessary to enable candidates to qualify for their citizenship papers" and the Council of National Defense and Committee on Public Information each had a temporary hand in Americanization, the Bureau of Education was, as Claxton saw it, "the proper legal and the logical agency" for the national program. Other figures associated with the Bureau of Education, Frances Kellor for one, also maintained a barrage of criticism implicitly directed at the rival bureau in relation to the complications of naturalization procedures. Colorado's James C. Stephens, while appreciative of the Naturalization Bureau's assistance, believed a national program should eventually be managed by an Americanization bureau in a Department of Education. If the Americanization movement was to become the great crusade of progressive education its backers hoped for, a clear national policy and the primacy of a single authoritative agency had to be established.[27]

Toward these ends, legislation designed to nationalize Americanization through the Bureau of Education made its way through Congress between 1915 and 1924. Members of the National Committee of One Hundred, the advisory body connected to the Bureau of Education, drafted legislation in 1917 after a lengthy investigation of perceived Americanization needs, but the proposed bills simply vanished in committees after being introduced.[28] A year later, a National Conference of Americanization convened in Washington, D.C., to again consider the bureau's legislative program for "a planned, far-sighted and comprehensive policy in America's reconstruction program during the war and thereafter." This particular gathering devoted its more practical energies to shepherding a national Americanization bill to passage as "a war-emergency measure." The proposed law, drafted again by members of the National Committee of One Hundred, gave the Bureau of Education and Council of National Defense primary responsibility to promote "the common use of the English language, patriotism, industrial efficiency and national unity." In addition, the Bureau of Education lobbied for a second bill to promote immigrant education and teacher training throughout the nation on a permanent basis. A committee appointed by Secretary of the Interior Franklin K. Lane and chaired by Montana governor Samuel V. Stewart concentrated on promoting the two Americanization bills. While the rhetoric invoked cooperation with the Bureau of Naturalization and the Committee on Public Information, the legislative approach essentially involved appropriating funds to the Bureau of Education so it—along with the Council of National Defense—could organize state and local Americanization programs along comprehensive, national lines.[29]

At the same time, Secretary Lane and Commissioner Claxton were also backing a bill, introduced by Senator Hoke Smith of Georgia and Representative William B. Bankhead of Alabama, "to require the Commissioner of Education to devise methods and promote plans for the elimination of adult illiteracy in the United States." Although the focus of the Smith-Bankhead legislation in 1918 was on men drafted into the armed forces, discussion at times turned to immigrants, resulting in an amendment to include aliens and naturalized citizens. In the course of debate, concern arose regarding the National Americanization Committee (NAC) paying special collaborators working in the Bureau of Education their yearly one-dollar fee. Opponents of the bill voiced their dismay at privately backed bureaucrats churning out propaganda under the government's franking privileges and duplicating the activities of the Bureau of Naturalization. Moreover, skeptical legislators, such as Senator George E. Chamberlain of Oregon, expressed fear that the

NAC-backed effort to secure a nominal appropriation at that time was simply an entering wedge to securing enormous amounts of funding later. Chamberlain saw the NAC as a Trojan horse and the Bureau of Education's Americanization campaign as federal interference in educational affairs reserved for the states. Commissioner Claxton also came under heavy fire for allegedly trying to muscle in on the Naturalization Bureau's turf and accrue inordinate bureaucratic power to himself. "Here is an undertaking," Chamberlain charged, "not only to kaiserize the public-school system of America but to take it out of the hands of the States and centralize it in the power and in the hands of Mr. Claxton." The bill never made it to a vote during that session.[30]

Leaders of the Americanization drive in the West also differed on the need for centralization. Simon J. Lubin hoped that the California Commission of Immigration and Housing's program would provide a model for a national Americanization agency and labored to drum up support. "The difficulties involved in the present decentralized and inarticulate situation," Lubin wrote in an October 1918 form letter, "is not so much on account of possible over-lapping, which in itself may not be very harmful, but rather on account of counteracting and antagonistic influences, and because important aspects of the problem are not covered, and chiefly because there is no directing mind in control." While careful not to specify problems or assign blame, Lubin undoubtedly had the counterproductive rivalry between the Naturalization and Education Bureaus in mind. He argued that increased efficiency and consistency would result if state councils of defense and other organizations had the luxury of dealing "in these matters directly with only one federal division." George Norlin in Colorado, however, found the prospect of a single national body more troubling than reassuring. "It is clearly objectionable," Norlin confided in Governor Julius Gunter, "that the detailed program of Americanization should be worked out in any central office and imposed upon all the states notwithstanding the very great variety of conditions in the different states." He feared that creation of a powerful federal agency, intent on fostering conformity to its "central plan," would doom the Americanization Committee of the State Council of Defense and deprive other state agencies of the initiative required to fashion programs to local conditions.[31]

With the war over and fears of industrial unrest rising, a significantly different set of circumstances obtained when Smith-Bankhead legislation was introduced again early in 1919. The bill was a significant expansion of previous proposals, "the most comprehensive and important educational measure ever presented to congress," according to the *New Mexico Journal of Education*. It "authorized and directed" the Bureau of Education, "with any other Federal agencies which may be able through their existing organizations to furnish assistance therein," to aid the states in educating illiterates, those "persons unable to understand, speak, read, or write the English language," and the foreign-born in general, as well as in "training and preparation of teachers, supervisors and directors for such educational work." Funding requests, as feared by Senator Chamberlain and other opponents the previous year, rose tremendously: $5 million for fiscal 1920 and $12.5 million annually thereafter through fiscal 1926; $250,000 for training in the remainder of fiscal 1919, then, $750,000 afterward; and $250,000 to the Bureau of Education for administering the act in fiscal 1919, with $1 million to be appropriated annually through fiscal 1926. States that wanted to be included in the program had to provide matching funds, the amounts to be determined based on the state's proportion of illiterates and non-English-speaking residents over ten years of age in relation to national figures provided in the most recent census.[32]

Predictably, opposition to the bill in 1919 centered on the cost. Senator William S. Kenyon of Iowa, a Smith-Bankhead supporter, begged his colleagues to ponder both the estimated 8.5 million illiterates over the age of ten and the 10 million unnaturalized immigrants then abroad in the land. "When men can not read the constitution, can not read the statutes, how can we inculcate ideas of government in them?" Kenyon asked. "How can they grasp the ideals of this Republic? There is your field for bolshevism." Kenyon earnestly tried to persuade the Senate "to put a fire under the melting pot to make Americans out of these illiterate people who have come to our shores." Yet, despite backing by Secretary of the Interior Lane and President Wilson, no action followed Kenyon's comments. With the exception of a Kenyon-sponsored bill in 1920, which passed the Senate only to disappear in the House, all efforts along the lines of forging a massive federal Americanization program went nowhere. By 1924, serious attempts at passing illiteracy and Americanization legislation in Congress had ended.[33]

The Federal Government and
Americanization in the 1920s

At the height of the Americanization crusade, Simon Lubin, in collaboration with Christina Krysto, a California Commission of Immigration and Housing employee, contributed a series of articles to the social work journal *The Survey*. Published over the winter of 1919–1920, Lubin and Krysto's "Strength of America" series called for a more systematic and patient incorporation of immigrants and their contributions as part of a conscious effort to build a unified nation. "America possesses the magic power of intensifying the talents, individual and national, of all of her people, the foreign-born no less than the native-born," they wrote. "But America also has the power to take from all national representatives the best they have . . . while preserving their national core, to transmute them into a new thing that is essentially American, the ideal towards which we are all building."

To that ambitious end, Lubin and Krysto proposed the establishment of a new federal agency, a "department of nation building" composed of seven bureaus. A Bureau of Schools would replace the Bureau of Education in the Department of the Interior, adapting the concept of the school as a community center so as to "reach the whole mass of the people." In addition, the diffuse and often counterproductive efforts of the present citizenship education and naturalization systems would be consolidated under a Bureau of Preparation for Citizenship. This bureau would have three divisions, one that oversaw the training of the native-born, "who must be prepared for citizenship first," a separate "alien division" for the specialized instruction of the foreign-born, and a "naturalization courts division" to assume the responsibilities then being managed by the Department of Labor's Bureau of Naturalization. Lubin and Krysto's proposed department would also include a Bureau of Community Organization, modeled on the California experiment that John Collier was directing at that time. "Under a system of well developed community life," they confidently maintained, "there could be no great political disturbances, there could be no great industrial upheavals, for man and his government would indeed be one."[34]

Three of the four remaining bureaus in Lubin and Krysto's super agency would concentrate on problems of labor and immigration. A Bureau of Labor Exchanges was meant to coordinate, in tandem with state and municipal employment agencies, the labor supply with the actual demand for workers. Provided "dependable information, scientifically obtained by impartial agencies," a Bureau of Selective Immigration would identify the prospective immigrants most relevant to actual labor needs and "invite them to come here." Such a bureau would replace the padrones and labor contractors that had so often exploited immigrant workers for personal profit. A Bureau of Immigrant Inspection would assure that selected immigrants were distributed to where they were needed. Rounding out the Department of Nation Building, the writers suggested a Bureau of National Culture, whose charge would be to "think through the whole problem of nation building."

In the spirit of John Quincy Adams, Lubin and Krysto even pictured a national university that would take charge of forging a national culture from diverse strains. Lubin and Krysto displayed abundant faith that, if conducted through a comprehensive federal agency, a coordinated blend of democratic schooling, citizenship education and naturalization, communities, labor exchanges and distribution systems, plus a think tank of national culture, could foster increased national coherence. "No other nation has a richer field in which to try experiments of a vast nature," they believed. The dreamed-for federal department, was, in certain respects, the California Commission of Immigration and Housing writ large. Lubin and Krysto's call for an agency devoted to a national domestic immigration policy represented a logical progression for liberal Americanization. The timing for their extraordinary proposal, however, could not have been less propitious.[35]

Lubin and Krysto's "Strength of America" proposal coincided with one of the most intense periods of antiradical and antiforeign outbreaks in American history. After the war, abject fear of communists, anarchists, and socialists drove the Red Scare of 1919–1920, and leading Americanizers either joined or helplessly observed the anticommunist crusades of Attorney General A. Mitchell Palmer, the National Security League, and industrialists. In such a charged atmosphere immigrant education retained its unifying appeal, and the existing national organizations and bureaus hoped support and money would continue. However, enthusiasm for Americanization had already peaked, and retrenchment, not reform, dominated politics in the early 1920s.

New federal legislation prohibited private backing for federal agencies, barring the National Americanization Committee from rendering financial assistance to the Bureau of Education's Division of Immigrant Education, which was absorbed, along with the War Work Extension, by the Americanization Division in 1919. The Bureau of Education subsequently incorporated its immigrant work into its adult education programs. Deprived of the Bureau of Education, Frances Kellor continued her citizenship education program from within the business-backed Inter-Racial Council, organized in March 1919. The council concerned itself with combating labor radicalism by providing appropriate stories and advertising copy for the foreign-language press, but it was not enough to revive the frenzied enthusiasm of the war years, and the organization folded in 1921. Reflecting the stepped-up pace of Americanization in the immediate postwar years, a Division of Citizenship Training within the Bureau of Naturalization, under a director of citizenship, was created in 1919 and remained in place until 1921. Under a 1923 reorganization, an expansion of citizenship training activities was planned, only to be abridged two years later with personnel "further reduced to what is an irreducible minimum."[36]

Antiradical hysteria dissipated, but as evidenced by disappearing agencies and cutbacks, the air had definitely gone out of the Americanization balloon. Yet, despite reorganization and downsizing, the Bureau of Naturalization continued its mission much as before in its Western districts. The scope of the regional offices' work is evident from the bulging files of correspondence and reports housed in the old National Archives building in Washington, D.C. One file concerns the cooperative effort between the bureau's staff in the District No. 11 office on the fourth floor of the federal building in Seattle and educators in Lewis County, just south of the Puget Sound region. In November 1919, Lewis County would gain much unwanted notoriety with the battle in Centralia between American Legion members and Wobblies that climaxed with the lynching of Wesley Everest. The far less dramatic and mundane workings of more effectively incorporating Lewis County within the national citizen-making system had commenced just a few months earlier.

"The bureau believes that even one unnaturalized alien creates the need for instruction," Commissioner of Naturalization Richard K. Campbell wrote in a February 1919 letter to the superintendent of Lewis County schools. To reach foreign-born adults outside of the urban centers, the cooperation of county superintendents became an urgent necessity. Campbell suggested that the superintendent urge teachers throughout the county to appraise their local conditions and inform foreigners of the "opportunity opened to them" for instruction in citizenship. "Once they understand that the citizenship class does not mean drudgery, but pleasant intercourse with friends, the making of new acquaintances, the fitting of themselves for better paying positions, a general broadening and uplifting," the commissioner promised, "they will be not only willing but eager to come."

The superintendent of schools for Lewis County, Z. May Meighen, responded with alacrity and "hearty cooperation" to the commissioner's suggestions. With information provided by school principals throughout the county, Meighen and a woman who was the county chairman of Americanization ascertained the locations and living conditions of foreigners in Lewis County. "We find in some of the logged off sections foreigners from Finland, Norway and Sweden who are cultivating the soil," Meighen informed the bureau. "These people," she presumed, "do not seem to have formed what we may call community groups to any great extent. We have some German farmers also." Groups of Poles, Finns, and Japanese resided in various logging camps. Meighen also formed a committee and secured the assistance of the superior court judge and county clerk.[37]

Naturalization examiners, educators, and clerks of the court composed a triad that sustained the bureau's mission of bringing all adult foreigners into the privileged status of citizen. In working the Lewis County Americanization program into shape, Chief Naturalization Examiner Jonathan Speed Smith relied on the clerk of the court. Once an alien made the initial application for citizenship, the declaration of intention (or "first papers"), or filed

the petition for naturalization ("final papers"), Smith informed Superintendent Meighen, the clerk of the court would immediately refer the applicant
to her "so that you may direct him (and his wife if he is married) to an appropriate teacher near his residence for instruction." According to Smith, the
county clerk plan had originated within his district "in a homestead section
of Montana." At the same time, in June 1920, Smith alerted the clerk of the
court in Chehalis, Washington, to refer declarants and petitioners to the
county superintendent. Two years later, he suggested to the superintendent
that the clerk of the court be deputized to assign applicants to citizenship instructors at times when the superintendent was absent.[38]

The Bureau of Naturalization's designs to match all citizenship applicants
to teachers through district courts and school superintendents, particularly
in counties with large rural populations, created problems in finding willing
instructors. For Superintendent Meighen's predicament in Lewis County,
Smith suggested that "some one should take it upon themselves, school
board or private citizens" to finance the work of rural teachers facing an inordinate amount of citizenship applicants seeking instruction. "It is not at all
surprising," Smith acknowledged "that some teachers find it difficult to take
up this work in addition to their school work for the day pupils." As for situations in which regular schoolteachers could not be secured or schools were
not in session, Smith suggested that the superintendent "designate some
other competent, discreet person not regularly employed in the schools to
give this instruction. A former teacher would no doubt be preferable."[39]

Examiner Paul B. Phillips assessed the results of the bureau's endeavors in
Lewis County after a naturalization hearing in the Superior Court at
Chehalis in February 1923. Superintendent Meighen had informed the Seattle office of a plan to train Lewis County teachers in the "ways and methods
of teaching citizenship" and asked Phillips how petitioners had fared in the
courtroom examination. He had to admit "that the showing was a poor one
on the whole" and that, while the bureau's "County Plan" had sparked considerable activity, it needed better direction in certain cases. Phillips agreed
to present the bureau's perspective on improving the county's citizenship
training at impending conferences of school superintendents and teachers. A
month later, Examiner Phillips addressed a meeting of the Chehalis section
of the Lewis County Educational Association. "I have addressed other
teacher's gatherings about this work," Phillips noted in his report to
Jonathan Speed Smith, "but I have never before followed quite the line of
thought or method of treatment that I did on this occasion."

Eschewing platitudes regarding educators' patriotic duty to assist in Americanization, Phillips instead used data compiled as part of the regional office's routine activity to impress upon the twenty teachers in attendance the

practical importance of the work. Phillips first described the "Americanization problem in Lewis County" revealed by the 1920 federal census, which
showed that more than three-fourths of the county's foreign-born white population lived outside of Chehalis and Centralia. Approximately two of every
five foreign-born whites in the county had not become naturalized by 1920,
with the majority of that category also living in rural areas. The examiner
next discussed materials, such as textbooks, charts, posters, and pamphlets,
provided by the bureau and the two basic options involving the public
schools—regular evening school classes and the individual instruction best
adapted to rural communities. Phillips also explained the "County Plan" and
acknowledged that Lewis County had earned a solid reputation for cooperation with the Naturalization Bureau. While private tutoring had achieved
good results, Phillips maintained that citizenship education would be enhanced "if Centralia and Chehalis would maintain regular citizenship classes
at least during part of the year." He concluded with advice on what to teach,
which amounted to as much knowledge of civics as expected of a student in
the eighth grade. "I felt when I got through that the teachers present had a
better insight into our work and a more real sympathy with our efforts than
they would have received from an address of a hortatory nature."[40]

While Chief Examiner Smith and Examiner Phillips carefully stroked
more effective Americanization out of communities in the Pacific Northwest
and northern Rockies, the employees of the Bureau of Naturalization's District No. 10 office in San Francisco strove to coordinate citizenship education within the diverse Bay Area. Even as immigration restriction made its
inexorable way toward realization, the bureau intensified its work with
school superintendents, county clerks, normal schools and universities, and
the wide variety of private organizations still devoting time and resources to
the cause. The depth of commitment and breadth of involvement by the San
Francisco office is apparent in reports submitted by Anne M. Godfrey, vari-
ously described as "Americanization Clerk," "Educational Representative,"
and "Educational Assistant." Not burdened with the added responsibility of
examining citizenship applicants in open court, Godfrey concentrated on
advising those cooperating with the bureau on educational matters.

Godfrey directed a considerable amount of attention to Santa Clara
County, just south of San Francisco, where, as she commented in a January
1922 report, "there are many foreign born." Godfrey aided in coordinating
Americanization programs in 1922 with two other women, County Superintendent of Schools Agnes Howe and Nellie Chope, a citizenship instructor and principal of the San Jose Evening High School. Howe succeeded in
establishing English and citizenship classes in a number of the county's small
communities, although, as Godfrey noted in reference to herself, "the Bureau

Representative has had to be very tactful but we are getting the results desired." Godfrey had addressed most of Mrs. Chope's classes and recommended the teacher as "a wonderful influence among the foreign born." In San Jose the following year, Godfrey addressed a district convention of the California Federation of Women's Clubs, held consultations on summer school Americanization courses with the presidents of the state Teachers' Colleges, discussed the possible expansion of home teaching with city school officials, and visited Mrs. Chope's classes. A man by the name of Joseph E. Hancock had replaced Agnes Howe as county superintendent of schools, and in "one of the most important interviews which I have had," Godfrey initiated Hancock into the mysteries of Americanization. Hancock had been named a member of the Americanization Committee of the State Council of Education and scheduled to present a talk on the problems and needs of work in the state. "He felt very helpless," Godfrey recounted, so she filled him in on "the state problem, together with some of the remedies," and, as she claimed in a subsequent report, prepared his address. "In doing this he became so imbued with the necessity of the work that he promised the appointment of a county director of Americanization as soon as possible."[41]

True to his word, Hancock appointed Cecilia Carmichael as director of Americanization for Santa Clara County. Beginning in September 1923, Carmichael organized classes in several rural communities as well as "a class of Russian janitors at Stanford University" and a County Council of Americanization composed of Americanization teachers. In an April 1924 issue of the San Jose Evening School's student newspaper, Carmichael interpreted the achievements of pupils enrolled in the new rural evening schools. At one, "seventeen young Portuguese dairymen enrolled and have been patiently wrestling with the English language from 8 to 10 o'clock, three nights a week." School trustees, impressed with the students' devotion, replaced the schoolroom's oil lamps with electricity. Carmichael described the twenty-five pupils in another evening school as "a happy lot of Americans in the making" and the fourteen enrolled at Los Gatos as "puffed up with pride" after the successful courtroom examinations of three class members. The director of Americanization projected the establishment of additional evening schools throughout the county and the employment of "a home teacher in every community where there is a need to implant American ideals of right living."[42]

Conclusion

Although the reported happiness and pride of Santa Clara County's adult immigrant students in 1924 cannot be corroborated, Cecilia Carmichael,

Anne M. Godfrey, and their Americanization colleagues perceived success in the expansion of evening schools and home teaching. Ironically, while the citizenship training system appeared to be hitting its stride in the Bay Area and other centers of immigrant population in the West, Congress readied passage of a permanent national origins quota system that promised to significantly reduce the numbers of presumably unassimilable aliens from Europe and exclude immigrants from Japan and other Asian sources. Nonetheless, despite two federal bureaus having reduced their citizenship education workloads, the federal government tried to sustain the momentum of the Americanization crusade. The creation, by executive order of President Harding, of the Federal Council of Citizenship Training in January 1923 signified a continuing effort within the national bureaucracy to coordinate "education for citizenship." Involving representatives from the Departments of the Interior, War, Navy, the Treasury, the Post Office, Agriculture, Labor, State, Justice, Commerce, the Federal Board of Vocational Education, and the Veterans Bureau, the Federal Council sought to lay the groundwork for effective community development through citizenship training, plus "whatever relates to mental development, health and physical development, vocational development, nurturing of patriotism, appreciation of our Government, and the social and moral development of the individual and the community." Limited to collecting and disseminating information and offering advice, the council accomplished little beyond organizing conferences and aiding the publication by its constituent agencies of more pamphlets on citizenship training.[43]

All the various pieces of the federal Americanization apparatus—the Bureau of Naturalization and Bureau of Education, in particular—attempted to shape programs in the West and, in so doing, reshape the region along national lines. This task fell largely on the shoulders of regional officials, particularly Bureau of Naturalization examiners. After the war, devotion to their mission and paychecks kept regional federal officials on the road, exhorting teachers and administrators of adult education programs to keep the fires under the melting pot burning. By distributing educational materials, networking with local Americanization teachers, and pushing and prodding school districts and universities to establish or expand adult immigrant education, federal officials took it upon themselves to promote the movement in all corners of the West. Like Paul B. Phillips, who used his naturalizing court trips in Montana to visit university campuses and attend education conferences, federal bureaucrats displayed admirable devotion to their mission of Americanizing the West. Lower-level officials like these, rather than desk-bound administrators in Washington, D.C., did the most to bring the West within the national citizen-making system. Americanization activists in the churches, schools, factories, labor camps, universities, and state agencies depended on federal officials and generally backed their efforts to impose order and standardization on a frequently chaotic enterprise. Although regional officials occasionally "colored outside the lines" in adjusting naturalization procedures to Western realities, the goal remained the same: to educate and naturalize the foreign-born and aid in the construction of an enduring and unified nation.

The inability of government to consolidate a national Americanization system within one federal agency did some damage to citizenship programs in the West. State Americanization committees, public schools, universities, and other interested parties certainly needed the money and level of support that a more smoothly functioning national bureaucracy might have provided. Nonetheless, the citizen-making went on even when the fervor of the Americanization crusade had faded. Naturalization officials continued to encourage educators in preparing candidates for citizenship, and Americanizers persisted, even in the face of diminishing financial aid and public interest, in "stirring the melting pot." Because the government thought it could make citizens of all the foreign-born who desired it, Chief Naturalization Examiner Paul Lee Ellerbe had, in 1916, cautiously asked his fellow citizens to help. In November 1917, Ellerbe sought to inspire members of the Colorado Education Association with the significance of transforming aliens into citizens. "When the unbelievable blessing of peace has returned to the tortured earth, it is not likely that a greater drama will be staged for some time than the making of America," he predicted. "And the aliens who came a million a year in nineteen thirteen and fourteen, 326,000 in 1915, 298,000 in 1916, the straggling few who are coming now, and the inestimable millions of those tides that will set this way after the war, will act some of the leading roles, have a hand in setting the stage, and a good deal to do with fashioning the play itself. What will they make of America? It will depend upon what America makes of them."[44]

6

"OUR OWN HOUSE NEEDS READJUSTMENT"

The Collapse of Americanization

The Americanization movement collapsed in the 1920s. For Romanian-born Carol Aronovici, at one time the director of housing programs for the California Commission of Immigration and Housing, "the spectacle of the rabid and ignorant Americanizing efforts was disheartening." Poisoned by an atmosphere of immigrant-bashing and red-baiting, Aronovici continued, Americanization became "a negative movement," the word "Americanization" itself now discredited. He bitterly recounted the fervor with which the foreign-born were stripped of the rights to use their languages and humiliated by the drumbeat of Anglo-Saxonism:

> The immigrant who had come to this country to find a great heterogeneous mass of people sharing a new political and social ideal found himself confronted with the problem of accepting as fact the presumptions that what is not Anglo-Saxon is not American, and that his race and national characters must conform to a strict code which is not the creation of a great synthetic mass of peoples from the four corners of the earth but the strict code of a civilization which controlled the destinies of this country a century and a half ago.

What emerged, therefore, out of America's wartime experience, according to this one disenchanted "hyphen," was a nation "less Americanized" than before the war because of an Americanization movement unequal to the task. "The weaving of national and racial characters of the alien into the fabric of American civilization is the real task of Americanization," Aronovici contended. "If we refuse to accept this doctrine we should close our doors to the immigrant or exclude him from ever becoming a part of this country's national life."[1]

Restrictionists, meanwhile, had come to the same conclusion based on far different assumptions. In *The Passing of the Great Race,* published in 1916, New York Zoological Society founder Madison Grant lent pseudoscientific cachet to the racism long directed toward southern and eastern Europeans. Grant pointed to America's earliest English settlers, who had supposedly been of Anglo-Saxon, Norse, and Danish "blood," as keepers of the highest civilization ever known. Self-government, brilliantly advanced by America's Anglo-Saxon Founding Fathers, had, he argued, originated among ancient Teutonic tribes in German forests before making its way across the English Channel. Grant and others feared, however, the replacement of the Anglo-Saxon "native American" by the "intrusive peoples drained from the lowest races of eastern Europe and western Asia." Unless they utilized their "superior intelligence" to counter the lower standards of living and higher birth rates of the new immigrants, the great Anglo-Saxon race would disappear, and with it liberty and democracy.[2]

The notion that high birth rates among new immigrant groups contributed to "race suicide" for the increasingly less prolific members of the "American race" haunted opponents of free immigration. Southern and eastern Europeans, if allowed to continue their migration to America, would outbreed native-born Americans of northern European stock.[3] California senator James D. Phelan and others involved in anti-Asian movements expressed concern as well that with the end of the frontier came the pinnacle of Western civilization and the accompanying decline in fertility. The Asian East, on the contrary, situated on a lower plane of civilization, was still prone to high birth rates, and that fact, in conjunction with Asian immigrants' supposed ability to "underlive" proud whites, would ultimately drive "the frugal, self-limiting white pioneer" from the land.[4] Supporters of California's alien land law initiative in 1920 laid particular stress on Japanese picture brides' allegedly mind-boggling fertility, accusing Japanese immigrants of conspiring to produce numberless American citizens "by the birth route" to take over the state's farmlands. As a summary of the picture bride scare in the *Literary Digest* put it, "the little Japanese lady is about the most sturdy opponent of race-suicide on the globe." University of California zoologist Samuel J. Holmes made a similar point about Mexican immigrants in 1929: "If we bring in large numbers of an alien people we are sacrificing our children for theirs." Holmes saw the Southwest in immediate danger of becoming "Mexicanized" by "the progeny of Mexican peons who will continue for centuries to afflict us with an embarrassing race problem."[5] The national character—and the national bloodstream, which, it was believed, defined that character—faced irrevocable alteration if these inferior types were not kept out or, at the very least, if they did not appropriate emerging American norms such as smaller families. Race suicide went to the heart of an apparently fading dominant culture's very sense of self and status as the fulcrum of American culture and society.

As part of the most advanced civilization in history, it also seemed vital to safeguard national homogeneity in terms of race purity. One presumably scientific means that appealed to a growing number of progressives was eugenics. Emphasizing quality over quantity, eugenicists conceded to some extent that the "best" stock could not be persuaded to breed prolifically. Nonetheless, through careful examination of heredity, the best human "breeds" could be determined and encouraged, perhaps through government programs, to have children. Meanwhile, the "unfit" could be dissuaded from multiplying or, failing in that endeavor, sterilized. Although the history of the eugenics movement, as well as its implications, is outside the scope of this study, it is important as an adjunct to fears of race suicide and race mixing. Frustrated by their overall failure to convince Americans of the racial doom inherent in race suicide and amalgamation, many of the alarmists turned to eugenics as "a sort of scientific reform" in the hopes of achieving a similar end—the preservation of the "American race."[6] In other words, eugenicists endeavored to restore the nation's homogeneous past through efficient breeding of the best stock and careful control of defective and immigrant stock. Many became strong supporters of immigration restriction as well.

Postwar fears that a devastated Europe would disgorge unprecedented numbers of desperate immigrants disturbed many restrictionists, already alarmed at the prospects of race suicide and deleterious racial amalgamation. "So long as foreigners are permitted to enter this country and segregate themselves," Kenneth Roberts, a former Army intelligence officer and disciple of Madison Grant, concluded in *Why Europe Leaves Home,* "just so long will they resist the rudiments of assimilation." As out of control as immigration had appeared before the war, Roberts contended, it would appear as nothing "compared with the serried ranks and the teeming multitudes which to-day are anxiously awaiting the opportunity to break all surging records between Europe and America." Roberts described Poles, Czechs, and Slavs as "oozing slowly but ceaselessly out of Central Europe to America; streams of under-sized, peculiar, alien people moving perpetually through consulates and steamship offices and delousing plants on their way from the slums of Europe to the slums of America." Though casting his argument in less sensational terms, Robert De Courcey Ward of the Immigration Restriction League also believed that the practical impossibility of assimilating and Americanizing millions of additional foreigners supported the fundamental logic of numerical restriction. "A real restriction of immigration," Ward maintained shortly after the end of World War I, "is a necessary and a logical part of the Americanization program."[7]

Many Americans, not just members of the Immigration Restriction League, shared the important broad assumption that the time had arrived to reduce the overall numbers of immigrants. Some believed that immigration restriction could improve the prospects for Americanization. Carol

Aronovici, for instance, sensed that, from a quantitative standpoint, restriction held the "possibility for a quick and effective adjustment to the American order of society which would give the immigrant the best opportunity for self-development and for intelligent participation and service in the building up of an American civilization." On the other hand, those with the greatest amount of influence on the matter disdained Americanization and demanded immigration restriction on racial grounds. In a 1918 form letter, Prescott F. Hall of the Immigration Restriction League noted the "very poor quality" of the impending flood of postwar immigration from Europe. At the same time, he predicted that the literacy test provision of the 1917 Immigration Act would become less effective "as primary education spreads in the more backward countries of Europe and Asia." Hall feared that more undesirable aliens would soon possess the rudimentary literacy skills required to enter the country. Given that situation, the immigration laws demanded further revision "in order to protect returning war workers from injurious competition and to promote our racial homogeneity in a way that no amount of 'Americanization' can do in a short time." Since Americanizers simply could not hope to pull off a miracle of wholesale assimilation of "unlike" types, numerical quotas "based on racial capacity for assimilation" promised to safeguard America's racial character.[8]

Intolerance, superpatriotism, and concerns for the national bloodstream do not explain completely the failure of Americanization as a national crusade. There were practical concerns as well and, as Aronovici admitted, Americanization generally went on without anybody's help. Despite the Americanizers' best efforts, Edward George Hartmann concluded in his 1948 study, "the number of immigrants who became Americanized along the formal lines advocated by the Americanization groups must have been small, indeed, when compared with the great bulk of their fellows who never saw the inside of an American schoolroom or settlement house." Gradual assimilation remained the norm, while immigrant education generally was absorbed into adult education programs. Many Americanizers were forced to admit, as one did, "that the process of Americanization has been going on automatically rather than consciously." As restriction won the day, Americanizers, ever faithful to their belief in professionalism, regrouped and began the task of "Americanizing all Americans" through the public schools.[9]

Americanization failed, too, because the desired centralization of education for citizenship never materialized. In his comprehensive study of immigrant education, Frank V. Thompson, superintendent of public schools in Boston, bemoaned the "present [1920] union of feeble public agencies and heterogeneous private enterprises" that compelled community forces interested in Americanization to confront "a situation disconcertingly confusing."

Americanization class in Rock Springs, Wyoming, ca. 1922. *Biennial Report of the State Department of Education of Wyoming, 1921–1922*, 56. Wyoming State Archives.

Sarka B. Hrbkova, former member of the Nebraska State Council of Defense and chairman of its Woman's Council, likened the confusing array of Americanizing forces to the "57 varieties" of Heinz ketchup. "To certain of them," Hrbkova explained, "it means merely the naturalization and attainment of citizenship by the foreigner. To others, it means the acceptance of a certain veneer or brand of religion along with the 'dose.' Some have a broad conception inclusive of every virtue under the sun." To quash labor activism, industrialists, often in league with "quasi-foreign or so-called inter-racial organizations," used Americanization as a weapon in their "fight on radicalism and bolshevism."[10]

Even the relatively self-contained federal effort was unable to offer a unified front. The Bureau of Naturalization's "standards are as various almost as the temperaments of the 62 examiners," Thompson observed, "certainly as the temperaments of the 11 chief examiners it employs." Thus, "no uniformity of view" applied to "our 2,265 naturalizing courts." For Paul Lee Ellerbe, the chief naturalization examiner in Denver during the war, the problems that plagued naturalization went well beyond individual temperaments and viewpoints. In 1922, Ellerbe, then living in New York City, published a set of articles describing the frustrations encountered in an increasingly mechanical and bureaucratic system. He discussed the terror even well-prepared citizenship applicants faced when put to the test in open court. "To be naturalized now you must show that you know enough to cast an intelligent vote," Ellerbe wrote. "It is pretty hard to do if you are very poor, badly dressed, speak English that makes everybody smile, and have never been in court." For Western homesteaders such as those Ellerbe had observed in eastern Colorado several years before, acquiring final title to their few hundred acres was "directly dependent upon the correctness of [their] answers to questions asked . . . during the terrifyingly few minutes [they] sit there before the judge." A humane and flexible judge could make all the difference in doing justice for an intelligent yet frightened applicant.[11]

Ellerbe also maintained that the extensive red tape involved in becoming naturalized—filing the declaration of intention and petition for naturalization, a thorough examination by a naturalization examiner, and, finally, the hearing before a judge—discouraged thousands of foreigners from following through on their desire to become citizens. Thousands more jumped through most or all of the bureaucratic hoops only to be denied at the end on technicalities discernible at the beginning. "There is no sense in feeding him through the mill of the law," Ellerbe argued, "just to tell him at the end that his first paper is invalid, that he is already a citizen, that he hasn't lived here long enough, that he has come to the wrong court, that the clerk forgot to get a certificate of arrival for him, that his first paper is not two years old, or that he is not a white man." Because naturalization statutes granted the right of naturalization only to "white" persons and Africans, twenty applicants during the 1921 fiscal year had had their petitions for naturalization denied when the courts involved held them to be "non-white." "If there's any doubt about you," commented Ellerbe, "you have to go through the mill to find out what you are." The statutory minutiae that had become woven into the naturalization system, Ellerbe complained, prevented too many able and willing foreigners from achieving their desire to become citizens. "Behind each paragraph of each subdivision of each section of each law and regulation," he wrote, "there are people, honest, intelligent, law-abiding, desirable people coming a cropper one after another at the hurdles. People I used to help annoy and retard for no good purpose whatever except loyalty to my oath of office."[12]

The mechanistic flaws of the federal naturalization system reflected, in part, the weakness of the educational programs that supposedly prepared applicants to survive their ordeal in court. Many Americanizers, Mary Gibson of the California Commission of Immigration and Housing among them, sadly noted the movement's overall failure to coalesce:

> Instead of approaching this delicate task of human adjustment with humility and studying the material with which we are to work, we presume to make plans without reference to the needs or aspirations of

foreigners of any sort, and then proceed like Procrustus of legend, to fit each individual to it by all the old methods of stretching and sawing off. Churches, schools, clubs and the general public all feel ordained to teach and to win love and loyalty to America. Each fashions its Procrustean belt, and in all love and loyalty proceed to teach it knows not what.

Gibson's comments concerning the movement's lack of coherence also touched on what emerged as a key flaw in the Americanization crusade. Try as many did to warn against ignoring the immigrants' perspectives on their assimilation, Americanizers in the main presumed they could charge ahead without studying the "needs or aspirations" of their students. Too often, therefore, Americanizers' lessons fell wide of the mark in addressing real lives lived by real people. "After visiting English classrooms all over America," Ethel Richardson, California's head of immigrant education, lamented, "I find that the old discarded system still prevails in most instances—a little effort at desultory conversation, and then the book." Only on rare occasion did "the book" pertain to the lives and interests of adult immigrant pupils. "The real purpose of the school is forgotten—the establishment of modes of communication between the foreign adult and his American life. The dictatorship of the teacher prevents that one activity which would contribute to the accomplishment of this real purpose—namely, practice in the art of speaking the language." Weary workers had understandable problems staying awake, much less finding relevance, when subjected to reading or copying such puerile twaddle as "I am a yellow bird. I can sing. I can fly. I can sing to you." Moreover, poorly prepared and incompetent teachers frequently undermined the most committed citizenship education programs. "The trouble is that the teaching does not follow any well matured plan and is not skillfully done," one analyst summarized. Sarka Hrbkova was more blunt: "Not only are these hundreds of Americanizers to a great degree guiltless of any knowledge of immigrant backgrounds but many do not even have a broad American knowledge of United States conditions into which they blithely undertake to fit the foreigner."[13]

Skillful teaching of adult immigrants required extensive training, and "Americanizing the Americanizers" in university courses represented one aspect of a belated attempt to institutionalize adult immigrant education as a profession. Yet, despite some initial enthusiasm immediately following the war, most Western states did little to systematize instruction in Americanization methodologies or provide adequate appropriations for teaching both immigrants and potential instructors. The states, in part impelled by the postwar hysteria, had passed legislation to take up the slack in federal support. "It is not too optimistic," an overly optimistic Americanizer claimed in

1920, "to predict that within a decade suitable legislation and adequate funds will be provided in all the states, and that states and communities will then co-operate in furnishing training for citizenship, each sharing equally in the responsibility, each bearing an equal portion of the expense, and each taking equal pride in the result—an intelligent, patriotic citizenry." State efforts to maintain the Americanizing momentum fell short, however, in the face of fading federal aid, the disappearance of supportive private groups, immigration restriction, postwar economic recession, and growing indifference. A Bureau of Education bulletin showed, as of 1923, that only eight states had anything resembling Americanization programs in place and these, for the most part, were poorly funded, which only served to strain local communities' abilities to actively encourage immigrant education. In many cases, state constitutions allowed mandatory free instruction only for pupils between six and twenty-one years of age, thereby inhibiting state support for adult night schools. In many rural areas, those interested in teaching English and citizenship to foreigners had to do so for free. "I am sorry to learn that the appropriations have been cut," a Danish-born teacher in Garfield County, Montana, wrote to his superintendent, "for I am afraid that there are few who will take the trouble to try to teach foreigners without any compensation whatsoever."[14]

On a deeper level, Americanization failed because of its internal duality. Though fearful of the social implosion that heavy immigration apparently presaged, the majority of Americanizers, it seems, never lost confidence in education as the one best method to salvage American homogeneity. Many Americanization teachers patronized their adult students and force-fed lessons on subjects that constituted mysteries to many native-born citizens and had little relevance to immigrants' lives. Therefore, attendance plummeted as classes wore on in many parts of the country. At the same time, others approached their task lacking a complex understanding of the diversity not only within an urbanizing, industrializing modern state, but also within immigrant groups themselves. For their part, many adult immigrants, whether they attended English and citizenship classes or not, had their doubts about the Americanizers from the public schools, universities, and federal bureaucracies. In Utah, for example, a 1924 state report acknowledged the failure of the compulsory Americanization law: "It creates an attitude of mind not conducive to learning. Its enforcement to the letter is expensive and uninviting to the communities with large numbers of the foreign population." In his 1933 University of Utah master's thesis, former state Americanization director Arch M. Thurman noted that only 1,628 of 22,000 aliens in the state registered for classes in 1921–1922. Utah's Americanization education program was suspended shortly afterward.[15]

The momentum of Americanization in the West petered out with the inauguration of the era of restriction and the onset of economic depression after 1929. Where funding and some measure of community support could be generated and sustained, education for citizenship persisted in viable forms. California's Americanization and home teaching programs survived postwar retrenchment efforts on the part of conservative administrations and actually expanded in the late 1920s. Elsewhere, as official state and national backing for adult immigrant education waned, settlement houses, private organizations, and public school systems resumed their earlier predominant role. In a climate grown more conducive to immigration restriction, some nonetheless succeeded at advancing liberal Americanization schemes. Friendly House in Phoenix, founded by the Phoenix Americanization Committee in 1921, operated along the lines of a settlement house in terms of its location (the city's predominantly Mexican south side) and pluralistic approach to assimilation. A social worker and former teacher named Carrie Green taught classes, first at an elementary school in south Phoenix and, beginning in 1922, at the actual Friendly House. Especially important for the ethnic Mexican community, Friendly House provided English and citizenship classes in addition to training and placement of females in domestic work. A pluralist in practice, Green allowed ample opportunity for the celebration of Mexican culture as a teacher and later as the full-time director of Friendly House before retiring in 1931.[16]

The scope of California's programs and the pluralist approach at Friendly House deserve notice because they were exceptional. Burdened by problems with "recruitment and retention," the lack of centralization, the arbitrary legalisms of the naturalization process, the dearth of effective instructors, lack of money, and the divergence between many educators' objectives and the goals of immigrants, the Americanization movement sputtered. While state departments of education had assumed responsibility for adult immigrant education throughout the Western states, outside of California few displayed sustained devotion to the work in terms of personnel and resources. In Wyoming, advocates of Americanization lobbied for several years before legislators agreed to authorize state support. James R. Coxen, the state director for vocational education who had helped organize a number of classes in coal mining areas of southwestern Wyoming, argued that the foreign-born were "very anxious to become citizens but the State provided no way in which they may secure the information which is necessary to secure their citizenship papers." As local governments should not be expected to foot the entire bill for providing citizenship training, it behooved the state government to assist. At last, a 1921 law appropriated $8,000 in the biennial budget to the state Board of Education for the purposes of Americanization education.[17]

The Wyoming Americanization Act of 1921 authorized the board to pay a portion of the salaries for evening school teachers "of English, American history, civics or other subjects which will 'promote better American Citizenship.'" The board decided in 1921 to refund two-thirds of the salaries for teachers employed by school districts that had agreed to organize evening schools and authorized Coxen "to establish and operate such classes where needed if the school district refused to sponsor the work." Despite increasing demand and the organization of new classes, the 1923 legislature halved the biennial appropriation (from $8,000 to $4,000), forcing the Board of Education to decrease the subsidy for teachers. By April 1924, on the eve of the enactment of immigration restriction, more than nine hundred students were registered in fifty-nine Americanization classes, and in 1925 the legislature increased the appropriation slightly (to $5,000). From that point on, though, the fortunes of state-subsidized Americanization in Wyoming ebbed. By 1930, with only about three hundred students enrolled in Americanization classes, the state director for vocational education noted that the program was "on a noticeable decline . . . due principally to the Federal regulation of immigration and the thoroughness of the past programs." He recommended a decrease (from $5,000 to $4,000) for the next biennium "because the Americanization problem in Wyoming is on the decline." In 1931, the director reported that the "group [of Americanization students] is becoming very small and classes are obtained with much more effort."[18]

A further indication of the declining state of adult immigrant education in the Rocky Mountain area was reflected in a study conducted in Greeley, Colorado, in the early 1930s. Mary Rebecca Darling, a master's student at the Colorado State Teachers' College, found that illiteracy among adult aliens remained a serious problem and that educational and cultural opportunities for the foreign-born were lacking. "Because of the separation which results from labor divisions and because of the lack of educational opportunities," she wrote, "many of these adults are untouched by the general factors which make for Americanization." Naturalization, Darling concluded, was "almost invariably left to the initiative of the foreigner." Like many an Americanizer fifteen years before, she recommended that careful investigations be conducted in Greeley's "Spanish colony," that "leaders among the Spanish people themselves" be trained, that "the need and desire for adult education especially among our foreign-born and Spanish-Americans" be determined, and that, if justified by the facts, a program be implemented.

Finally, Darling advocated the transformation of the Fourth of July into International Day, "with special recognition of other nations in the form of music, addresses, pageants, or other appropriate exercises given by those who represent those nations" and a "formal and distinctive presentation of citizenship papers by the proper officials to all persons who have acquired this honor during the year just closed." Since Greeley's Americanization school for adults, organized by local women's club members in 1921, had just closed due to budget cuts, Darling's grandiose plans for International Day represented perhaps wishful thinking in the midst of the Great Depression. Still, her recommendations also show how, in the afterglow of the Americanization movement, educators living in proximity to the West's immigrant communities continued to fret over the social impact of unassimilated foreigners.[19]

Race and Citizenship: The Immigration Act of 1924

Grace Raymond Hebard, besides teaching the precepts of Americanization to University of Wyoming students well into the 1930s, continued to find time to preach about the benefits of educating immigrants and extol Americanization and naturalization. Yet, as the United States worked its way toward restricting immigration in the early 1920s, Hebard also made her views concerning certain groups known in Wyoming and nationally. At a Wyoming Federation of Women's Clubs convention at Casper in 1920, she warned clubwomen of an "expanding foreign population, which consists largely of Italians, Slovaks, Czecks [sic], Rumanians, Poles and Russians" lured to the United States because of postwar conditions in Europe and high wages in America. Hebard again expressed her underlying doubts about these immigrants' willingness to throw off their "restless spirit" and "become American citizens." If unwilling to become American citizens, display interest in democracy, and learn English, constitutional ideals, and American history, then these aliens should be considered for deportation, Hebard maintained. With an oversupply of labor and the threat of radicalism posed by jobless and restless men, she suggested "a crisis" had arrived "that will warrant the cry of 'halt' and the consideration of America for Americans." Hebard also reiterated that Americanization and naturalization were not identical, and patriotic citizens needed to redouble their efforts. If the nation would awaken and "devote herself to the work of Americanization," she exhorted, foreign neighborhoods, newspapers, churches, and schools could be abolished, hyphenation banished, and a "United America" restored.

In an issue of the *Woman Citizen* in 1921, Hebard maintained that "our own house needs readjustment just now" and commended the recently passed federal immigration law, which limited the number of new immigrants from each nationality to 3 percent of those resident in the United States in 1910. That provision favored immigration from northern and western Europe and greatly reduced the numbers coming from southern and eastern Europe. "Homogeneity," Hebard asserted, "can only be maintained by admitting in greatest numbers those who are acceptable for assimilation with our American people. . . . The new law aims to restrict the tide from countries which would give us a population difficult of assimilation and give preference to countries whose emigrants are eager to become Americans, with whom we would intermarry." Perhaps, as examples of those eager to become Americans, Dr. Hebard had in mind the "German, Irishman, Englishman" whom she transformed into Americans several years before. She also gave "Americanization" talks as the 1924 Immigration Act, which ultimately restricted European immigration on the basis of the 1890 census, further reducing the quota for southern and eastern Europeans, approached passage.[20]

Hebard's doubts about unrestricted immigration were echoed by other Westerners, especially during the uncertain and turbulent years following World War I. In a speech given at the annual meeting of the National Education Association in Salt Lake City in July 1920, University of Nevada president Walter E. Clark, who had been a member of the Committee on Americanization of the Nevada State Council of Defense, pointed to "the mere volume of immigrant inflow in recent years" as a clear peril to the nation. Clark concentrated his remarks on southern and eastern Europeans, whom he claimed possessed "an alienness which checks our democratic progress at every step." Halting the flow of "incoming alien laborers," he argued, "will not solve any of our greater American democratic problems, but it will greatly simplify the solution of every one of these problems." Wisdom dictated necessity; the time had arrived "to close the door against further alien incomers."[21]

The immigration from southern and eastern Europe that so concerned Hebard and Clark was indeed subjected to restriction based, in 1917, on literacy requirements and, beginning in 1921, quotas. Henry Cabot Lodge of Massachusetts, a leading figure in the Immigration Restriction League, first introduced a literacy test bill in the Senate in 1895. It passed both houses in 1897, but Grover Cleveland, in one of his final acts as president, vetoed the legislation. For a number of years thereafter, the literacy test occasionally dominated congressional deliberations on immigration, regaining momentum once the U.S. Immigration Commission, in its 1911 report, recommended it as the best means of restriction. After vetoes by William Howard Taft in 1913 and Woodrow Wilson in 1915, the literacy test finally became law with a congressional override of a second Wilson veto in 1917.

In 1921 Congress enacted and President Harding signed a temporary law limiting annual immigration to about 357,000 people. Each European nation was entitled to send 3 percent of the number of its nationals who had been residents of the United States in the base year of 1910. In 1924, an amended version of the 1921 legislation reduced the number of immigrants from outside the Americas to 150,000, the quota to 2 percent, and changed the base year to 1890. Because most southern and eastern Europeans had begun to emigrate to the United States only after 1890, the quotas of such poor countries as Poland and Italy were very low. By contrast, 70 percent of the quotas applied to the comparatively prosperous countries of northern and western Europe, the nations of the "old" immigrants. Under a provision of the 1924 act, the 1890 base year for quotas was to be changed in 1927 to a national origins system based on the composition of the entire white American population in 1920. After two years of debate, the national origins plan went into effect in 1929. The National Origins Act, as the immigration law of 1924 became known, represented a complete about-face in American immigration policy, rejecting the idea of free immigration.[22]

Western congressmen and senators took leading roles in advancing immigration restriction. Albert Johnson, a representative from Washington State, chaired the House Committee on Immigration and Naturalization and led congressional support for the 1924 law. Johnson, who was also president of the Eugenics Research Association, argued for restriction on racial grounds. Claiming that the temporary quota law of 1921 had contributed to economic recovery, he pressed skeptical members of the U.S. Chamber of Commerce to support restriction on a permanent basis. "Our fibre is being saved. We are cleaning house," he insisted. In the foreword to a study on immigration restriction, Johnson held that the "capacity to maintain our cherished institutions stands diluted by a stream of alien blood, with all its inherited misconceptions respecting the relationships of the governing power to the governed." To persist in the "indiscriminate acceptance of all races" would destroy forever the republic's viability. In other words, careful selection among those desiring to enter the United States was vital to the survival of self-government and liberty in America. Johnson's colleagues in the West agreed and stood solidly behind restriction. The votes on the Immigration Act of 1924 displayed almost unanimous support for the legislation by members from states west of the Mississippi River. Of the seventy-one votes against the measure in the House of Representatives, one came from a Missourian and one from a Nebraskan. All other Western congressmen present for the vote supported restriction. In the Senate, a mere six members voted against the bill, with William H. King of Utah the sole Westerner. The other twenty-six trans-Mississippi senators present for the vote backed reducing immigration from southern and eastern Europe.[23]

"The United States is our land," Albert Johnson declared in defense of immigration restriction. "If it was not the land of our fathers, at least it may be, and it should be, the land of our children. We intend to maintain it so." For Johnson and other Westerners who opposed unrestricted immigration of southern and eastern Europeans, the presumed end of the frontier era signaled the erosion of the nation's assimilative capacity. Once, the frontier had lured hardy Anglo-Americans and able immigrants from the the north and west of Europe to carry civilization into the wilderness. Frederick Jackson Turner's frontier thesis had pivoted on the idea that the westward movement of immigrants had transformed northern Europeans into Americans. The mixture of northern European peoples into a composite American "race" had coincided with the westward movement and expedited the rapid transformation of the West from an undeveloped wasteland inhabited by listless natives and mixed-race Mexicans into an orderly and stable region of thriving communities and bustling cities. To allow unrestricted entry to the masses from the most backward, impoverished, and undemocratic corners of Europe promised nothing short of disaster. Faced with the daunting task of trying to assimilate the thousands of "new" immigrants already present in the West, while simultaneously lacking the formative and ameliorative effects of the frontier, Westerners had no intention of permitting alien newcomers to undo the stability crafted so painstakingly by pioneer ancestors.[24]

If aliens from southern and eastern Europe threatened the West's fragile social order, those from across the Pacific presented an even greater menace. As anti-Asian speakers and writers maintained, national homogeneity rested on racial purity and only certain immigrant groups could effectively assimilate. California's Senator John F. Miller, in guiding his exclusion bill through Congress in 1882, had set forth the typical assumption (prior to the advent of increased immigration from southern and eastern Europe) in contrasting Asian and European immigration. "European immigrants are men of the like mental and physical characteristics of the American laborer," Miller assured his colleagues. "They assimilate with American society and become a part of the American people." Ten years later, during Senate debate on the 1892 exclusion act, Colorado's Henry Teller addressed the assimilability issue, holding that Americans could assimilate "with the most objectionable classes that come here from Europe," forming in the long run "a harmonious people" with "no distinction between the children of the immigrant of to-day and the children of the immigrant of 200 years ago." As for the Chinese, "we never shall assimilate with them, because even if we would they will not."[25]

When the disruptions of the world war and its aftermath helped make Americanization a national obsession, Westerners adhered to themes of danger regarding Japanese immigrants. Senator James D. Phelan, upon submitting an amendment to the eventual Immigration Act of 1917 to bar Japanese picture brides, argued that the brown and black races did not amalgamate, even when thrown into the American "melting pot." Damning Japanese immigrants with fulsome praise, Phelan remarked, "They are so industrious, so thrifty, so, if you please, superior in industry and thrift to our own people, that they beat them at their own game." Industry and thrift, laudable qualities that they were, did not translate into assimilability. Instead, Japanese success meant, to Phelan and so many other concerned Anglo-Americans in the West, the prospect of abandoning the West Coast to them. When queried as to whether as citizens, Japanese-American offspring would not be less influenced by Japanese customs and loyalties, Phelan insisted that Japanese Americans, though born in the United States, could not be transformed into real Americans.

Several years later, in remarks to state legislators in Oregon, Governor Ben W. Olcott attached the threat of Japanese immigration to the state's white pioneer identity. "Here in Oregon the pioneer blood flows more purely and in a more nearly undiluted stream than in any other state of the union," the governor asserted. "As a precious heritage, passed down to us from those heroic fathers who braved the perils and trials and tribulations of pioneer days, it should be preserved unsullied, as they gave it to us." Grace Raymond Hebard, the ardent Americanizer from Wyoming, characterized the "hydra-headed question of Japanese immigration" as "a greater problem" than those relating to "guarding our eastern coast" from substandard Europeans.[26]

As a process, assimilation culminated in citizenship, arguably the central defining characteristic of an American, native-born or naturalized, according to those engaged in the immigration debates of the late nineteenth and early twentieth centuries. In relation to Asian immigrants, Senator Samuel B. Maxie of Texas offered colleagues a civics lesson during the 1882 exclusion debate: "The Constitution of the United States, in my judgment, never contemplated the bringing of all people of all colors, climes, races, and conditions into this country and making of them citizens." At the time, federal law bestowed the right of naturalization on any "white" alien and natives of Africa. For the Chinese, the question was whether they were "Caucasian" or "Mongolian," confusion over which led to the naturalization of a number of Chinese immigrants in the late nineteenth century and beyond. The maintenance of race purity reflected a clear meaning of the Constitution, Maxie concluded, and "should a dominating element as to numbers from that exhaustless human hive of China become citizens this country is destroyed." If a danger to America's racial purity and incapable of assimilation, it followed that Asian immigrants, as one veteran observer of the Chinese in California put it in 1884, were "not qualified for citizenship as a race."[27]

The successes of the anti-Japanese movement, alien land legislation in particular, likewise depended on interpretations of naturalization statutes that denied citizenship to the immigrant generation, or issei. Senator Phelan also sought a means by which to "deny citizenship to the children of those who themselves are ineligible to citizenship," an endeavor that, while unsuccessful, pleased the most radical elements of the anti-Japanese movement. Confusion about the racial identity of the Japanese had resulted in an unknown number of Japanese immigrants being naturalized by 1911, when the Bureau of Immigration and Naturalization ordered clerks of the courts to cease accepting declarations of intention and petitions for naturalization other than from aliens who were white or of African nativity or descent. Despite the uncertainty, Japanese immigrants still enrolled in Americanization classes, at the very least to improve their skills in the English language, if not to prepare for citizenship.[28]

The uncertainty ended in 1922, when the U.S. Supreme Court, in the case of *Ozawa v. United States,* dealt a death blow to Japanese immigrants' hopes to redefine naturalization. The high court upheld the original district court determination that Takao Ozawa, a Japanese-born resident of Hawaii, was "ineligible to citizenship" because he "was not a free white person."[29] Federal law, once clarified, only codified what the guardians of the racial frontier believed to be immutable truth from long experience with Asian immigrants. The exclusion of Japanese immigrants made possible by the 1924 National Origins Act, according to Sacramento newspaper publisher V. S. McClatchy, had nothing to do with ill will, politics, racial prejudice, or discrimination. Rather, it was part of a new national policy to restrict immigration of the unassimilable. Therefore, McClatchy reasoned, "It is certainly logical to exclude those who under our own laws may not become citizens and are therefore hopelessly unassimilable."[30]

McClatchy, one of the few Californians capable of outdemagoguing James D. Phelan on the Japanese issue, insisted as well that regardless of how many generations were born on American soil, Japanese Americans would always be Japanese subjects. The problem of dual citizenship for American-born children of immigrants, or nisei, which rested on Japanese law stipulating that any children of Japanese males, regardless of the father's residence, were Japanese citizens, offered the anti-Japanese movement additional fodder for agitation. The Japanese parliament, acquiescing to issei leaders' urgings, amended the law in 1916 to allow parents to renounce the Japanese citizenship of children fourteen years old and younger; youngsters aged fifteen and sixteen could do the same on their own, but those males seventeen and older were required to complete mandatory military service before renunciation, an expectation that only stoked the fires of anti-Japanese hysteria. Finally, in 1924, Japan abolished Japanese citizenship for nisei altogether. To McClatchy and other anti-Japanese spokespeople, Japan's amended expatriation laws were meaningless since Japanese in America, issei and nisei alike, possessed no desire to assimilate anyway. "Where the parents are alien born," Mc-Clatchy asserted, "they will probably elect to have the children retain the rights of citizenship in both countries." He claimed as well that the Japanese, whether immigrant or American-born, possessed an ineradicable sense of racial superiority. Therefore, McClatchy insisted that any apparent desire on the part of Japanese nationals or even nisei to prove their worth for American citizenship occurred only "that they may better serve Japan and the Mikado."[31]

Congratulating himself and fellow exclusionists upon passage of the Immigration Act of 1924, Senator Hiram W. Johnson proudly affirmed, "California's cherished policy is now the nation's maturely determined policy."[32] The homogeneous ideal in the West, articulated by powerful interests for many decades as Chinese immigrants were replaced by Japanese immigrants and as one legislative triumph for restriction or exclusion followed upon another, was now enshrined as a key element in the presumed final triumph for American homogeneity. Survival of the American republic called for the safeguarding of the nation's racial purity, which could only be maintained by allowing immigration from countries that could assimilate with "real" Americans while restricting or preventing that of unassimilable peoples. It was impossible, moreover, to transform Asian immigrants into American citizens, an assumption conveniently codified by federal naturalization statutes and Supreme Court decisions. As for the immigrants' American-born offspring, they were "citizens" in name only, tarnished by their unassimilable racial inheritance and, in the case of the nisei, dual citizenship and therefore ineradicable dual loyalties. The national state, of which the West was such an important component, could only endure, according to racial frontier rhetoric, as a racially homogeneous entity. Citizenship, with the unfortunate but historically necessary exception of Africans and African Americans, belonged only to those deemed racially deserving.

The Immigration Act of 1924, which drastically reduced entry into the United States for southern and eastern Europeans and effectively excluded all immigrants from Asia, exempted the western hemisphere from its quota provisions. Throughout the 1920s, pressure exerted by Southwestern growers and industrialists acted as a powerful economic counterweight to racialist arguments for the restriction of immigration from Mexico and Latin America. In addition, Protestant missionaries encouraged immigration from Mexico as a morally necessary means to rescue more souls from the oppressive dogmas and superstitions of Catholicism, while the Catholic Church saw Mexican immigrants as necessary to its expansion in the West. Republican foreign policy, which favored improved relations with Mexico in the interest of investment and trade, further strengthened the cause of unrestricted immigration during the 1920s.[33]

Nonetheless, Western nativists continued to express deep misgivings about the effects of unchecked immigration from the south and to lobby for restriction. "The Mexican peon is racially as alien as the Chinese coolie," Chester H. Rowell maintained, "and is not so good a workman." Even less assimilable than the dregs of southern and eastern Europe, Mexican peasants, while eagerly sought by American farmers and railroads, would become a permanent, multigenerational caste of degraded labor. Furthermore, since the peon was an Indian, Rowell feared that "our Anglo-Puritan tradition" stood to gain nothing by incorporating such impoverished and defeated specimens. Aghast that national origins quotas did not apply to Mexico, C. M. Goethe, president of the Immigration Study Commission, a privately financed nativist organization in Sacramento, alerted Americans to the dire impact of allowing "the peon . . . to come and to breed among us." The differential birth rates between Mexican laborers, who, according to Goethe, averaged nine or ten children per family, and white American citizens would swamp the Southwest with low-grade "racial hybrids." "He is of a colored race—either wholly or partially Amerind. His standards are those of a Chinese coolie. He can take a blanket, a frying pan, and a few beans and exist indefinitely," Goethe asserted. The Mexican's debased morality, superstition, and savage instinct for revenge, furthermore, threatened the foundations of American society.[34]

Prior to the onset of the Great Depression and the repatriation campaigns of the early 1930s, opponents of Mexican immigration had to endure a steady influx of migrants into California, the Southwest, the southern Great Plains, and even the industrial cities of the Upper Midwest. As more Mexican immigrants became permanent residents in the 1920s and 1930s, the problem of assimilation took on greater significance. "A migrant labor class is inimical to stable social order," wrote Emory Bogardus in 1934. "Migratoriness creates unrest, makes home life difficult, hinders the proper education of children, and arrests the growth of constructive citizenship." Despite the best efforts of Americanizers and others concerned with assimilation, few immigrants from Mexico became American citizens between 1900 and 1930. An 1897 federal court ruling, *In re Rodriguez,* had affirmed the right to naturalization for Mexican nationals under the original terms of the 1848 treaty but prompted little motivation on the part of immigrants to seek American citizenship. "The immigrants, even if they make their home in this country, seldom become naturalized," observed Victor S. Clark in his 1908 report for the Department of Commerce and Labor. The desire to someday return to Mexico certainly had a profound effect on many immigrants' reluctance or refusal to become

American citizens. Americans' attitudes toward ethnic Mexicans cast further doubt on the value of naturalization. Manuel Gamio, in acknowledging the general tendency to avoid assimilation and acculturation, noted racial prejudice and cultural and geographical differences as key elements in Mexican immigrants' lives in the United States. Drawn north by economic opportunity or the chance to escape the turmoil of revolution, Mexican immigrants found themselves stuck in an ambivalent borderland of identity that even the most determined Americanizers would find a frustrating impediment to achieving homogeneity in the West.[35]

Tensions between immigrant Mexicans and Mexican Americans on American citizenship further complicated the question of assimilation. The immigrants often regarded the American-born, as well as immigrants who assimilated, as renegades, while Mexican Americans considered the immigrants as inferior (and "darker"). Manuel Gamio documented a number of songs that illustrated the conflicts within Mexican immigrant and ethnic communities. One song, "The Renegade," underscored the contempt that Mexican nationals held for immigrants who adopted the trappings of American culture and, in effect, betrayed their Mexican heritage:

> You go along showing off
> In a big automobile.
> You call me a pauper
> And dead with hunger,
> And what you don't remember is
> That on my farm
> You went around almost naked
> And without sandals.
> That happens to many
> That I know here
> When they learn a little American
> And dress up like dudes,
> And go to the dance.
> But he who denies his race
> Is the most miserable creature.
> There is nothing in the world
> So vile as he,
> The mean figure of the renegade.

For their part, Mexican Americans often perceived immigrants as stubbornly resistant to assimilation and obsessed with Mexican patriotism. A "Spanish American" public school teacher quoted in Paul Taylor's 1930 report on Colorado commented upon the immigrants' unyielding patriotic devotion to Mexico: "The Mexicans think the Spanish Americans should be patriotic for Mexico because of blood and history. They say that the Spanish Americans were sold in 1848, but the Spanish Americans feel themselves to be American and one hundred years ahead of the Old Mexico Mexicans." Moreover, many Mexican Americans feared the economic effects of increased immigration as well as the deleterious impact of Mexican immigrants on their own problematic relationship with Anglo America. Although empathy and mutual assistance often characterized relations within the ethnic Mexican communities, the differences in attitudes about citizenship reflected persistent tensions and ambivalence concerning assimilation and ethnic identity. Many immigrants and Mexican Americans favored maintenance of culture and ethnic identity as mechanisms to cope with racism and growing restrictionist sentiment, while others concluded that assimilation offered a more effective, if uncertain, path toward eventual acceptance as Americans.[36]

In 1920, after a tour of the borderlands sponsored by an organization called the International Reform Bureau, Colonel L. M. Maus reported on the overall lack of progress in assimilating "Spanish-Americans." Disdained and "ostracized, as it were, by their American neighbors," Maus noted, "they have little opportunity to learn our language or to become useful American citizens." An interview of an Americanization teacher in Santa Ana, California, in 1928 revealed Mexican immigrants' perception of their racial subordination. The teacher reported that Mexican women asked about or even purchased bleaching cream in the belief that they could make their children lighter. Upon reassuring a class that there was little difference between English and Spanish, a student "put her fingers on her cheek and said, 'but our skin is different.'" The students in this instance understood a hard truth that a number of Americanization advocates in the West apparently sought to obscure. Lessons in English, American history, and civics, along with tutoring in the domestic arts or whatever else fit one's definition of Americanism, did not alter the calculus of racial privilege and power in the New West. To nonwhite immigrants in particular, whether naturalized, unnaturalized, or "ineligible to citizenship," the ideals of democracy and equality preached by Americanizers rang hollow. Making citizens of "undesirable" aliens did not prevent immigration restriction, alter court decisions that denied the right of naturalization to Asians, or reorder economic regimes that exploited Mexican labor.[37]

Consciously or not, Americanizers in the dynamic regions of the West played an important role in pushing racialized readings of citizenship and assimilation, especially with the treatment of those nonwhites deemed most "foreign." Defined as racially different, separate, or inferior in relation to

"real" Americans or assimilable immigrants, Asians and Mexicans in particular had little to gain from an "education for citizenship." In creating a
Western identity, Americanization intersected with the efforts to restrict, exclude, and deport undesirable and unassimilable foreigners. Given who they
were and what they were attempting to accomplish, even the most cosmopolitan assimilationists contributed to the forging of a fundamentally
"white" national and regional identity.

Conclusion

Like engineers harnessing a wild river's flow behind an elaborate system of
dams, the Americanization movement had attempted to control the chaotic,
diverse, and mobile immigrant populations of the West. It is hardly surprising that Americanizers in the West largely failed in their endeavor, since
many immigrants considered their own agendas when deciding whether or
not to enroll in Americanization classes. Members of immigrant and ethnic
communities entering or already present in the diverse Western subregions
often felt little inclination to, in the words of Paul Lee Ellerbe, "drink of the
spirit" of citizenship as defined by Americanization educators and bureaucrats.[38] Only a fraction of all the adult foreign-born eligible to register for
English and citizenship training ever bothered to do so. Increasingly associated with conformity and intolerance, the movement collapsed in the 1920s
as federal leadership and aid faded and Congress passed immigration restriction laws.

Despite the persistent calls for centralizing the disparate menagerie of
Americanization agencies and organizations, the movement—much like the
immigrants it sought to assimilate—failed to melt into one cohesive national
operation. It failed as well because efforts to professionalize the teaching of
Americanization fell short, leaving poorly prepared and incompetent teachers in charge of many citizenship education programs. Too often failing to
make the distinction between their adult students and children, many Americanizers patronized and often embarrassed their adult immigrant pupils.
Another factor in the movement's failure involved the divergent expectations
of instructors, many of whom brought a certain evangelistic zeal and ideal-
ism to their work, and students, who generally had more practical needs in
pursuing education.

Nativists, meanwhile, who had never believed in or had given up on the
notion that "new" immigrants could or would accede to Anglo-Americanization, saw restriction and exclusion as the sole methods by which to save
American civilization from unassimilable immigrants. The Immigration Act

Citizenship class at Grant Junior High School in Denver, 1933. Denver Public Library, Western History Department.

of 1924, it is true, represented a watershed in the nation's immigration policy as well as the triumph of years of exertions by restrictionists. In a very real sense, however, immigration restriction was anticlimactic. Because Americanizers failed to show that all newcomers could be quickly melted into a composite nationality, restrictionists' arguments about the dangers associated with unassimilable immigrants became more convincing. The relative ease with which national origins quotas became the basis of immigration law suggests a certain widespread dissatisfaction with Americanizers' assimilation project. As part of the centralizing tendencies of the war years and their immediate aftermath, that project involved the federal government and several states. All tried to consolidate a plethora of Americanization endeavors into efficient and predictable assimilation bureaucracies, an impossible and futile task almost by definition. Most generally clung to an optimistic, "melting pot" conception of the nation's assimilative powers. Progressive era homogeneity thus climaxed during the Americanization campaigns—a last gasp of faith in America's melting pot prowess before the pessimists stepped in and shut the gates.

If the Americanization movement did not Americanize many immigrants in the West through its organized channels, it nonetheless helped Americanize the West, when larger processes of national integration are considered. Through the exertions of local and state councils of defense and "four-minute men," Students' Army Training Corps (SATC) activities, antiradical campaigns, and other nationalizing activities, Westerners participated in the consolidation of bureaucratic management and progressive social control during and after World War I. With its emphases on efficiency, expertise, and professionalism, Americanization represented a key component in elites' attempts to manage people, manage change, and, ultimately, manage society. Americanization had a profound effect on bureaucrats, teachers, reformers, and others who took part; for one individual, it was considered "perhaps most precious" of a lifetime of notable achievement.[39] But participation in the movement was also a lesson in how to marshal power through organization and expertise, a lesson many learned via failure, some by success. Regardless, however, Americanization in the West laid foundations for subsequent, more enduring projects in managing human resources.

In their search for order, Westerners brought distinctive approaches to Americanization. Ideas about the boundaries of citizenship, premised on Western attitudes about race, ethnicity, gender, class, nation, and knowledge, impinged on Westerners' programs of assimilation. Prerogatives of reform rubbed up against the myths of Westerners' histories and identities. While many preferred to ignore or exclude the "other" who skirted the margins of Western communities, Americanizers tried, to the extent their attitudes and agendas allowed, to incorporate the region's foreign-born into a national citizenry. From their point of view, Americanization was a democratic enterprise, freeing individuals from the constraints of alien and backward cultures and allowing them to be reborn as self-reliant and independent American citizens. With devoted teachers and officials, along with innovations such as Colorado's America First Societies, California's home teachers, and various industrial Americanization plans, the West made a genuine contribution to a national movement dominated by reformers and bureaucrats from the East.

As "a great movement to *nationalize America*,"[40] Americanization played a major part in speeding the nationalization of the West, in incorporating an isolated and complex area into the mainstream of American economic and social life. Contemporary observers noticed this nationalizing of the West. As the country mobilized for war in 1917, an Eastern journalist commented approvingly on the region's maturation. "Foremost in the influences that have changed the mental attitude of the Westerner has been his recognition of the oneness of the nation," Charles Moreau Harger wrote. Populist nonsense about abusive capitalists had given way to a sensible realization of the benefits to be derived from manufacturing and finance. "Provincialism passed away, and in its place came a fuller understanding of the nation at large." Having completed its pioneer era, a grown-up West was coming to appreciate the advantages of permanency. "The evolution of the West has been toward sanity," Harger believed, "and with this has gone an acceptance of its real relation to older sections; its more or less volatile public has settled down to the steady progress of existence."[41]

In terms of protecting the mature and modern West from the forces that continued to threaten its permanence and progress—immigrants and labor conflict foremost among them—Americanization held considerable promise. The Americanization movement appeared, for a time, capable of smoothing the rough edges by Americanizing, if not the immigrants to any appreciable degree, the West itself. In a sense, the Americanization movement sought to corral the West and its diverse population, to organize and manage a disorderly region, to divest it of its distinctiveness, and to reconcile the Western myth of rugged individualism with the demands of a planned society and activist state. In its multiple guises—element of progressive reform, key to wartime unity, component of corporate welfare or union membership, educational prerogative, or federal management—Americanization reflected the combination of continuity concerning the pioneer past and change with formation of a modern West.[42]

EPILOGUE

At the dawn of the twenty-first century, there is considerable anxiety over a fragmenting American citizenry and identity, similar to that which prompted the Americanization movement in the first decades of the twentieth century. Nativism and support for immigration restriction have reemerged in the wake of changes in the composition of immigration over the past several decades. Much of the most intense controversy has been provoked by illegal immigration from Mexico and other Latin American countries. Proposition 187, approved by California voters in 1994, barred illegal aliens from receiving welfare benefits and gaining access to the state's public education system and nonemergency medical care. A federal judge blocked enforcement of Proposition 187 on the basis of the unconstitutionality of denying educational benefits to illegal aliens. Nonetheless, the overwhelming votes in favor of the measure by white Californians and Asian Americans, along with Latinos' solid opposition, revealed the widening fissures between and among groups in the nation's most populous and diverse state. In addition, federal immigration and welfare reform laws that deny government benefits to noncitizens, the "English Only" movement, rollbacks of affirmative action, the militarization of the border with Mexico, and ongoing concerns about refugees are just a few of the pressing questions that parallel those of seventy or eighty years ago. The American West, in which these issues often predominate, remains an incredibly diverse and contentious crossroads of cultures.[1]

Immigration has a prominent place in a public discourse most often notable for the harshness of its tones, not unlike the debates regarding "new" immigrants and American identity eighty years ago and more. Present-day restrictionists argue that the immigration system has broken down; that the American economy and environment suffer from unrestricted immigration; and, like the supporters of restriction in the 1910s and 1920s, that "new" immigrants do not assimilate and mainstream American culture will be irremediably damaged by the influx of nonwhite, non-European, and growing numbers of non-Christian immigrants. Many modern restriction advocates maintain that the time has arrived for another hiatus in immigration to allow the millions already resident in the United States to become more thoroughly acculturated, if not completely assimilated. Reducing immigration is also perceived by many new restrictionists as a key step toward making English the official language of the nation and eliminating bilingual education programs in public schools. The overt racism and intolerance of the earlier era are largely absent, yet the burgeoning numbers of nonwhite immigrants since passage of the Hart-Celler Immigration Act of 1965 ended the national origins system subtly impact the current debates about immigration and assimilation.[2]

The racial connotations that attached themselves to Americanization campaigns in the early-twentieth-century West have become national in scope: Asian- and Latin-American immigrants predominate and are far more widely distributed than was the case during World War I and the 1920s. Current demands for reducing the numbers of immigrants can carry racial implications simply because the bulk of immigrants are not white. For the most part, the issue of race in restrictionist rhetoric is muted, and restriction supporters insist that they are not racists. Be that as it may, the sentiments expressed by some contemporary advocates of immigration reform or restriction differ only in degree from the thoughts of James D. Phelan or Grace Raymond Hebard. Journalist Peter Brimelow, in his *Alien Nation,* warns that the "racial and ethnic balance of America is being radically altered through public policy." For Brimelow, a naturalized citizen from England, the "mass immigration so thoughtlessly triggered in 1965" threatens to destroy Americans' sense of themselves as a cohesive nation. Instead, the United States is becoming an "alien nation" inflicting "a demographic mutation" upon itself. Brimelow and other critics of recent immigration policy foresee a future in which whites will become a minority if immigration from Africa, Asia, the Caribbean, and Latin America remains at present levels. White flight and the dramatic growth of the Hispanic population (including illegal immigrants) in California are often cited as precursors to a more general alteration in the country's fundamental character and identity. The nation's historic ethnic core, defined by Brimelow as the white immigrants from northern and western Europe who predominated in the colonial era and early nineteenth century, is being transformed into a decidedly multicultural, but dangerously balkanized, polity.[3]

In subtle ways, too, the mystique of the white pioneer past maintains a powerful hold on ideas of American identity and thoughts about immigration, certainly in the West. Chilton Williamson Jr. is a Colorado-based author and editor for *Chronicles,* which is published by the Rockford Institute, a conservative think tank. In his 1993 book, *The Immigration Mystique,* Williamson recast an idea purveyed by an earlier generation of Western chroniclers—that the genuine achievements of conquering a continent and creating a nation redounded exclusively to the credit of a certain exalted segment of western civilization. The legacies of the American experience can be imparted to immigrants from the Third World, but because they are in no way intimately associated with constructing those legacies, they can never properly experience the meaning of the American past. "Immigrants can be taught their adoptive nation's history, its literature, its customs," Williamson writes. "They cannot, however, experience its past in the way that a native of the same country, whose ancestors fought in the American Revolution, pioneered the West, or attended Princeton with Scott Fitzgerald and Edmund Wilson can experience it. Nor can they, in the degree that their countries of origin differ from the found one, appreciate the meaning of that past."[4]

For the millions of American citizens whose ancestors did not fight in the Revolution or head west in a covered wagon or attend Princeton, Williamson defines the range of the nation's significant historical experiences rather narrowly. Nor is it likely that Williamson's native-born Anglo-Americans can find branches on their family trees that recall the experience of actually building—with bare hands, pickaxs, shovels, and dynamite rather than watered stock and government loans—the Central Pacific Railroad. Chinese "aliens" did. Nor did they "experience" the dismal work of draining swamps and building levees in the Sacramento–San Joaquin river deltas, transforming them into some of the most productive agricultural regions known to history. Chinese, Japanese, East Indian, and Filipino "aliens" did. Nor did they "experience" picking beans in the broiling heat of the Imperial Valley or topping sugar beets on Colorado's dry eastern prairies. Mexican and Volga German "aliens" did. Nor did they "experience" toiling thousands of feet below ground for low wages in an Arizona copper mine. Asian, Mexican, and European "aliens" did. Nor did they "experience" being forced to kiss the American flag or get beaten up by patriotic vigilantes during World War I. Nor did they ever have to "experience" growing pressures to become Americanized, to "talk the language of America," to learn to cook and eat "American" food, to dress like an American, or to be made into citizens and cease posing a threat to somebody or other's "America." Why should membership in the DAR, a pioneer organization, or Princeton's alumni association be considered more "American" than tracing one's ancestry to a Chinese railroad laborer, a Japanese farmer, a Mexican field hand, or a Slavic miner? Williamson's odes to "real" Americans are just as much nonsense now as they were one hundred years ago. Whatever the merits or flaws in Williamson's and other restrictionists' arguments to reduce the flow of immigrants may be, their characterization of the American experience is, if not racist, ahistorical, arrogant, and elitist.

The issue of Americanization has enjoyed less prominence as part of the contemporary discussions concerning the quantity and quality of immigration than what occurred during the previous era of mass immigration. There is no Americanization "movement" today. Many of the new restrictionists operate according to the assumption, common with many of the old restrictionists, too, that cutting the numbers could hasten the assimilation of the unnaturalized foreigners now living in the United States.[5] Questions of the assimilability of large numbers of immigrants from the Third World, on the other hand, will lead some to again question the usefulness of an Americanization approach. Still, there are a few voices trying to rise above the din of the immigration reform/restriction debates and revive Americanization, to restore "its good name" and make it "a national priority," as writer John J. Miller hopes. In accounting for the country's inability to fashion a renewed commitment to assimilation, Miller and a number of others who are still optimistic about the promise of Americanization fault the presumed excesses of multiculturalism. Regardless, Americanization as a salient public question has been submerged by the controversies surrounding the more fundamental immigration issues of numbers, sources, and effects.[6]

As suggested by a 1997 report to Congress by the U.S. Commission on Immigration Reform (CIR), issues of Americanization, naturalization, and citizenship are also provoking serious reevaluations of national immigrant and immigration policies. Created by Congress in 1990, the bipartisan CIR (also referred to as the Jordan Commission in honor of its first chairperson, former Texas congresswoman Barbara Jordan, who died in 1996) acknowledged the pervasive problems of American immigration policy and reflected a growing consensus that reform was needed in the areas of "unlawful migration, legal immigration, and refugee and asylum policy." The Commission's commentaries on Americanization and naturalization, in general, hearken back to the more optimistic strains peculiar to progressive Americanizers of the World War I era. "The process of becoming an American," the report stated in its introduction, "is most simply called 'Americanization,' which must always be a two-way street." The desired end result is a "national community" that both the native-born and the immigrant help construct through commitment to a "shared civic culture." "Americanization," the commission announced, "is the process of integration by which immigrants become part of our communities and by which our communities and the nation learn from and adapt to their presence."[7]

Interestingly, in 1920, Carol Aronovici provided an idealistic definition of Americanization quite in keeping with the commission philosophy in 1997. "In Americanization," Aronovici wrote, "a peaceful merging and co-operative development of a nation can be obtained when out of depths of each people comes a desire for participation and common benefit that is born out of equality, that is devoid of fear, that looks to the future and not to the past, that considers tradition a stepping-stone and not a chain, and that looks upon the culture of the world as an achievement to be conserved and developed rather than as a menace." Seeking to rescue the very word "Americanization" from the abuses of overzealous patriots and anti-immigrant demagogues that so disenchanted Aronovici, the CIR expressed the need to resurrect Americanization as a positive force, a "covenant between immigrant and nation." Therefore, Americanization cannot be effected by force and must be understood in terms of both mutual obligations and individual rights. The commission also called upon "federal, state, and local governments to provide renewed leadership and resources to a program to promote Americanization." A comprehensive new Americanization campaign would begin by providing coordinated information and orientation for immigrants and "their receiving communities."[8]

Additionally, immigrants and the local communities in which they reside need further government support for education in English language skills and civics. Just as Americanizers lamented eighty years ago, adult immigrant education presently suffers from inadequate resources. Similarly, adult immigrant education is hampered by a dearth of teachers trained in English as a Second Language (ESL) instruction or basic adult education methods. Americanization education is further impeded by the "general quality of adult education programs," which typically "have no defined objectives, valid assessment instruments, or accurate program data." Unlike the period of Americanization enthusiasm in the early twentieth century, state departments of education, local school boards, and local businesses are now far less involved in educational programs for adult immigrants. As did leaders in the old Americanization movement, the CIR calls on businesses and corporations, religious schools and institutions, charities, foundations, community organizations, public and private schools, and colleges and universities to "contribute resources, facilities, and expertise."[9]

Finally, the commission calls for ensuring the integrity and meaning of naturalization, stating that "the naturalization process must be credible, and it must be accorded the formality and ceremony appropriate to its importance." Many of the same complaints voiced by critics of the Bureau of Naturalization decades before still apply to the modern Immigration and Naturalization Service (INS). The tests used to determine naturalization applicants' knowledge of U.S. history and civics and ability to communicate in English "do not adequately assess such understanding or abilities." The INS civics test, according to the report, emphasizes rote memorization of facts in lieu of a "substantive understanding of the basic concepts of civic participation." The district offices, as in the days of Paul Lee Ellerbe and Paul B. Phillips, utilize different methods and apply varying standards in examining applicants. "The lack of uniform standards governing whether an applicant has satisfactorily fulfilled the requirements is disturbing," the commission concludes in a statement reminiscent of conditions during the 1920s. The CIR recommends instituting standardized tests that would "evaluate a common core of information to be understood by all new citizens," including such basic principles of American government as the freedom of speech or assembly guaranteed by the First Amendment. Moreover, the INS English test "should accurately and fairly measure an immigrant's ability to speak, read, and write; the current practice of dictating English sentences for applicants to write is not an effective means of testing English proficiency."[10]

The Jordan Commission's declaration on naturalization also recalls the emphasis earlier Americanization advocates placed on lending symbolic importance to the immigrant's achievement in attaining citizenship. Indicative of the symbiotic relationship between federal, state, and local Americanization programs, ritualized ceremonies commemorating immigrants' advancement to citizenship frequently involved a federal official examining several students before appreciative audiences. Simple ceremonies conducted as part of the actual granting of naturalization in courtrooms also appealed to many as an appropriate means to lend dignity and honor to the proceedings. "It is time for us to see," remarked Anne M. Godfrey of the Bureau of Naturalization office in San Francisco in 1923, "that citizenship, the most valuable of all things, is at least as dignified and impressive a procedure as the ceremony connected with the bestowal of educational degrees." For early-twentieth-century Americanizers, these ceremonies signified the inclusive nature of America's melting pot and the existence of a shared national identity achievable through education and naturalization. Likewise, the late-twentieth-century commission proposed expediting the scheduling of swearing-in ceremonies and conducting them in a "dignified" manner. According to the commission, the "solemnity and pomp of the current judicial ceremonies should be maintained and could be enhanced by the inclusion of distinguished speakers. However, would-be citizens who have passed all requirements for naturalization should not be denied timely citizenship because of processing delays in scheduling swearing-in ceremonies."[11]

The successes and failures of the Americanization movement in the early-twentieth-century West raise questions concerning revived efforts to launch nationally organized citizenship education programs. Any new drive to foster a federally backed Americanization movement would have to address the extent to which either a centralized bureaucracy or the decentralized structure favored by the Commission on Immigration Reform can realistically cope with an endless array of unique local situations. Regional distinctiveness has perhaps lessened thanks to interstate highways, fast-food outlets, discount stores, and the Internet. Nonetheless, problems that the earlier generation of Americanizers confronted in Western regions are reflected in the continuing reliance of Western agribusiness on migratory, often undocumented labor; on the persistence of ethnic enclaves; on controversies concerning language; and on the racial undertones of renewed nativism that still questions nonwhite immigrant groups' desire and ability to become "real" citizens. In addition, corporate foundations, politicians, government agencies, and everyone involved in a new Americanization movement would be hard-pressed to restrain larger agendas that transcend simply naturalizing a few more immigrants. Finally, regardless of intentions, is assimilation a process that is even controllable? Does Americanization occur or not of its own volition and in its own time, given any individual's attitudes, experiences, hopes, fears, or objectives? Is consensus on what Americanization means any more possible now than it was then? Americanization, as more than one Americanizer conceded, occurred naturally for most immigrants without much professional assistance. It occurs yet, despite renewed calls for restriction or more forceful attempts to speed assimilation and thereby achieve the still chimerical ideal of a homogeneous and orderly society.

NOTES

Abbreviations used:

AHC	American Heritage Center, University of Wyoming, Laramie
ASA	Arizona State Archives, Phoenix
ASL	Arizona State Library, Phoenix
CSA	Colorado State Archives, Denver
CSHS	Colorado State Historical Society, Stephen H. Hart Library, Denver
CSL	California State Library, Government Publications, Sacramento
KSHS	Kansas State Historical Society, Topeka
MSHSA	Montana State Historical Society Archives, Helena
NARA	National Archives and Records Administration, Washington, D.C., and College Park, Maryland
NMSRCA	New Mexico State Records Center and Archives, Santa Fe
UCB	University of California, Berkeley
UCBL	University of Colorado, Boulder, Libraries
USA	Utah State Archives, Salt Lake City
USHS	Utah State Historical Society, Salt Lake City
UUSC	University of Utah Special Collections, Marriott Library, Salt Lake City
WSA	Wyoming State Archives, Cheyenne

Preface

1. *Rocky Mountain News,* 18 September 1999.

2. Sarah Deutsch, "Landscape of Enclaves: Race Relations in the West, 1865–1990," in *Under an Open Sky: Rethinking America's Western Past,* ed. William Cronon, George Miles, and Jay Gitlin (New York: Norton, 1992), 131.

Introduction

1. Theodore Roosevelt, "Americanism," in *The Works of Theodore Roosevelt,* ed. Hermann Hagedorn (New York: Charles Scribner's Sons, 1926), 18:401.

2. [George Norlin], "A Life," 2, typed manuscript in Box 1, Norlin Family Material, Genealogy and Personal History folder, George Norlin Papers, Archives, UCBL. Norlin got over the childhood insults, took his A.B. at Hastings College in Nebraska, and then earned a Ph.D. at the University of Chicago in 1900. After a year at the Sorbonne in Paris in 1901–1902, Norlin resumed his duties as professor of Greek at the University of Colorado, where he had joined the faculty in 1899. Named acting president in 1917, just as the Americanization movement was heating up, he became university president in 1919, a post he held until 1939.

3. George Norlin, *What Is America?* (Americanization Committee of the Colorado State Council of Defense, 1917), 7, in Box 3, Norlin Pamphlets, 1911–1918 folder, Norlin Papers. In 1924, Norlin earned high praise for courageously standing up to Ku Klux Klan–backed governor Clarence J. Morley, who threatened to cut off the university's appropriations if the president did not fire Jewish and Catholic faculty members. Norlin refused to do the governor's bidding and Morley backed down. After spending parts of 1932 and 1933 lecturing in Berlin, Norlin warned, long before many others, of the dangers of Nazism and Fascism. Ralph E. Ellsworth, ed., *A Voice from Colorado's Past for the Present: Selected Writings of George Norlin* (Boulder: Colorado Associated University Press, 1985), 47; *Boulder Daily Camera,* 31 March 1942, clipping in Box 5, Folder 29, Norlin Papers; William E. Davis, *Glory Colorado! A History of the University of Colorado, 1858–1963* (Boulder, Colo.: Pruett Press, 1965), 263–66, 332–36; Dixon Wecter, "A President in Action: George Norlin," *Atlantic Monthly,* June 1939, 785–93.

4. Ellis W. Hawley, *The Great War and the Search for a Modern Order: A History of the American People and Their Institutions, 1917–1933* (New York: St. Martin's Press, 1979), 6–9, 20–37; Barry D. Karl, *The Uneasy State: The United States from 1915 to 1945* (Chicago: University of Chicago Press, 1983), 16–49; David M. Kennedy, *Over Here: The First World War and American Society* (New York: Oxford University Press, 1980), 93–143; Ronald Schaffer, *America in the Great War: The Rise of the War Welfare State* (New York: Oxford University Press, 1991), 3–63; Meirion and Susie Harries, *The Last Days of Innocence: America at War, 1917–1918* (New York: Random House, 1997), 154–77.

5. Frederick P. Woellner, "Practical Suggestions for the Organization of Citizenship Classes to Bring About Citizen's Participation—Abstract," *Addresses and Proceedings of the Sixty-First Annual Meeting Held at Oakland–San Francisco, California, July 1–6, 1923* (Washington, D.C.: National Education Association, 1923), 677. See Robert H. Wiebe, *The Search for Order, 1877–1920* (New York: Hill and Wang, 1967); Stephen Skowronek, *Building a New American State: The Expansion of National Administrative Capacities, 1877–1920* (Cambridge: Cambridge University Press, 1982); Morton Keller, *Regulating a New Society: Public Policy and Social Change in America, 1900–1933* (Cambridge, Mass.: Harvard University Press, 1994).

6. Informed by Robert Wiebe's organizational or bureaucratic interpretation of progressivism, John F. McClymer, *War and Welfare: Social Engineering in America, 1890–1925* (Westport, Conn.: Greenwood Press, 1980), for one, has focused on the role of experts in trying to engineer social change; Wiebe, *Search for Order,* 145–59.

7. McClymer, *War and Welfare,* 84–100; On social and settlement worker attitudes toward immigrants, see Howard Jacob Karger, *Sentinels of Order: A Study of Social Control and the Minneapolis Settlement House Movement, 1915–1950* (Lanham, Md.: University Press of America, 1987); Rivka Shpak Lissak, *Pluralism and Progressives: Hull House and the New Immigrants, 1890–1919* (Chicago: University of Chicago Press, 1989); Mina Carson, *Settlement Folk: Social Thought and the American Settlement Movement, 1885–1930* (Chicago: University of Chicago Press, 1990); Ruth Hutchinson Crocker, *Social Work and Social Order: The Settlement Movement in Two Industrial Cities, 1889–1930* (Urbana: University of Illinois Press, 1992).

8. Walter Nugent, *Into the West: The Story of Its People* (New York: Alfred A. Knopf, 1999), 131–33; see Michael P. Malone and Richard W. Etulain, *The American West: A Twentieth-Century History* (Lincoln: University of Nebraska Press, 1989), 1–10.

9. Frederick M. Davenport, "On the Trail of Progress and Reaction in the West: The Persistence of the Pioneer Conscience," *Outlook,* 16 June 1915, 365; Nugent, *Into the West,* 174. Woodrow Wilson's comments are discussed in David M. Wrobel, "Beyond the Frontier-Region Dichotomy," *Pacific Historical Review* 65 (August 1996): 417–18. The article to which Wrobel refers is "The Making of the Nation," *Atlantic Monthly,* July 1897, 1–14.

10. Edward Hyatt to school superintendents of California, 5 May 1916, press release copy in File 420, Box 44, "Americanization" folder, Immigrant Education, Records of the Office of the Commissioner, Historical File, 1870–1950, Records of the Office of Education, RG 12, NARA. The letter was also published in *School and Society,* 24 June 1916, 931. For commentary on the atomizing tensions supposedly unique to the West in the World War I period, see Malone and Etulain, *The American West,* 54, 73–74.

11. George L. Bell, *Americanization as a Necessity to National Defense; Address at State Convention of C.F.W.C., Pasadena, Cal. [1918],* in CSL.

12. George Bell, "What the State and Nation Can Do to Help the Community in Americanization," Department of the Interior, Bureau of Education, *Proceedings Americanization Conference* (Washington, D.C.: Government Printing Office, 1919), 336, 338.

13. For the most illuminating discussions of early-twentieth-century contests over workplace control, see David Montgomery, *Workers' Control in America: Studies in the History of Work, Technology, and Labor Struggles* (Cambridge: Cambridge University Press, 1979), and *The Fall of the House of Labor: The Workplace, the State, and American Labor Activism, 1865–1925* (Cambridge: Cambridge University Press, 1987); Joseph A. McCartin, *Labor's Great War: The Struggle for Industrial Democracy and the Origins of Modern American Labor Relations, 1912–1921* (Chapel Hill: University of North Carolina Press, 1997). See, too, Edward George Hartmann, *The Movement to Americanize the Immigrant* (New York: Columbia University Press, 1948), 140–46, 261–64; William M. Leiserson, *Adjusting Immigrant and Industry* (New York: Harper, 1924; reprint, New York: Arno Press and *New York Times,* 1969).

14. Most helpful in tracing the background of Americanization as an educational movement are Hartmann, *Movement to Americanize;* Robert A. Carlson, "Americanization as an Early Twentieth-Century Adult Education Movement," *History of Education Quarterly* 10 (Winter 1970): 440–64; Carlson, *The Quest for Conformity: Americanization through Education* (New York: John Wiley, 1975); John F. McClymer, "The Americanization Movement and the Education of the Foreign-Born Adult," in *American Education and the European Immigrant: 1840–1940,* ed. Bernard J. Weiss (Urbana: University of Illinois Press, 1982), 96–116; Lucy Eve Kerman, "Americanization: The History of an Idea, 1700–1860" (Ph.D. diss., University of California, Berkeley, 1983).

15. The Americanization of Mexican immigrants was, for the most part, limited geographically to the Southwest but was nonetheless very important to Americanizers in that section of the country. Although there were isolated reports of Asian immigrants attending citizenship classes, the generally accepted notion that Chinese, Japanese, and other Asians were not "white" and thus "ineligible to citizenship" meant the Americanization movement largely ignored them. The 1922 Supreme Court decision in the *Ozawa* case confirmed the ineligible status of Asian immigrants in relation to naturalization. And considering the aims of the Americanization movement, questions remain as to why blacks, although not immigrants, were not included. For the most part, the movement was Europe-focused; even in their constant reference to "races" and "racial relations," Americanizers did not mean blacks. See Nathan Glazer, "Is Assimilation Dead?" *Annals of the American Academy of Political and Social Science*

530 (November 1993): 122–36; Desmond King, *Making Americans: Immigration, Race, and the Origins of the Diverse Democracy* (Cambridge, Mass.: Harvard University Press, 2000).

16. Hartmann, *Movement to Americanize*, 8.

17. Arch M. Thurman, "Americanization in Utah," *Bulletin of the University of Utah*, Vol. 11, No. 8, October 1920, Extension Division Series, Vol. 2, No. 1 (Salt Lake City: University of Utah Press, 1920), 6.

18. Chester H. Rowell, "The Japanese in California," *World's Work*, June 1913, 196.

19. Grace Raymond Hebard, "Why We Exclude the Ninety-Seven," *Woman Citizen*, 18 June 1921, 14; Theodore Roosevelt, *Fear God and Take Your Own Part*, in *Works*, 18:392.

20. Walter Nugent underscores this point as well: "We move from homesteaders to miners to city dwellers, including the incredible diversity of ethnics from Asia as well as Europe—an even greater range than in Ellis Island–era New York." He also notes that, although the West had been "richly multicultural . . . since at least Gold Rush times," middle-class whites made no distinctions among the various groups and "evenhandedly discriminated against blacks, Asians, Mexicans, and European immigrants alike" (*Into the West*, 133, 218).

21. [Oscar Rohn], "Americanization," typed manuscript, 10, in File 106, Box 7, Americanization folder, Council of National Defense—Combating Illiteracy, Records of the Office of Education, RG 12, NARA.

22. *Thirteenth Report of the Superintendent of Public Instruction of the State of Utah for the Biennial Period Ending June 30, 1920*, 65, Public Documents Serial Set, Series 240, Reels 36–37, USA.

1. "The Stuff from Which Citizens Are Made"

1. Robert G. Athearn, *The Mythic West in Twentieth-Century America* (Lawrence: University Press of Kansas, 1986); Clyde A. Milner II, "The Shared Memory of Montana Pioneers," *Montana: The Magazine of Western History* 37 (Winter 1987): 2–13, and "The View from Wisdom: Four Layers of History and Regional Identity," in *Under an Open Sky: Rethinking America's Western Past*, ed. William Cronon, George Miles, and Jay Gitlin (New York: Norton, 1992), 213–15; David M. Wrobel, "Beyond the Frontier-Region Dichotomy," *Pacific Historical Review* 65 (August 1996): 409–14. For general discussions of history and memory in American culture, see Michael Kammen, *Mystic Chords of Memory: The Transformation of Tradition in American Culture* (New York: Alfred A. Knopf, 1991), and John Bodnar, *Remaking America: Public Memory, Commemoration, and Patriotism in the Twentieth Century* (Princeton, N.J.: Princeton University Press, 1992); Kammen treats developments in the West in *Mystic Chords of Memory*, 273–76, 393–403, 492–93.

2. This is a reference to commercially published compilations of local history and biographical sketches of the prominent, typically financed through prepublication subscriptions. These volumes were particularly abundant between 1880 and 1900. See Carol Kammen, *On Doing Local History: Reflections on What Local Historians Do, Why, and What It Means* (Nashville, Tenn.: American Association for State and Local History, 1986), 24–27.

3. *History of Fresno County, California* . . . (San Francisco: Wallace W. Elliott, 1882), 46; Rev. Jonathan Edwards, *An Illustrated History of Spokane County, State of Washington* (n.p.: W. H. Lever, 1900), iv; Ira L. Bare and Will H. McDonald, eds., *An Illustrated History of Lincoln County, Nebraska, and Her People* (Chicago: American Historical Society, 1920), iii, 307.

4. *Daily Iowan,* June 1932; Grace Raymond Hebard to Aven Nelson, 18 May 1929. Both sources quoted in Janell M. Wenzell, "Dr. Grace Raymond Hebard as Western Historian" (M.A. thesis, University of Wyoming, 1960), 7.

5. Grace Raymond Hebard and E. A. Brininstool, *The Bozeman Trail* (Cleveland: Arthur H. Clark, 1922), 2:266; Grace Raymond Hebard, *The Pathbreakers from River to Ocean: The Story of the Great West from the Time of Coronado to the Present* (Chicago: University Publishing, 1917), 253.

6. Emerson Hough, "The Settlement of the West: A Study in Transportation," *Century,* November 1901, 91, and *The Passing of the Frontier: A Chronicle of the Old West* (New Haven, Conn.: Yale University Press, 1918), 1–3.

7. Remington quoted in G. Edward White, *The Eastern Establishment and the Western Experience* (New Haven, Conn.: Yale University Press, 1968), 109; Edward Alsworth Ross, "The Middle West. I. The Fiber of the People," *Century,* February 1912, 611–15; John A. Johnson, "The Call of the West," *World's Work,* October 1909, 12139–40; Athearn, *Mythic West,* 53–56.

8. For an excellent introduction to studies on Western race relations published prior to the mid-1980s, see Richard White, "Race Relations in the American West," *American Quarterly* 38 (Bibliography 1986): 396–416. See, too, Sarah Deutsch, "Landscape of Enclaves: Race Relations in the West, 1865–1990," in *Under an Open Sky,* 110–31. Important works published since the mid-1980s include Sarah Deutsch, *No Separate Refuge: Culture, Class, and Gender on an Anglo-Hispanic Frontier in the American Southwest, 1880–1940* (New York: Oxford University Press, 1988); Tomás Almaguer, *Racial Fault Lines: The Historical Origins of White Supremacy in California* (Berkeley: University of California Press, 1994); Lisbeth Haas, *Conquests and Historical Identities in California, 1769–1936* (Berkeley: University of California Press, 1995).

9. The following references comprise several of the standard sources on immigrants in the West. Carlton C. Qualey, "Ethnic Groups and the Frontier," in *American Frontier and Western Issues: A Historiographical Review,* ed. Roger L. Nichols (New York: Greenwood Press, 1986), 199–216; Frederick Luebke, ed., *European Immigrants in the American West: Community Histories* (Albuquerque: University of New Mexico Press, 1998); Sucheng Chan, *Asian Americans: An Interpretive History* (Boston: Twayne, 1991); Roger Daniels, *Asian America: Chinese and Japanese in the United States since 1850* (Seattle: University of Washington Press, 1988); Ronald Takaki, *Strangers from a Different Shore: A History of Asian Americans* (New York: Penguin, 1990); Rodolfo Acuña, *Occupied America: A History of Chicanos,* 2d ed. (New York: Harper and Row, 1981); Richard Griswold del Castillo and Arnoldo De León, *North to Aztlán: A History of Mexican Americans in the United States* (New York: Twayne, 1996).

10. Jon Gjerde, *From Peasants to Farmers: The Migration from Balestrand, Norway, to the Upper Middle West* (Cambridge: Cambridge University Press, 1988); Dino Cinel, *From Italy to San Francisco: The Immigrant Experience* (Stanford, Calif.: Stanford University Press, 1982), 101–33; Timothy J. Kloberdanz, "Plainsmen of Three Continents: Volga German Adaptation to Steppe, Prairie, and Pampas," in *Ethnicity on the Great Plains,* ed. Frederick C. Luebke (Lincoln: University of Nebraska Press, 1980), 62; Deutsch, *No Separate Refuge;* Gunther Peck, "Mobilizing Community: Migrant Workers and the Politics of Labor Mobility in the North American West, 1900–1920," in *Labor Histories: Class, Politics, and the Working-Class Experience,* ed. Eric Arnesen, Julie Greene, and Bruce Laurie (Urbana: University of Illinois Press, 1998), 175–200; Carlos A. Schwantes, "The Concept of the Wageworkers' Frontier: A Framework for Future Research," *Western Historical Quarterly* 18 (January 1987). 39–55.

11. See Cinel, *From Italy to San Francisco,* 162–95; Mario T. García, *Desert Immigrants: The Mexicans of El Paso, 1880–1920* (New Haven, Conn.: Yale University Press, 1981), 197–236; Gilbert G. González, *Labor and Community: Mexican Citrus Worker Villages in a Southern California County, 1900–1950* (Urbana: University of Illinois Press, 1994), 77–98.

12. The Italian "mugbook," Marcello Gandolfo, *Gli Italiani Nel Colorado: Librio Dedicato Agli Italiani, 1899–1900* (Denver: Dove Press, 1900), is briefly discussed in Rebecca Ann Hunt, "Urban Pioneers: Continuity and Change in the Ethnic Communities in Two Denver, Colorado, Neighborhoods: 1875–1998" (Ph.D. diss., University of Colorado, 1999), 108–09. Michinari Fujita, "The Japanese Association in America," *Sociology and Social Research* 13 (1928–1929): 211–28; Yuji Ichioka, "Japanese Associations and the Japanese Government: A Special Relationship, 1909–1926," *Pacific Historical Review* 46 (August 1977): 409–37. Also see García, *Desert Immigrants,* 223–30.

13. Jon Gjerde, *The Minds of the West: Ethnocultural Evolution in the Rural Middle West, 1830–1917* (Chapel Hill: University of North Carolina Press, 1997), 53–64, 227–29, 240–47, 279–81; Kathleen Neils Conzen, David A. Gerber, Ewa Morawska, George E. Pozzetta, and Rudolph J. Vecoli, "The Invention of Ethnicity: A Perspective from the U.S.A.," *Journal of American Ethnic History* 12 (Fall 1992): 3–41.

14. Peri Ander [John Chetwood Jr.], "Our Foreign Immigration. Its Social Aspects," *Arena,* August 1890, 271; Sydney G. Fisher, "Alien Degradation of American Character," *Forum,* January 1893, 608–15. See Thomas L. Hartshorne, *The Distorted Image: Changing Conceptions of the American Character since Turner* (Cleveland: The Press of Case Western Reserve University, 1968), esp. chap. 2. On the historical currents of nativism in the United States, see John Higham, *Strangers in the Land: Patterns of American Nativism, 1860–1925* (New Brunswick, N.J.: Rutgers University Press, 1955); David H. Bennett, *The Party of Fear: From Nativist Movements to the New Right in American History* (Chapel Hill: University of North Carolina Press, 1988); Dale T. Knobel, *"America for the Americans": The Nativist Movement in the United States* (New York: Twayne, 1996).

15. Edward Alsworth Ross, *The Old World in the New: The Significance of Past and Present Immigration to the American People* (New York: Century, 1914), 216. See Bronwen J. Cohen, "Nativism and Western Myth: The Influence of Nativist Ideas on the American Self-Image," *Journal of American Studies* 8 (April 1974): 23–39; Matthew Frye Jacobson, *Whiteness of a Different Color: European Immigrants and the Alchemy of Race* (Cambridge, Mass.: Harvard University Press, 1998), 155–61.

16. Josiah Strong, *Our Country: Its Possible Future and Its Present Crisis,* rev. ed. (New York: Baker and Taylor, 1885, 1891), 60, 200; Dorothea R. Muller, "Church Building and Community Making on the Frontier, a Case Study: Josiah Strong, Home Missionary in Cheyenne, 1871–1873," *Western Historical Quarterly* 10 (April 1979): 191–216. Rogers M. Smith, *Civic Ideals: Conflicting Visions of Citizenship in U.S. History* (New Haven, Conn.: Yale University Press, 1997), 6, 353–57, discusses Strong as an example of the complex and contradictory mix of "liberal, democratic republican, and inegalitarian ascriptive elements" that typified political conceptions of citizenship in the United States as white, Anglo-Saxon, Protestant, and male. In that sense, Strong is an important precursor to many early-twentieth-century progressives involved with Americanization. See also John Chetwood Jr., *Immigration Fallacies* (Boston: Arena Publishing, 1896), 16–19.

17. Roger Daniels, *Coming to America: A History of Immigration and Ethnicity in American Life* (New York: Harper Collins, 1990), 121–26, 183–84, and *Not Like Us: Immigrants*

and Minorities in America, 1880–1924 (Chicago: Ivan R. Dee, 1997), 61. In addition to Daniels, I have drawn on a number of works regarding immigration, including Marcus Lee Hansen, *The Immigrant in American History* (Cambridge, Mass.: Harvard University Press, 1940); Oscar Handlin, *Boston's Immigrants: A Study in Acculturation* (Cambridge, Mass.: Belknap Press of Harvard University Press, 1941, 1959), and *The Uprooted: The Epic Story of the Great Migrations That Made the American People* (Boston: Little, Brown, 1951); Higham, *Strangers in the Land,* Stephen Thernstrom, ed., *Harvard Encyclopedia of American Ethnic Groups* (Cambridge, Mass.: Belknap Press of Harvard University Press, 1980); Thomas Archdeacon, *Becoming American: An Ethnic History* (New York: Free Press, 1983); John Higham, *Send These to Me: Immigrants in Urban America,* rev. ed. (Baltimore: Johns Hopkins University Press, 1984); John Bodnar, *The Transplanted: A History of Immigrants in Urban America* (Bloomington: Indiana University Press, 1985); Alan M. Kraut, *The Huddled Masses: The Immigrant in American Society, 1880–1921* (Arlington Heights, Ill.: Harlan Davidson, 1982); Leonard Dinnerstein, Roger L. Nichols, and David M. Reimers, *Natives and Strangers: Blacks, Indians, and Immigrants in America,* 3d ed. (New York: Oxford University Press, 1996).

18. [J. B. Bishop], "Quality of Our Latest Immigration," *Nation,* 5 February 1891, 108; [J. H. Noble], "The New Immigration," *Nation,* 17 September 1891, 209–10. For a good summary and discussion of anti-immigrant sentiment between 1865 and 1924, see Archdeacon, *Becoming American,* 151–64.

19. Guy Raymond Halifax, "The Immigration Scourge," *Overland Monthly,* January 1904, 65–69; Kent quoted in Leslie Wayne Koepplin, "A Relationship of Reform: Immigrants and Progressives in the Far West" (Ph.D. diss., University of California, Los Angeles, 1971), 211.

20. Elwood P. Cubberley, *Public Education in the United States: A Study and Interpretation of American Educational History* (Boston: Houghton Mifflin, 1919), 333, 336–37. A devotee of Frederick Taylor, Cubberley was a progressive insofar as he believed in and helped develop a professional administrative approach to running schools. See Jesse B. Sears and Adin B. Henderson, *Cubberley of Stanford and His Contribution to American Education* (Stanford, Calif.: Stanford University Press, 1957).

21. California State Commission of Immigration and Housing, *Report on Fresno's Immigration Problem with Particular Reference to Educational Facilities and Requirements* (Sacramento: State Printing Office, 1918), 8–10, CSL; Grace Raymond Hebard, "Americanization of the Immigrant," typewritten draft of speech given at Sheridan, Wyoming, 6 October 1916, before Wyoming Federation of Women's Clubs, in Naturalization Folder 1, Subject Files, Hebard Papers, AHC; Hebard used this text, with only minor modifications, in many subsequent Americanization talks and also published it as an article in the *General Federation of Women's Clubs Magazine* for February 1917, a copy of which is in Naturalization Folder 3; *Sheridan Post,* 6, 10 October 1916.

22. Chester H. Rowell, "Chinese and Japanese Immigrants—A Comparison," *Annals of the American Academy of Political and Social Science* 34 (September 1909): 230, and "The Japanese in California," *World's Work,* June 1913, 196. Years later, Rowell was still arguing along similar lines, extending the idea to encompass race relations in British Columbia, Australia, and New Zealand as well as to warn against the erection of caste systems. "They regard their borders as a racial frontier," he wrote in 1926, "which they are determined to maintain inviolate. . . . Unless the racial frontier is drawn on the borders of the Pacific, there is nowhere

else to draw it horizontally. It would be drawn, instead vertically down the middle of our institutions, to rend them into segments with which the world has not yet learned how to deal" ("Western Windows to the East," *Survey,* 1 May 1926, 174–75).

23. E. P. Hutchinson, *Legislative History of American Immigration Policy, 1798–1965* (Philadelphia: University of Pennsylvania Press, 1981), 80–82, 85–86, 92–93, 103–04, 129–30, 134–35; Mary Roberts Coolidge, *Chinese Immigration* (New York: Henry Holt, 1909; reprint, New York: Arno Press and *New York Times,* 1969), 168–233, 244–52. According to Roger Daniels, *Not Like Us,* 17, the Chinese Exclusion Act "became the hinge on which all American immigration policy turned" and paved the way for creation of a federal immigration bureaucracy to enforce restriction. For a detailed consideration of Chinese immigrants' efforts to neutralize enforcement of the exclusion laws through federal courts, see Lucy E. Salyer, *Laws Harsh as Tigers: Chinese Immigrants and the Shaping of Modern Immigration Law* (Chapel Hill: University of North Carolina Press, 1995).

24. Yuji Ichioka, *The Issei: The World of the First Generation Japanese Immigrants, 1885–1924* (New York: Free Press, 1988), 71–72. Though dated, Thomas A. Bailey, *Theodore Roosevelt and the Japanese-American Crises* (Palo Alto, Calif.: Stanford University Press, 1934), is still a good starting point for examining the diplomatic ramifications of the early anti-Japanese movement in California. Another useful overview of the topic is Raymond A. Esthus, *Theodore Roosevelt and Japan* (Seattle: University of Washington Press, 1966).

25. For an overview of the Alien Land Act of 1913, see Roger Daniels, *The Politics of Prejudice: The Anti-Japanese Movement in California and the Struggle for Japanese Exclusion* (Berkeley: University of California Press, 1962), 46–64.

26. Yuji Ichioka, "The Japanese Immigrant Response to the 1920 California Alien Land Law," *Agricultural History* 58 (April 1984): 157–78; Chan, *Asian Americans,* 47.

27. Roy L. Garis, *Immigration Restriction: A Study of the Opposition to and Regulation of Immigration into the United States* (New York: Macmillan, 1927), 128–30; Hutchinson, *Legislative History,* 166–67.

28. U.S. House Select Committee on the Causes of the Present Depression of Labor, *Chinese Immigration,* 46th Cong., 2d sess., 1880, H. Report 572, serial 1935, 25. For a discussion of how American perceptions about China colored attitudes about the immigrants (and vice versa) after the Chinese Exclusion Act of 1882, see Robert McClellan, *The Heathen Chinee: A Study of American Attitudes toward China, 1890–1905* (Columbus: Ohio State University Press, 1971); *Congressional Record,* 46th Cong., 1st sess., 9, pt. 2: 2262; *Congressional Record,* 47th Cong., 1st sess., 13, pt. 2: 1483–84. See also John F. Miller, "Certain Phases of the Chinese Question," *Californian,* March 1880, 237–42; McClellan, *Heathen Chinee,* 72–106; Senate Committee on Immigration, *Chinese Exclusion,* 57th Cong., 1st sess., 1902, S. Report 776, serial 4265, 296.

29. Rowell, "Japanese in California," 196; *Statement of Hon. James D. Phelan of California before the Committee on Immigration and Naturalization, House of Representatives, Friday, June 20, 1919* (Washington, D.C.: Government Printing Office, 1920), 12, in James D. Phelan Papers, Bancroft Library, UCB.

30. *Congressional Record,* 4th Cong., 1st sess., 13, pt. 2: 1487; Francis E. Sheldon, "The Chinese Immigration Discussion," *Overland Monthly,* February 1886, 118; House Select Committee, *Chinese Immigration,* 27; Wilbur F. Sanders in *Congressional Record,* 52d Cong., 1st sess., 23, pt. 4: 3566; *Rocky Mountain News,* 8 May 1892.

31. Senate Committee on Immigration, *Chinese Exclusion,* 300; *Congressional Record,*

· 64th Cong., 2d sess., 54, pt. 1: 272; "By Senator James D. Phelan," undated statement in Japanese File, 1920, Carton 15, Phelan Papers.

32. *Congressional Record,* 45th Cong., 1st sess., 6, pt. 1: 392, quoted in Jacobson, *Whiteness of a Different Color,* 157; Paul S. Taylor, *Mexican Labor in the United States,* vol. I (Berkeley: University of California Press, 1930), 154; Samuel J. Holmes, "Perils of the Mexican Invasion," *North American Review* (May 1929): 620; Col. L. M. Maus, "What Should Be Done to Americanize and Make Useful Citizens of the Spanish-American Population of Our Border States," File 106, Box 11, Records of the Office of Education, NARA.

33. Victor S. Clark, "Mexican Labor in the United States," Department of Commerce and Labor, Bureau of Labor *Bulletin,* No. 78 (Washington, D.C.: Government Printing Office, 1908), reprinted in *Mexican Labor in the United States* (New York: Arno Press, 1974), 485; U.S. Immigration Commission, *Reports of the Immigration Commission, Abstracts of Reports of the Immigration Commission* (Washington, D.C.: Government Printing Office, 1911), 1:691.

34. Alfred White, "The Apperceptive Mass of Foreigners as Applied to Americanization, the Mexican Group" (M.A. thesis, University of California, 1923; reprint, San Francisco: R and E Research Associates, 1971), 38–39; Emory S. Bogardus, *The Mexican in the United States* (Los Angeles: University of Southern California Press, 1934; reprint, New York: Arno Press, 1970), 76.

35. Manuel Gamio, *Mexican Immigration to the United States: A Study of Human Migration and Adjustment* (Chicago: University of Chicago Press, 1930; reprint, New York: Arno Press and *New York Times,* 1969), 57, 64–65; Taylor, *Mexican Labor in the United States,* 208; Deutsch, *No Separate Refuge,* 128–42. On the development of a segregated urban barrio, see Richard Griswold del Castillo, *The Los Angeles Barrio, 1850–1890: A Social History* (Berkeley: University of California Press, 1979), 139–70.

36. Carey McWilliams, *North from Mexico: The Spanish-Speaking People of the United States* (New York: Greenwood Press, 1968), 214, 221–23, argued that Mexicans, not being indigenous to Midwestern industrial cities, were in effect just "another immigrant group." In Chicago, Detroit, Lorain, Ohio, and elsewhere, Mexicans faced less discrimination, assimilated and acculturated more readily, and applied for citizenship in higher proportions than in the Southwest. See also Taylor, *Mexican Labor in the United States,* 224.

37. House Committee on Immigration, *Hearings on Immigration from Countries of the Western Hemisphere* (1928), 289, quoted in Mark Reisler, *By the Sweat of Their Brow: Mexican Immigrant Labor in the United States, 1900–1940* (Westport, Conn.: Greenwood Press, 1976), 140; Hon. James L. Slayden, "Some Observations on Mexican Immigration," *Annals of the American Academy of Political and Social Science* 93 (January 1921): 125.

38. Reisler, *By the Sweat of Their Brow,* 140. See Neil Foley, *The White Scourge: Mexicans, Blacks, and Poor Whites in Texas Cotton Culture* (Berkeley: University of California Press, 1997), chap. 2; Clark, "Mexican Labor in the United States," 466; Bogardus, *Mexican in the United States,* 16. See also Robert F. Foerster, *The Racial Problems Involved in Immigration from Latin America and the West Indies to the United States* (Washington, D.C.: Government Printing Office, 1925; reprint, San Francisco: R and E Research Associates, 1971), 8–14.

39. William E. Borah to W. G. Swendson, June 9, 1928, Box 288, Immigration File, Borah Papers, Library of Congress, quoted in Reisler, *By the Sweat of Their Brow,* 132. According to Reisler, anti-Catholicism was not much of a factor in anti-Mexican nativism, in part due to the anticlericalism of the Mexican Revolution (157–58). Bogardus, *Mexican in the United States,* 9, 23, 33, 46–47, 61.

40. Bogardus, *Mexican in the United States,* 36; California State Commission of Immigration and Housing, *Report on an Experiment Made in Los Angeles in the Summer of 1917 for the Americanization of Foreign-born Women* (Sacramento: California State Printing Office, 1917), 21; White, "Apperceptive Mass," 34–37; George J. Sanchez, "'Go After the Women': Americanization and the Mexican Immigrant Woman, 1915–1929," in *Unequal Sisters: A Multicultural Reader in U.S. Women's History,* ed. Ellen Carol DuBois and Vicki L. Ruiz (New York: Routledge, 1990), 250–63.

41. Andrew F. Rolle, *The Immigrant Upraised: Italian Adventurers and Colonists in an Expanding America* (Norman: University of Oklahoma Press, 1968) is most notable in this regard. Rolle's book is decidedly Turnerian in tone, seeking to advance a corrective to Oscar Handlin's "uprooted" and alienated immigrants languishing in urban ghettoes by emphasizing that many Italian immigrants thrived when they ventured west. "The Italians in the West found there more of the outdoor rusticity of life familiar in rural Italy than did their compatriots who settled in larger cities of the East. Also, they encountered an acculturation usually based upon less friction than immigrants to the eastern cities or the midwestern urban centers of Chicago or Kansas City faced. As viniculturists, cotton-raisers, hostelers, miners, or restauranteurs . . . they were accepted quite readily as members of the society in which they lived" (p. 10).

42. In a study of ethnic group formation on the Kansas prairies, D. Aidan McQuillan writes: "Ethnogenesis, the creation of a distinctive ethnic identity, was part of this maturing transition from immigrant settlement to ethnic community. Families no longer saw themselves as immigrants in the bewildering mass of a polyglot American society but as members of a cohesive group with a distinctive culture that shared a common language, religion, and national origin" (*Prevailing Over Time: Ethnic Adjustment on the Kansas Prairies, 1875–1925* [Lincoln: University of Nebraska Press, 1990], 85).

43. U.S. House Select Committee on the Depression of Labor, *Land Monopoly and Chinese Immigration,* 46th Cong., 2d sess., 1879, H. Mis. Doc. 5, serial 1928, 260.

44. Grace Raymond Hebard, "Immigration and Needed Ballot Reform," *Illinois Wesleyan Magazine,* October 1896, 230.

45. House Committee on Immigration and Naturalization, *Japanese Immigration: Hearings before the Committee on Immigration and Naturalization,* 66th Cong., 2d sess., 1921, H. Report 459, serial 7799, 33.

2. Progressives, Americanization, and War

1. David George Herman, "Neighbors on the Golden Mountain: The Americanization of Immigrants in California. Public Instruction as an Agency of Ethnic Assimilation, 1850 to 1933" (Ph.D. diss., University of California, Berkeley, 1981), 163–70, 374; Jonas Alex Gurvis, "Elementary Education of Adult Immigrants in California: An Historical and Descriptive Study" (Ed.D. diss., University of California, Los Angeles, 1976), 47–51. According to a 1919 assessment of Americanization, California remained the only state with a reference to evening schools in its constitution; Howard C. Hill, "The Americanization Movement," *American Journal of Sociology* 24 (May 1919): 620. The standard overviews of the Americanization movement are Edward George Hartmann, *The Movement to Americanize the Immigrant* (New York: Columbia University Press, 1948), and John Higham, *Strangers in the Land:*

Patterns of American Nativism, 1860–1925 (New Brunswick, N.J.: Rutgers University Press, 1955), 234–63. For a useful overview and critique of the historiography of Americanization, see Otis L. Graham Jr. and Elizabeth Koed, "Americanizing the Immigrant, Past and Future: History and Implications of a Social Movement," *Public Historian* 15 (Fall 1993): 24–45. See also Gary Gerstle, "Liberty, Coercion, and the Making of Americans," *Journal of American History* 84 (September 1997): 524–58.

2. Gerald D. Nash, *The American West in the Twentieth Century: A Short History of an Urban Oasis* (Englewood Cliffs, N.J.: Prentice-Hall, 1973), 43–51; Michael P. Malone and Richard W. Etulain, *The American West: A Twentieth Century History* (Lincoln: University of Nebraska Press, 1989), 54–66; William D. Rowley, "The West as Laboratory and Mirror of Reform," in *The Twentieth-Century West: Historical Interpretations,* ed. Gerald D. Nash and Richard W. Etulain (Albuquerque: University of New Mexico Press, 1989), 341–47.

3. Clarence H. Matson, "The Immigration Problem: A New View," *Outlook,* 25 June 1904, 461.

4. Gary Gerstle describes many progressives' difficulties in crafting a cohesive cultural politics, stating that progressives were perplexed by "the bewildering array and unexpected vigor of ethnic cultures among the working people." "Immigrants had to be 'Americanized,'" he continues, "culturally and morally transformed from aliens into citizens, and given a sense of membership in and loyalty to the nation. . . . Because of these broad differences in background and aspiration, the Progressives had difficulty fashioning a cultural politics to which they could all adhere. The issue of immigration illustrates the problem" ("The Protean Character of American Liberalism," *American Historical Review* 99 [October 1994]: 1049, 1051). See also Rogers M. Smith, *Civic Ideals: Conflicting Visions of Citizenship in U.S. History* (New Haven, Conn.: Yale University Press, 1997), 412–24.

5. Edward Alsworth Ross, "The Value Rank of the American People," *Independent,* 3 November 1904, 1063, and *Seventy Years of It: An Autobiography* (New York: D. Appleton-Century, 1936), 276–77; his origination of the "race suicide" concept is in "The Causes of Race Superiority," *Annals of the American Academy of Political and Social Science* 18 (July–December 1901): 86–88. For a general discussion of Ross's nativism and racism, see Julius Weinberg, *Edward Alsworth Ross and the Sociology of Progressivism* (Madison: State Historical Society of Wisconsin, 1972), 149–75. Rowell's comments appeared in the *Fresno Republican,* 20 November 1906.

6. William Carlson Smith, *Americans in the Making: The Natural History of the Assimilation of Immigrants* (New York: D. Appleton-Century, 1939), 115; Ellwood P. Cubberley, *Changing Conceptions of Education* (Boston: Houghton Mifflin, 1909), 15. For an excellent review of the development of assimilation theories, see Russell A. Kazal, "Revisiting Assimilation: The Rise, Fall, and Reappraisal of a Concept in American Ethnic History," *American Historical Review* 100 (April 1995): 437–71. Other good discussions of competing assimilation models are in John Higham, *Send These to Me: Immigrants in Urban America,* rev. ed. (Baltimore: Johns Hopkins University Press, 1984), 175–232; Milton Gordon, *Assimilation in American Life: The Role of Race, Religion, and National Origins* (New York: Oxford University Press, 1964), 84–141; Arthur Mann, *The One and the Many: Reflections on the American Identity* (Chicago: University of Chicago Press, 1979), 100–148; Harold J. Abramson, "Assimilation and Pluralism," in *Harvard Encyclopedia of American Ethnic Groups,* ed. Stephen Thernstrom (Cambridge, Mass.: Belknap Press of Harvard University Press, 1980), 150–55.

7. Issac B. Berkson, *Theories of Americanization: A Critical Study with Special Reference to the Jewish Group* (New York: Teachers, College, Columbia University, 1920; reprint, New York:

Arno Press and *New York Times,* 1969), 77. For illuminating discussions on the melting pot idea, consult Philip Gleason, *Speaking of Diversity: Language and Ethnicity in Twentieth-Century America* (Baltimore: Johns Hopkins University Press, 1992), 3–90; Werner Sollors, *Beyond Ethnicity: Consent and Descent in American Culture* (New York: Oxford University Press, 1986), 66–101. A similar concept, most commonly associated with sociologist Robert E. Park and becoming more popular after the period in question, defined assimilation in terms of a mutually enriching reciprocal interaction between natives and immigrants, ultimately blending various cultural activities into a continually renewed and refined common culture. Park and others later revised this process of interaction into the "race relations cycle" of competition, conflict, accommodation, and assimilation. See Robert E. Park and Herbert A. Miller [original author, William I. Thomas], *Old World Traits Transplanted* (New York: Harper, 1921); Robert E. Park and Ernest W. Burgess, *Introduction to the Science of Sociology* (Chicago: University of Chicago Press, 1921).

8. *Thirteenth Report of the Superintendent of Public Instruction of the State of Utah for the Biennial Period Ending June 30, 1920,* 65, Public Documents Serial Set, Series 240, Reels 36–37, USA; George L. Bell, *Americanization as a Necessity to National Defense; Address at State Convention of C.F.W.C., Pasadena, Cal.* [1918], in CSL.

9. Roosevelt quoted in Arthur M. Schlesinger Jr., *The Disuniting of America: Reflections on a Multicultural Society* (New York: Norton, 1992), 35; Horace Kallen, "Democracy Versus the Melting Pot: A Study of American Nationality. Part Two," *Nation,* 18 February 1915, 220; Randolph S. Bourne, "Trans-National America," *Atlantic Monthly,* June 1916, 89. Schlesinger discusses Kallen and these earlier expressions of cultural pluralism in *Disuniting of America,* 36–38. Another recent assessment of cultural pluralism and diversity is David A. Hollinger, *Postethnic America: Beyond Multiculturalism* (New York: Basic Books, 1995). Kallen and Bourne elaborated on ideas relating to human diversity that others, including John Stuart Mill and W. E. B. Du Bois, had addressed for many years. See Jeff Spinner, *The Boundaries of Citizenship: Race, Ethnicity, and Nationality in a Liberal State* (Baltimore: Johns Hopkins University Press, 1994), 78–80. Another pre-Kallen pluralist was Israel Friedlander of the Educational Alliance, a Jewish organization in New York City that began Americanization programs for adult immigrants in the 1890s; Joseph Dorinson, "The Educational Alliance: An Institutional Study in Americanization and Acculturation," in *Immigration and Ethnicity: American Society—"Melting Pot" or "Salad Bowl"?* ed. Michael D'Innocenzo and Josef P. Sirefman (Westport, Conn.: Greenwood Press, 1992), 94–107.

10. Horace Kallen, "Democracy Versus the Melting Pot: A Study of American Nationality. Part One," *Nation,* 11 February 1915, 116; Christopher Lasch, *The New Radicalism in America: [1889–1963] The Intellectual as a Social Type* (New York: Alfred A. Knopf, 1965); Bruce Clayton, *Forgotten Prophet: The Life of Randolph Bourne* (Baton Rouge: Louisiana State University Press, 1984); Edward Abraham, *The Lyrical Left: Randolph Bourne, Alfred Stieglitz, and the Origin of Cultural Radicalism in America* (Charlottesville: University Press of Virginia, 1988); Leslie J. Vaughan, "Cosmopolitanism, Ethnicity, and American Identity: Randolph Bourne's 'Trans-National America,'" *Journal of American Studies* 25 (December 1991): 443–59. Conceiving American identity as essentially white, the Anglo-conformist, melting pot, and cultural pluralist approaches of the 1910s and 1920s all ignored African Americans as well as other nonwhites. See Desmond King, *Making Americans: Immigration, Race, and the Origins of the Diverse Democracy* (Cambridge, Mass.: Harvard University Press, 2000), 14–36.

11. Hartmann, *Movement to Americanize,* 24–37; Allen F. Davis, *Spearheads for Reform: The Social Settlements and the Progressive Movement, 1890–1914* (New York: Oxford University Press, 1967); Ruth Hutchinson Crocker, *Social Work and Social Order: The Settlement Movement in Two Industrial Cities, 1889–1930* (Urbana: University of Illinois Press, 1992); Mina Carson, *Settlement Folk: Social Thought and the American Settlement Movement, 1885–1930* (Chicago: University of Chicago Press, 1990); Rivka S. Lissak, *Pluralism and Progressives: Hull House and the New Immigrants, 1890–1919* (Chicago: University of Chicago Press, 1989); Rebecca Ann Hunt, "Urban Pioneers: Continuity and Change in the Ethnic Communities in Two Denver, Colorado, Neighborhoods: 1875–1998" (Ph.D. diss., University of Colorado, 1999), 214.

12. Gurvis, "Elementary Education of Adult Immigrants in California," 52; Mary E. Stilson, "Dana Bartlett: The Modern Mission Father," *Out West,* 1912, 222; Emory S. Bogardus, *Essentials of Americanization,* rev. ed. (Los Angeles: University of Southern California Press, 1920); Leslie Wayne Koepplin, "A Relationship of Reform: Immigrants and Progressives in the Far West" (Ph.D. diss., University of California, Los Angeles, 1971), 161–78.

13. Hartmann, *Movement to Americanize,* 24–37. On domestic immigration policy, see Ann Marie Woo-Sam, "Domesticating the Immigrant: California's Commission of Immigration and Housing and the Domestic Immigration Policy Movement, 1910–1945" (Ph.D. diss., University of California, Berkeley, 1999), 17–57.

14. Hartmann, *Movement to Americanize,* 38; Henry Beardsell Leonard, *The Protest against the Movement to Restrict European Immigration, 1896–1924* (New York: Arno Press, 1980), 165–70; U.S. Congress, *Reports of the Immigration Commission,* Vol. 41: *Statements and Recommendations Submitted by Societies and Organizations Interested in the Subject of Immigration,* 61st Cong., 3d sess., S. Doc. 764, 97–99. Chicago's Immigrants' Protective League, organized in 1908, provided services similar to those offered by the North American Civic League. See Rivka S. Lissak, "Liberal Progressives and 'New Immigrants': The Immigrants' Protective League of Chicago, 1908–1919," *Studies in American Civilization* 32 (1987): 79–103. Concerning Frances Kellor's career, see William Joseph Maxwell, "Frances Kellor in the Progressive Era: A Case Study in the Professionalization of Reform" (Ed.D. diss., Columbia University, 1968); Ellen Fitzpatrick, *Endless Crusade: Women Social Scientists and Progressive Reform* (New York: Oxford University Press, 1990), 17–20, 58–66, 130–65.

15. Koepplin, "A Relationship of Reform," 172–78; Donald Bruce Johnson, comp., *National Party Platforms, Vol. I: 1840–1956,* rev. ed. (Urbana: University of Illinois Press, 1978), 181.

16. On progressivism in California, see George Mowry, *The California Progressives* (Berkeley: University of California Press, 1951); Spencer C. Olin, *California's Prodigal Sons: Hiram Johnson and the Progressives, 1911–1917* (Berkeley: University of California Press, 1968); Tom Sitton and William Deverell, eds., *California Progressivism Revisited* (Berkeley: University of California Press, 1994). For a discussion of the Alien Land Act of 1913, see Roger Daniels, *The Politics of Prejudice: The Anti-Japanese Movement in California and the Struggle for Japanese Exclusion* (Berkeley: University of California Press, 1962), 46–64. Spencer C. Olin, "European Immigrant and Oriental Alien: Acceptance and Rejection by the California Legislature of 1913," *Pacific Historical Review* 35 (August 1966): 303–15, dwells on the race-conscious ambivalence of the state's progressives toward immigrants expressed in the simultaneous establishment of the CCIH and passage of the Alien Land Act.

17. Samuel Edgerton Wood, "The California State Commission of Immigration and Housing: A Study of Administrative Organization and the Growth of Function" (Ph.D. diss., University of California, Berkeley, 1942), 91–104; Woo-Sam, "Domesticating the Immigrant," 37–45; Herman, "Neighbors on the Golden Mountain," 329–30. The text of section 6 is in California State Commission of Immigration and Housing, *First Annual Report* (Sacramento: State Printing Office, 1915), 8.

18. California State Commission of Immigration and Housing, *Ninth Annual Report* (Sacramento: State Printing Office, 1924), 87; Mrs. Frederick C. Bagley, "The Woman Citizen in Action," *Woman Citizen,* 20 October 1917, 396; Herman, "Neighbors on the Golden Mountain," 350, 372–76; Wood, "California State Commission of Immigration and Housing," 171–74; Woo-Sam, "Domesticating the Immigrant," 138–39. On Gibson's background and career, see Judith Raftery, "Los Angeles Clubwomen and Progressive Reform," in Sitton and Deverell, *California Progressivism Revisited,* 153–58.

19. Herman, "Neighbors on the Golden Mountain," 377–78; Gurvis, "Elementary Education of Adult Immigrants in California," 61–67; Diane Claire Wood, "Immigrant Mothers, Female Reformers, and Women Teachers: The California Home Teacher Act of 1915" (Ph.D. diss., Stanford University, 1996), 28–78; California State Commission of Immigration and Housing, *A Manual for Home Teachers* (Sacramento: California State Printing Office, 1918), in CSL; Mary S. Gibson, "The Education of Immigrant Women in California," *Immigrants in America Review,* June 1915, 13–17, and "Schools for the Whole Family," *Survey,* 1 June 1926, 300–303; Gayle Gullett, "Women Progressives and the Politics of Americanization in California, 1915–1920," *Pacific Historical Review* 64 (February 1995): 71–94; Judith Rosenberg Raftery, *Land of Fair Promise: Politics and Reform in Los Angeles Schools, 1885–1941* (Stanford: Stanford University Press, 1992), 68–75.

20. Hartmann, *Movement to Americanize,* 97; Frank Trumbull, Chairman, National Americanization Committee, New York City, to Dr. P. P. Claxton, Commissioner of Education, Washington, D.C., 1 April 1919, File 106, Box 11, Records of the Office of the Commissioner, Historical File, 1870–1950, Records of the Office of Education, RG 12, NARA; Darrell Hevenor Smith, *The Bureau of Education: Its History, Activities and Organization* (Baltimore: Johns Hopkins University Press, 1923), 39; National Committee of One Hundred, "The Story of the 'America First' Campaign," Box 5, Folder 9: Subject File 1916–1919 and N.D., U.S. Interior Deptartment, Council of Defense Records, Record Series 19, MSHSA.

21. Richard K. Campbell, "Americanization," in *Immigration and Americanization: Selected Readings,* comp. and ed. Philip Davis (Boston: Ginn, 1920), 673–701, quote on 678; "Educating the Immigrants," *World's Work,* April 1916, 600–601; "Your Government of the United States: Making New Americans," *World's Work,* May 1916, 30–33; Darrell Hevenor Smith, *The Bureau of Naturalization: Its History, Activities and Organization* (Baltimore: Johns Hopkins Press, 1926), 11–12. The Naturalization Act of 29 June 1906 established the Bureau of Immigration and Naturalization within the Department of Commerce and Labor and specified the proceedings through which immigrants declared their intention to seek citizenship and, between two and seven years after their declaration ("first papers"), petitioned for naturalization. The act also stated that knowledge of English was required to be admitted to citizenship. *U.S. Statutes at Large* 34 (1906): 596–97, 599.

22. P. P. Claxton, "Americanization," in Davis, *Immigration and Americanization,* 622; Thompson, *Schooling of the Immigrant,* 6–7.

23. "Making Aliens into Citizens," *Independent,* 28 February 1916, 294; "Lending a Hand to the Immigrant," *Outlook,* 21 June 1916, 397.

24. Ray Stannard Baker and William E. Dodd, eds., *The Public Papers of Woodrow Wilson: The New Democracy,* 2 vols. (New York: Harper, 1926), 319. See Ronald Fernandez, "Getting Germans to Fight Germans: The Americanizers of World War I," *Journal of Ethnic Studies* 9 (Summer 1981): 53–68.

25. The 1915 affair was based on a 1914 Cleveland celebration, at which newly naturalized citizens were invited to a special reception. After receiving a small American flag and a seal of the city with "Citizen" emblazoned upon it, they were seated on the stage and listened to patriotic songs and speeches. "Americanization Day," *Outlook,* 30 June 1915, 485; "Americanization Day," *Immigrants in America Review,* June 1915, 74–75; Hartmann, *Movement to Americanize,* 112–23; Frances A. Kellor, "National Americanization Day—July 4th," *Immigrants in America Review,* September 1915, 20–22. See also Chester Ferris, "The Los Angeles Example," *Review of Reviews,* January 1916, 82.

26. [Frances Kellor], "America's Problem," *Immigrants in America Review,* January 1916, 3–5; "Immigrant Education," *School and Society,* 9 September 1916, 397–98. In July 1916, the Bureau of Naturalization sponsored a competing Citizenship Convention in Washington, D.C.; Hartmann, *Movement to Americanize,* 158.

27. John F. McClymer, *War and Welfare: Social Engineering in America, 1890–1925* (Westport, Conn.: Greenwood Press, 1980), 116–17; Hartmann, *Movement to Americanize,* 164–215; Franklin K. Lane, Secretary of the Interior, "Americanization Agencies Coordinated," Department of the Interior, Bureau of Education, Americanization Division, *Americanization,* 1 January 1919, 1; Trumbull to Claxton [P. P. Claxton], Commissioner of Education, Washington, D.C., "Reply to Memorandum of Elliott Dunlap Smith in Regard to Conflict between Federal Agencies for Americanization," 5, File 106, Box 12, Council of National Defense, 1917–1921, RG 12, NARA; Council of National Defense, Washington, *Bulletin No. 86. Americanization of Aliens,* 12 February 1918, File 106, Box 7, Council of National Defense—Combating Illiteracy, RG 12.

28. William J. Breen, *Uncle Sam at Home: Civilian Mobilization, Wartime Federalism, and the Council of National Defense, 1917–1919* (Westport, Conn.: Greenwood Press, 1984); Robert D. Cuff, *The War Industries Board: Business-Government Relations during World War I* (Baltimore: Johns Hopkins University Press, 1973), 13–43.

29. George Creel, "The Hopes of the Hyphenated," *Century,* January 1916, 350; Stephen Vaughn, *Holding Fast the Inner Lines: Democracy, Nationalism, and the Committee on Public Information* (Chapel Hill: University of North Carolina Press, 1980), 14–22, 32–34, 49–51; George Creel, *How We Advertised America* (New York: Harper, 1920), 184–99; James R. Mock and Cedric Larson, *Words That Won the War: The Story of the Committee on Public Information* (Princeton, N.J.: Princeton University Press, 1939), 3–47, 213–32; Hartmann, *Movement to Americanize,* 205–10.

30. Larry Joe Smith, "The Gubernatorial Career of Julius C. Gunter, 1917–1919" (M.A. thesis, University of Denver, 1973), 38–59; Arthur Capper, "Kansas in the Great War," in *History of the Kansas State Council of Defense,* ed. Frank W. Blackmar (Topeka: Kansas State Printing Plant, 1920), 13. As to Colorado's claim as the first state council of defense, the Commonwealth of Massachusetts had formed a Committee on Public Safety in February 1917. Breen, *Uncle Sam at Home,* 7.

31. Carl Abbott, Stephen J. Leonard, and David McComb, *Colorado: A History of the*

Centennial State, rev. ed. (Boulder: Colorado Associated University Press, 1982), 254–55.

32. Benjamin Goddard, comp., *Pertinent Facts on Utah's Loyalty and War Record* (Salt Lake City, Utah: 1918), 1; Breen, *Uncle Sam at Home,* 100.

33. Henry Wray, "America's Unguarded Gateway," *North American Review,* August 1918, 312–14.

34. "A Proud and Loyal State," *North American Review,* October 1918, 487–93.

35. Warren A. Beck, *New Mexico: A History of Four Centuries* (Norman: University of Oklahoma Press, 1962), 304–11; Paul D. Young, "The Kansas State Council of Defense in World War I" (M.A. thesis, Emporia State University, 1988), 36, 52, 89.

36. Arizona State Council of Defense, *A Record of the Activities of the Arizona State Council of Defense* (Phoenix: Republican Print Shop, 1919), 18; Ellis Parker Butler, "Tories and Copperheads," *Council of Defense Chronicle,* April 1918, KSHS Library; *Wyoming Tribune,* 2 March 1918, in Box 37, Grace Raymond Hebard Papers, AHC.

37. *Big Horn County Rustler,* 6 April 1917; Lyle W. Dorsett, "The Ordeal of Colorado's Germans during World War I," *Colorado Magazine* 51 (Fall 1974): 281–82. See Frederick C. Luebke, *Bonds of Loyalty: German-Americans and World War I* (DeKalb: Northern Illinois University Press, 1974). See Helen Z. Papanikolas, "Immigrants, Minorities, and the Great War," *Utah Historical Quarterly* 58 (Fall 1990): 351–70.

38. W. S. Gifford, Director, Council of National Defense, and George F. Porter, Chief of State Councils Section, to the Several State Councils of Defense, "Bulletin No. 82: Reaching the German-Speaking Population," 4 January 1918, Box 7, Folder 105: Americanization, 4 January 1918–17 February 1919, RG 35, Council of Defense, Reel 4, ASA; Robert N. Manley, "The Nebraska State Council of Defense: Loyalty Programs and Policies During World War I" (M.A. thesis, University of Nebraska, 1959); William G. Ross, *Forging New Freedoms: Nativism, Education, and the Constitution, 1917–1927* (Lincoln: University of Nebraska Press, 1994); Dorsett, "Ordeal of Colorado's Germans," 285; William C. Sherman and Playford V. Thorson, eds., *Plains Folk: North Dakota's Ethnic History* (Fargo: North Dakota Institute for Regional Studies, 1986), 92; K. Ross Toole, *Twentieth-Century Montana: A State of Extremes* (Norman: University of Oklahoma Press, 1972), 139–93. See Arnon Gutfeld, *Montana's Agony: Years of War and Hysteria, 1917–1921* (Gainesville: University Press of Florida, 1979).

39. Breen, *Uncle Sam at Home,* 161–65; Hartmann, *Movement to Americanize,* 174–76, 188; Young, "Kansas State Council of Defense," 53; Newton D. Baker, Secretary of War and Chairman of the Council of National Defense, to President, 24 July 1918, in Box 26958, Reports, 1917–1919, Julius C. Gunter Papers, CSA. This letter was part of an effort begun several months before to enhance recognition of the state councils and the State Councils Section. Baker's letter and a reply by Wilson were actually ghosted by Frederick Lewis Allen, then a staffer in the State Councils Section. Breen, *Uncle Sam at Home,* 48–50.

40. James C. Stephens to A. W. Grant, 11 January 1918, Gunter Papers, Box 26744, Correspondence 1918; A. W. Grant to Professor J. C. Stephens, 19 January 1918, A. W. Grant to George Norlin, 21, 26 March 1918, Norlin to Grant, 29 March 1918, Colorado State Council of Defense, General Letter 6, 18 June 1918, all in Box 1237, Americanization, January–August 1918 folder, Governor's Council of Defense, World War I and II Collection, CSA; Colorado Council of Defense, *Weekly News Letter No. 25,* March 1918, and *Weekly News Letter No. 46,* August 1918, Box 1245, State Council of Defense Weekly News Letter, October 1917–November 1918, CSA; James C. Stephens, "Report of Committee on Amer-

icanization, November 18, 1918," Box 1, Continuing Education, 1918–1919 folder, Extension Division Papers, Archives, UCBL.

41. State of Utah Council of Defense, *Bulletin No. 4* (1918), 27; Minutes, 22 June 1918, Box 1, Folder 2: Minutes of Executive Committee Meetings, 22 December 1917–29 June 1918, Utah State Council of Defense Collection, MS 107, UUSC; Minutes, State Council of Defense, 11 May 1918, World War I Utah State Council of Defense, Correspondence, Minutes, Reports, Misc., Acc. 15163, Military Dept. 3170-71, USA.

42. *Acts, Resolutions, and Memorials of the First Special Session, Third Legislature of the State of Arizona*, Phoenix, 1918, 28–29; Arizona State Council of Defense, *Record of Activities*, 32–36.

43. F. W. Blackmar, "Organization of State Council of Defense," In Blackmar, *History of the Kansas State Council of Defense*, 33; *Report of the Council of Defense of the State of New Mexico*, Santa Fe, 1918, 41–42, Box 10911, Administrative Records, Council of Defense, Adjutant General's Collection, NMSRCA. See Lansing B. Bloom, "New Mexico in the Great War. I: The Breaking of the Storm," *New Mexico Historical Review* 1 (January 1926): 3–14; Frank H. H. Roberts, "New Mexico in the Great War. II: The War Executive," *New Mexico Historical Review* 1 (January 1926): 15–22; Walter M. Danburg, "New Mexico in the Great War. III: The State Council of Defense," *New Mexico Historical Review* 1 (April 1926): 103–20.

44. Report of the Montana Council of Defense to the Sixteenth Legislative Assembly, 28 January 1919, Box 10: Legislative Series, 1918 Extraordinary Session, 1919 Session, Governors' Papers, Manuscript Collection 35, MSHSA; Chamber of Commerce of the United States of America, "Bulletin No. 17 of the Immigration Committee," 15 December 1917, 1–3, Box 10910, Americanization Programs, Council of Defense, Adjutant General's Collection, NMSRCA.

45. Norlin to Gunter, 22 June 1918, Norlin to H. A. Buchtel, 22 June 1918, Correspondence 1918, Gunter Papers; Colorado Council of Defense, *Weekly News Letter No. 38*, June 1918, Box 1245, State Council of Defense Weekly News Letter, October 1917–November 1918, CSA.

46. C. J. Ernst, *Are You Sorry You Came to This Country: An Address to Citizens of the United States of German Birth or Ancestry*, Nebraska State Council of Defense, 1917, 9–10, Box 1262, War Activities of Other States folder, Governor's Council of Defense, World War I and II Collection, CSA; Noble Warrum, *Utah in the World War*, Utah State Council of Defense, 1924, 105–07; Minutes, Executive Committee, 13 April 1918, World War I Utah State Council of Defense, Correspondence, Minutes, Reports, Misc., USA; James C. Stephens to State Council of Defense, 27 September 1918, Box 1237, Americanization, September 1918–March 1919 folder, CSA.

47. Victor Neuhaus to State Council of Defense, 18 June, 9 July 1918, George Norlin to Executive Committee of the Colorado State Council of Defense, 10 July 1918, H. R. Welton to Victor Neuhaus, 16 July, 21 October 1918, Welton to Norlin, 11 October 1918, all in Box 1237, Americanization, September 1918–March 1919 folder, CSA; Minutes, Meeting of Americanization Committee, Colorado State Council of Defense, 22 June 1918, Box 11, Folder 6—Americanization, University Archives, President's Office Papers, Archives, UCBL.

48. Minutes, 23 July 1918, Minute Book No. Two, Box 1278A, State Council of Defense, CSA; James C. Stephens to H. R. Welter, 20 August 1918; "The Use of the German Language in America," by the Committee on Americanization of the Colorado State Council of Defense; Colorado State Council of Defense, General Letter 76, 3 October 1918, and Gen-

eral Letter 84, 5 October 1918, all in Box 1237, Americanization, September 1918–March 1919 folder, CSA.

49. Young, "Kansas State Council of Defense in World War I," 45–47, 50–57; Blackmar, *History of the Kansas State Council of Defense,* 70–71.

50. Breen, *Uncle Sam at Home,* 72, 81; Washington State Council of Defense, *Report of the State Council of Defense to the Governor of Washington Covering Its Activities during the War, June 16, 1917 to January 9, 1919* (Olympia, Wash.: Frank M. Lamborn, 1919), 60–61; Margaret A. Hall, "Henry Suzzalo and the Washington State Council of Defense" (M.A. thesis, University of Washington, 1975), 3–39; Gutfeld, *Montana's Agony,* 37–69. The Montana Council of Defense survived until August 1921, when Governor Stewart's successor, Joseph Dixon, terminated its powers and canceled its appropriations.

51. California State Commission of Immigration and Housing, *Americanization: The California Program* (Sacramento: State Printing Office, 1919), 7, in CSL. Along with Oregon, California became a big disappointment in terms of its State Council of Defense. An enthusiastic beginning, with the legislature's establishment of a thirty-three-member body shortly before American entry, was negated by Governor William D. Stephens's choice for chairman, who proved to be incompetent in the eyes of the State Councils Section of the Council of National Defense. Breen, *Uncle Sam at Home,* 100.

52. California State Commission of Immigration and Housing, *Americanization: The California Program,* 8–12, quotes on 10–11.

53. Frederick Lewis Allen, "The American Tradition and the War," *Nation,* 26 April 1917, 485.

54. Sarka B. Hrbkova, *Bridging the Atlantic: A Discussion of the Problems and Methods of Americanization* (Lincoln: Nebraska State Council of Defense, 1919), 3–4, 6, 17, 23.

55. Richard K. Campbell, Commissioner of Naturalization, Bureau of Naturalization, to Governor S. V. Stewart, Chairman, State Council of Defense, 25 November 1918, Box 3, Folder 23: Americanization, Council of Defense Records (Record Series 19), MSHSA; Elliott Dunlap Smith, Chief, Organization and Information Section, Field Division, Council of National Defense, to State Council of Defense, Topeka, Kansas, 13 December 1918, Franklin K. Lane, Chairman, Field Division, Council of National Defense, to Arthur Capper, 17 December 1918, Arthur Capper Collection, Correspondence Files, General Correspondence—Numerical File 1917–1918, Box 14, Governor's Office, Kansas State Archives, KSHS; Grosvenor B. Clarkson, Director of the Field Division and Acting Director of the Council, Council of National Defense, to the Several State Councils and State Divisions of the Woman's Committee, "Bulletin No. 17, Circular No. 35: Americanization," 21 December 1918, Box 3, Folder 23, Council of Defense Records, MSHSA. The Field Division of the Council of National Defense was organized in fall 1918, incorporating the work previously done by the Woman's Committee and the State Councils Section.

56. Blackmar, *History of the Kansas State Council of Defense,* 72–73; J. C. Mohler, Secretary, Kansas State Council of Defense, to Henry J. Allen, 16 January 1919, Henry J. Allen Papers, Correspondence—Subject File, Box 8, Council of Defense 1918–1919, Governor's Office Collection, Kansas State Archives, KSHS.

57. *Laws, Resolutions, and Memorials of the State of Montana Passed by the Sixteenth Regular Session of the Legislative Assembly* (Helena: State Publishing, 1919), 90–91; May Trumper, "Summary of Montana School Legislation," *Inter-Mountain Educator,* March 1919, 16; *Laws of the State of New Mexico Passed by the Fourth Regular Session, 1919* (Albuquerque: Albright and Anderson, 1919), 298.

58. *Laws of the State of Utah Passed at the Thirteenth Regular Session of the Legislature* (Salt

Lake City: F. W. Gardiner, 1919), 285–87, Pubic Document Serial Set, Series 83155, Reel 15, and *Laws of the State of Utah Passed at the Fourteenth Regular Session of the Legislature* (Salt Lake City: Arrow Press, 1921), 301–02, Series 83155, Reel 16, both in USA. Interestingly, after passage of the 1921 amendments, Japanese comprised the majority of those paying the fee and attending the classes in Carbon County. Philip F. Notarianni, "Utah's Ellis Island: The Difficult 'Americanization' of Carbon County," *Utah Historical Quarterly* 47 (Spring 1979): 192.

59. James R. Coxen, State Director for Vocational Education, to Raymond Crist, Director of Citizenship, U.S. Department of Labor, 23 April 1920, File 27682/62, Box 410, University of Wyoming, Universities and Colleges, Correspondence, RG 85, NARA. *Wyoming House Journal, Fifteenth Legislature* (Laramie: Laramie Republican, 1919), 38, 394; Frances Birkhead Beard, ed., *Wyoming from Territorial Days to the Present* (Chicago: American Historical Society, 1933), 1:628; *Wyoming Educational Bulletin,* February 1921, 1.

60. "Americanization Work Assuming Definite Shape in Arizona," *Arizona Service Bulletin,* 1 February 1919, 1–2, ASL; Arizona State Council of Defense, *A Record of the Activities of the Arizona State Council of Defense,* 43.

61. *Americanization in Arizona,* State Committee on Americanization Work in Arizona, 1920, File 106: Council of National Defense—Combating Illiteracy, Entry 6, Box 11, RG 12, NARA; State Committee on Americanization Work in Arizona, *Americanization in Arizona,* Bulletin No. 1, June 1920, 4, ASL; "Reaching the Women in the Homes," *Arizona Service Bulletin,* 1 February 1919, 9.

62. *Seventh Biennial Report of the State Superintendent of Public Instruction for the Period July 1, 1922, to June 30, 1924* (Phoenix, 1924), 24; *Eighth Biennial Report of the State Superintendent of Public Instruction for the Period July 1, 1924, to June 30, 1926* (Phoenix, 1926), 42.

63. Breen, *Uncle Sam at Home,* 164; California State Commission of Immigration and Housing, *Americanization: California's Answer* (Sacramento: California State Printing Office, 1920), in CSL. See File 27682/4, Box 407, University of California, Re: Americanization Work in Universities and Colleges (A General File), Education and Americanization Files, 1914–1936, RG 85, NARA; Lawrence C. Kelly, *The Assault on Assimilation: John Collier and the Origins of Indian Policy Reform* (Albuquerque: University of New Mexico Press, 1983), 106–07; Wood, "California State Commission of Immigration and Housing," 176–79.

64. General Federation of Women's Clubs Americanization Committee, 1918–1920, *A Suggested Program for Americanization; Reprinted by Permission of the G.F.W.C. and presented by the California Commission of Immigration and Housing,* 7–8, in CSL.

65. Herman, "Neighbors on the Golden Mountain," 460–594; Kelly, *Assault on Assimilation,* 109–10; Gurvis, "Elementary Education of Adult Immigrants in California," 149–51; Wood, "California State Commission of Immigration and Housing," 130–37.

66. California State Commission of Immigration and Housing, *Ninth Annual Report,* 10–11, quoted in Smith, *Americans in the Making,* 202–03; Herman, "Neighbors on the Golden Mountain," 348, 386–87. For a succinct critique of what Lubin considered "pseudo-Americanization" efforts, see Simon J. Lubin and Christina Krysto, "The Strength of America: V. The Menace of Americanization," *Survey,* 21 February 1920, 610–12.

67. Robert E. Hennings, *James D. Phelan and the Wilson Progressives of California* (New York: Garland, 1985), 75–76, 192, 194, 198–99; *Amendments to the Constitution and Proposed Statutes with Arguments Respecting the Same to be Submitted to the Electors of the State of California at the General Election on Tuesday, November 2, 1920* (Sacramento: Department of State Printing, 1920), pamphlet in Japanese File, 1920, Carton 15, James D. Phelan Papers, Bancroft Library, UCB.

68. "Americanization," *Arizona Service Bulletin,* 1 February 1919, 6.

69. On the trials of the Greek population in Utah during this period, see Helen Z. Papanikolas, "The Exiled Greeks," in *The Peoples of Utah,* ed. Helen Z. Papanikolas (Salt Lake City: Utah State Historical Society, 1976), 427–31, and *Toil and Rage in a New Land: The Greek Immigrants in Utah* (Salt Lake City: Utah State Historical Society, 1970), originally published as *Utah Historical Quarterly* 38 (Spring 1970).

70. For context on the rise of the Ku Klux Klan in areas of the West during the 1920s, see Charles C. Alexander, *The Ku Klux Klan in the Southwest* (Lexington: University Press of Kentucky, 1965), 11–17; Kenneth T. Jackson, *The Ku Klux Klan in the City, 1915–1930* (New York: Oxford University Press, 1967), 10–11, 18–23, 187–231; Robert Alan Goldberg, *Hooded Empire: The Ku Klux Klan in Colorado* (Urbana: University of Illinois Press, 1981); Larry R. Gerlach, *Blazing Crosses in Zion: The Ku Klux Klan in Utah* (Logan: Utah State University Press, 1982); Shawn Lay, *War, Revolution, and the Ku Klux Klan: A Study of Intolerance in a Border City* (El Paso: Texas Western Press, 1985); Shawn Lay, ed., *The Invisible Empire in the West: Toward a New Appraisal of the Ku Klux Klan of the 1920s* (Urbana: University of Illinois Press, 1992).

3. "Sane Information on Capital and Labor"

1. Two-thirds of all male coal mine operatives and roughly three of every five steam railroad laborers in Colorado listed in the 1910 census were foreign-born white. In Montana, four out of five copper miners were foreign-born white, as were over three-fourths of all steam railroad workers. Foreign-born whites made up more than three-fourths of all coal miners in both Utah and Wyoming. U.S. Bureau of the Census, *Thirteenth Census, Vol. 4: Population* (Washington, D.C.: Government Printing Office, 1913), 441, 484, 523, 533; U.S. Immigration Commission, *Reports of the Immigration Commission. Immigrants in Industries, Part 25: Japanese and Other Immigrant Races in the Pacific Coast and Rocky Mountain States,* vol. 2, 61st Cong., 2d sess., S. Doc. 633, serial 5684-3: 151. See Carlton H. Parker, "The Casual Laborer," in Parker, *The Casual Laborer and Other Essays* (New York: Harcourt, Brace and Howe, 1920), 61–89. For a comprehensive historical analysis of the Western economy and workforce, see Carlos A. Schwantes, "Wage Earners and Wealth Makers," in *The Oxford History of the American West,* ed. Clyde A. Milner II, Carol A. O'Conner, and Martha A. Sandweiss (New York: Oxford University Press, 1994), 431–67.

2. A. Dudley Gardner and Verla R. Flores, *Forgotten Frontier: A History of Wyoming Coal Mining* (Boulder, Colo.: Westview Press, 1989), 113. See Mario T. García, *Desert Immigrants: The Mexicans of El Paso, 1880–1920* (New Haven, Conn.: Yale University Press, 1981); Gunther Peck, "Padrones and Protest: 'Old' Radicals and 'New' Immigrants in Bingham, Utah, 1905–1912," *Western Historical Quarterly* 24 (May 1993): 157–78, "Reinventing Free Labor: Immigrant Padrones and Contract Laborers in North America, 1885–1925," *Journal of American History* 83 (December 1996): 848–71, and "Mobilizing Community: Migrant Workers and the Politics of Labor Mobility in the North American West, 1900–1920," in *Labor Histories: Class, Politics, and the Working-Class Experience,* ed. Eric Arnesen, Julie Greene, and Bruce Laurie (Urbana: University of Illinois Press, 1998), 175–200.

3. Edward Alsworth Ross, *The Old World in the New: The Significance of Past and Present Immigration to the American People* (New York: Century, 1914), 96, 209; quote on Chinese

in Spencer C. Olin, "European Immigrant and Oriental Alien: Acceptance and Rejection by the California Legislature of 1913," *Pacific Historical Review* 35 (August 1966): 309–10; Chester H. Rowell, "Chinese and Japanese Immigrants—A Comparison," *Annals of the American Academy of Political and Social Science* 34 (September 1909): 223–26; U.S. Immigration Commission, *Reports of the Immigration Commission. Abstracts of Reports of the Immigration Commission* (Washington, D.C.: Government Printing Office, 1911), 1:672.

4. Victor S. Clark, "Mexican Labor in the United States," U.S. Department of Commerce and Labor, *Bureau of Labor Bulletin,* No. 78, Washington, D.C., 1908, reprinted in *Mexican Labor in the United States* (New York: Arno Press, 1974), 466; U.S. Department of Commerce and Labor, *Annual Report of the Commissioner-General of Immigration* (Washington, D.C.: Government Printing Office, 1911), 121, quoted in Mark Reisler, *By the Sweat of Their Brow: Mexican Immigrant Labor in the United States, 1900–1940* (Westport, Conn.: Greenwood Press, 1976), 4.

5. Lawrence A Cardoso, *Mexican Emigration to the United States, 1897–1931: Socio-Economic Patterns* (Tucson: University of Arizona Press, 1980), 1–95; Carey McWilliams, *North from Mexico: The Spanish-Speaking People of the United States* (New York: Greenwood Press, 1968), 162–88; Reisler, *By the Sweat of Their Brow,* 24–48; Paul S. Taylor, *Mexican Labor in the United States* (Berkeley: University of California Press, 1930), 1:41. See also U.S. Immigration Commission, *Abstracts of Reports of the Immigration Commission,* 1:683.

6. U.S. Senate Committee on Immigration, *Chinese Exclusion,* 57th Cong., 1st sess., 1902, S. Report 776, serial 4265, 296–99, 309; *San Francisco Chronicle,* 2 March 1905.

7. Carlos A. Schwantes, "The Concept of the Wageworkers' Frontier: A Framework for Future Research," *Western Historical Quarterly* 18 (January 1987): 44–45; David M. Emmons, "Constructed Province: History and the Making of the Last American West," *Western Historical Quarterly* 25 (Winter 1994): 457; Alexander Saxton, *The Indispensable Enemy: Labor and the Anti-Chinese Movement in California* (Berkeley: University of California Press, 1971); Michael Kazin, *Barons of Labor: The San Francisco Building Trades and Union Power in the Progressive Era* (Urbana: University of Illinois Press, 1987), 162–70; Dino Cinel, *From Italy to San Francisco: The Immigrant Experience* (Stanford, Calif.: Stanford University Press, 1982), 115; Allan Kent Powell, "The 'Foreign Element' and the 1903–4 Carbon County Coal Miners' Strike," *Utah Historical Quarterly* 43 (Spring 1975): 125–54; David M. Emmons, *The Butte Irish: Class and Ethnicity in an American Mining Town, 1875–1925* (Urbana: University of Illinois Press, 1989), 255–91; Andrea Yvette Huginnie, "'Strikitos': Race, Class, and Work in the Arizona Copper Industry, 1870–1920" (Ph.D. diss., Yale University, 1991), 52–62, 155–57.

8. Catherine Collomp, "Unions, Civics, and National Identity: Organized Labor's Reaction to Immigration, 1881–1897," *Labor History* 29 (Fall 1988): 453, 463; Herbert Hill, "Anti-Oriental Agitation and the Rise of Working-Class Racism," *Society* 10 (January/February 1973): 53; *San Francisco Chronicle,* 15 November 1904. Gompers was willing to grant a charter to the Beet Workers if Japanese and Chinese were kept out. The Mexican head of the union refused to accede to that condition; Huginnie, "'Strikitos,'" 165–70.

9. Huginnie, "'Strikitos,'" 236–64; James W. Byrkit, *Forging the Copper Collar: Arizona's Labor-Management War of 1901–1921* (Tucson: University of Arizona Press, 1982), 52–53. Southern progressives, as several historians have shown, premised their reform programs on first consolidating segregation and the disfranchisement of black and poor white voters. See C. Vann Woodward, *Origins of the New South, 1877–1913* (Baton Rouge: Louisiana State University Press, 1951), 321–95, 456–81; Jack D. Kirby, *Darkness at the Dawning: Race and*

Reform in the Progressive South (Philadelphia: Lippincott, 1972); J. Morgan Kousser, *The Shaping of Southern Politics: Suffrage Restriction and the Establishment of the One-Party South* (New Haven, Conn.: Yale University Press, 1974); Dewey W. Grantham, *Southern Progressivism: The Reconciliation of Progress and Tradition* (Knoxville: University of Tennessee Press, 1983); Edward L. Ayers, *The Promise of the New South: Life after Reconstruction* (New York: Oxford University Press, 1992), 418–20, 424–26, 434–37.

10. Huginnie, "'Strikitos,'" 264–89, 305–20.

11. Harvey A. Levenstein, "The AFL and Mexican Immigration in the 1920s: An Experiment in Labor Diplomacy," *Hispanic American Historical Review* 48 (May 1968): 206–19.

12. There are those, like the socialist historian Theodore W. Allen, who argue that social control by the ruling class was possible only by investing in the racial privileges of the laboring class, for instance through laws on trades, tenancy, and homesteading. Irish-American attacks on abolition and black equal rights before the Civil War, Allen suggests, were carried out in part as a "white" workers' front via the Democratic Party aligned with southern slaveholders (*The Invention of the White Race,* vol. 1, *Racial Oppression and Social Control* [New York: Verso, 1994]). For a viewpoint that emphasizes working-class racism as more of a grassroots phenomenon, see Michael Omi and Howard Winant, *Racial Formation in the United States from the 1960s to the 1980s* (New York: Routledge and Kegan Paul, 1986). For additional discussions of working-class racial beliefs and policies, see Gwendolyn Mink, *Old Labor and New Immigrants in American Political Development: Union, Party, and State, 1875–1920* (Ithaca, N.Y.: Cornell University Press, 1986); David Roediger, *The Wages of Whiteness: Race and the Making of the American Working Class* (London: Verso, 1991); Eric Arneson, "'Like Banquo's Ghost, It Will Not Down': The Race Question and the American Railroad Brotherhoods, 1880–1920," *American Historical Review* 99 (December 1994): 1601–33; Noel Ignatiev, *How the Irish Became White* (New York: Routledge, 1995).

13. The worst labor violence occurred in Colorado, climaxing with the 1903–1904 Cripple Creek strike, which originated with WFM efforts to organize mill and smelter workers at Colorado City. When miners in the Cripple Creek district struck in August 1903, a business-government alliance led by Colorado's antilabor governor James Peabody responded with determination. Peabody dispatched state militia troops, whose commander announced his intention "to do up this damned anarchistic federation." The strike spread to Telluride, and Peabody, citing some minor incidents crafted by company detectives to implicate the union, declared martial law in the strike regions. When the dynamiting of a railroad station in Cripple Creek killed thirteen nonunion miners on 6 June 1904, corporate interests quickly pinned responsibility upon the WFM. More than two hundred union miners were marched into Kansas and New Mexico and abandoned. Subsequently, workers could only get jobs in Colorado mines if they held an official Mine Owners' Association card and did not belong to a union. Melvyn Dubofsky, *We Shall Be All: A History of the Industrial Workers of the World,* 2d ed. (Urbana: University of Illinois Press, 1988), 28–35, 42–56; Schwantes, "Wage Earners and Wealth Makers," 443–44; Mark Wyman, *Hard-Rock Epic: Western Miners and the Industrial Revolution, 1860–1910* (Berkeley: University of California Press, 1989).

14. On the Western Federation of Miners' ethnic exclusiveness prior to 1910, see Philip F. Notarianni Jr. and Joseph Stipanovich, "Immigrants, Industry, and Labor Unions: The American West, 1890–1916," *Journal of Historical Studies* 3 (Fall/Winter 1978): 10–12. See also Dubofsky, *We Shall Be All,* 81–87, 146–70; Patrick Renshaw, *The Wobblies: The Story of the IWW and Syndicalism in the United States* (Chicago: Ivan R. Dee, 1999), 21–74; Joseph R.

Conlin, *Bread and Roses Too: Studies of the Wobblies* (Westport, Conn.: Greenwood Publishing, 1969), 66–94.

15. Frank S. Hamilton, "A Screed and a Suggestion," *Solidarity,* 21 November 1914, 2–3, quoted in Dubofsky, *We Shall Be All,* 313; see Carlton H. Parker, "The I.W.W.," in Parker, *The Casual Laborer and Other Essays,* 91–124. For discussion and references pertaining to the Wobblies' ethnic and racial toleration and relative failure to organize among minorities, see Phil Mellinger, "How the IWW Lost Its Western Heartland: Western Labor History Revisited," *Western Historical Quarterly* 27 (Autumn 1996): 308–11, 319–24.

16. Dubofsky, *We Shall Be All,* 173–97; Renshaw, *The Wobblies,* 84–87; Conlin, *Bread and Roses Too,* 71–76; Robert L. Tyler, *Rebels of the Woods: The I.W.W. in the Pacific Northwest* (Eugene: University of Oregon Books, 1967), 33–43.

17. See Cletus E. Daniel, *Bitter Harvest: A History of California Farmworkers, 1870–1941* (Berkeley: University of California Press, 1981), 88–94; Dubofsky, *We Shall Be All,* 294–300.

18. House Committee on Immigration, *Hearings on Temporary Admission of Illiterate Mexican Laborers,* 302, quoted in Reisler, *By the Sweat of Their Brow,* 159; Neil Foley, *The White Scourge: Mexicans, Blacks, and Poor Whites in Texas Cotton Culture* (Berkeley: University of California Press, 1997), 108–15; James A. Sandos, *Rebellion in the Borderlands: Anarchism and the Plan of San Diego, 1904–1923* (Norman: University of Oklahoma Press, 1992); Ricardo Romo, *East Los Angeles: History of a Barrio* (Austin: University of Texas Press, 1983), 89–111; Robert E. Ireland, "The Radical Community: Mexican and American Radicalism, 1900–1910," *Journal of Mexican-American History* 2 (Fall 1971): 22–29; Huginnie, "'Strikitos,'" 297–98, 300, 332. Prosecuted and convicted by the federal government under the Espionage Act of 1918, Flores Magón was imprisoned again from 1918 to 1922. For more information and references on Mexican labor and radical organizing in the West, see Mellinger, "How the IWW Lost Its Western Heartland," 313–16.

19. H. Lee Scamehorn, *Mill and Mine: The CF&I in the Twentieth Century* (Lincoln: University of Nebraska Press, 1992); George S. McGovern and Leonard F. Guttridge, *The Great Coalfield War* (Boston: Houghton Mifflin, 1972); Zeese Papanikolas, *Buried Unsung: Louis Tikas and the Ludlow Massacre* (Salt Lake City: University of Utah Press, 1982); H. M. Gitelman, *Legacy of the Ludlow Massacre: A Chapter in Industrial Relations* (Philadelphia: University of Pennsylvania Press, 1988).

20. Dubofsky, *We Shall Be All,* 333–43 (quote on 334); Tyler, *Rebels of the Woods,* 62–84.

21. Joseph A. McCartin, *Labor's Great War: The Struggle for Industrial Democracy and the Origins of Modern American Labor Relations, 1912–1921* (Chapel Hill: University of North Carolina Press, 1997), 38–63.

22. Dubofsky, *We Shall Be All,* 313–18, 359–61; Nigel Anthony Sellars, *Oil, Wheat, and Wobblies: The Industrial Workers of the World in Oklahoma, 1905–1930* (Norman: University of Oklahoma Press, 1998), 35–76.

23. *Utah Mining Review,* 15 August 1917, in Helen Z. Papanikolas, "Immigrants, Minorities, and the Great War," *Utah Historical Quarterly* 58 (Fall 1990): 355; Dubofsky, *We Shall Be All,* 360–65; Washington State Council of Defense, *Report of the State Council of Defense to the Governor of Washington Covering Its Activities during the War, June 16, 1917 to January 9, 1919* (Olympia, Wash.: Frank M. Lamborn, 1919), 44; *Omaha Evening Bee,* 15 November 1917, quoted in David G. Wagaman, "'Rausch Mit': The I.W.W. in Nebraska during World War I," in *At the Point of Production: The Local History of the I.W.W.,* ed. Joseph R. Conlin (Westport, Conn.: Greenwood Press, 1981), 127.

24. Dubofsky, *We Shall Be All*, 301–07, 366–69, 391–93; Arnon Gutfeld, *Montana's Agony: Years of War and Hysteria, 1917–1921* (Gainesville: University Press of Florida, 1979), 14–36; Emmons, *Butte Irish*, 277–86, 364–86.

25. Byrkit, *Forging the Copper Collar*, 1–9, 138–215; Dubofsky, *We Shall Be All*, 369–74, 384–91; Philip Taft, "The Bisbee Deportation," *Labor History* 13 (Winter 1972): 3–40; Huginnie, "'Strikitos,'" 294–338; President's Mediation Commission, *Report on the Bisbee Deportations*, 6 November 1917, Box 3, Folder 44: IWW 25 April 1917–14 June 1918, RG 35, Council of Defense, Reel 2, ASA.

26. J. S. Douglas to Dwight B. Heard, President, Arizona Council of Defense, 27 July 1917, Box 3, Folder 44: IWW 25 April 1917–14 June 1918, RG 35, ASA. The governors of California, Arizona, Utah, Nevada, Idaho, Colorado, Oregon, and Wyoming comprised the organization of Western governors. Dubofsky, *We Shall Be All*, 393–422; William Preston Jr., *Aliens and Dissenters: Federal Suppression of Radicals, 1903–1933* (Cambridge, Mass.: Harvard University Press, 1963), 124–26; Samuel Edgerton Wood, "The California State Commission of Immigration and Housing: A Study of Administrative Organization and the Growth of Function" (Ph.D. diss., University of California, Berkeley, 1942), 265–73.

27. James R. Green, *Grass-Roots Socialism: Radical Movements in the Southwest, 1895–1943* (Baton Rouge: Louisiana State University Press, 1978), 360–66; Sellars, *Oil, Wheat, and Wobblies*; Robert L. Morlan, *Political Prairie Fire: The Nonpartisan League, 1915–1922* (Minneapolis: University of Minnesota Press, 1955); Carl H. Chrislock, *Ethnicity Challenged: The Upper Midwest Norwegian-American Experience in World War I* (Northfield, Minn.: Norwegian-American Historical Association, 1981), 89, 91; Gutfeld, *Montana's Agony*, 93–101.

28. Chrislock, *Ethnicity Challenged*, 97–98; Wood, "California Commission of Immigration and Housing," 263–65; C. L. Cross to Arthur Capper, 27 February 1918, and Capper to Cross, 4 March 1918, Arthur Capper Collection, Box 14, File 222, Non-Partisan League, Kansas State Archives, KSHS.

29. Capper to J. C. Mack, 9 March 1918, W. J. Rumald to the Adjutant General, 11 March 1918, T. A. Case to Capper, 12 March 1918, M. L. Ames to Capper, 23 March 1918, Capper to Case, 23 March 1918, Capper to Ames, 28 March 1918, Capper to B. A. Belt, 1 April 1918, Capper to Elmer T. Peterson, 27 April 1918, all in Capper Collection, Box 14, File 222, Non-Partisan League. There was an interesting exchange between Capper and a P. E. Zimmerman of Lindsborg, a fanatical antiradical. Zimmerman repeatedly expressed disappointment with Capper's lack of zeal and threatened political retribution for politicians who did not join his crusade; see Capper to Zimmerman, 30 March, 26 August 1918, Zimmerman to Capper, 6 April, 19 August 1918, Capper Collection, Box 14, File 222, Non-Partisan League. For discussion of the Nebraska State Council of Defense's campaign against the NPL, see Robert N. Manley, "The Nebraska State Council of Defense: Loyalty Programs and Policies during World War I" (M.A. thesis, University of Nebraska, 1959), 242–80. On NPL recruitment in Washington State and the State Council of Defense's efforts to thwart it, see Margaret A. Hall, "Henry Suzzallo and the Washington State Council of Defense" (M.A. thesis, University of Washington, 1975), 34–36, 66–67.

30. Dubofsky, *We Shall Be All*, 423–78; Renshaw, *The Wobblies*, 163–67; Tyler, *Rebels of the Woods*, 155–84, 187–94, 199–206; Earl Bruce White, "*The United States v. C. W. Anderson et al.*: The Wichita Case, 1917–1919," in Conlin, *At the Point of Production*, 143–64. The Wichita trial was transferred to Kansas City on 1 December 1919 because of the deplorable

condition of the Wichita jail in which defendants had been held for two years; Clayton R. Koppes, "The Kansas Trials of the IWW, 1917–1919," *Labor History* 16 (Summer 1975): 348. David M. Kennedy points out that "nearly half the prosecutions under the espionage and sedition acts had taken place in thirteen of the eighty-seven federal districts. Not surprisingly, those thirteen districts were to be found primarily in the Western states, especially where the IWW was most active" (*Over Here: The First World War and American Society* [New York: Oxford University Press, 1980], 83).

31. Preston, *Aliens and Dissenters,* 118–51, 163–80, 191–237; Robert K. Murray, *Red Scare: A Study in National Hysteria* (Minneapolis: University of Minnesota Press, 1955); Eldridge F. Dowell, *A History of Criminal Syndicalism Legislation in the United States* (Baltimore: Johns Hopkins University Press, 1939); On the Colorado coal strike of 1927–1928, see Donald J. McClurg, "The Colorado Coal Strike of 1927—Tactical Leadership of the IWW," *Labor History* 4 (Winter 1963): 68–92; Charles J. Bayard, "The 1927–1928 Colorado Coal Strike," *Pacific Historical Review* 32 (August 1963): 235–50; Ronald L. McMahan, "'Rang-U-Tang': The I.W.W. and the 1927 Colorado Coal Strike," in Conlin, *At the Point of Production,* 191–212.

32. Hywel Davies, U.S. Labor Administrator, to W. B. Wilson, Secretary of Labor, 28 March 1918, Box 3, Folder 44: IWW 25 April 1917–14 June 1918, RG 35, ASA.

33. National Committee of 100, "War Facts on Americanization;" George Norlin to Governor Julius C. Gunter, 27 March 1918, James C. Stephens to Dr. George Norlin, 15 April 1918, Box 26774, Correspondence 1918, File Folder AM Americanization, Julius C. Gunter Papers, CSA.

34. James C. Stephens, "Report of Committee on Americanization, November 18, 1918," Box 1, Continuing Education, 1918–1919 folder, Extension Division Papers, Archives, UCBL; Stephens to A. U. Mayfield, 17 January 1919, Box 1237, September 1918–March 1919 folder, Governor's Council of Defense World War I and II Collection, CSA; *Wyoming Educational Bulletin,* October 1919, 1.

35. Preston, *Aliens and Dissenters,* 45–46, 64, 70–75, 83–85. See *U.S. Statutes at Large* 39 (1917): 889.

36. Stephen Meyer III, "Adapting the Immigrant to the Line: Americanization in the Ford Factory, 1914–1921," *Journal of Social History* 14 (1980): 67–82, and *The Five Dollar Day: Labor Management and Social Control in the Ford Motor Company, 1908–1921* (Albany: State University of New York Press, 1981), 149–68; Ruth Hutchinson Crocker, *Social Work and Social Order: The Settlement Movement in Two Industrial Cities, 1889–1930* (Urbana: University of Illinois Press, 1992), 103, 106–07, 133–38; Gerd Korman, *Industrialization, Immigrants, and Americanizers: The View from Milwaukee, 1866–1921* (Madison: State Historical Society of Wisconsin, 1967), 104–05, 110–16, 130–31, 136–47, 161–65; William M. Leiserson, *Adjusting Immigrant and Industry* (New York: Harper, 1924; reprint, New York: Arno Press and *New York Times,* 1969), 120–25.

37. Department of the Interior, Bureau of Education, "Schedule 7: A Pro-American Drive for Industries Employing Immigrants," Box 5, Folder 9: Subject File 1916–1919 and N.D., U.S. Interior Department, Council of Defense Records, MSHSA.

38. *Annual Report of the Sociological Department of the Colorado Fuel and Iron Company for 1901–1902,* 32–33, Colorado Fuel and Iron Company Collection, MSS 1057, Box 6, File Folder 108, CSHS; P. P. Colgrove, "Night Schools of the Iron Range of Minnesota," *Immigrants in America Review,* January 1916, 65–69; "The Iron Melting Pot," *American City,* April

1917, 350–53; Emory S. Bogardus, *Essentials of Americanization* (Los Angeles: University of Southern California Press, 1920), 286–87; C. F. Switzer, "Larger Plans for Americanizing the Foreigner," *Elementary School Journal* 19 (January 1919): 371; "Teaching Americanism in the Factory," *Literary Digest*, 1 February 1919, 29.

39. Loren Stiles Minckley, *Americanization through Education* (Frontenac, Kans., privately published, 1917), 228–44, quotes on 231–33. See William E. Powell, "European Settlement in the Cherokee-Crawford Coal Fields of Southeastern Kansas," *Kansas Historical Quarterly* 41 (Summer 1975): 150–65.

40. Frances Kellor, "How to Americanize a City," *American City*, February 1916, 164. See also Kellor, "Americanization: A Conservation Policy for Industry," *Annals of the American Society of Political and Social Science* 65 (May 1916): 240–44, and "Americanization by Industry," *Immigrants in America Review*, April 1916, 15–26.

41. "America First Conference," *School and Society*, 27 January 1917, 106; M. E. Ravage, "Standardizing the Immigrant," *New Republic*, 31 May 1919, 145. See also "Chambers of Commerce in 'America First' Campaign," *American City*, December 1916, 680.

42. Arthur H. Fleming, Chief of State Council Section, Council of National Defense, to the Several State Councils of Defense, "Americanization: Supplementing Bulletins Nos. 86 and 92," 11 July 1918, P. P. Claxton, Commissioner, Bureau of Education, to Gentlemen, 5 July 1918, Box 3, Folder 23: Americanization, Council of Defense Records, Record Series 19, MSHSA; Department of the Interior, Bureau of Education, "America First Campaign. To Increase School Attendance of Non-English-Speaking Immigrants. How Industries Can Cooperate," Division of Immigrant Education Circular No. 12, Box 5, Folder 9: Subject File 1916–1919 and N.D., U.S. Interior Department, Council of Defense Records, MSHSA.

43. Department of the Interior, Bureau of Education, "America First Campaign. How Labor Unions Can Cooperate," Division of Immigrant Education Circular No. 16, Box 5, Folder 9: Subject File 1916–1919 and N.D., U.S. Interior Department, Council of Defense Records, MSHSA; Ruby Baughman, "Elementary Education for Adults," *Annals of the American Academy of Political and Social Science* 93 (January 1921): 165; John Bodnar, *The Transplanted: A History of Immigrants in Urban America* (Bloomington: Indiana University Press, 1985), 98–104; David Montgomery, "Nationalism, American Patriotism, and Class Consciousness among Immigrant Workers in the United States in the Epoch of World War I," in *"Struggle a Hard Battle": Essays on Working-Class Immigrants*, ed. Dirk Hoerder (DeKalb: Northern Illinois University Press, 1986), 327–51; Gary Gerstle, *Working-Class Americanism: The Politics of Labor in a Textile City, 1914–1960* (Cambridge: Cambridge University Press, 1989), 19–91; James R. Barrett, *Work and Community in the Jungle: Chicago's Packinghouse Workers, 1894–1922* (Urbana: University of Illinois Press, 1987), 118–53, and "Americanization from the Bottom Up: Immigration and the Remaking of the Working Class in the United States, 1880–1930," *Journal of American History* 79 (December 1992): 1014–18; McCartin, *Labor's Great War*, 104–18.

44. David Montgomery, *Workers' Control in America: Studies in the History of Work, Technology, and Labor Struggles* (Cambridge: Cambridge University Press, 1979), 32–33, 40–44, 93–108, *The Fall of the House of Labor: The Workplace, the State, and American Labor Activism, 1865–1925* (Cambridge: Cambridge University Press, 1987), 6, 214–56, 330–410, and "Nationalism, American Patriotism, and Class Consciousness," in Hoerder, *"Struggle a Hard Battle,"* 328. See also Lizabeth Cohen, *Making a New Deal: Industrial Workers in Chicago, 1919–1939* (Cambridge: Cambridge University Press, 1990), 159–211; McCartin, *Labor's Great War*, 199–220.

45. Frank B. Lenz, "The Assimilation of the Immigrant," *Overland Monthly*, September 1915, 243; Leiserson, *Adjusting Immigrant and Industry*, 244–45.

46. Huginnie, "'Strikitos,'" 318. See James R. Barrett and David Roediger, "Inbetween Peoples: Race, Nationality and the 'New Immigrant' Working Class," *Journal of American Ethnic History* 16 (Spring 1997): 3–44.

47. The company declared bankruptcy and reorganized in 1936 as the Colorado Fuel and Iron Corporation; the Rockefellers sold out to Wall Street investment banker Charles Allen Jr. in 1944. H. Lee Scamehorn, *Pioneer Steelmaker in the West: The Colorado Fuel and Iron Company, 1872–1903* (Boulder, Colo.: Pruett Publishing, 1976), and *Mill and Mine*.

48. John Thomas Hogle, "The Rockefeller Plan: Workers, Managers, and the Struggle over Unionism in Colorado Fuel and Iron, 1915–1942" (Ph.D. diss., University of Colorado, 1992), 70–99; Denise Pan, "Peace and Conflict in an Industrial Family: Company Identity and Class Consciousness in a Multi-ethnic Community, Colorado Fuel and Iron's Cameron and Walsen Coal Camps, 1913–1928" (M.A. thesis, University of Colorado, 1994), 26–30; Scamehorn, *Mill and Mine*, 56–81.

49. *Annual Report of the Sociological Department . . . 1901–1902*, 14–16, 32–33; *Annual Report of the Sociological Department of the Colorado Fuel and Iron Company, 1903–1904*, 25–26; *Annual Report of the Sociological Department of the Colorado Fuel and Iron Company, 1906–1907*, 16, all in Colorado Fuel and Iron Company Collection, MSS 1057, Box 6, File Folders 108–110, CSHS.

50. *Annual Report of the Sociological Department of the Colorado Fuel and Iron Company, 1904–1905*, 11–12, MSS 1057, Box 6, File Folder 109, CSHS.

51. Hogle, "Rockefeller Plan," 108; Pan, "Peace and Conflict in an Industrial Family," 72–73, 76; "Alien Miners Learn English Language," *Colorado Fuel and Iron Company Industrial Bulletin* (hereafter cited as *Industrial Bulletin*), 31 October 1916, 4; "Y.M.C.A. Making Forward Strides," *Industrial Bulletin*, 31 January 1917, 9, 12; "Y.M.C.A. at Minnequa Steel Works," *Industrial Bulletin*, 30 April 1917, 4; "A Talk with Men Who Love America," *Industrial Bulletin*, 31 October 1917, 3; "Making Americans in Coal Camps," *Industrial Bulletin*, 31 October 1918, 6.

52. "Training for American Citizenship," *Industrial Bulletin*, 30 April 1919, 5; "Experts Plan Americanization Campaign," *Industrial Bulletin*, 27 April 1920, 11; "Citizenship School at Steel Works 'Y,'" *Industrial Bulletin*, 15 February 1924, 25.

53. Hogle, "Rockefeller Plan," 100–140; Gitelman, *Legacy of the Ludlow Massacre*, 320–22.

54. Horace W. Kruse, *Americanizing an Industrial Center: An Account of Experience and Procedure in the Towns of the St. Louis, Rocky Mountain and Pacific Company in Colfax County, New Mexico* (Raton, N.M.: Raton Publishing, 1920), 7–8. Organized in 1905 by Henry and Hugo Koehler of St. Louis, Missouri, the company owned the large Raton Coal Field in Colfax County. See Craig Alan Ratcher, "A Brief History of the St. Louis, Rocky Mountain and Pacific Company" (M.A. thesis, University of New Mexico, 1971).

55. Kruse, *Americanizing an Industrial Center*, 8–10.

56. Kruse, *Americanizing an Industrial Center*, 12–14.

57. Kruse, *Americanizing an Industrial Center*, 16–18.

58. Kruse, *Americanizing an Industrial Center*, 18–20.

59. Kruse, *Americanizing an Industrial Center*, 26.

60. George B. Hodgkin, "Americanization in a Labor Camp," *School and Society*, 26 No-

vember 1921, 492; Ethel Richardson, "Doing the Thing That Couldn't Be Done," *Survey,* 1 June 1926, 298; Gilbert G. González, *Labor and Community: Mexican Citrus Worker Villages in a Southern California County, 1900–1950* (Urbana: University of Illinois Press, 1994), 117–20.

61. Hodgkin, "Americanization in a Labor Camp," 493; Baughman, "Elementary Education for Adults," 165; González, *Labor and Community,* 126.

62. Chamber of Commerce of the United States of America, *Bulletin No. 17 of the Immigration Committee,* 15 December 1917, and *Bulletin No. 23x of the Immigration Committee,* 1 June 1918, Box 1237, Americanization, January–August 1918 folder, Governor's Council of Defense World War I and II Collection, CSA; see also Ellen Schoening Aiken, "Japanese Immigrant Women and the Union Pacific Towns of Wyoming in the 1920s" (M.A. thesis, University of Colorado, Boulder, 1994).

63. "Alien Miners Learn English Language," 4.

64. González, *Labor and Community,* 120, 122, 128, 130.

65. State Commission of Immigration and Housing of California, *Americanization: The California Program* (Sacramento: State Printing Office, 1919), 11, CSL; Wood, "California Commission of Immigration and Housing," 263–65.

66. *Thirteenth Report of the Superintendent of Public Instruction of the State of Utah for the Biennial Period Ending June 30, 1920,* 63–65, Public Documents Serial Set, Series 240, Reels 36–37, USA.

67. Report of Director for the Americanization Committee of the State Council of Defense, for April and May 1918; James C. Stephens to Dr. George Norlin, 13 August, 25 September, 14 December 1918; "Americanization of Foreigners in Colorado," undated, typed manuscript; all in Box 11, Folder 6—Americanization, University Archives, President's Office Papers, Archives, UCBL. Stephens, "Report of Committee on Americanization, November 18, 1918"; "Report of Work Carried on by the Committee on Americanization of the Colorado State Council of Defense, April 1, 1918, to April 1, 1919," Box 1, Continuing Education, 1918–1919 Folder, Extension Division Papers, Archives, UCBL. James C. Stephens to Julius C. Gunter, 31 May, 10 July 1918, Stephens to Elliott D. Smith, 19 June 1918, Box 26744, Correspondence 1918, File Folder AM Americanization, Gunter Papers, CSA; Stephens to State Council of Defense, 27 September 1918, Box 1237, Americanization, September 1918–March 1919 folder, Governor's Council of Defense, World War I and II Collection, CSA. See too "Making Americans in Coal Camps," *Industrial Bulletin,* 31 October 1918, 6.

68. "Report of the Director of the Committee on Americanization of the Colorado State Council of Defense," 26 August 1918, Box 11, Folder 6—Americanization, University Archives, President's Office Papers, Archives, UCBL; Stephens, "Report of Committee on Americanization, November 18, 1918," James C. Stephens, "Report of Activities of Committee on Americanization, Colorado State Council of Defense, March 1918 to January 1919," and Stephens to State Council of Defense, 27 September 1918, all in Box 1237, Americanization, September 1918–March 1919 folder, Governor's Council of Defense, World War I and II Collection, CSA.

69. Stephens to State Council of Defense, 27 September 1918; James C. Stephens, "To the Members of the Committee on Americanization of the Colorado State Council of Defense," Box 1, Continuing Education, 1918–1919 Folder, Extension Division Papers, Archives, UCBL.

70. *Denver Post,* 1 January 1920; for samples of commentaries critical of industrial Americanization, see Glenn Frank, "The Fad of Americanization," *Century,* June 1920, 221; Edward Hale Bierstadt, "Pseudo-Americanization," *New Republic,* 25 May 1921, 371–73, and 1 June 1921, 19–23.

71. Bierstadt, "Pseudo-Americanization," 371.

72. George Bell, "What the State and Nation Can Do to Help the Community in Americanization," Department of the Interior, Bureau of Education, *Proceedings Americanization Conference* (Washington, D.C.: Government Printing Office, 1919), 337; "Denver Opportunity School," *Colorado Manufacturer and Consumer,* undated clipping in Emily Griffith biographical file, AHC.

4. "Education for Citizenship"

1. Paul Lee Ellerbe, Chief Naturalization Examiner, Denver, to Commissioner of Naturalization, 2 November 1917; unidentified newspaper clipping; Paul Lee Ellerbe, speech draft; all in File 27671/4747, Box 189, Colorado Education Association, General Educational Correspondence, Education and Americanization Files, 1914–1936, Records of the Immigration and Naturalization Service, RG 85, NARA; Paul Lee Ellerbe, "Education for Citizenship," *Outlook,* 11 September 1918, 65.

2. Grace Raymond Hebard to Mrs. David, 2 November 1916, Grace Raymond Hebard Papers, AHC; Charles M. Reinoehl, "Mrs. Crow and the Cross School, Montana," *Inter-Mountain Educator,* January 1920, 209.

3. Ruby Baughman, "Elementary Education for Adults," *Annals of the American Academy of Political and Social Science* 93 (January 1921): 164–66.

4. Frank V. Thompson, *Schooling of the Immigrant* (New York: Harper, 1920), 3, 7. Department of the Interior, Bureau of Education, *Bulletin No. 35: Adult Illiteracy* (Washington, D.C.: Government Printing Office, 1916). The problem of adult illiteracy among native-born and immigrant populations appeared to have reached epidemic proportions once the United States entered World War I. Tests revealed that, on average, one of every four draftees was "illiterate to the extent of being unable to read a newspaper or write a letter." Department of the Interior, Bureau of Education, *Report of the Commissioner of Education for the Year Ending June 30, 1919* (Washington, D.C.: Government Printing Office, 1919), 44; Bagdasar Krekor Baghdigian, *Americanism in Americanization* (Kansas City, Mo.: Burton Publishing, 1921), 131–33.

5. "Sen. Winsor Reports Progress of the Americanization Survey," *Arizona Service Bulletin,* 1 February 1919, 2, ASL; Arch M. Thurman, "Americanization in Utah," *Bulletin of the University of Utah,* vol. 11, no. 8, October 1920, Extension Division Series, vol. 2, no. 1 (Salt Lake City: University of Utah Press, 1920), 2; *Thirteenth Report of the Superintendent of Public Instruction of the State of Utah for the Biennial Period Ending June 30, 1920,* 63, Public Documents Serial Set, Series 240, Reels 36–37, USA; State of New Mexico Department of Education, "Proposed Program of Procedure Adopted by the Administrative School Officials and Teachers in Conference with the State Department of Education at Santa Fe, New Mexico, August 15 to 17 inclusive, 1918," Box 8, 1917–1918, Serial Number 14117, Folder 129: State Board of Education, 1917–1918, Governor Washington E. Lindsey Collection, special investigations—penal papers, NMSRCA; California State Commission of Immigration and

Housing, *A Manual for Home Teachers* (Sacramento: California State Printing Office, 1918), 46, CSL.

6. Thompson, *Schooling of the Immigrant,* 164–66. The New York State Department of Education was the first to address the problems of English and illiteracy in a systematic way. After surveying immigrant education statewide, New York State established a "teachers' training institute" at Albany in fall 1915. Permanent training programs were subsequently incorporated within the curriculum at the State College for Teachers, while other temporary "institutes" operated in New York City, Syracuse, Buffalo, and Rochester. "New York State and the Americanization Problem," File 420, Box 44, Americanization folder, Immigrant Education, Records of the Office of the Commissioner, Historical File, 1870–1950, Records of the Office of Education, RG 12, NARA.

7. Department of the Interior, Bureau of Education, Division of Immigrant Education, "Standards and Methods in the Education of Immigrants, Part II: Organization and Administration," Americanization folder, RG 12, NARA. See too William Sharlip and Albert A. Owens, *Adult Immigrant Education: Its Scope, Content, and Methods* (New York: Macmillan, 1925), 22–39.

8. Mark Hall, "A Remarkable Americanization Record: The Great Good Being Accomplished by One Woman," *Today's Housewife,* February 1924, 8; Specimens of the Work of Pupils, File 27671/23/2, Box 5, General Educational Correspondence, Education and Americanization Files, 1914–1936, RG 85, NARA; Loren Stiles Minckley, *Americanization through Education* (Frontenac, Kan.: privately published, 1917), 248–49, 255.

9. *Eighth Biennial Report of the State Superintendent of Public Instruction for the Period July 1, 1924 to June 30, 1926,* Phoenix, 1926, 41; Department of the Interior, Bureau of Education, Washington, "Syllabus of a Tentative Course in Elementary Civics for Immigrants," Hebard Papers, AHC.

10. Joel M. Roitman, "The Progressive Movement: Education and Americanization" (Ph.D. diss., University of Cincinnati, 1981), iv.

11. Thompson, *Schooling of the Immigrant,* 2; "Making Americans," *Nation,* 31 May 1919, 878. The classic study of progressive education reform is Lawrence A. Cremin, *The Transformation of the School: Progressivism in American Education, 1876–1957* (New York: Alfred A. Knopf, 1961). See also Rush Welter, *Popular Education and Democratic Thought in America* (New York: Columbia University Press, 1962), 245–82; Henry J. Perkinson, *The Imperfect Panacea: American Faith in Education, 1865–1965* (New York: Random House, 1968), 183–97. The "community school" ideal was very nearly realized in the Gary system, pioneered in the industrial Indiana city of that name. The Gary plan emphasized, in typical progressive style, efficiency and democracy. Ultimately, the system's paternalism backfired when the emphasis on vocational education in New York City schools alienated Jewish immigrant parents, who rioted against the system in 1917; Roitman, "Progressive Movement," 180–205. For discussions of progressive education with particular emphases on immigrants, see Paula S. Fass, *Outside In: Minorities and the Transformation of American Education* (New York: Oxford University Press, 1989), 13–35.

12. Thurman, "Americanization in Utah," 3–6. From 1921 until retirement in 1953, Thurman was a teacher and administrator in Salt Lake City schools. He earned a masters' degree from the University of Utah in 1934 and did doctoral work at the University of Chicago. Thurman died in May 1959. *Salt Lake City Tribune,* 10 April 1953, 4 May 1959, Arch M. Thurman—Biography Clippings File, Utah History Information Center, USHS; W. C.

Ebaugh to W. W. Armstrong, 10 August 1918, Box 2, Folder 3: General Correspondence, 10 June 1917–30 September 1918, Utah State Council of Defense Collection, MS 107, UUSC.

13. Robert A. Carlson, *The Quest for Conformity: Americanization through Education* (New York: Wiley, 1975), 79.

14. Emory S. Bogardus, *Essentials of Americanization,* rev. ed. (Los Angeles: University of Southern California Press, 1920), 20, 21–26, 92–107.

15. P. P. Claxton, "Americanization," in *Immigration and Americanization: Selected Readings,* comp. and ed. Philip Davis (Boston: Ginn, 1920), 622; Thompson, *Schooling of the Immigrant,* 6–7; State Committee on Americanization Work in Arizona, *Americanization in Arizona,* Bulletin No. 1, June 1920, 3, ASL; Minckley, *Americanization through Education,* 250.

16. George L. Bell, *Americanization as a Necessity to National Defense; Address at State Convention of C.F.W.C., Pasadena, Cal.* [1918], in CSL; *Boston Herald and Tribune,* 3 September 1918, clipping in Box 35, Hebard Papers, AHC; Ethel Richardson, "Socializing the Method, Content, and Procedure," *Addresses and Proceedings of the Sixtieth Annual Meeting Held at Boston, Massachusetts, July 3–8, 1922* (Washington, D.C.: National Education Association, 1922), 922.

17. Division of Immigrant Education, "Standards and Methods," 1–11. A completed, official "Schedule of Standards and Methods in the Education of Immigrants" was released by the Bureau in February 1917. Department of the Interior, Bureau of Education, *Report of the Commissioner of Education for the Year Ended June 30, 1917,* vol. I (Washington, D.C.: Government Printing Office, 1917), 62.

18. *Arizona Service Bulletin,* 1 February 1919, 12, ASL; Frances A. Kellor, "How to Increase Night School Attendance among the Foreign-Born," *School and Society,* 15 April 1916, 572.

19. Bogardus, *Essentials of Americanization,* 285; Frederic Ernest Farrington, "Campaign for Americanization," *School and Society,* 10 June 1916, 863.

20. *U.S. Statutes at Large* 34 (1907): 1228; Candice Lewis Bredbenner, *A Nationality of Her Own: Women, Marriage, and the Law of Citizenship* (Berkeley: University of California Press, 1998), 4–5, 57–60.

21. Grace Raymond Hebard, "Americanization of Alien Woman," *Vanguard,* March 1918, in Hebard Papers. The Naturalization Act of 1855 conferred derivative citizenship on foreign women who married American citizens; Bredbenner, *A Nationality of Her Own,* 4–5, 15–16.

22. [Grace Raymond Hebard], "America for Americans," 2–4, typewritten speech draft in Hebard Papers.

23. *U.S. Statutes at Large* 42 (1922): 1021–22. Technically referred to as the Married Women's Independent Citizenship Act, the legislation took on the name of its chief sponsor in the House of Representatives, John L. Cable of Ohio. House passage took place on 20 June 1922, with the Senate following suit on 9 September. President Warren G. Harding signed the bill into law on 22 September. One problematic consequence of the Cable Act concerned the creation of "stateless" foreign women who, expatriated by marriage to Americans according to their native country's statutes, no longer enjoyed automatic naturalization in the United States. Between the moment they married and the day they completed naturalization requirements, such women held no citizenship whatsoever; Bredbenner, *A Nationality of Her Own,* 80–112.

24. "Americanization Work of Women's Clubs," *Immigrants in America Review,* January

1916, 64; National Americanization Committee, "Americanization of Immigrant Women," Box 10910, Adjutant General's Collection, Americanization Program, Council of Defense folder, NMSRCA.

25. "Americanization of Aliens Is Urged," unidentified and undated newspaper clipping, Box 37, Hebard Papers. See Hebard to Hon. V. J. Tidball, 15 September 1916, Hebard to Paul Lee Ellerbe, 15 September 1916, Ellerbe to Hebard, 25 September 1916, Hebard to Mrs. John C. Pearson, undated, all in Naturalization Files, Folder 4, Hebard Papers. Also see John F. McClymer, "Gender and the 'American Way of Life': Women in the Americanization Movement," *Journal of American Ethnic History* 10 (Spring 1991): 7–9; Frank B. Lenz, "The Education of the Immigrant," *Educational Review,* May 1916, 473; "Home Economics Evening School Classes for Spanish-American Women," *New Mexico School Review,* April 1925, 15; Sharlip and Owens, *Adult Immigrant Education,* 192–202. For a notably tolerant, commonsense approach to teaching English to immigrant girls and women, see Edith Terry Bremer, "Foreign Community and Immigration Work of the National Young Women's Christian Association," *Immigrants in America Review,* January 1916, 73–82.

26. W. H. W. (?), Acting Commissioner of Naturalization, to Professor E. J. Iddings, Extension Division, University of Idaho, 5 June 1919, Box 407, Folder U10, Entry 30, File 27682 (U) Re: Americanization Work in Universities and Colleges (A General File), RG 85, NARA.

27. Outline of Work Department of Applied Education, 1924–1925, Division of Illiteracy (Chairman—Mrs. Bertha Van Devender, Basin), Box 1: Board Records, Wyoming Federation of Women's Clubs Papers (hereafter cited as WFWC Papers), WSA; *Wyoming Clubwoman,* November 1925, 23. In 1916, under an agreement with the U.S. commissioner of immigration, the GFWC established its first Americanization program. A special GFWC Americanization division was set up under Alice James Winter in 1919 "to coordinate the work of all departments." When Winter advanced to the General Federation presidency in 1920, former president Anna J. H. Pennybacker of Texas became the first chairman of an American Citizenship Department. With its slogan "Every Club a Training Ground for Citizenship," Pennybacker's department promoted Americanization institutes and conferences, encouraged attendance at naturalization court hearings by local Americanization committees, proposed classes, and suggested the holding of "immigrant gifts"–style gatherings where the native-born and foreign-born could meet. Mildred White Wells, *Unity in Diversity: The History of the General Federation of Women's Clubs* (Washington, D.C.: GFWC, 1953), 246–47, 250–51. See Karen J. Blair, *The Clubwoman as Feminist: True Womanhood Redefined, 1868–1914* (New York: Holmes and Meier Publishers, 1980).

28. See 1924 Handbook, Folder 5, Handbooks for the Local Unions of the Kansas WCTU, and Folder 2, Programs for the Local Unions, Kansas WCTU 1917–1918, both in Box 6, Mary Evelyn Dobbs/Kansas Women's Christian Temperance Union (KWCTU) Collection, KSHS.

29. Bell, *Americanization as a Necessity to National Defense;* David George Herman, "Neighbors on the Golden Mountain: The Americanization of Immigrants in California. Public Instruction as an Agency of Ethnic Assimilation, 1850 to 1933" (Ph.D. diss., University of California, Berkeley, 1981), 378–84; Ann Marie Woo-Sam, "Domesticating the Immigrant: California's Commission of Immigration and Housing and the Domestic Immigration Policy Movement, 1910–1945" (Ph.D. diss., University of California, Berkeley, 1999), 144–47; Judith Rosenberg Raftery, *Land of Fair Promise: Politics and Reform in Los Angeles Schools,*

1885–1941 (Stanford, Calif.: Stanford University Press, 1992), 75–81; California State Commission of Immigration and Housing, *Report on an Experiment Made in Los Angeles in the Summer of 1917 for the Americanization of Foreign-born Women* (Sacramento: California State Printing Office, 1917); Amanda Chase, "A Practical Program for the Home Teacher," in Commission of Immigration and Housing, *Manual for Home Teachers,* 22–23. See too Amanda Matthews Chase, "The 'Official' Home Teacher," *Out West,* January 1916, 33–37.

30. California State Commission of Immigration and Housing, *Manual for Home Teachers,* 29–30, 39. With the exception of Oakland, home teaching found little sustained success outside of southern California. Diane Claire Wood, "Immigrant Mothers, Female Reformers, and Women Teachers: The California Home Teacher Act of 1915" (Ph.D. diss., Stanford University, 1996), 64–69.

31. *Report of the Woman's Committee of the Council of Defense for Kansas: From July 6, 1917, to December 30, 1918* (Topeka: Kansas State Printing Press, 1919), 48; Paul D. Young, "The Kansas State Council of Defense in World War I" (M.A. thesis, Emporia State University, 1988), 71; "Americanization Work Assuming Definite Shape in Arizona," *Arizona Service Bulletin,* 1 February 1919, 2, ASL; *Americanization in Arizona,* State Committee on Americanization Work in Arizona, 1920, File 106: Council of National Defense—Combating Illiteracy, Entry 6, Box 11, RG 12, NARA.

32. Wood, "Immigrant Mothers, Female Reformers, and Women Teachers," 1–9, 29–35; see Eileen Boris, "Reconstructing the 'Family': Women, Progressive Reform, and the Problem of Social Control," in *Gender, Class, Race, and Reform in the Progressive Era,* ed. Noralee Frankel and Nancy S. Dye (Lexington: University Press of Kentucky, 1991), 73–86; Seth Koven and Sonya Michel, eds., *Mothers of a New World: Maternalist Politics and the Origins of the Welfare State* (New York: Routledge, 1993); Gwendolyn Mink, *The Wages of Motherhood: Inequality in the Welfare State, 1917–1942* (Ithaca, N.Y.: Cornell University Press, 1995).

33. Wood, "Immigrant Mothers, Female Reformers, and Women Teachers," 91–98; Baughman, "Elementary Education for Adults," 167.

34. George J. Sanchez, "'Go After the Women': Americanization and the Mexican Immigrant Woman, 1915–1929," in *Unequal Sisters: A Multicultural Reader in U.S. Women's History,* ed. Ellen Carol DuBois and Vicki L. Ruiz (New York: Routledge, 1994), 288–91, and *Becoming Mexican American: Ethnicity, Culture, and Identity in Chicano Los Angeles, 1900–1945* (New York: Oxford University Press, 1993), 87–107. Historian Ricardo Romo, *East Los Angeles: History of a Barrio* (Austin: University of Texas Press, 1983), 130–37, posits that the barrio in east Los Angeles was important to progressives' practical experiments in legislating morality and, most decidedly with World War I, fostering assimilation via home teachers, mothers' classes, and evening schools. He states, without a citation, that "suspicious of the home teachers, Mexican women rarely attended the organized sessions at the evening school. As a result, the home teacher found it necessary to arrange visits to each of the homes of the Mexican families for the purpose of recruiting students in English and industrial crafts classes" (p. 133).

35. Sanchez, "'Go After the Women,'" 292–93; Wood, "Immigrant Mothers, Female Reformers, and Women Teachers," 99–105. On immigrant women's responses to Americanization, see Maxine Seller, "The Education of the Immigrant Woman," *Journal of Urban History* 4 (May 1978): 316–20.

36. Richardson, "Socializing the Method, Content, and Procedure," 925; Boris, "Reconstructing the 'Family,'" 82; Woo Sam, "Domesticating the Immigrant," 179–85.

37. Gilbert G. González, *Chicano Education in the Era of Segregation* (Philadelphia: Balch Institute Press, 1990), 59–60.

38. Welter, *Popular Education and Democratic Thought,* 258–63.

39. See Carol S. Gruber, *Mars and Minerva: World War I and the Uses of the Higher Learning in America* (Baton Rouge: Louisiana State University Press, 1975). For extension divisions' activities conducted through land-grant institutions see Edward Danforth Eddy Jr., *Colleges for Our Land and Time: The Land-Grant Idea in American Education* (Westport, Conn.: Greenwood Press, 1973), 148–200; "The University and the National Service and Defense: The Extension Division of the University of Utah," World War I Utah State Council of Defense, Miscellaneous Correspondence, Papers, Speeches, Acc. 15164, Military Dept. 3172, USA.

40. Frank W. Blackmar, ed., *History of the Kansas State Council of Defense* (Topeka: Kansas State Printing Plant, 1920), 73–74; "Program of Americanization, Kansas City, Kansas, 1920–1921," Kansas State Library, KSHS.

41. Thompson, *Schooling of the Immigrant,* 269–74.

42. *Thirteenth Report of the Superintendent of Public Instruction,* 63–64; Philip F. Notarianni Jr., "Utah's Ellis Island: The Difficult 'Americanization' of Carbon County," *Utah Historical Quarterly* 47 (Spring 1979): 190.

43. University Extension Division, Bureau of Americanization, "Americanization Course," *University of Colorado Bulletin,* vol. 20, no. 3, March 1920, File 27682/5, Box 407, University of Colorado, Universities and Colleges, Correspondence, RG 85, NARA; R. D. Harriman, "Suggestions for Americanization Teachers," *Bulletin of the University of Utah,* vol. 10, no. 16, March 1920, Extension Division Series, vol. I, no. 3 (Salt Lake City: University of Utah Press, 1920), 8; James R. Coxen, State Director for Vocational Education, Laramie, to Raymond Crist, Director of Citizenship, Washington, D.C., 23 April 1920, File 27682/62, Box 410, University of Wyoming, Universities and Colleges, Correspondence, RG 85, NARA. See Robert Floyd Gray, "The Training of Americanization Teachers," *Educational Review,* March 1921, 224–29.

44. Wood, "Immigrant Mothers, Female Reformers, and Women Teachers," 69–72, 126–29, 134–40; Baughman, "Elementary Education for Adults," 167; Mary S. Gibson, "Schools for the Whole Family," *Survey,* 1 June 1926, 303.

45. Wood, "Immigrant Mothers, Female Reformers, and Women Teachers," 114–41. On the development of professionalism in education, see David B. Tyack, *The One Best System: A History of American Urban Education* (Cambridge, Mass.: Harvard University Press, 1974), 135–36, 182–98. For a more thorough discussion of how professionalism impacted women social workers, see Robyn Muncy, *Creating a Female Dominion of Reform, 1890–1935* (New York: Oxford University Press, 1991).

46. "Attorney General Makes Ruling on Senate Bill Number Nineteen," *Arizona Service Bulletin,* 1 February 1919, 7, ASL; Wood, "Immigrant Mothers, Female Reformers, and Women Teachers," 85–91, quote on 90.

47. Paul Armstrong, Chief Naturalization Examiner, Denver, to Commissioner of Naturalization, Educational, 10 March 1924, Conference—Americanization Teachers, Denver, Colorado, File 27671/42/1, Box 14, Correspondence, RG 85, NARA; Harriman, "Suggestions for Americanization Teachers," 20.

48. *Wyoming News,* 3 August 1935, clipping in Box 35, Hebard Papers; see also Cora M. Beach, *Women of Wyoming* (Casper, Wyo.: S. E. Boyer, 1927?), 119–23; I. S. Bartlett, *History of Wyoming,* vol. 3 (Chicago: S. J. Clarke Publishing, 1918), 319–20; *In Memoriam: Grace*

Raymond Hebard, 1861–1936 (Laramie: Faculty of the University of Wyoming, 1937); Janell M. Wenzell, "Dr. Grace Raymond Hebard as Western Historian" (M.A. thesis, University of Wyoming, 1960); Ellerbe, "Education for Citizenship," 64; Mary Antin to Grace Raymond Hebard, undated letter, Hebard Papers, AHC. Antin wrote to Hebard about her work while staying at the cabin of the author Elinore Pruitt Stewart (*Letters of a Woman Homesteader*) in Burnt Fork, Wyoming.

49. Grace Raymond Hebard, "Immigration and Needed Ballot Reform," *Illinois Wesleyan Magazine,* October 1896, 230, in Box 33, Hebard Papers. Hebard's Ph.D. thesis was listed in the University of Wyoming faculty records as "Immigration: Its Relation to Citizenship"; Wenzell, "Dr. Grace Raymond Hebard as Western Historian," 30–33. For Francis Amasa Walker's views, see his *Discussions in Economics and Statistics,* 2 vols., ed. Davis R. Dewey (New York: Henry Holt, 1899).

50. Hebard, "Immigration and Ballot Reform," 226, 228–29, emphasis in the original.

51. Hebard, "Immigration and Ballot Reform," 229, 231–34, 238–43.

52. "Immigration" was one of the topics listed in a description of the Department of Political Economy's "Sociology and Social Problems" course in prewar catalogues. See, for example, "Catalogue, 1914," *University of Wyoming Bulletin* 11 (Laramie: University of Wyoming, April 1914), 95.

53. For the January through April 1916 letters to the Committee on Immigrants in America et al., see Naturalization vertical files; Grace Raymond Hebard to Paul Lee Ellerbe, 10 May 1916, both in Folder 4, AHC.

54. Quotes from Grace Raymond Hebard to Paul Lee Ellerbe, 20 September 1916, and Ellerbe to Hebard, 25 September 1916; see also Hebard to Honorable V. J. Tidball, 15 September 1916; Hebard to Ellerbe, 15 September 1916, all in Naturalization vertical files, Folder 4, AHC.

55. Grace Raymond Hebard, "Americanization of the Immigrant," typewritten draft of speech given at Sheridan, Wyoming, 6 October 1916, before Wyoming Federation of Women's Clubs, 2–3, in Hebard Papers. Several months after the convention, the General Federation published a slightly revised version of Hebard's speech; see Dr. Grace Raymond Hebard, "Americanization of the Immigrant," *General Federation of Women's Clubs Magazine,* February 1917. Anne Ruggles Gere includes a very brief analysis of Hebard's article in *Intimate Practices: Literacy and Cultural Work in U.S. Women's Clubs, 1880–1920* (Urbana: University of Illinois Press, 1997), 90.

56. Hebard, "Americanization of the Immigrant," 3–4, 7; Minutes of the Thirteenth Annual Convention of the Wyoming State Federation of Women's Clubs, Sheridan, Wyoming, 4 October 1916, 28–29, 31, Box 6, Minutes, 1916–1920 folder, WFWC Papers, WSA; *Sheridan Post,* 10 October 1916.

57. Hebard to Ellerbe, 9 October 1916, and Ellerbe to Hebard, 11, 23 October 1916, in Naturalization files, Folder 4, AHC; *Laramie Daily Boomerang,* 25 October 1916, clipping in Box 37, Hebard Papers. See also Hebard to Richard K. Campbell (Commissioner of Naturalization, U.S. Department of Labor), 31 October 1916, also in Folder 4. On cooperation between the Bureau of Naturalization's chief examiners and local judges, see John F. McClymer, "The Federal Government and the Americanization Movement, 1915–24," *Prologue: The Journal of the National Archives* 10 (Spring 1978): 36; Hebard to Mrs. David, 2 November 1916, Hebard to Mrs. Walter McNab Miller, 25 November 1916, Naturalization files, Folder 4.

58. "Americanization Service of the Suffragists," *National Suffrage News,* undated clipping in Box 35, Hebard Papers; "Citizenship. Outline Lessons to Be Used in the Class for Preparation for Naturalization. Grace Raymond Hebard, Laramie, Wyo.," in Naturalization files, Folder 2, AHC. Students had to be able to read English to take Hebard's course. Otherwise, a citizenship candidate would "receive special instruction in another course." See John F. McClymer, "The Americanization Movement and the Education of the Foreign-Born Adult," in *American Education and the European Immigrant: 1840–1940,* ed. Bernard J. Weiss (Urbana: University of Illinois Press, 1982), 105–10, for a general critique of Americanization classes.

59. "Americanization Service"; "Interesting Westerners," *Sunset,* September 1918, 46; *Laramie Boomerang,* 8 March 1917. The German, of course, was Hansen; the Irishman, Joe L. Madigan; and the Englishman, Walter Teesdale. Hansen was indeed drafted into the armed forces. See Grace Raymond Hebard to A. N. Hasenkamp, 17 January 1919, in Naturalization files, Folder 4, AHC.

60. Information on students gleaned from enrollment cards in Naturalization vertical files, Folder 1, AHC. McLay, despite missing the first few meetings of Dr. Hebard's class due to a "very bad cold," was naturalized on 19 March 1919, along with Peter Ketelson, a German, Razi Najjar from Syria, Frederick G. James, a barber from the British West Indies, and Chris Andersen, a Dane who worked as a hostler for the Union Pacific. See Jennie McLay to Grace Raymond Hebard, 4 February 1919, in Naturalization files, Folder 2. Moreover, McLay, who taught for a period of time at Tie Siding School, about twenty miles south of Laramie, was Albany County superintendent of schools from 1923 to 1925. See Albany County Cow-Belles, *Cow-Belles Ring School Bells: A History of Rural Schools in Albany County, Wyoming* (Laramie, Wyo.: Albany County Cow-Belles Club, 1976), xviii, 34.

61. "In a Suffrage Garden," *Woman Citizen,* 10 November 1917, 458, clipping, and "Dr. Hebard Urges Americanization of Aliens," unidentified newspaper clipping, dated 14 November 1917, both in Box 35, Hebard Papers; "Interesting Westerners," 46; Minutes of the State Board of Education for 12 November 1917, in *Minutes of and Reports to the State Board of Education,* WSA.

62. Grace Raymond Hebard to Richard K. Campbell, 9 January 1919, Entry 30, Box 151, File 27671/1973, University of Wyoming, Education and Americanization Files, RG 85, NARA.

63. Hebard also anticipated the state's public schools and the university's Department of Education taking control of Americanization. Grace Raymond Hebard to Raymond Martin, 26 February 1919; Hebard to Paul Armstrong, 26 February, 21 March 1919; Hebard to V. J. Tidball, 17 March 1919; Hebard to Richard K. Campbell, 21 March 1919; Hebard to Paul Lee Ellerbe, 21 March 1919, all in Naturalization files, Folder 4, AHC.

64. "Division of Correspondence Study," *University of Wyoming Bulletin* 15 (Laramie: University of Wyoming, December 1918), 42; "Catalogue, 1921," *UW Bulletin* 18 (Laramie: University of Wyoming, April 1921), 76; "Summer School Number, June 19 to July 29, 1922," *UW Bulletin* 18 (Laramie: University of Wyoming, April 1922), 30. See course outlines for training Americanization workers in Naturalization files, Folder 1, AHC.

65. Undated, typed letter (possibly a copy), and Kate Banner to Grace Raymond Hebard, 5 June 1917, both in Naturalization files, Folder 2, AHC; "Dr. Hebard Honored on Anniversary of Service," *Branding Iron,* 1 July 1929, clipping in Box 35, Hebard Papers.

66. Grace Raymond Hebard to Mr. J. E. Thayer, 18 March 1929, in Naturalization vertical file, Folder 2, AHC; see also, in same location, Hebard to Honorable V. J. Tidball, 18

March 1929; A. L. Burgoon to Dr. Grace Raymond Hebard, 1 August 1922, Box 36, and Sister M. Veronica to Hebard, 23 March 1924, Box 35, Hebard Papers.

67. "Interesting Westerners," 46.

68. "Educators' rhetoric of Americanization was often messianic," David Tyack writes, "a mixture of fear outweighed by hope, of a desire for social control accompanied by a quest for equality of opportunity for the newcomers under terms dictated by the successful Yankee" (*The One Best System*, 232).

69. Department of Labor, Bureau of Naturalization, *Student's Textbook*, comp. Raymond F. Crist (Washington, D.C.: Government Printing Office, 1918), 11.

70. Carol Aronovici, "Americanization: Its Meaning and Function," *American Journal of Sociology* 25 (May 1920): 713.

71. Baughman, "Elementary Education for Adults," 168.

72. Charles Moreau Harger, "The West's New Vision," *Atlantic Monthly*, July 1917, 125.

73. Daughters of the American Revolution of Wyoming, report dated Sheridan, Wyoming, 4 October 1916, in Box 1, DAR Folder, Hebard Papers; *Sheridan Post*, 6 October 1916.

74. Hall, "A Remarkable Americanization Record," 8.

5. "Our Government Thinks We Can"

1. For discussion of the federal government's role in shaping the West, see David Emmons, "Constructed Province: History and the Making of the Last American West," *Western Historical Quarterly* 25 (Winter 1994): 437–59. See, too, Patricia Nelson Limerick, *The Legacy of Conquest: The Unbroken Past of the American West* (New York: W. W. Norton, 1987); Richard White, *"It's Your Misfortune and None of My Own": A History of the American West* (Norman: University of Oklahoma Press, 1991); Clyde A. Milner II, "National Initiatives," in *The Oxford History of the American West*, ed. Clyde A. Milner II, Carol A. O'Conner, and Martha Sandweiss (New York: Oxford University Press, 1994), 155–93; Carl Abbott, "The Federal Presence," in *Oxford History of the American West*, 468–99.

2. Other district offices were at Boston, New York City, Philadelphia, Pittsburgh, and Chicago. Department of Labor, Bureau of Naturalization, *Report of the Commissioner of Naturalization to the Secretary of Labor for the Year Ending June 30, 1924* (Washington, D.C.: Government Printing Office, 1924), 29. In 1925, the bureau was reorganized into twenty-three districts plus four subdistricts, for twenty-seven stations in all. New regional offices were established at Buffalo, Cleveland, Detroit, Cincinnati, Birmingham, New Orleans, Omaha, Kansas City, Ft. Worth, Salt Lake City, Portland, and Los Angeles. Department of Labor, Bureau of Naturalization, *Report of the Commissioner of Naturalization to the Secretary of Labor for the Year Ending June 30, 1925* (Washington, D.C.: Government Printing Office, 1925); Darrell Hevenor Smith, *The Bureau of Naturalization: Its History, Activities, and Organization* (Baltimore: Johns Hopkins University Press, 1926), 37–42. For an overview of the federal government's role in Americanization, see John F. McClymer, "The Federal Government and the Americanization Movement, 1915–1924," *Prologue: Journal of the National Archives* 10 (Spring 1978): 22–41.

3. Paul Lee Ellerbe, "Denver's Aid to Naturalization of Alien Residents," *Rocky Mountain News*, 27 February 1916. Ellerbe and his wife, Alma Estabrook Ellerbe, published a short

story about the difficulties in becoming naturalized experienced by a Volga German farmer in eastern Colorado. In 1918 Ellerbe left Denver and the Bureau of Naturalization to take a position in the Americanization Section of the Council of National Defense. After the war the couple moved to New York City to concentrate on their writing careers. In 1922 Ellerbe also wrote a series of articles critical of the federal government's naturalization bureaucracies and courts. Alma Estabrook Ellerbe and Paul Lee Ellerbe, "The Citizen Paper," *Century,* February 1918, 605–17; Paul Lee Ellerbe, "The Adopted Nephews of Samuel: Treating 'Em Human," *Outlook,* 15 February 1922, 263–65, "The Goats: Our Foreign-Born Who Can't Be Naturalized, and Why," *Outlook,* 22 February 1922, 296–98, and "Red, White and Blue Tape," *Survey,* 29 April 1922, 156–61, 189.

4. Commissioner of Naturalization to Director, Extension Division, University of Colorado, 13 February 1919, File 27682/5, Box 407, University of Colorado, Americanization Work in Universities and Colleges, General Educational Correspondence, Education and Americanization Files, 1914–1936, Records of the Immigration and Naturalization Service, RG 85, NARA.

5. Commissioner of Naturalization to Director, Extension Division, University of Colorado, 29 March 1919, File 27682/5, Box 407, University of Colorado, Americanization Work in Universities and Colleges, RG 85, NARA (emphasis in the original).

6. P. P. Claxton, *Immigrant Education Letter No. 5: Training for Americanization Service,* File 420, Box 44, Americanization folder, Immigrant Education, Records of the Office of the Commissioner, Historical File, 1870–1950, Records of the Office of Education, RG 12, NARA; "The Immigrant Problem in the Colleges," File 420, Box 44, Americanization folder; Department of the Interior, Bureau of Education, *Bulletin No. 18: Public Facilities for Educating the Alien* (Washington, D.C.: Government Printing Office, 1916).

7. Paul B. Phillips, Naturalization Examiner, Seattle, to Chief Examiner, Seattle, 22 April 1919, File 27671/7557, Box 206, Conference of County Superintendent of Schools, Montana, Correspondence, RG 85, NARA.

8. Paul B. Phillips, Naturalization Examiner, Seattle, to Chief Examiner, Seattle, 20 April 1919, A. L. Stone, Dean of Journalism, University of Montana, Missoula, to Raymond F. Crist, Director of Citizenship, Bureau of Naturalization, Washington, 18 November 1919, File 27682/25, Box 408, University of Montana, Missoula, Americanization Work in Universities and Colleges, RG 85, NARA. On the impact of World War I on the University of Montana, consult H. G. Merriam, *The University of Montana, A History* (Missoula: University of Montana Press, 1970), 50–59.

9. Paul B. Phillips, Naturalization Examiner, to Chief Examiner, Seattle, 24 April 1919, File 27682/26, Box 408, College of Agriculture and Mechanic Arts of Montana, Bozeman, Americanization Work in Universities and Colleges, RG 85, NARA. The most recent history of Montana State University has a good section on the school's World War I activities and some discussion of its Cooperative Extension Division, but no mention of Americanization. Robert Rydell, Jeffrey Safford, and Pierce Mullen, *In the People's Interest: A Centennial History of Montana State University* (Bozeman: Montana State University Foundation, 1992).

10. Paul B. Phillips, Naturalization Examiner, Seattle, to Chief Examiner, Seattle, 5 April 1919, Jonathan Speed Smith, Chief Naturalization Examiner, Seattle, to Commissioner of Naturalization, Washington, 7 July 1919, File 27682/27, Box 408, Montana State School of Mines, Americanization Work in Universities and Colleges, RG 85, NARA.

11. Paul B. Phillips, Naturalization Examiner, Seattle, to Chief Naturalization Examiner,

Seattle, 17 July 1919, File 27671/7557, Box 206, Conference of County Superintendent of Schools, Montana, Correspondence, RG 85, NARA.

12. Deputy Commissioner of Naturalization to Mr. W. D. Baker, Superintendent of Schools, Prescott, Arizona, 15 October 1915; W. D. Baker, Superintendent of City Schools, Prescott, Arizona, to U.S. Department of Labor, Bureau of Naturalization, Washington, D.C., 18 December 1915; Frederick Jones, Naturalization Examiner, Los Angeles, to Chief Examiner, San Francisco, 28 March, 10 October 1916; George A. Crutchfield, Chief Examiner, San Francisco, to Commissioner of Naturalization, Washington, D.C., 14 February 1917, all in File 27671/31, Box 8, Educational Work at Prescott, Arizona, Education and Americanization Files, RG 85, NARA.

13. Paul Armstrong, Chief Naturalization Examiner, Denver, to Commissioner of Naturalization, 23 May 1919, File 27671/30, Box 5, General File for Educational Work, Part II, April 1919 to February 1920, Education and Americanization Files, 1914–1936; Paul Armstrong, Chief Naturalization Examiner, Denver, to J. R. Coxen, Director of Vocational Education, State University, Laramie, 12 December 1919, File 27682/62, Box 410, University of Wyoming, Americanization Work in Universities and Colleges, both in RG 85, NARA.

14. *Immigrants in America Review,* June 1915, 79; "Americanization Service of the Suffragists," *National Suffrage News,* undated clipping in Box 35, Grace Raymond Hebard Papers, AHC.

15. Commissioner of Naturalization to Chief Examiner, Denver, 14 November 1917, Paul Lee Ellerbe, Chief Naturalization Examiner, Denver, to Commissioner of Naturalization, 17 November 1917, File 27671/4747, Box 189, Colorado Education Association, Correspondence, RG 85, NARA.

16. Commissioner of Naturalization to Chief Examiner, Denver, 7 January 1918, File 27671/4747, Box 189, Colorado Education Association, RG 85, NARA (emphasis in the original). Campbell, in a 1916 report, wrote: "The public schools are not sufficiently in touch with the candidate for citizenship, throughout the five year period—except in the rarest instances—to warrant the issuance of a certificate carrying with it such responsibilities" ("Americanization," in *Immigration and Americanization: Selected Readings,* comp. and ed. Philip Davis [Boston: Ginn, 1920], 688). Frank V. Thompson, on the other hand, found the bureau's stand on certificates "unfortunate" because schoolteachers would actually be better qualified for evaluating the qualifications of citizenship applicants than "the examiners, who have had no pedagogical training or even clear instructions" (*Schooling of the Immigrant* [New York: Harper, 1920], 344–45).

17. Commissioner of Naturalization to Chief Examiner, Denver, 1 December 1917, Paul Lee Ellerbe, Chief Naturalization Examiner, Denver, to Commissioner of Naturalization, 12 January 1918; File 27671/4747, Box 189, Colorado Education Association, RG 85, NARA.

18. Director of Citizenship, Washington, to James R. Coxen, State Director for Vocational Education, Laramie, 13 May 1920, File 27682/62, Box 410, University of Wyoming, Americanization Work in Universities and Colleges, RG 85, NARA; *Report of the Commissioner of Naturalization to the Secretary of Labor for the Year Ending June 30, 1920* (Washington, D.C.: Government Printing Office, 1920), 74; Jonathan Speed Smith, Chief Naturalization Examiner, Seattle, to Miss Z. May Meighan, County Superintendent of Schools, Chehalis, Washington, 11 February 1920, File 27671/3751, Lewis County, Washington, Education and Americanization Files, RG 85, NARA; Raymond F. Crist, "Citizens in the Making," *Independent,* 5 February 1921, 146. The Certificates of Proficiency were discontinued in 1922.

Report of the Commissioner of Naturalization to the Secretary of Labor for the Year Ending June 30, 1922 (Washington, D.C.: Government Printing Office, 1920), 28.

19. Coxen's Americanization resumé included appointment as chairman of the Americanization committee of the State Council of Defense and authorship of an Americanization bill passed in 1919. The legislation mandated compulsory evening school attendance for non-English-speaking residents with state funds provided for the schools; it was vetoed by Governor Robert Carey. An Americanization act sans compulsory attendance requirements passed and became law in 1921. Coxen was subsequently named state director of Americanization education. James R. Coxen, State Director for Vocational Education, Laramie, to Raymond Crist, Director of Citizenship, U.S. Department of Labor, Washington, 23 April 1920; Director of Citizenship, Washington, to James R. Coxen, State Director for Vocational Education, Laramie, 13 May 1920, File 27682/62, Box 410, University of Wyoming, Americanization Work in Universities and Colleges, RG 85, NARA.

20. Raymond F. Crist, Commissioner of Naturalization, to Dolly Dean Burgess, 23 November 1927, File 27671/18358, Montana Federation of Women's Clubs 1924–1927, General Educational Correspondence, Education and Americanization Files, 1914–1936, RG 85, NARA (emphasis in the original).

21. Paul Armstrong, Chief Naturalization Examiner, Denver, to Commissioner of Naturalization, 12 June 1919, Loran D. Osborn, Director, Extension Division, University of Colorado, to Paul Armstrong, Chief Naturalization Examiner, Denver, 20 June 1919, File 27682/5, Box 407, University of Colorado, Americanization Work in Universities and Colleges, RG 85, NARA; Osborn to President George Norlin, 15 August 1919, Box 18, Folder 6, President's Office Papers, Archives, UCBL.

22. George Norlin, President, University of Colorado, Boulder, to Hon. Franklin K. Lane, Secretary of the Interior, Washington, D.C., 11 April 1918, Franklin K. Lane to Dr. George Norlin, President, University of Colorado, Boulder, 11 May 1918, File 106, Box 7, Americanization Folder, Council of National Defense—Combating Illiteracy, Records of the Office of the Commissioner, Historical File, 1870–1950, RG 12, NARA. Other states asked Lane to finance their efforts in terms of franking privileges and transportation costs. See, for example, John S. Chambers, Controller, State Board of Control of California, Sacramento, to Hon. Franklin K. Lane, Secretary of the Interior, Washington, D.C., 24 April 1918 and Lane's reply, dated 15 May 1918, also in File 106, Box 7, Americanization Folder.

23. George Bell, "What the State and Nation Can Do to Help the Community in Americanization," Department of the Interior, Bureau of Education, *Proceedings Americanization Conference* (Washington, D.C.: Government Printing Office, 1919), 336; Carol Aronovici, "Americanization: Its Meaning and Function," *American Journal of Sociology* 25 (May 1920): 726.

24. Jonathan Speed Smith, Chief Naturalization Examiner, Naturalization Service, Seattle, to Mr. Charles D. Greenfield, Secretary, Montana State Council of National Defense, 12 October 1918, Box 3, Folder 8, Council of Defense Records, Record Series 19, MSHSA; James C. Stephens, "Report to Americanization Committee," 16 January 1919, Box 1, Continuing Education, 1918–1919 Folder, Extension Division Papers, Archives, UCBL. See *U.S. Statutes at Large* 40 (1918): 544.

25. Department of Labor, Bureau of Naturalization, *Student's Textbook. A Standard Course of Instruction for Use in the Public Schools,* comp. Raymond F. Crist (Washington, D.C.: Government Printing Office, 1918); Joyce Paine Lewis, "The Schools' Role in Americanizing the Immigrant: 1910–1920" (Ph.D. diss., University of Rochester, 1986), 58–68; Howard C.

Hill, "The Americanization Movement," *American Journal of Sociology* 24 (May 1919): 640–41.

26. Lewis, "Schools' Role in Americanizing," 69–83. The Bureau of Education was hampered, however, by infighting involving Kellor's Department on Extension of Americanization and Wheaton's Department on Immigrant Education. William J. Breen, *Uncle Sam at Home: Civilian Mobilization, Wartime Federalism, and the Council of National Defense, 1917–1919* (Westport, Conn.: Greenwood Press, 1984), 164.

27. [P. P. Claxton], "Reply to Memorandum of Elliott Dunlap Smith in Regard to Conflict Between Federal Agencies for Americanization," 3, 12, File 106, Box 12, Council of National Defense, 1917–1921, RG 12, NARA; Stephens, "Report to Americanization Committee."

28. P. P. Claxton, Commissioner of Education, Bureau of Education, Washington, D.C., to George Norlin, Chairman, Americanization Committee, Colorado Council of Defense, Boulder, 18 June 1918, File 106, Box 7, Council of National Defense—Combatting Illiteracy, RG 12, NARA; *Congressional Record,* 64th Cong., 2d sess., 54, pt. 2: 1730, 2023; *Cong. Rec.,* 65th Cong., 1st sess., 55, pt. 1: 196. Two bills introduced in 1918 to create a Bureau of Citizenship and Americanization in the Department of Labor also went nowhere. *Cong. Rec.,* 65th Cong., 2d sess., 56, pt. 9: 8602, pt. 11: 11401.

29. David Rosenstein, "A Crucial Issue in War-Time Education—Americanization," *School and Society,* 1 June 1918, 633–35; Department of the Interior, Bureau of Education, *Bulletin, 1918, No. 18: Americanization as a War Measure* (Washington, D.C.: Government Printing Office, 1918); Department of the Interior, Bureau of Education, *Report of the Commissioner of Education for the Year Ending June 30, 1918* (Washington, D.C.: Government Printing Office, 1918), 132; H. H. Wheaton, Chairman, Executive Committee, National Committee of One Hundred, Washington, D.C., to Honorable Julius C. Gunter, Governor of Colorado, Denver, 4 May 1918, Box 26774, Correspondence 1918, File Folder AM Americanization, Gunter Papers, CSA. The Council of National Defense quickly acted to dispel the displeasure of the Bureau of Naturalization by advising its state affiliates to assist the bureau in promoting citizenship classes. Council of National Defense, Washington, D.C., *Bulletin No. 91—Americanization—Cooperation with the United States Bureau of Naturalization; Supplementary to Bulletin No. 86, 18 April 1918,* File 106, Box 12, Council of National Defense, 1917–1921, RG 12, NARA.

30. *Congressional Record,* 65th Cong., 2d sess., 56, pt. 4: 3942, 3999, pt. 5: 4366–67, 4369, 4478–4504, quote on 4481.

31. Simon J. Lubin, President, State Commission of Immigration and Housing of California, to Honorable Julius C. Gunter, Governor of Colorado, 14 October 1918, George Norlin to His Excellency, the Governor of Colorado, 15 May 1918, Box 26774, Correspondence 1918, File Folder AM Americanization, Gunter Papers.

32. *Congressional Record,* 65th Cong., 3d sess., 57, pt. 3: 2191; "The Hoke Smith Americanization Bill," *New Mexico Journal of Education,* February 1919, 15–16.

33. *Congressional Record,* 65th Cong., 3d sess., 57, pt. 5: 4391–92, 4563–65, quotes on 4564; Frank Trumbull, Chairman, National Americanization Committee, New York City, to Dr. P. P. Claxton, Commissioner of Education, Washington, D.C., 1 April 1919, File 106, Box 11, Council of National Defense—Combating Illiteracy, RG 12, NARA; Virginia Yeaman Remnitz, "The Story of Senate Bill 5464," *North American Review,* August 1919, 203–11; "Great Interest Shown in Smith-Bankhead Bill," Department of the Interior, Bureau

of Education, Americanization Division, *Americanization,* 1 March 1919, 1. For debate on Kenyon's Americanization bill, S. 3315, see *Cong. Rec.,* 66th Cong., 2d sess., 59, pt. 2: 1649–70, 1708–10, 1777–80, 1873–88, 1939–50, 1983–96, 2050–59.

34. Simon J. Lubin and Christina Krysto, "The Strength of America. I. Cracks in the Melting Pot," *Survey,* 20 December 1919, 259; Lubin and Krysto, "The Strength of America. VI. Nation Building," *Survey,* 8 March 1920, 692, 695.

35. Lubin and Krysto, "The Strength of America. VI. Nation Building," 692, 695, 719. See Anne Marie Woo-Sam, "Domesticating the Immigrant: California's Commission of Immigration and Housing and the Domestic Immigration Policy Movement, 1910–1945" (Ph.D. diss., University of California, Berkeley, 1999), 39–41.

36. John Higham, *Strangers in the Land: Patterns of American Nativism, 1860–1925* (New Brunswick, N.J.: Rutgers University Press, 1955), 254–63; Ellis Hawley, *The Great War and the Search for a Modern Order: A History of the American People and Their Institutions, 1917–1933* (New York: St. Martin's Press, 1979), 48–52; Edward George Hartmann, *The Movement to Americanize the Immigrant* (New York: Columbia University Press, 1948), 225–52; Smith, *Bureau of Naturalization,* 12; Department of Labor, Bureau of Naturalization, *Report of the Commissioner of Naturalization for the Year Ending June 30, 1925,* 5.

37. Commissioner of Naturalization to Superintendent of Lewis County Schools, Chehalis, Washington, 19 February 1919, Z. May Meighen, Superintendent, Lewis County Public Schools, to U.S. Department of Labor, Bureau of Naturalization, Washington, D.C., 13 March 1919, File 27671/3751, Lewis County, Washington, Education and Americanization Files, RG 85, NARA.

38. Chief Naturalization Examiner to County Superintendent of Schools, Chehalis, Washington, 10 June 1920; Chief Naturalization Examiner to Clerk of Courts, Chehalis, 10 June 1920; Chief Naturalization Examiner to Miss Mary Grimm, Clerk of Court, Chehalis, 16 June 1922, all in File 27671/3751, Lewis County, Washington, Education and Americanization Files, RG 85, NARA.

39. Chief Naturalization Examiner to Miss Z. May Meighen, County School Superintendent, Chehalis, Washington, 14, 18 December 1920, 25 February 1921, File 27671/3751, Lewis County, Washington, Education and Americanization Files, RG 85, NARA.

40. Interview with Miss Z. May Meighen, County Superintendent of Schools, Chehalis, Lewis County, Washington, 8 February 1923, Report dated 12 February 1923, U.S. Naturalization Examiner to Chief Examiner, Seattle, 12 March 1923, File 27671/3751, Lewis County, Washington, Education and Americanization Files, RG 85, NARA.

41. Anne M. Godfrey, Clerk, San Francisco, to Richard K. Campbell, Commissioner of Naturalization, Washington, D.C., 30 January 1922; Anne M. Godfrey, Educational Representative, San Francisco, Memorandum for File E-3608, excerpt from educational report, 1922; Anne M. Godfrey, Report for San Jose, Santa Clara County, California, 15 March 1923; Anne M. Godfrey, "Resume of Trip to San Jose, Santa Clara County," 17 April 1923; Mrs. Anne M. Godfrey, Educational Assistant, San Francisco, Memorandum for File E-3608, 30 May 1923; Anne M. Godfrey to Chief Naturalization Examiner, 22 December 1923, all in File 27671/3608, Santa Clara County, California, Education and Americanization Files, RG 85, NARA.

42. Godfrey to Chief Naturalization Examiner, 22 December 1923; *San Jose Evening School Echo,* 9 April 1924, clipping attached to Memorandum for File E-3608; M. R. Bevington, District Director of Naturalization, San Francisco, excerpt from "Annual report of the

citizenship training work of the San Francisco District for the fiscal year ended June 30, 1924," Memorandum for File E-3608, 28 July 1924, File 27671/3608, Santa Clara County, California, Education and Americanization Files, RG 85, NARA.

43. Federal Council of Citizenship Training, *Community Score Card: Preliminary Draft for Criticism and Experimental Try-out*, File 27671/17314, Box 261, Pamphlets Relative to the Federal Council of Citizenship Training, General Educational Correspondence, Education and Americanization Files, 1914–1936, RG 85, NARA.

44. Paul Lee Ellerbe, speech draft, File 27671/4747, Box 189, Colorado Education Association, RG 85, NARA.

6. "Our Own House Needs Readjustment"

1. Carol Aronovici, "Americanization," *Annals of the American Academy of Political and Social Science* 93 (January 1921): 134–37. A noted city planner, Aronovici had immigrated in 1900, becoming naturalized in 1906. Earning a doctorate from Brown University, he conducted numerous studies of housing conditions in several East Coast cities. He served as chairman of the Americanization Committee of Minnesota between 1917 and 1919 before taking the CCIH position, which he occupied in 1919–1920. *Who Was Who in America with World Notables,* vol. 6 (Chicago: Marquis Who's Who, 1976), 12; *National Cyclopædia of American Biography,* vol. 45 (New York: James T. White, 1962), 460.

2. Madison Grant, *The Passing of the Great Race or the Racial Basis of European History,* rev. ed. (New York: Charles Scribner's Sons, 1918; reprint, New York: Arno Press and *New York Times,* 1970), 110; John Higham, *Strangers in the Land: Patterns of American Nativism, 1860–1925* (New Brunswick, N.J.: Rutgers University Press, 1955), 155–57.

3. Higham, *Strangers in the Land,* 147, characterizes the race suicide controversy as a "minor national phobia." Barbara Solomon, *Ancestors and Immigrants: A Changing New England Tradition* (Cambridge, Mass.: Harvard University Press, 1956), explains the theories and profiles the theoretician—Francis Amasa Walker—most responsible for fueling race suicide propaganda. Linda Gordon, *Woman's Body, Woman's Right: A Social History of Birth Control in America* (New York: Grossman Books, 1976), 136–58, discusses race suicide primarily in its relation to feminism; Elaine Tyler May, *Barren in the Promised Land: Childless Americans and the Pursuit of Happiness* (New York: Basic Books, 1995), devotes a chapter to race suicide, emphasizing the campaign's connections to eugenics and pressure on "old stock" American women to have more children. Gail Bederman, in a very brief section of *Manliness and Civilization: A Cultural History of Gender and Race in the United States, 1880–1917* (Chicago: University of Chicago Press, 1995), 200–206, interprets Theodore Roosevelt's fears of race suicide as reflective of middle-class white male anxieties (which she likens to neurasthenia) regarding overcivilization through effeminacy and racial decadence. Also see Robert Eldridge Bouwman, "Race Suicide: Some Aspects of Race Paranoia in the Progressive Era" (Ph.D. diss., Emory University, 1975); Thomas Dyer, *Theodore Roosevelt and the Idea of Race* (Baton Rouge: Louisiana State University Press, 1980), 143–67; Miriam King and Stephen Ruggles, "American Immigration, Fertility, and Race Suicide at the Turn of the Century," *Journal of Interdisciplinary History* 20 (Winter 1990): 347–69.

4. Fred H. Matthews, "White Community and 'Yellow Peril,'" *Mississippi Valley Historical Review* 50 (March 1964): 614.

5. *Statement of Hon. James D. Phelan of California before the Committee on Immigration and Naturalization, House of Representatives, Friday, 20 June 1919* (Washington, D.C.: Government Printing Office, 1920), 9, in James D. Phelan Papers, Bancroft Library, UCB; "Japanese 'Picture Brides' Become Frights in California," *Literary Digest*, 9 August 1919, 53. See also V. S. McClatchy, *Japanese Immigration and Colonization: Brief Prepared for Consideration of the State Department, October 1, 1921* (San Francisco: R and E Research Associates, 1970), 46–52; S. J. Holmes, "Perils of the Mexican Invasion," *North American Review*, May 1929, 622.

6. Francis Galton of England, a relative of Charles Darwin, transformed an obsession with the heredity of genius into the "science" of eugenics, which concerned itself with attempting to reverse the decline in the birth rate of the white, wealthy, and innately intelligent types while impeding the allegedly out-of-control fertility of the darker, poorer, and duller. See Higham, *Strangers in the Land*, 150–53, 273–76; Gordon, *Woman's Body, Woman's Right*, 116–35; Mark H. Haller, *Eugenics: Hereditarian Attitudes in American Thought* (New Brunswick, N.J.: Rutgers University Press, 1963), quote on 76; Donald K. Pickins, *Eugenics and the Progressives* (Nashville, Tenn.: Vanderbilt University Press, 1968); Kenneth M. Ludmerer, *Genetics and American Society: A Historical Appraisal* (Baltimore: Johns Hopkins University Press, 1972); Allan Chase, *The Legacy of Malthus: The Social Costs of the New Scientific Racism* (New York: Alfred A. Knopf, 1977); Hamilton Cravens, *The Triumph of Evolution: American Scientists and the Heredity-Environment Controversy, 1900–1941* (Baltimore: Johns Hopkins University Press, 1978), especially chap. 5; Daniel J. Kevles, *In the Name of Eugenics: Genetics and the Uses of Human Heredity* (New York: Knopf, 1985).

7. Kenneth L. Roberts, *Why Europe Leaves Home* (New York: Bobbs-Merrill, 1922; reprint, New York: Arno Press, 1977), 6, 35; Robert De C. Ward, "Americanization and Immigration," *Review of Reviews*, May 1919, 514.

8. Carol Aronovici, "Americanization: Its Meaning and Function," *American Journal of Sociology* 25 (May 1920): 707. This article had been published several months earlier in St. Paul, Minnesota, as a booklet. Carol Aronovici, *Americanization* (St. Paul: Keller Publishing, 1919); Prescott F. Hall to Edward A. Ross, 16 October 1918, Edward A. Ross Papers (microfilm edition, 1982), Reel 10, State Historical Society of Wisconsin, Madison.

9. Edward George Hartmann, *The Movement to Americanize the Immigrant* (New York: Columbia University Press, 1948; reprint, New York: AMS Press, 1967), 264–73, quote on 271. For speculation concerning how many immigrants enrolled in and attended Americanization classes between 1914 and 1925, see John F. McClymer, "The Americanization Movement and the Education of the Foreign-Born Adult," in *American Education and the European Immigrant: 1840–1940*, ed. Bernard J. Weiss (Urbana: University of Illinois Press, 1982), 102–05; Higham, *Strangers in the Land*, 254–63; Frank V. Thompson, *Schooling of the Immigrant* (New York: Harper, 1920), 60.

10. Thompson, *Schooling of the Immigrant*, 37–38; Sarka B. Hrbkova, "'Bunk' in Americanization: A Laudable Propaganda Infected by Ignorance," *Forum*, April–May 1920, 429. Hrbkova, a native of Czechoslovakia, was head of the Slavic languages department at the University of Nebraska. Robert N. Manley, "The Nebraska State Council of Defense: Loyalty Programs and Policies during World War I" (M.A. thesis, University of Nebraska, 1959), 34–36.

11. Thompson, *Schooling of the Immigrant*, 337; Paul Lee Ellerbe, "The Adopted Nephews of Samuel: Treating 'Em Human," *Outlook*, 15 February 1922, 263–64.

12. Paul Lee Ellerbe, "The Goats: Our Foreign-Born Who Can't Be Naturalized, and Why," *Outlook,* 22 February 1922, 296–98, and "Red, White and Blue Tape," *Survey,* 29 April 1922, 156–61, 189.

13. General Federation of Women's Clubs Americanization Committee, 1918–1920, *A Suggested Program for Americanization; Reprinted by Permission of the G.F.W.C. and Presented by the California Commission of Immigration and Housing,* 9–10, in CSL; Ethel Richardson, "Socializing the Method, Content, and Procedure," *Addresses and Proceedings of the Sixtieth Annual Meeting Held at Boston, Massachusetts, July 3–8, 1922* (Washington, D.C.: National Education Association, 1922), 918; Herbert Adolphus Miller, *The School and the Immigrant* (Cleveland: Survey Committee of the Cleveland Foundation, 1916), 90–92; Hrbkova, "'Bunk' in Americanization," 431.

14. Robert A. Carlson, *The Quest for Conformity: Americanization through Education* (New York: Wiley, 1975),128; Thompson, *Schooling of the Immigrant,* 323; John T. Mahoney, U.S. Bureau of Education, *Bulletin No. 31: Americanization in the United States* (Washington, D.C.: Government Printing Office, 1923), 15–17, in *Immigration: Select Documents and Case Records,* ed. Edith Abbott (Chicago: University of Chicago Press, 1924), 560–63; H. H. Wheaton, "Education of Immigrants," in *Immigration and Americanization: Selected Readings,* comp. and ed. Philip Davis (Boston: Ginn, 1920), 570–73, originally published in Department of the Interior, Bureau of Education, *Report of the Commissioner of Education for the Year Ending June 30, 1916,* vol. I (Washington, D.C.: Government Printing Office, 1916), 339–51; Charles M. Reinoehl, "Americanization Work," *Inter-Mountain Educator,* June 1920, 468–69.

15. State of Utah, *Fifteenth Report of the Superintendent of Public Instruction* (Salt Lake City: State Printing Office, 1924), 109, Public Document Serial Set, Series 240, Reel 40, USA; Arch M. Thurman, "Adult Education with Reference to a Program for Salt Lake City" (M.S. thesis, University of Utah, 1933), 15.

16. Ann Marie Woo Sam, "Domesticating the Immigrant: California's Commission of Immigration and Housing and the Domestic Immigration Policy Movement, 1910–1945" (Ph.D. diss., University of California, Berkeley, 1999), 177–79; Bradford Luckingham, *Minorities in Phoenix: A Profile of Mexican American, Chinese American, and African American Communities, 1860–1992* (Tucson: University of Arizona Press, 1994), 34–36; Mary Ruth Titcomb, "Americanization and Mexicans in the Southwest: A History of Phoenix's Friendly House, 1920–1983" (M.A. thesis, University of California, Santa Barbara, 1984), 37–41.

17. *Biennial Report of the State Department of Education of Wyoming, 1918–1920* (Sheridan, Wyo.: Mills, 1920), 40; "Report of State Director for Vocational Education for Year Ending March 31, 1920," 6, Box 1, Superintendent of Public Instruction/Department of Education Records, RG 0005, WSA; *Wyoming Educational Bulletin,* February 1921, 1.

18. *Wyoming Educational Bulletin,* April 1921, 3, November 1921, 2, February 1924, 1, April 1924, 1, May 1925, 2; *Biennial Report of the State Department of Education of Wyoming, 1922–1924* (Cheyenne: Wyoming Labor Journal Publishing, 1924), 62–63; "Report of State Director for Vocational Education for Year Ending March 31, 1924," 17–18, Box 1, RG 0005, WSA; *Biennial Report of the State Department of Education of Wyoming, 1928–1930* (Sheridan, Wyo.: Mills, 1930), 133–34; Minutes, State Board of Education, 24 October 1921, 57–58, 28 March 1930, 327, 13 October 1931, Box 1, RG 0005, WSA.

19. Mary Rebecca Darling, "Americanization of the Foreign-Born in Greeley, Colorado" (M.A. thesis, Colorado State Teachers' College, 1932), iv–vi.

20. "Americanization and Naturalization in Wyoming, 1921–22," *Clubwoman*, October–November 1922, 12–13; [Grace Raymond Hebard], "America for Americans," 2–4, typewritten draft in Naturalization files, Folder 3, AHC; *Casper Daily Tribune*, 29–30 September 1920; *Casper Herald*, 30 September 1920; Grace Raymond Hebard, "Why We Exclude the Ninety-Seven," *Woman Citizen*, 18 June 1921, 14; unidentified and undated newspaper clipping, probably April 1924, Box 37, Grace Raymond Hebard Papers, AHC.

21. Walter E. Clark, "The Stranger within Our Gates," *Addresses and Proceedings of the Fifty-Eighth Annual Meeting Held at Salt Lake City, Utah, July 4–10, 1920* (Washington, D.C.: National Education Association, 1920), 60–62.

22. Roger Daniels, *Coming to America: A History of Immigration and Ethnicity in American Life* (New York: Harper Collins, 1990), 276–77; Higham, *Strangers in the Land*, 300–324; Robert A. Divine, *American Immigration Policy, 1924–1952* (New Haven, Conn.: Yale University Press, 1957), 1–18; E. P. Hutchinson, *Legislative History of American Immigration Policy, 1798–1965* (Philadelphia: University of Pennsylvania Press, 1981), 465–68; Desmond King, *Making Americans: Immigration, Race, and the Origins of the Diverse Democracy* (Cambridge, Mass.: Harvard University Press, 2000), 199–228.

23. *New York Times*, 9 May 1923; Albert Johnson, foreword to *Immigration Restriction: A Study of the Opposition to and Regulation of Immigration into the United States,* by Roy L. Garis (New York: Macmillan, 1927), vii–viii; *Congressional Record*, 68th Cong., 1st sess., 65, pt. 6: 6257–58; *Cong. Rec.*, 68th Cong., 1st sess., 65, pt. 7: 6649; King, *Making Americans,* 201–04.

24. Johnson, foreword to *Immigration Restriction*, viii; Turner, "The Significance of the Frontier in American History," in *Frontier and Section: Selected Essays of Frederick Jackson Turner*, with an Introduction by Ray Allen Billington (Englewood Cliffs, N.J.: Prentice-Hall, 1961), 51. Concerning questions of ethnic group assimilation, neither Turner nor his thesis offered much beyond superficial confidence in the frontier's environmental forces as a factor in transforming Europeans into Americans. Frederick C. Luebke, "Ethnic Minority Groups in the American West," in *Historians and the American West*, ed. Michael P. Malone (Lincoln: University of Nebraska Press, 1983), 387–413, argues, on the other hand, that Turner's other thesis dealing with sectionalism did suggest a methodology that was congenial to a sophisticated study of ethnic minorities in the West. For further discussion connecting the end of the frontier to immigration restriction, see David M. Wrobel, *The End of American Exceptionalism: Frontier Anxiety from the Old West to the New Deal* (Lawrence: University Press of Kansas, 1993), 47–50, 75–77, 118–21; Bronwen J. Cohen, "Nativism and Western Myth: The Influence of Nativist Ideas on the American Self-Image," *Journal of American Studies* 8 (April 1974): 29.

25. *Congressional Record*, 13, pt. 2: 1485; *Cong. Rec.*, 23, pt. 4: 3558.

26. *Congressional Record,* 54, pt. 1: 270–72; unidentified, undated newspaper clipping, Box 1, Serial Number 14132, Folder 42: Question of Japanese Immigration, 1921–1922, Governor Merrit C. Mecham Collection, Correspondence 1921–1922, NMSRCA; [Hebard], "America for Americans," 5.

27. *Congressional Record,* 13, pt. 2: 1583, 1747–48; James O'Meara, "The Chinese in Early Days," *Overland Monthly,* May 1884, 480.

28. *Congressional Record,* 66th Cong., 2d sess., 1920, 59, pt. 1: 1815–16; House Committee on Immigration and Naturalization, *Japanese Immigration,* 66th Cong., 2d sess., 1921, H. Report 459, serial 7799, 25; Roy Malcolm, "American Citizenship and the Japanese," *An-*

nals of the American Academy of Political and Social Science 93 (January 1921): 79. In a 1920 publication, Arizona's State Committee on Americanization Work referred to an English class in Winslow "for Japanese." See State Committee on Americanization Work in Arizona, *Americanization in Arizona,* Bulletin No. 1, June 1920, 11, ASL.

29. Frank F. Chuman, *The Bamboo People: The Law and Japanese Americans* (Del Mar, Calif.: Publishers, Inc., 1976); Jeffrey Lesser, "Always Outsiders: Asians, Naturalization, and the Supreme Court," *Amerasia Journal* 12 (1985–1986): 83–100; Yuji Ichioka, *The Issei: The World of the First Generation Japanese Immigrants, 1885–1924* (New York: Free Press, 1988), 210–26; Ian F. Haney López, *White by Law: The Legal Construction of Race* (New York: New York University Press, 1996), 79–86; Matthew Frye Jacobson, *Whiteness of a Different Color: European Immigrants and the Alchemy of Race* (Cambridge, Mass.: Harvard University Press, 1998), 234–40; Mae M. Ngai, "The Architecture of Race in American Immigration Law: A Reexamination of the Immigration Act of 1924," *Journal of American History* 86 (June 1999), 80–88. In 1923, only a few months after the Ozawa ruling, the Supreme Court ruled that Asian Indians were racially ineligible for naturalization in *United States v. Thind.* See Haney López, *White by Law,* 86–92. Congress repealed Chinese exclusion in 1943, which opened naturalization to Chinese immigrants. Aliens from India and the newly independent Philippines were granted eligibility to citizenship in 1946, while Japanese and all other theretofore ineligible groups were cleared as part of the McCarren-Walter Act of 1952. That law also added the requirement that applicants had to demonstrate proficiency in English by reading and writing "simple words and phrases" as well as providing proof of ability to speak and understand the language. See Reed Ueda, *Postwar Immigrant America: A Social History* (Boston: Bedford Books of St. Martin's Press, 1994).

30. [V. S. McClatchy], *California's Answer to Japan; Japan's Honor Not Hurt by the Immigration Act; Story of the Facts: A Reply to the Special Edition of the Japan Times (of Tokyo) and Its Friendly "Message from Japan to America"* (San Francisco: California Joint Immigration Committee, 1924), 10, Japanese Exclusion Pamphlets, no. 27, UCBL; see also McClatchy, "Japanese in the Melting-Pot: Can They Assimilate and Make Good Citizens?" *Annals of the American Academy of Political and Social Science* 93 (January 1921): 29–34.

31. California Joint Immigration Committee, "Japan's Cure for Dual Citizenship," San Francisco, 17 November 1924, typed draft of statement in California Joint Immigration Committee Collection, folder 2, and V. S. McClatchy, *Assimilation of Japanese: Can They Be Moulded into American Citizens? Remarks before the Honolulu Rotary Club, October 27th, 1921,* Japanese Exclusion Pamphlets, no. 26, both in UCBL; McClatchy, "Japanese in the Melting-Pot," 31–33.

32. *New York Times,* 27 May 1924. In his classic study of the Far West states, Earl Pomeroy summarized the significance of Japanese exclusion: "In stopping Japanese immigration, Congress accepted the Western argument that it was impossible to assimilate Orientals into American society. At the same time, by refusing to let Orientals become American citizens or buy land, the national and state governments retarded assimilation and thus proved themselves right" (*The Pacific Slope: A History of California, Oregon, Washington, Idaho, Utah, and Nevada* [New York: Knopf, 1965], 276).

33. Lawrence A Cardoso, *Mexican Emigration to the United States, 1897–1931: Socio-Economic Patterns* (Tucson: University of Arizona Press, 1980), 119–31; Divine, *American Immigration Policy,* 52–66. Demand for agricultural labor increased significantly with the Immigration Acts of 1921 and 1924. Once *braceros* paid a ten-dollar fee for a visa and an

eight-dollar head tax, passed a literacy test, proved they were not paupers, and underwent a medical exam, they could legally enter the United States. Given the difficulty with which most Mexican laborers desiring entry could meet the demands of the law, the smuggling of immigrants into the United States increased significantly. In turn, the U.S. government created the Border Patrol in 1924. See Mark Reisler, *By the Sweat of Their Brow: Mexican Immigrant Labor in the United States, 1900–1940* (Westport, Conn.: Greenwood Press, 1976), 59–60.

34. Chester H. Rowell, "Why Make Mexico an Exception?" *Survey,* May 1931, 180; C. M. Goethe, "Peons Need Not Apply," *World's Work,* November 1930, 47–48.

35. Emory S. Bogardus, *The Mexican in the United States* (Los Angeles: University of Southern California Press, 1934; reprint edition, New York: Arno Press, 1970), 37, 45; Ngai, "Architecture of Race," 88–89; Victor S. Clark, "Mexican Labor in the United States," U.S. Department of Commerce and Labor, *Bureau of Labor Bulletin,* No. 78, Washington, D.C., 1908; reprinted in *Mexican Labor in the United States* (New York: Arno Press, 1974), 521; Manuel Gamio, *Mexican Immigration to the United States: A Study of Human Migration and Adjustment* (Chicago: University of Chicago Press, 1930; reprint, New York: Arno Press and *New York Times,* 1969), 177. For a more recent interpretation of migratory labor as part of a Hispanic strategy to ensure the survival of village communities, see Sarah Deutsch, *No Separate Refuge: Culture, Class, and Gender on an Anglo-Hispanic Frontier in the American Southwest, 1880–1940* (New York: Oxford University Press, 1987), 35–40.

36. Gamio, *Mexican Immigration to the United States,* 93–94; Paul S. Taylor, *Mexican Labor in the United States,* vol. I (Berkeley: University of California Press, 1930), 213. One manifestation of Mexican Americans' concern with assimilation involved the formation of citizens' organizations in Texas during the 1920s. Determined to promote Americanism and the rights and duties of citizenship as well as to fight against segregation and discrimination, these groups combined in 1929 as the League of United Latin American Citizens or LULAC. See David G. Gutiérrez, *Walls and Mirrors: Mexican Americans, Mexican Immigrants, and the Politics of Ethnicity* (Berkeley: University of California Press, 1995), 56–65, 74–78.

37. Colonel L. M. Maus, "What Should Be Done to Americanize and Make Useful Citizens of the Spanish-American Population of Our Border States," 6, File 106, Box 11, Records of the Office of Education, RG 12, NARA; Camille Guerin-Gonzales, *Mexican Workers and American Dreams: Immigration, Repatriation, and California Farm Labor, 1900–1939* (New Brunswick, N.J.: Rutgers University Press, 1994), 69.

38. Paul Lee Ellerbe, speech draft, File 27671/4747, Box 189, Colorado Education Association, General Educational Correspondence, Education and Americanization Files, 1914–1936, Records of the Immigration and Naturalization Service, RG 85, NARA.

39. *Wyoming News,* 3 August 1935, in Hebard Papers.

40. Frank Trumbull, Chairman, National Americanization Committee, New York City, to Dr. P. P. Claxton, Commissioner of Education, Washington, D.C., 1 April 1919, File 106, Box 11, Council of National Defense—Combating Illiteracy, RG 12, NARA.

41. Charles Moreau Harger, "The West's New Vision," *Atlantic Monthly,* July 1917, 121–22, 126.

42. For consideration of the theme of continuity and change in the West, see Michael P. Malone and Richard W. Etulain, *The American West: A Twentieth-Century History* (Lincoln: University of Nebraska Press, 1989), 1–10.

Epilogue

1. David M. Reimers, *Unwelcome Strangers: American Identity and the Turn against Immigration* (New York: Columbia University Press, 1998) 25–41; Gary Gerstle, "Liberty, Coercion, and the Making of Americans," *Journal of American History* 84 (September 1997): 556; Charles Jaret, "Troubled by Newcomers: Anti-Immigrant Attitudes and Action during Two Eras of Mass Immigration to the United States," *Journal of American Ethnic History* 18 (Spring 1999): 9–39. See also David M. Reimers, *Still the Golden Door: The Third World Comes to America* (New York: Columbia University Press, 1985); James Crawford, *Hold Your Tongue: Bilingualism and the Politics of "English Only"* (Reading, Mass.: Addison-Wesley, 1992); Raymond Tatalovich, *Nativism Reborn? The Official English Language Movement and the American States* (Lexington: University Press of Kentucky, 1995); Timothy J. Dunn, *The Militarization of the U.S.–Mexico Border, 1978–1992: Low-Intensity Conflict Doctrine Comes Home* (Austin, Tex.: Center for Mexican American Studies, 1996).

2. Reimers, *Unwelcome Strangers,* passim. For titles related to recent immigration debates, see David M. Reimers, "The New Restrictionism: Reviewing the Literature," *Immigration and Ethnic History Newsletter,* November 1999, 1, 8–9. See also George J. Sanchez, "Face the Nation: Immigration and the Rise of Nativism in Late Twentieth-Century America," *International Migration Review* 31 (Winter 1997): 1009–30, and "Race, Nation, and Culture in Recent Immigration Studies," *Journal of American Ethnic History* 74 (Summer 1999): 68–84.

3. Peter Brimelow, *Alien Nation: Common Sense about America's Immigration Disaster* (New York: Random House, 1995), xvii. Charles Jaret likens the importance of Brimelow's book to that of Madison Grant's *Passing of the Great Race* (1916), characterizing each as a "widely read 'classic text' that fuses nativist fears and accusations with racist notions of white supremacy" ("Troubled by Newcomers," 10). See Daniel Kanstroom, "Dangerous Undertones of the New Nativism: Peter Brimelow and the Decline of the West," in Juan F. Perea, ed., *Immigrants Out! The New Nativism and the Anti-Immigrant Impulse in the United States* (New York: New York University Press, 1997), 300–317.

4. Chilton Williamson Jr., *The Immigration Mystique: America's False Conscience* (New York: Basic Books, 1996), 199.

5. Jaret, "Troubled by Newcomers," 19.

6. John J. Miller, *The Unmaking of Americans: How Multiculturalism Has Undermined the Assimilation Ethic* (New York: Free Press, 1998), x; See Arthur M. Schlesinger Jr., *The Disuniting of America: Reflections on a Multicultural Society* (New York: Norton, 1992).

7. Reimers, *Unwelcome Strangers,* 135–36; Desmond King, *Making Americans: Immigration, Race, and the Origins of the Diverse Democracy* (Cambridge, Mass.: Harvard University Press, 2000), 25–26; U.S. Commission on Immigration Reform, *Becoming an American: Immigration and Immigrant Policy. 1997 Report to Congress,* i, vi.

8. Carol Aronovici, "Americanization: Its Meaning and Function," *American Journal of Sociology* 25 (May 1920): 716; Commission on Immigration Reform, *Becoming an American,* vi–ix.

9. Commission on Immigration Reform, *Becoming an American,* ix–xii, 43–45.

10. Commission on Immigration Reform, *Becoming an American,* 47–48.

11. Commission on Immigration Reform, *Becoming an American,* xii–xiii, 49; Mrs. Anne M. Godfrey, "Citizenship Ceremonies—Abstract," *Addresses and Proceedings of the Sixty-First Annual Meeting Held at Oakland San Francisco, California, July 1–6, 1923* (Washington

D.C.: National Education Association, 1923), 699. On the symbolism of Americanization pageantry in the early twentieth century, see Michael R. Olneck, "Americanization and the Education of Immigrants, 1900–1925: An Analysis of Symbolic Action," *American Journal of Education* 97 (August 1989): 413–16.

SELECTED BIBLIOGRAPHY

Primary Sources

Manuscript Collections and Other Archival Sources

Allen, Henry J. Papers. Governor's Office Collection. Kansas State Archives, Kansas State Historical Society, Topeka.

Arizona State Council of Defense Records. Record Group 35. Arizona State Archives, Phoenix.

Biography Clippings File. Utah History Information Center, Utah State Historical Society, Salt Lake City.

California Joint Immigration Committee Collection. Bancroft Library, University of California, Berkeley.

Capper, Arthur. Papers. Governor's Office Collection. Kansas State Archives, Kansas State Historical Society, Topeka.

Colorado Fuel and Iron Company Collection. MSS 1057. John M. Hart Library, Colorado State Historical Society, Denver.

Dobbs, Mary Evelyn/Kansas Women's Christian Temperance Union (KWCTU) Collection. Kansas State Historical Society, Topeka.

Governor's Council of Defense World War I and II Collection. Colorado State Archives, Denver.

Governors' Papers. Manuscript Collection 35. Montana State Historical Society Archives, Helena.

Gunter, Julius C. Papers. Colorado State Archives, Denver.

Hebard, Grace Raymond. Papers. American Heritage Center, University of Wyoming, Laramie.

Japanese Exclusion Pamphlets. Bancroft Library, University of California, Berkeley.

Japanese Pamphlets. California State Library, Sacramento.

Lindsey, Governor Washington E. Collection. New Mexico State Records Center and Archives, Santa Fe.

Mecham, Governor Merrit C. Collection. New Mexico State Records Center and Archives.

Montana State Council of Defense Records. Record Series 19. Montana State Historical Society Archives, Helena.

New Mexico State Council of Defense. Adjutant General's Collection. New Mexico State Records Center and Archives, Santa Fe.

Norlin, George. Papers. Archives, University of Colorado at Boulder Libraries.

Pamphlet File. Archives, University of Colorado at Boulder Libraries.

Phelan, James Duval. Papers. Bancroft Library, University of California, Berkeley.

Records of the Immigration and Naturalization Service. Record Group 85. National Archives, Washington, D.C.

Records of the Office of Education. Record Group 12. National Archives, College Park, Maryland.

Records of the Wyoming State Department of Education. Record Group 0005. Wyoming State Archives, Cheyenne.

University Archives. Extension Division Papers. Archives, University of Colorado at Boulder Libraries.

———. President's Office Papers. Archives, University of Colorado at Boulder Libraries.

Utah State Council of Defense Collection. MS 107. University of Utah Special Collections, Marriott Library, Salt Lake City.

World War I Utah State Council of Defense Records. Utah State Archives, Salt Lake City.

Wyoming Federation of Women's Clubs. Papers. Wyoming State Archives, Cheyenne.

Government Publications

Acts, Resolutions, and Memorials of the First Special Session, Third Legislature of the State of Arizona. Phoenix, 1918.

Arizona Service Bulletin, 1 February 1919.

Arizona State Council of Defense. *A Record of the Activities of the Arizona State Council of Defense.* Phoenix: Republican Print Shop, 1919.

Bell, George L. *Americanization as a Necessity to National Defense; Address at State Convention of C.F.W.C., Pasadena, Cal. [1918].* California State Library, Government Publications, Sacramento.

Biennial Reports of the State Department of Education of Wyoming. 1916–1930.

Blackmar, Frank W, ed. *History of the Kansas State Council of Defense.* Topeka: Kansas State Printing Plant, 1920.

California State Commission of Immigration and Housing. *Americanization: The California Program.* Sacramento: State Printing Office, 1919. California State Library, Government Publications, Sacramento.

———. *Americanization: California's Answer.* Sacramento: California State Printing Office, 1920. California State Library, Government Publications, Sacramento.

———. *First Annual Report.* Sacramento: State Printing Office, 1915.

———. *A Manual for Home Teachers.* Sacramento: California State Printing Office, 1918. California State Library, Government Publications, Sacramento.

———. *Ninth Annual Report.* Sacramento: State Printing Office, 1924.

———. *Report on an Experiment Made in Los Angeles in the Summer of 1917 for the Americanization of Foreign-born Women.* Sacramento: California State Printing Office, 1917.

———. *Report on Fresno's Immigration Problem with Particular Reference to Educational Facilities and Requirements.* Sacramento: State Printing Office, 1918.

Clark, Victor S. "Mexican Labor in the United States." Department of Commerce and Labor. Bureau of Labor *Bulletin,* No. 78. Washington, D.C.: Government Printing Office, 1908; reprinted in *Mexican Labor in the United States.* New York: Arno Press, 1974.

Congressional Record. 1879–1924. Washington, D.C.

Council of Defense Chronicle. 1917–1919. Kansas State Historical Society Library.

Foerster, Robert F. *The Racial Problems Involved in Immigration from Latin America and the West Indies to the United States.* Washington, D.C.: Government Printing Office, 1925. Reprint, San Francisco: R and E Research Associates, 1971.

General Federation of Women's Clubs Americanization Committee, 1918–1920. *A Suggested Program for Americanization. Reprinted by Permission of the G.F.W.C. and presented by the*

California Commission of Immigration and Housing. California State Library, Government Publications, Sacramento.

Guhin, M. M. *Americanization in South Dakota.* South Dakota State Department of Public Instruction, August 1919.

Harriman, R. D. "Suggestions for Americanization Teachers." *Bulletin of the University of Utah.* Vol. 10, No. 16, March 1920; Extension Division Series, Vol. I, No. 3. Salt Lake City: University of Utah Press, 1920.

Hrbkova, Sarka B. *Bridging the Atlantic: A Discussion of the Problems and Methods of Americanization.* Lincoln: Nebraska State Council of Defense, 1919.

Laws of the State of New Mexico Passed by the Fourth Regular Session, 1919. Albuquerque: Albright and Anderson, 1919.

Laws of the State of Utah Passed at the Thirteenth Regular Session of the Legislature. Salt Lake City: F. W. Gardiner, 1919.

Laws of the State of Utah Passed at the Fourteenth Regular Session of the Legislature. Salt Lake City: Arrow Press, 1921.

Laws, Resolutions, and Memorials of the State of Montana Passed by the Sixteenth Regular Session of the Legislative Assembly. Helena: State Publishing, 1919.

Report of the Council of Defense of the State of New Mexico. Santa Fe, 1918.

Report of the Woman's Committee of the Council of Defense for Kansas, From July 6, 1917, to December 30, 1918. Topeka: Kansas State Printing Press, 1919.

Reports of the State Superintendent of Public Instruction. Phoenix, 1924, 1926.

Reports of the Superintendent of Public Instruction of the State of Utah. Public Documents Serial Set, Series 240, Reels 36–37. Utah State Archives, Salt Lake City.

State Committee on Americanization Work in Arizona. *Americanization in Arizona,* Bulletin No. 1, June 1920.

Thurman, Arch M. "Americanization in Utah." *Bulletin of the University of Utah.* Vol. 11, No. 8, October 1920; Extension Division Series, Vol. 2, No. 1. Salt Lake City: University of Utah Press, 1920.

U.S. Commission on Immigration Reform. *Becoming an American: Immigration and Immigrant Policy. 1997 Report to Congress.*

U.S. Congress. *Reports of the Immigration Commission. Immigrants in Industries, Part 25: Japanese and Other Immigrant Races in the Pacific Coast and Rocky Mountain States.* Vol. 2, 61st Cong., 2d sess., S. Doc. 633, serial 5684-3.

———. *Reports of the Immigration Commission, Vol. 41: Statements and Recommendations Submitted by Societies and Organizations Interested in the Subject of Immigration.* 61st Congress, 3d sess., S. Doc. 764, serial 5881.

U.S. Department of the Interior. Bureau of Education. *Bulletin, 1916, No. 18: Public Facilities for Educating the Alien.* Washington, D.C.: Government Printing Office, 1916.

———. *Bulletin, 1916, No. 35: Adult Illiteracy.* Washington, D.C.: Government Printing Office, 1916.

———. *Bulletin, 1918, No. 18: Americanization as a War Measure.* Washington, D.C.: Government Printing Office, 1918.

———. *Proceedings Americanization Conference.* Washington, D.C.: Government Printing Office, 1919.

———. *Reports of the Commissioner of Education.* Washington, D.C.: Government Printing Office, 1916–1919.

U.S. Department of the Interior. Bureau of Education. Americanization Division. *Americanization*. Vols. 1–2.

U.S. Department of Labor. Bureau of Naturalization. *Citizenship Training of Adult Immigrants in the United States: Its Status in Relation to the Census of 1920*. Prepared by Margaret D. Moore with a foreword by James J. Davis, Secretary of Labor. Washington, D.C.: Government Printing Office, 1925.

———. *Reports of the Commissioner of Naturalization to the Secretary of Labor*. Washington, D.C.: Government Printing Office, 1920–1925.

———. *Student's Textbook. A Standard Course of Instruction for Use in the Public Schools*. Raymond F. Crist, comp. Washington, D.C.: Government Printing Office, 1918.

U.S. House Committee on Immigration and Naturalization. *Japanese Immigration: Hearings before the Committee on Immigration and Naturalization*. 66th Cong., 2d sess., 1921, H. Report 459, serial 7799.

U.S. House Select Committee on the Causes of the Present Depression of Labor. *Chinese Immigration*. 46th Cong., 2d sess., 1880, H. Report 572, serial 1935.

U.S. House Select Committee on the Depression of Labor. *Land Monopoly and Chinese Immigration*. 46th Cong., 2d sess., 1879, H. Misc. Doc. 5, serial 1928.

U.S. Immigration Commission. *Reports of the Immigration Commission, Abstracts of Reports of the Immigration Commission*. Vol. 1. Washington, D.C.: Government Printing Office, 1911.

U.S. Joint Special Committee to Investigate Chinese Immigration. *Chinese Immigration*. 44th Cong., 2d sess., 1877, S. Report 689, serial 1734.

U.S. Senate Committee on Immigration. *Chinese Exclusion*. 57th Cong., 1st sess., 1902, S. Report 776, serial 4265.

Warrum, Noble. *Utah in the World War*. Utah State Council of Defense, 1924.

Washington State Council of Defense. *Report of the State Council of Defense to the Governor of Washington Covering Its Activities during the War, June 16, 1917 to January 9, 1919*. Olympia, Wash.: Frank M. Lamborn, 1919.

Wyoming House Journal, Fifteenth Legislature. Laramie, Wyo.: Laramie Republican, 1919.

Books

Abbott, Edith, ed. *Immigration: Select Documents and Case Records*. Chicago: University of Chicago Press, 1924.

Aronovici, Carol. *Americanization*. St. Paul, Minn.: Keller Publishing, 1919.

Baghdigian, Bagdasar Krekor. *Americanism in Americanization*. Kansas City, Mo.: Burton Publishing, 1921.

Berkson, Isaac B. *Theories of Americanization: A Critical Study with Special Reference to the Jewish Group*. New York: Teachers, College, Columbia University, 1920. Reprint, New York: Arno Press and *New York Times,* 1969.

Bogardus, Emory S. *Essentials of Americanization*. Rev. ed. Los Angeles: University of Southern California Press, 1920.

———. *The Mexican in the United States*. Los Angeles: University of Southern California Press, 1934. Reprint, New York: Arno Press, 1970.

Chetwood, John, Jr. *Immigration Fallacies*. Boston: Arena Publishing, 1896.

Creel, George. *How We Advertised America*. New York: Harper, 1920.

Cubberley, Elwood P. *Changing Conceptions of Education*. Boston: Houghton Mifflin, 1909.

————. *Public Education in the United States: A Study and Interpretation of American Educational History.* Boston: Houghton Mifflin, 1919.

Davis, Philip, comp. and ed. *Immigration and Americanization: Selected Readings.* Boston: Ginn, 1920.

Gamio, Manuel. *Mexican Immigration to the United States: A Study of Human Migration and Adjustment.* Chicago: University of Chicago Press, 1930. Reprint, New York: Arno Press and *New York Times,* 1969.

Garis, Roy L. *Immigration Restriction: A Study of the Opposition to and Regulation of Immigration into the United States.* New York: Macmillan, 1927.

Goddard, Benjamin, comp. *Pertinent Facts on Utah's Loyalty and War Record.* Salt Lake City, Utah, 1918.

Grant, Madison. *The Passing of the Great Race or the Racial Basis of European History.* Rev. ed. New York: Charles Scribner's Sons, 1918. Reprint, New York: Arno Press and *New York Times,* 1970.

Hebard, Grace Raymond. *The Pathbreakers from River to Ocean: The Story of the Great West from the Time of Coronado to the Present.* Chicago: University Publishing, 1917.

Hebard, Grace Raymond, and E. A. Brininstool. *The Bozeman Trail.* 2 vols. Cleveland: Arthur H. Clark, 1922.

Hough, Emerson. *The Passing of the Frontier: A Chronicle of the Old West.* New Haven, Conn.: Yale University Press, 1918.

Kallen, Horace M. *Culture and Democracy in the United States.* New York: Boni and Liveright, 1924. Reprint, New York: Arno Press and *New York Times,* 1970.

Kruse, Horace W. *Americanizing an Industrial Center: An Account of Experience and Procedure in the Towns of the St. Louis, Rocky Mountain and Pacific Company in Colfax County, New Mexico.* Raton, N.M.: Raton Publishing, 1920.

Leiserson, William M. *Adjusting Immigrant and Industry.* New York: Harper, 1924. Reprint, New York: Arno Press and *New York Times,* 1969.

McClatchy, V. S. *Japanese Immigration and Colonization: Brief Prepared for Consideration of the State Department, October 1, 1921.* San Francisco: R and E Research Associates, 1970.

Miller, Herbert Adolphus. *The School and the Immigrant.* Cleveland: Survey Committee of the Cleveland Foundation, 1916.

Minckley, Loren Stiles. *Americanization through Education.* Frontenac, Kan.: privately published, 1917.

Parker, Carlton H. *The Casual Laborer and Other Essays.* New York: Harcourt, Brace and Howe, 1920.

Roberts, Kenneth. *Why Europe Leaves Home.* New York: Bobbs-Merrill, 1922. Reprint, New York: Arno Press, 1977.

Roosevelt, Theodore. *The Letters of Theodore Roosevelt.* Ed. Elting Morrison. Cambridge, Mass.: Harvard University Press, 1951.

————. *The Works of Theodore Roosevelt.* Ed. Hermann Hagedorn. 20 vols. New York: Charles Scribner's Sons, 1926.

Ross, Edward A. *The Old World in the New: The Significance of Past and Present Immigration to the American People.* New York: Century, 1914.

Sharlip, William, and Albert A. Owens. *Adult Immigrant Education: Its Scope, Content, and Methods.* New York: Macmillan, 1925.

Smith, Darrell Hevenor. *The Bureau of Education: Its History, Activities, and Organization.* Baltimore: Johns Hopkins University Press, 1923.

————. *The Bureau of Naturalization: Its History, Activities, and Organization.* Baltimore: Johns Hopkins Press, 1926.

Strong, Josiah. *Our Country: Its Possible Future and Its Present Crisis.* Rev. ed. New York: Baker and Taylor, 1885, 1891.

Taylor, Paul S. *Mexican Labor in the United States.* Vol. 1. Berkeley: University of California Press, 1930.

Thompson, Frank V. *Schooling of the Immigrant.* New York: Harper, 1920.

Turner, Frederick Jackson. *Frontier and Section: Selected Essays of Frederick Jackson Turner.* With an introduction by Ray Allen Billington. Englewood Cliffs, N.J.: Prentice-Hall, 1961.

Wilson, Woodrow. *The Public Papers of Woodrow Wilson: The New Democracy.* Ed. Ray Stannard Baker and William E. Dodd. 2 vols. New York: Harper, 1926.

Selected Articles

Aronovici, Carol. "Americanization." *Annals of the American Academy of Political and Social Science* 93 (January 1921): 134–38.

————. "Americanization: Its Meaning and Function." *American Journal of Sociology* 25 (May 1920): 695–730.

Baughman, Ruby. "Elementary Education for Adults." *Annals of the American Academy of Political and Social Science* 93 (January 1921): 161–66.

Chase, Amanda Matthews. "The 'Official' Home Teacher." *Out West,* January 1916, 33–37.

Ellerbe, Paul Lee. "The Adopted Nephews of Samuel: Treating 'Em Human." *Outlook,* 15 February 1922, 263–65.

————. "Education for Citizenship." *Outlook,* 11 September 1918, 64–65.

————. "The Goats: Our Foreign-Born Who Can't Be Naturalized, and Why." *Outlook,* 22 February 1922, 296–98.

————. "Red, White and Blue Tape." *Survey,* 29 April 1922, 156–61, 189.

Gibson, Mary S. "The Education of Immigrant Women in California." *Immigrants in America Review,* June 1915, 13–17.

————. "Schools for the Whole Family." *Survey,* 1 June 1926, 300–303.

Hebard, Grace Raymond. "Why We Exclude the Ninety-Seven." *Woman Citizen,* 18 June 1921, 14.

Hill, Howard C. "The Americanization Movement." *American Journal of Sociology* 24 (May 1919): 609–42.

Hodgkin, George B. "Americanization in a Labor Camp." *School and Society,* 26 November 1921, 492–94.

Hrbkova, Sarka B. "'Bunk' in Americanization: A Laudable Propaganda Infected by Ignorance." *Forum,* April–May 1920, 428–39.

Lenz, Frank B. "The Education of the Immigrant." *Educational Review,* May 1916, 469–77.

Lubin, Simon J., and Christina Krysto. "The Strength of America. I. Cracks in the Melting Pot." *Survey,* 20 December 1919, 258–59.

————. "The Strength of America: V. The Menace of Americanization." *Survey,* 21 February 1920, 610–12.

————. "The Strength of America. VI. Nation Building." *Survey,* 8 March 1920, 690–95, 719.

McClatchy, V. S. "Japanese in the Melting-Pot: Can They Assimilate and Make Good Citizens?" *Annals of the American Academy of Political and Social Science* 93 (January 1921): 29–34.

Malcolm, Roy. "American Citizenship and the Japanese." *Annals of the American Academy of Political and Social Science* 93 (January 1921): 77–81.

Richardson, Ethel. "Doing the Thing That Couldn't Be Done." *Survey,* 1 June 1926, 297–99.

———. "Socializing the Method, Content, and Procedure." *Addresses and Proceedings of the Sixtieth Annual Meeting Held at Boston, Massachusetts, July 3–8, 1922* (Washington, D.C.: National Education Association, 1922), 914–28.

Rowell, Chester H. "California and the Japanese Problem." *New Republic,* 15 September 1920, 64–65.

———. "Chinese and Japanese Immigrants—A Comparison." *Annals of the American Academy of Political and Social Science* 34 (September 1909): 223–30.

———. "The Japanese in California." *World's Work,* June 1913, 195–201.

Periodicals

Addresses and Proceedings of the National Education Association
American City
Annals of the American Academy of Political and Social Science
Arena
Atlantic Monthly
Century
Colorado Fuel and Iron Company Industrial Bulletin
Educational Review
Elementary School Journal
Forum
Harper's
Immigrants in America Review
Independent
Inter-Mountain Educator
Literary Digest
Nation
New Mexico School Review
New Republic
North American Review
Outlook
Out West
Overland Monthly
Review of Reviews
School and Society
Sunset
Survey
Woman Citizen
World's Work
Wyoming Clubwoman

Secondary Sources

Books

Abbott, Carl, Stephen J. Leonard, and David McComb. *Colorado: A History of the Centennial State.* Rev. ed. Boulder: Colorado Associated University Press, 1982.

Acuña, Rodolfo. *Occupied America: A History of Chicanos.* 2d ed. New York: Harper and Row, 1981.

Alexander, Charles C. *The Ku Klux Klan in the Southwest.* Lexington: University Press of Kentucky, 1965.

Allen, Theodore W. *The Invention of the White Race.* Vol. 1, *Racial Oppression and Social Control.* New York: Verso, 1994.

Almaguer, Tomás. *Racial Fault Lines: The Historical Origins of White Supremacy in California.* Berkeley: University of California Press, 1994.

Archdeacon, Thomas J. *Becoming American: An Ethnic History.* New York: Free Press, 1983.

Arnesen, Eric, Julie Greene, and Bruce Laurie. *Labor Histories: Class, Politics, and the Working-Class Experience.* Urbana: University of Illinois Press, 1998.

Athearn, Robert G. *The Mythic West in Twentieth-Century America.* Lawrence: University Press of Kansas, 1986.

Barrett, James R. *Work and Community in the Jungle: Chicago's Packinghouse Workers, 1894–1922.* Urbana: University of Illinois Press, 1987.

Barth, Gunther. *Bitter Strength: A History of the Chinese in the United States, 1850–1870.* Cambridge, Mass.: Harvard University Press, 1964.

Bates, James Leonard. *The United States, 1898–1928: Progressivism and a Society in Transition.* New York: McGraw-Hill, 1976.

Beck, Warren A. *New Mexico: A History of Four Centuries.* Norman: University of Oklahoma Press, 1962.

Bederman, Gail. *Manliness and Civilization: A Cultural History of Gender and Race in the United States, 1880–1917.* Chicago: University of Chicago Press, 1995.

Bennett, David H. *The Party of Fear: From Nativist Movements to the New Right in American History.* Chapel Hill: University of North Carolina Press, 1988.

Blair, Karen J. *The Clubwoman as Feminist: True Womanhood Redefined, 1868–1914.* New York: Holmes and Meier Publishers, 1980.

Bodnar, John. *The Transplanted: A History of Immigrants in Urban America.* Bloomington: Indiana University Press, 1985.

Bredbenner, Candice Lewis. *A Nationality of Her Own: Women, Marriage, and the Law of Citizenship.* Berkeley: University of California Press, 1998.

Breen, William J. *Uncle Sam at Home: Civilian Mobilization, Wartime Federalism, and the Council of National Defense, 1917–1919.* Westport, Conn.: Greenwood Press, 1984.

Brimelow, Peter. *Alien Nation: Common Sense about America's Immigration Disaster.* New York: Random House, 1995.

Byrkit, James W. *Forging the Copper Collar: Arizona's Labor-Management War of 1901–1921.* Tucson: University of Arizona Press, 1982.

Camarillo, Albert. *Chicanos in a Changing Society: From Mexican Pueblos to American Barrios in Santa Barbara and Southern California, 1848–1930.* Cambridge, Mass.: Harvard University Press, 1979.

Cardoso, Lawrence A. *Mexican Emigration to the United States, 1897–1931: Socio-Economic Patterns.* Tucson: University of Arizona Press, 1980.

Carlson, Robert A. *The Quest for Conformity: Americanization through Education.* New York: Wiley, 1975.

Carson, Mina. *Settlement Folk: Social Thought and the American Settlement Movement, 1885–1930.* Chicago: University of Chicago Press, 1990.

Chambers, John Whiteclay, II. *The Tyranny of Change: America in the Progressive Era, 1900–1917.* New York: St. Martin's Press, 1980.

Chan, Sucheng. *Asian Americans: An Interpretive History.* Boston: Twayne, 1991.

———. *This Bittersweet Soil: The Chinese in California Agriculture, 1860–1910.* Berkeley: University of California Press, 1986.

Chase, Allan. *The Legacy of Malthus: The Social Costs of the New Scientific Racism.* New York: Knopf, 1977.

Chrislock, Carl H. *Ethnicity Challenged: The Upper Midwest Norwegian-American Experience in World War I.* Northfield, Minn.: Norwegian-American Historical Association, 1981.

Cinel, Dino. *From Italy to San Francisco: The Immigrant Experience.* Stanford, Calif.: Stanford University Press, 1982.

Cohen, Lizabeth. *Making a New Deal: Industrial Workers in Chicago, 1919–1939.* Cambridge: Cambridge University Press, 1990.

Conlin, Joseph R. *Bread and Roses Too: Studies of the Wobblies.* Westport, Conn.: Greenwood Publishing, 1969.

———, ed. *At the Point of Production: The Local History of the I.W.W.* Westport, Conn.: Greenwood Press, 1981.

Cononelos, Louis James. *In Search of Gold Paved Streets: Greek Immigrant Labor in the Far West, 1900–1920.* New York: AMS Press, 1989.

Coolidge, Mary Roberts. *Chinese Immigration.* New York: Henry Holt and Company, 1909. Reprint, New York: Arno Press and *New York Times,* 1969.

Cravens, Hamilton. *The Triumph of Evolution: American Scientists and the Heredity-Environment Controversy, 1900–1941.* Baltimore: Johns Hopkins University Press, 1978.

Cremin, Lawrence. *The Transformation of the School: Progressivism in American Education, 1876–1957.* New York: Alfred A. Knopf, 1961.

Crocker, Ruth Hutchinson. *Social Work and Social Order: The Settlement Movement in Two Industrial Cities, 1889–1930.* Urbana: University of Illinois Press, 1992.

Cronon, William, George Miles, and Jay Gitlin, eds. *Under an Open Sky: Rethinking America's Western Past.* New York: W. W. Norton, 1992.

Cuff, Robert D. *The War Industries Board: Business-Government Relations during World War I.* Baltimore: Johns Hopkins University Press, 1973.

Curran, Thomas J. *Xenophobia and Immigration, 1820–1930.* Boston: Twayne, 1975.

Daniel, Cletus E. *Bitter Harvest: A History of California Farmworkers, 1870–1941.* Berkeley: University of California Press, 1981.

Daniels, Roger. *Asian Americans: Chinese and Japanese in the United States since 1850.* Seattle: University of Washington Press, 1988.

———. *Coming to America: A History of Immigration and Ethnicity in American Life.* New York: Harper Collins, 1990.

———. *Not Like Us: Immigrants and Minorities in America, 1880–1924.* Chicago: Ivan R. Dee, 1997.

————. *The Politics of Prejudice: The Anti-Japanese Movement in California and the Struggle for Japanese Exclusion.* Berkeley: University of California Press, 1962.

Davis, Allen F. *Spearheads for Reform: The Social Settlements and the Progressive Movement, 1890–1914.* New York: Oxford University Press, 1967.

Debouzy, Marianne, ed. *In the Shadow of the Statue of Liberty: Immigrants, Workers, and Citizens in the American Republic, 1880–1920.* Urbana: University of Illinois Press, 1992.

del Castillo, Richard Griswold. *The Los Angeles Barrio, 1850–1890: A Social History.* Berkeley: University of California Press, 1979.

del Castillo, Richard Griswold, and Arnoldo De León. *North to Aztlán: A History of Mexican Americans in the United States.* New York: Twayne, 1996.

De Santis, Vincent. *The Shaping of Modern America, 1877–1916.* Boston: Allyn and Bacon, 1973.

Deutsch, Sarah. *No Separate Refuge: Culture, Class, and Gender on an Anglo-Hispanic Frontier in the American Southwest, 1880–1940.* New York: Oxford University Press, 1987.

Deverell, William, and Tom Sitton, eds. *California Progressivism Revisited.* Berkeley: University of California Press, 1994.

Dinnerstein, Leonard, Roger L. Nichols, and David M. Reimers. *Natives and Strangers: Blacks, Indians, and Immigrants in America.* 3d ed. New York: Oxford University Press, 1996.

D'Innocenzo, Michael, and Josef P. Sirefman. *Immigration and Ethnicity: American Society— "Melting Pot" or "Salad Bowl"?* Westport, Conn.: Greenwood Press, 1992.

Divine, Robert A. *American Immigration Policy, 1924–1952.* New Haven, Conn.: Yale University Press, 1957.

Dubofsky, Melvyn. *We Shall Be All: A History of the Industrial Workers of the World.* 2d ed. Urbana: University of Illinois Press, 1988.

DuBois, Ellen Carol, and Vicki L. Ruiz, eds. *Unequal Sisters: A Multicultural Reader in U.S. Women's History.* New York: Routledge, 1994.

Emmons, David M. *The Butte Irish: Class and Ethnicity in an American Mining Town, 1875–1925.* Urbana: University of Illinois Press, 1989.

Etulain, Richard W., ed. *Writing Western History: Essays on Major Western Historians.* Albuquerque: University of New Mexico Press, 1991.

Fass, Paula S. *Outside In: Minorities and the Transformation of American Education.* New York: Oxford University Press, 1989.

Fitzpatrick, Ellen. *Endless Crusade: Women Social Scientists and Progressive Reform.* New York: Oxford University Press, 1990.

Foley, Neil. *The White Scourge: Mexicans, Blacks, and Poor Whites in Texas Cotton Culture.* Berkeley: University of California Press, 1997.

Frankel, Noralee, and Nancy S. Dye, eds. *Gender, Class, Race, and Reform in the Progressive Era.* Lexington: University Press of Kentucky, 1991.

Fuchs, Lawrence H. *The American Kaleidoscope: Race, Ethnicity, and the Civic Culture.* Middletown, Conn.: Wesleyan University Press, 1990.

García, Mario T. *Desert Immigrants: The Mexicans of El Paso, 1880–1920.* New Haven, Conn.: Yale University Press, 1981.

Gardner, A. Dudley, and Verla R. Flores. *Forgotten Frontier: A History of Wyoming Coal Mining.* Boulder, Colo.: Westview Press, 1989.

Gerlach, Larry R. *Blazing Crosses in Zion: The Ku Klux Klan in Utah.* Logan: Utah State University Press, 1982.

Gerstle, Gary. *Working-Class Americanism: The Politics of Labor in a Textile City, 1914–1960.* Cambridge: Cambridge University Press, 1989.

Gitelman, H. M. *Legacy of the Ludlow Massacre: A Chapter in Industrial Relations.* Philadelphia: University of Pennsylvania Press, 1988.

Gjerde, Jon. *From Peasants to Farmers: The Migration from Balestrand, Norway, to the Upper Middle West.* Cambridge: Cambridge University Press, 1988.

———. *The Minds of the West: Ethnocultural Evolution in the Rural Middle West, 1830–1917.* Chapel Hill: University of North Carolina Press, 1997.

Gleason, Philip. *Speaking of Diversity: Language and Ethnicity in Twentieth-Century America.* Baltimore: Johns Hopkins University Press, 1992.

Goldberg, Robert Alan. *Hooded Empire: The Ku Klux Klan in Colorado.* Urbana: University of Illinois Press, 1981.

González, Gilbert G. *Chicano Education in the Era of Segregation.* Philadelphia: Balch Institute Press, 1990.

———. *Labor and Community: Mexican Citrus Worker Villages in a Southern California County, 1900–1950.* Urbana: University of Illinois Press, 1994.

Gordon, Linda. *Woman's Body, Woman's Right: A Social History of Birth Control in America.* New York: Grossman Books, 1976.

Gordon, Milton. *Assimilation in American Life: The Role of Race, Religion, and National Origins.* New York: Oxford University Press, 1964.

Gossett, Thomas F. *Race: The History of an Idea in America.* Dallas: Southern Methodist University Press, 1963.

Green, James R. *Grass-Roots Socialism: Radical Movements in the Southwest, 1895–1943.* Baton Rouge: Louisiana State University Press, 1978.

Gruber, Carol S. *Mars and Minerva: World War I and the Uses of the Higher Learning in America.* Baton Rouge: Louisiana State University Press, 1975.

Guerin-Gonzales, Camille. *Mexican Workers and American Dreams: Immigration, Repatriation, and California Farm Labor, 1900–1939.* New Brunswick, N.J.: Rutgers University Press, 1994.

Gutfeld, Arnon. *Montana's Agony: Years of War and Hysteria, 1917–1921.* Gainesville: University Press of Florida, 1979.

Gutiérrez, David G. *Walls and Mirrors: Mexican Americans, Mexican Immigrants, and the Politics of Ethnicity.* Berkeley: University of California Press, 1995.

Haas, Lisbeth. *Conquests and Historical Identities in California, 1769–1936.* Berkeley: University of California Press, 1995.

Haller, John S. *Outcasts from Evolution: Scientific Attitudes of Racial Inferiority, 1859–1900.* Urbana: University of Illinois Press, 1971.

Haller, Mark H. *Eugenics: Hereditarian Attitudes in American Thought.* New Brunswick, N.J.: Rutgers University Press, 1963.

Handlin, Oscar. *Race and Nationality in American Life.* Boston: Little, Brown, 1957.

———. *The Uprooted: The Epic Story of the Great Migrations That Made the American People.* Boston: Little, Brown, 1951.

Haney López, Ian F. *White by Law: The Legal Construction of Race.* New York: New York University Press, 1996.

Hansen, Marcus Lee. *The Immigrant in American History.* Cambridge, Mass.: Harvard University Press, 1940.

Harper, Richard Conant. *The Course of the Melting Pot Idea to 1910.* New York: Arno Press, 1980.

Harries, Meirion, and Susie Harries. *The Last Days of Innocence: America at War, 1917–1918.* New York: Random House, 1997.

Hartmann, Edward G. *The Movement to Americanize the Immigrant.* New York: Columbia University Press, 1948.

Hartshorne, Thomas L. *The Distorted Image: Changing Conceptions of the American Character Since Turner.* Cleveland: Press of Case Western Reserve University, 1968.

Hendrickson, Gordon Olaf, ed. *Peopling the High Plains: Wyoming's European Heritage.* Cheyenne: Wyoming State Archives and Historical Department, 1977.

Hennings, Robert E. *James D. Phelan and the Wilson Progressives of California.* New York: Garland Publishing, 1985.

Higham, John. *Send These to Me: Immigrants in Urban America.* Rev. ed. Baltimore: Johns Hopkins University Press, 1984.

———. *Strangers in the Land: Patterns of American Nativism, 1860–1925.* New Brunswick, N.J.: Rutgers University Press, 1955.

Hoerder, Dirk, ed. *"Struggle a Hard Battle": Essays on Working-Class Immigrants.* DeKalb, Ill.: Northern Illinois University Press, 1986.

Hollinger, David A. *Postethnic America: Beyond Multiculturalism.* New York: Basic Books, 1995.

Horsman, Reginald. *Race and Manifest Destiny: The Origins of American Racial Anglo-Saxonism.* Cambridge, Mass.: Harvard University Press, 1981.

Hutchinson, E. P. *Legislative History of American Immigration Policy, 1798–1965.* Philadelphia: University of Pennsylvania Press, 1981.

Ichihashi, Yamato. *Japanese in the United States: A Critical Study of the Problems of the Japanese Immigrants and Their Children.* Palo Alto, Calif.: Stanford University Press, 1932.

Ichioka, Yuji. *The Issei: The World of the First Generation Japanese Immigrants, 1885–1924.* New York: Free Press, 1988.

Jackson, Kenneth T. *The Ku Klux Klan in the City, 1915–1930.* New York: Oxford University Press, 1967.

Jacobson, Matthew Frye. *Whiteness of a Different Color: European Immigrants and the Alchemy of Race.* Cambridge, Mass.: Harvard University Press, 1998.

Karger, Howard Jacob. *Sentinels of Order: A Study of Social Control and the Minneapolis Settlement House Movement, 1915–1950.* Lanham, Md.: University Press of America, 1987.

Karl, Barry D. *The Uneasy State: The United States from 1915 to 1945.* Chicago: University of Chicago Press, 1983.

Kazin, Michael. *Barons of Labor: The San Francisco Building Trades and Union Power in the Progressive Era.* Urbana: University of Illinois Press, 1987.

Keller, Morton. *Regulating a New Society: Public Policy and Social Change in America, 1900–1933.* Cambridge, Mass.: Harvard University Press, 1994.

Kelly, Lawrence C. *The Assault on Assimilation: John Collier and the Origins of Indian Policy Reform.* Albuquerque: University of New Mexico Press, 1983.

Kennedy, David M. *Over Here: The First World War and American Society.* New York: Oxford University Press, 1980.

Kevles, Daniel J. *In the Name of Eugenics: Genetics and the Uses of Human Heredity.* New York: Knopf, 1985.

King, Desmond. *Making Americans: Immigration, Race, and the Origins of the Diverse Democracy.* Cambridge, Mass.: Harvard University Press, 2000.

Knobel, Dale T. *"America for the Americans": The Nativist Movement in the United States.* New York: Twayne, 1996.

Korman, Gerd. *Industrialization, Immigrants, and Americanization: The View from Milwaukee, 1886–1921.* Madison: State Historical Society of Wisconsin, 1967.

Kraut, Alan M. *The Huddled Masses: The Immigrant in American Society, 1880–1921.* Arlington Heights, Ill.: Harlan Davidson, 1982.

Lay, Shawn. *War, Revolution and the Ku Klux Klan: A Study of Intolerance in a Border City.* El Paso: Texas Western Press, 1985.

———, ed. *The Invisible Empire in the West: Toward a New Appraisal of the Ku Klux Klan of the 1920s.* Urbana: University of Illinois Press, 1992.

Leonard, Henry Beardsell. *The Protest against the Movement to Restrict European Immigration, 1896–1924.* New York: Arno Press, 1980.

Limerick, Patricia Nelson. *The Legacy of Conquest: The Unbroken Past of the American West.* New York: W. W. Norton, 1987.

Limerick, Patricia Nelson, Clyde A. Milner II, and Charles E. Rankin, eds. *Trails: Toward a New Western History.* Lawrence: University Press of Kansas, 1991.

Lissak, Rivka S. *Pluralism and Progressives: Hull House and the New Immigrants, 1890–1919.* Chicago: University of Chicago Press, 1989.

Luebke, Frederick. *Bonds of Loyalty: German-Americans and World War I.* DeKalb: Northern Illinois University Press, 1974.

Luebke, Frederick, C. ed. *Ethnicity on the Great Plains.* Lincoln: University of Nebraska Press, 1980.

———. *European Immigrants in the American West: Community Histories.* Albuquerque: University of New Mexico Press, 1998.

Luckingham, Bradford. *Minorities in Phoenix: A Profile of Mexican American, Chinese American, and African American Communities, 1860–1992.* Tucson: University of Arizona Press, 1994.

Ludmerer, Kenneth M. *Genetics and American Society: A Historical Appraisal.* Baltimore: Johns Hopkins University Press, 1972.

McBride, Paul W. *Culture Clash: Immigrants and Reformers, 1880–1920.* San Francisco: R and E Research Associates, 1975.

McCartin, Joseph A. *Labor's Great War: The Struggle for Industrial Democracy and the Origins of Modern American Labor Relations, 1912–1921.* Chapel Hill: University of North Carolina Press, 1997.

McClellan, Robert. *The Heathen Chinee: A Study of American Attitudes toward China, 1890–1905.* Columbus: Ohio State University Press, 1971.

McClymer, John F. *War and Welfare: Social Engineering in America, 1890–1925.* Westport, Conn.: Greenwood Press, 1980.

McGovern, George S., and Leonard F. Guttridge. *The Great Coalfield War.* Boston: Houghton Mifflin, 1972.

McQuillan, D. Aiden. *Prevailing over Time: Ethnic Adjustment on the Kansas Prairies, 1875–1925.* Lincoln: University of Nebraska Press, 1990.

McWilliams, Carey. *North from Mexico: The Spanish-Speaking People of the United States.* New York: Greenwood Press, 1968.

Malone, Michael P., ed. *Historians and the American West.* Lincoln: University of Nebraska Press, 1983.

Malone, Michael P., and Richard W. Etulain. *The American West: A Twentieth-Century History.* Lincoln: University of Nebraska Press, 1989.

Mann, Arthur. *The One and the Many: Reflections on the American Identity.* Chicago: University of Chicago Press, 1979.

May, Dean L. *Utah: A People's History.* Salt Lake City: University of Utah Press, 1987.

Meyer, Stephen, III. *The Five Dollar Day: Labor Management and Social Control in the Ford Motor Company, 1908–1921.* Albany: State University of New York Press, 1981.

Miller, John J. *The Unmaking of Americans: How Multiculturalism Has Undermined the Assimilation Ethic.* New York: Free Press, 1998.

Miller, Stuart Creighton. *The Unwelcome Immigrant: The American Image of the Chinese, 1785–1882.* Berkeley: University of California Press, 1969.

Milner, Clyde A., II, Carol A. O'Conner, and Martha A. Sandweiss, eds. *The Oxford History of the American West.* New York: Oxford University Press, 1994.

Mink, Gwendolyn. *Old Labor and New Immigrants in American Political Development: Union, Party, and State, 1875–1920.* Ithaca, N.Y.: Cornell University Press, 1986.

Mock, James R., and Cedric Larson. *Words That Won the War: The Story of the Committee on Public Information.* Princeton, N.J.: Princeton University Press, 1939.

Montgomery, David. *The Fall of the House of Labor: The Workplace, the State, and American Labor Activism, 1865–1925.* Cambridge: Cambridge University Press, 1987.

———. *Workers' Control in America: Studies in the History of Work, Technology, and Labor Struggles.* Cambridge, Cambridge University Press, 1979.

Morlan, Robert L. *Political Prairie Fire: The Nonpartisan League, 1915–1922.* Minneapolis: University of Minnesota Press, 1955.

Murray, Robert K. *Red Scare: A Study in National Hysteria.* Minneapolis: University of Minnesota Press, 1955.

Nash, Gary B., and Richard Weiss. *The Great Fear: Race in the Mind of America.* New York: Holt, Rinehart and Winston, 1970.

Nash, Gerald D. *The American West in the Twentieth Century: A Short History of an Urban Oasis.* Englewood Cliffs, N.J.: Prentice-Hall, 1973.

———. *Creating the West: Historical Interpretations, 1890–1990.* Albuquerque: University of New Mexico Press, 1991.

Nash, Gerald D., and Richard W. Etulain, eds. *The Twentieth-Century West: Historical Interpretations.* Albuquerque: University of New Mexico Press, 1989.

Nichols, Roger L. *American Frontier and Western Issues: A Historiographical Review.* New York: Greenwood Press, 1986.

Noble, David W. *The Progressive Mind, 1890–1917.* Chicago: Rand McNally, 1970.

Nugent, Walter. *Into the West: The Story of Its People.* New York: Alfred A. Knopf, 1999.

Olin, Spencer C. *California's Prodigal Sons: Hiram Johnson and the Progressives, 1911–1917.* Berkeley: University of California Press, 1968.

Omi, Michael, and Howard Winant. *Racial Formation in the United States from the 1960s to the 1980s.* New York: Routledge and Kegan Paul, 1986.

Painter, Nell Irvin. *Standing at Armageddon: The United States, 1877–1919.* New York: W. W. Norton, 1987.

Papanikolas, Helen Z., ed. *The Peoples of Utah.* Salt Lake City: Utah State Historical Society, 1976.

―――. *Toil and Rage in a New Land: The Greek Immigrants in Utah.* Salt Lake City: Utah State Historical Society, 1970.

Papanikolas, Zeese. *Buried Unsung: Louis Tikas and the Ludlow Massacre.* Salt Lake City: University of Utah Press, 1982.

Patterson, George James, Jr. *The Unassimilated Greeks of Denver.* New York: AMS Press, 1989.

Perkinson, Henry J. *The Imperfect Panacea: American Faith in Education, 1865–1965.* New York: Random House, 1968.

Pickins, Donald K. *Eugenics and the Progressives.* Nashville, Tenn.: Vanderbilt University Press, 1968.

Pomeroy, Earl. *The Pacific Slope: A History of California, Oregon, Washington, Idaho, Utah, and Nevada.* New York: Knopf, 1965.

Preston, William, Jr. *Aliens and Dissenters: Federal Suppression of Radicals, 1903–1933.* Cambridge, Mass.: Harvard University Press, 1963.

Raftery, Judith Rosenberg. *Land of Fair Promise: Politics and Reform in Los Angeles Schools, 1885–1941.* Stanford, Calif.: Stanford University Press, 1992.

Reimers, David M. *Unwelcome Strangers: American Identity and the Turn against Immigration.* New York: Columbia University Press, 1998.

Reisler, Mark. *By the Sweat of Their Brow: Mexican Immigrant Labor in the United States, 1900–1940.* Westport, Conn.: Greenwood Press, 1976.

Renshaw, Patrick. *The Wobblies: The Story of the IWW and Syndicalism in the United States.* Chicago: Ivan R. Dee, 1999.

Roediger, David. *The Wages of Whiteness: Race and the Making of the American Working Class.* London: Verso, 1991.

Rolle, Andrew F. *The Immigrant Upraised: Italian Adventurers and Colonists in an Expanding America.* Norman: University of Oklahoma Press, 1968.

Romo, Ricardo. *East Los Angeles: History of a Barrio.* Austin: University of Texas Press, 1983.

Ross, Dorothy. *The Origins of American Social Science.* Cambridge: Cambridge University Press, 1992.

Ross, William G. *Forging New Freedoms: Nativism, Education, and the Constitution, 1917–1927.* Lincoln: University of Nebraska Press, 1994.

Salyer, Lucy E. *Laws Harsh as Tigers: Chinese Immigrants and the Shaping of Modern Immigration Law.* Chapel Hill: University of North Carolina Press, 1995.

Sanchez, George J. *Becoming Mexican American: Ethnicity, Culture, and Identity in Chicano Los Angeles, 1900–1945.* New York: Oxford University Press, 1993.

Sandmeyer, Elmer C. *The Anti-Chinese Movement in California.* Urbana: University of Illinois Press, 1939.

Sandos, James A. *Rebellion in the Borderlands: Anarchism and the Plan of San Diego, 1904–1923.* Norman: University of Oklahoma Press, 1992.

Sarasohn, Eileen Sunada. *The Issei, Portrait of a Pioneer: An Oral History.* Palo Alto, Calif.: Pacific Books, 1983.

Saveth, Edward N. *American Historians and European Immigrants, 1875–1925.* New York: Russell and Russell, 1965.

Saxton, Alexander. *The Indispensable Enemy: Labor and the Anti-Chinese Movement in California.* Berkeley: University of California Press, 1971.

―――. *The Rise and Fall of the White Republic: Class Politics and Mass Culture in Nineteenth-Century America.* New York: Verso, 1990.

Scamehorn, H. Lee. *Mill and Mine: The CF&I in the Twentieth Century.* Lincoln: University of Nebraska Press, 1992.

Schaffer, Ronald. *America in the Great War: The Rise of the War Welfare State.* New York: Oxford University Press, 1991.

Schlesinger, Arthur M., Jr. *The Disuniting of America: Reflections on a Multicultural Society.* New York: Norton, 1992.

Sellars, Nigel Anthony. *Oil, Wheat, and Wobblies: The Industrial Workers of the World in Oklahoma, 1905–1930.* Norman: University of Oklahoma Press, 1998.

Sherman, William C., and Playford V. Thorson, eds. *Plains Folk: North Dakota's Ethnic History.* Fargo: North Dakota Institute for Regional Studies, 1986.

Slotkin, Richard. *Gunfighter Nation: The Myth of the Frontier in Twentieth-Century America.* New York: HarperCollins, 1992.

Smedley, Audrey. *Race in North America: Origin and Evolution of a Worldview.* Boulder, Colo.: Westview Press, 1993.

Smith, Henry Nash. *Virgin Land: The American West as Symbol and Myth.* Cambridge, Mass.: Harvard University Press, 1950.

Smith, Rogers M. *Civic Ideals: Conflicting Visions of Citizenship in U.S. History.* New Haven, Conn.: Yale University Press, 1997.

Smith, William Carlson. *Americans in the Making: The Natural History of the Assimilation of Immigrants.* New York: D. Appleton-Century, 1939.

Sollors, Werner. *Beyond Ethnicity: Consent and Descent in American Culture.* New York: Oxford University Press, 1986.

Solomon, Barbara. *Ancestors and Immigrants: A Changing New England Tradition.* Cambridge, Mass.: Harvard University Press, 1956.

Spinner, Jeff. *The Boundaries of Citizenship: Race, Ethnicity, and Nationality in the Liberal State.* Baltimore: Johns Hopkins University Press, 1994.

Stanton, William R. *The Leopard's Spots: Scientific Attitudes toward Race in America, 1815–1859.* Chicago: University of Chicago Press, 1960.

Stipanovich, Joseph. *The South Slavs in Utah: A Social History.* San Francisco: R and E Research Associates, 1975.

Stocking, George, Jr. *Race, Culture, and Evolution: Essays in the History of Anthropology.* New York: Free Press, 1968.

Takaki, Ronald T. *A Different Mirror: A History of Multicultural America.* Boston: Little, Brown, 1993.

———. *From Different Shores: Perspectives on Race and Ethnicity in America.* 2d ed. New York: Oxford University Press, 1994.

———. *Iron Cages: Race and Culture in Nineteenth-Century America.* New York: Alfred A. Knopf, 1979.

———. *Strangers from a Different Shore: A History of Asian Americans.* New York: Penguin, 1990.

Thernstrom, Stephen, ed. *Harvard Encyclopedia of American Ethnic Groups.* Cambridge, Mass.: Belknap Press of Harvard University Press, 1980.

Toole, K. Ross. *Twentieth-Century Montana: A State of Extremes.* Norman: University of Oklahoma Press, 1972.

Tyler, Robert L. *Rebels of the Woods: The I.W.W. in the Pacific Northwest.* Eugene: University of Oregon Books, 1967.

Ubbelohde, Carl, Maxine Benson, and Duane A. Smith, eds. *A Colorado History*. Boulder, Colo.: Pruett Publishing, 1982.

Ueda, Reed. *Postwar Immigrant America: A Social History*. Boston: Bedford Books of St. Martin's Press, 1994.

Vaughn, Stephen. *Holding Fast the Inner Lines: Democracy, Nationalism, and the Committee on Public Information*. Chapel Hill: University of North Carolina Press, 1980.

Weinberg, Julius. *Edward Alsworth Ross and the Sociology of Progressivism*. Madison: State Historical Society of Wisconsin, 1972.

Weiss, Bernard J., ed. *American Education and the European Immigrant, 1840–1940*. Urbana: University of Illinois Press, 1982.

Wells, Mildred White. *Unity in Diversity: The History of the General Federation of Women's Clubs*. Washington, D.C.: GFWC, 1953.

Welter, Rush. *Popular Education and Democratic Thought in America*. New York: Columbia University Press, 1962.

White, Richard. *"It's Your Misfortune and None of My Own": A History of the American West*. Norman: University of Oklahoma Press, 1991.

Wiebe, Robert. *The Search for Order, 1877–1920*. New York: Hill and Wang, 1967.

Williamson, Chilton, Jr. *The Immigration Mystique: America's False Conscience*. New York: Basic Books, 1996.

Wrobel, David M. *The End of American Exceptionalism: Frontier Anxiety from the Old West to the New Deal*. Lawrence: University Press of Kansas, 1993.

Wyman, Mark. *Hard-Rock Epic: Western Miners and the Industrial Revolution, 1860–1910*. Berkeley: University of California Press, 1989.

Yans-McLaughlin, Virginia, ed. *Immigration Reconsidered: History, Sociology, Politics*. New York: Oxford University Press, 1990.

Articles

Arnesen, Eric. "'Like Banquo's Ghost, It Will Not Down': The Race Question and the American Railroad Brotherhoods, 1880–1920." *American Historical Review* 99 (December 1994): 1601–33.

Barrett, James R. "Americanization from the Bottom Up: Immigration and the Remaking of the Working Class in the United States, 1880–1930." *Journal of American History* 79 (December 1992): 996–1020.

Barrett, James R., and David Roediger. "Inbetween Peoples: Race, Nationality and the 'New Immigrant' Working Class." *Journal of American Ethnic History* 16 (Spring 1997): 3–44.

Berrol, Selma C. "In Their Image: German Jews and the Americanization of the Ost Juden in New York City." *New York History* 63 (October 1982): 417–33.

Bolin, Winifred Wandersee. "Heating Up the Melting Pot: Settlement Work and Americanization in Northeast Minneapolis." *Minnesota History* 45 (Summer 1976): 58–69.

Cardoso, Lawrence A. "Nativism in Wyoming, 1868 to 1930: Changing Perceptions of Foreign Immigrants." *Annals of Wyoming* 58 (Spring 1986): 20–35.

Carlson, Robert A. "Americanization as an Early Twentieth-Century Adult Education Movement." *History of Education Quarterly* 10 (Winter 1970): 440–64.

Cohen, Bronwen J. "Nativism and Western Myth: The Influence of Nativist Ideas on the American Self-Image." *Journal of American Studies* 8 (April 1974): 23–39.

Collomp, Catherine. "Unions, Civics, and National Identity: Organized Labor's Reaction to Immigration, 1881–1897." *Labor History* 29 (Fall 1988): 450–74.

Conzen, Kathleen Neils. "Immigrants, Immigrant Neighborhoods, and Ethnic Identity: Historical Issues." *Journal of American History* 66 (December 1979): 603–15.

Conzen, Kathleen Neils, David A. Gerber, Ewa Morawska, George E. Pozzetta, and Rudolph J. Vecoli. "The Invention of Ethnicity: A Perspective from the U.S.A." *Journal of American Ethnic History* 12 (Fall 1992): 3–63.

Dorsett, Lyle W. "The Ordeal of Colorado's Germans during World War I." *Colorado Magazine* 51 (Fall 1974): 277–93.

Emmons, David. "Constructed Province: History and the Making of the Last American West." *Western Historical Quarterly* 25 (Winter 1994): 437–59.

Fernandez, Ronald. "Getting Germans to Fight Germans: The Americanizers of World War I." *Journal of Ethnic Studies* 9 (Summer 1981): 53–68.

Gerstle, Gary. "Liberty, Coercion, and the Making of Americans." *Journal of American History* 84 (September 1997): 524–58.

———. "The Protean Character of American Liberalism." *American Historical Review* 99 (October 1994): 1043–73.

Glazer, Nathan. "Is Assimilation Dead?" *Annals of the American Academy of Political and Social Science* 530 (November 1993): 122–36.

Graham, Otis L., Jr., and Elizabeth Koed. "Americanizing the Immigrant, Past and Future: History and Implications of a Social Movement." *Public Historian* 15 (Fall 1993): 24–50.

Gullett, Gayle. "Women Progressives and the Politics of Americanization in California, 1915–1920." *Pacific Historical Review* 64 (February 1995): 71–94.

Higgs, Robert. "Landless by Law: Japanese Immigrants in California Agriculture to 1941." *Journal of Economic History* 38 (March 1978): 205–25.

Hill, Herbert. "Race and Ethnicity in Organized Labor: The Historical Sources of Resistance to Affirmative Action." *Journal of Intergroup Relations* 12 (Winter 1984): 5–49.

Hollinger, David A. "Ethnic Diversity, Cosmopolitanism, and the Emergence of the American Liberal Intelligentsia." *American Quarterly* 27 (May 1975): 133–51.

Ichioka, Yuji. "The Early Japanese Immigrant Quest for Citizenship: The Background of the 1922 Ozawa Case." *Amerasia Journal* 4 (Spring 1977): 409–37.

———. "Japanese Associations and the Japanese Government: A Special Relationship, 1909–1926." *Pacific Historical Review* 46 (August 1977): 409–37.

———. "The Japanese Immigrant Response to the 1920 California Alien Land Law." *Agricultural History* 58 (April 1984): 157–78.

Ireland, Robert E. "The Radical Community, Mexican and American Radicalism, 1900–1910." *Journal of Mexican-American History* 2 (Fall 1971): 22–29.

Iwata, Masakazu. "The Japanese Immigrant in California Agriculture." *Agricultural History* 36 (January 1962): 25–37.

Jaret, Charles. "Troubled by Newcomers: Anti-Immigrant Attitudes and Action during Two Eras of Mass Immigration to the United States." *Journal of American Ethnic History* 18 (Spring 1999): 9–39.

Kazal, Russell A. "Revisiting Assimilation: The Rise, Fall, and Reappraisal of a Concept in American Ethnic History." *American Historical Review* 100 (April 1995): 437–71.

King, Miriam, and Steven Ruggles. "American Immigration, Fertility, and Race Suicide at the Turn of the Century." *Journal of Interdisciplinary History* 20 (Winter 1990): 347–69.

Korelitz, Seth. "'A Magnificent Piece of Work': The Americanization Work of the National Council of Jewish Women." *American Jewish History* 83 (June 1995): 177–203.

Kuhlman, Erika. "'Greetings From This Coalvillage': Finnish Immigrants of Red Lodge." *Montana: The Magazine of Western History* 40 (Spring 1990): 32–45.

Lesser, Jeffrey. "Always Outsiders: Asians, Naturalization, and the Supreme Court." *Amerasia Journal* 12 (1985–86): 83–100.

Levenstein, Harvey A. "The AFL and Mexican Immigration in the 1920s: An Experiment in Labor Diplomacy." *Hispanic American Historical Review* 48 (May 1968): 206–19.

Lissak, Rivka S. "Liberal Progressives and 'New Immigrants': The Immigrants' Protective League of Chicago, 1908–1919." *Studies in American Civilization* 32 (1987): 79–103.

McClymer, John F. "The Federal Government and the Americanization Movement, 1915–24." *Prologue: Journal of the National Archives* 10 (Spring 1978): 22–41.

———. "Gender and 'The American Way of Life': Women in the Americanization Movement." *Journal of American Ethnic History* 10 (Spring 1991): 3–20.

Matthews, Fred H. "The Revolt against Americanism: Cultural Pluralism and Cultural Relations as an Ideology of Liberation." *Canadian Review of American Studies* 1 (Spring 1970): 4–31.

———. "White Community and 'Yellow Peril.'" *Mississippi Valley Historical Review* 50 (March 1964): 612–33.

Mellinger, Phil. "How the IWW Lost Its Western Heartland: Western Labor History Revisited." *Western Historical Quarterly* 27 (Autumn 1996): 303–24.

Meyer, Stephen, III. "Adapting the Immigrant to the Line: Americanization in the Ford Factory, 1914–1921." *Journal of Social History* 14 (1980): 67–82.

Milner, Clyde A., II. "The Shared Memory of Montana Pioneers." *Montana: The Magazine of Western History* 37 (Winter 1987): 2–13.

Nash, Gary B. "The Hidden History of Mestizo America." *Journal of American History* 82 (December 1995): 941–64.

Ngai, Mae M. "The Architecture of Race in American Immigration Law: A Reexamination of the Immigration Act of 1924." *Journal of American History* 86 (June 1999): 67–92.

Notarianni, Philip F., Jr. "Utah's Ellis Island: The Difficult 'Americanization' of Carbon County." *Utah Historical Quarterly* 47 (Spring 1979): 178–93.

Notarianni, Philip F., Jr., and Joseph Stipanovich. "Immigrants, Industry, and Labor Unions: The American West, 1890–1916." *Journal of Historical Studies* 3 (Fall/Winter 1978): 1–14.

Olin, Spencer C. "European Immigrant and Oriental Alien: Acceptance and Rejection by the California Legislature of 1913." *Pacific Historical Review* 35 (August 1966): 303–15.

Olneck, Michael R. "Americanization and the Education of Immigrants, 1900–1925: An Analysis of Symbolic Action." *American Journal of Education* 97 (August 1989): 398–423.

Papanikolas, Helen Z. "Immigrants, Minorities, and the Great War." *Utah Historical Quarterly* 58 (Fall 1990): 351–70.

Peck, Gunther. "Padrones and Protest: 'Old' Radicals and 'New' Immigrants in Bingham, Utah, 1905–1912." *Western Historical Quarterly* 24 (May 1993): 157–78.

———. "Reinventing Free Labor: Immigrant Padrones and Contract Laborers in North America, 1885–1925." *Journal of American History* 83 (December 1996): 848–71.

Powell, Allan Kent. "The 'Foreign Element' and the 1903–4 Carbon County Coal Miners' Strike." *Utah Historical Quarterly* 43 (Spring 1975): 125–54.

Schwantes, Carlos A. "The Concept of the Wageworkers' Frontier: A Framework for Future Research." *Western Historical Quarterly* 18 (January 1987): 39–55.

Seller, Maxine. "The Education of the Immigrant Woman." *Journal of Urban History* 4 (May 1978): 307–30.

Taft, Philip. "The Bisbee Deportation." *Labor History* 13 (Winter 1972): 3–40.

Vaughn, Leslie J. "Cosmopolitanism, Ethnicity, and American Identity: Randolph Bourne's 'Trans-National America.'" *Journal of American Studies* 25 (December 1991): 443–59.

Wacker, R. Fred. "Assimilation and Cultural Pluralism in American Social Thought." *Phylon* 40 (December 1979): 325–33.

White, Richard. "Race Relations in the American West." *American Quarterly* 38 (Bibliography 1986): 396–416.

Wrobel, David M. "Beyond the Frontier-Region Dichotomy." *Pacific Historical Review* 65 (August 1996): 401–29.

Zellick, Anna. "Fire in the Hole: Slovenians, Croatians, and Coal Mining on the Musselshell." *Montana: The Magazine of Western History* 40 (Spring 1990): 16–31.

———. "'We All Intermingled': The Childhood Memories of South Slavic Immigrants in Red Lodge and Bearcreek, Montana, 1904–1943." *Montana: The Magazine of Western History* 44 (Summer 1994): 34–45.

Theses and Dissertations

Abrams, Bruce A. "A Muted Cry: White Opposition to the Japanese Exclusion Movement, 1911–24." Ph.D. diss., City University of New York, 1987.

Aiken, Ellen Schoening. "Japanese Immigrant Women and the Union Pacific Towns of Wyoming in the 1920s." M.A. thesis, University of Colorado, Boulder, 1994.

Bouwman, Robert Eldridge. "Race Suicide: Some Aspects of Race Paranoia in the Progressive Era." Ph.D. diss., Emory University, 1975.

Darling, Mary Rebecca. "Americanization of the Foreign-Born in Greeley, Colorado." M.A. thesis, Colorado State Teachers' College, 1932.

Gurvis, Jonas Alex. "Elementary Education of Adult Immigrants in California: An Historical and Descriptive Study." Ed.D. diss., University of California, Los Angeles, 1976.

Hall, Margaret A. "Henry Suzzalo and the Washington State Council of Defense." M.A. thesis, University of Washington, 1975.

Herman, David George. "Neighbors on the Golden Mountain: The Americanization of Immigrants in California. Public Instruction as an Agency of Ethnic Assimilation, 1850 to 1933." Ph.D. diss., University of California, Berkeley, 1981.

Hogle, John Thomas. "The Rockefeller Plan: Workers, Managers and the Struggle over Unionism in Colorado Fuel and Iron, 1915–1942." Ph.D. diss., University of Colorado, 1992.

Huginnie, Andrea Yvette. "'Strikitos': Race, Class, and Work in the Arizona Copper Industry, 1870–1920." Ph.D. diss., Yale University, 1991.

Hunt, Rebecca Ann. "Urban Pioneers: Continuity and Change in the Ethnic Communities in Two Denver, Colorado, Neighborhoods: 1875–1998." Ph.D. diss., University of Colorado, 1999.

Kerman, Lucy Eve. "Americanization: The History of an Idea, 1700–1860." Ph.D. diss., University of California, Berkeley, 1983.

Koepplin, Leslie Wayne. "A Relationship of Reform: Immigrants and Progressives in the Far West." Ph.D. diss., University of California, Los Angeles, 1971.

Leonard, Stephen J. "Denver's Foreign-Born Immigrants, 1859–1900." Ph.D. diss., Claremont Graduate School and University, 1971.

Lewis, Joyce Paine. "The Schools' Role in Americanizing the Immigrant: 1910–1920." Ph.D. diss., University of Rochester, 1986.

Manley, Robert N. "The Nebraska State Council of Defense: Loyalty Programs and Policies during World War I." M.A. thesis, University of Nebraska, 1959.

Pan, Denise. "Peace and Conflict in an Industrial Family: Company Identity and Class Consciousness in a Multi-ethnic Community, Colorado Fuel and Iron's Cameron and Walsen Coal Camps, 1913–1928." M.A. thesis, University of Colorado, 1994.

Roitman, Joel M. "The Progressive Movement: Education and Americanization." Ph.D. diss., University of Cincinnati, 1981.

Smith, Larry Joe. "The Gubernatorial Career of Julius C. Gunter, 1917–1919." M.A. thesis, University of Denver, 1973.

Teeuwen, Randall C. "Public Rural Education and the Americanization of the Germans from Russia in Colorado: 1900–1930." M.A. thesis, Colorado State University, 1993.

Thurman, Arch M. "Adult Education with Reference to a Program for Salt Lake City." M.S. thesis, University of Utah, 1933.

Titcomb, Mary Ruth. "Americanization and Mexicans in the Southwest: A History of Phoenix's Friendly House, 1920–1983." M.A. thesis, University of California, Santa Barbara, 1984.

Wenzell, Janell M. "Dr. Grace Raymond Hebard as Western Historian." M.A. thesis, University of Wyoming, 1960.

White, Alfred. "The Apperceptive Mass of Foreigners as Applied to Americanization, the Mexican Group." M.A. thesis, University of California, 1923. Reprint, San Francisco: R and E Research Associates, 1971.

Wood, Diane Claire. "Immigrant Mothers, Female Reformers, and Women Teachers: The California Home Teacher Act of 1915." Ph.D. diss., Stanford University, 1996.

Wood, Samuel Edgerton. "The California State Commission of Immigration and Housing: A Study of Administrative Organization and the Growth of Function." Ph.D. diss., University of California, Berkeley, 1942.

Woo-Sam, Ann Marie. "Domesticating the Immigrant: California's Commission of Immigration and Housing and the Domestic Immigration Policy Movement, 1910–1945." Ph.D. diss., University of California, Berkeley, 1999.

Young, Paul D. "The Kansas State Council of Defense in World War I." M.A. thesis, Emporia State University, 1988.

INDEX